The Voice That Thinks

The Voice That Thinks

Heidegger Studies with a Bibliography of English Translations, 1949-2015

Second Edition, Revised and Enlarged

Miles Groth

ENI Press
New York, NY

Table of Contents

Heidegger Studies

Heidegger Bibliography, 1949-2015

Note on the Texts

Earlier versions of the first two chapters were published as *Preparatory Thinking in Heidegger's Teaching* (New York: Philosophical Library, 1987). Chapter Three and the "Appendix" to that chapter comprise a whole, "The Telling Word," serving as an introduction to my translation of the *Eisgeschichte* by Adalbert Stifter, one of Heidegger's favorite writers. The original text read by Heidegger to a radio audience in 1964 may be found in Volume 13 of the *Gesamtausgabe* of Heidegger's writings (Frankfurt: Klostermann, 1983), pp. 185-195. An earlier version of Chapter Five appeared in *Philosophy Today* 25(2), Summer 1981, pp. 139-147, as "On the Fundamental Experience of Voice in Language" and in a French translation the following year as "L'Expérience Fondamentale de la Voix dans le Langage," in *Spirales. Journal International de Culture* (Paris and Milan), No. 16, June 1982, pp. 54-56.[1] Chapters 4 and 6 were published for the first time in the first edition of *The Voice That Thinks* (Greensburg: Eadmer Press, 1997). The Heidegger Bibliography has been a work in progress for forty years. Versions of it appeared in *Preparatory Thinking in Heidegger's Teaching* and in *Translating Heidegger* (New York: Prometheus Books, 1997), but it has been thoroughly revised, corrected and supplemented for this volume.

---

[1] I am proud to say that I am listed in *Cartel International de Collaborateurs* for *Spirales* with, among others, Christopher Bollas, Aaron Esterson, Gabriel Garcia Marquez, Julia Kristeva, Milan Kundera, Maud Mannoni, Alain Robbe-Grillet, Luciano Berio, Alberto Moravia, Lina Wertmuller, Harold Bloom, William S. Burroughs, John Cage, Noam Chomsky, Merce Cunningham, Lawrence Ferlinghetti, Allen Ginsberg, Silvere Lotringer, Thomas Szasz and Gore Vidal.

Heidegger Studies

ONE

Preparatory Thinking and Heidegger's Teaching

IT HAS BECOME INCREASINGLY EVIDENT to me that Heidegger's entire career as a thinker is preparational. The dominant feature of preparatory thinking is that it is not metaphysical. This means it proceeds without the tendency toward closure, which conformity to an underlying principle implies. The hallmark of metaphysical thinking is its relation to a guiding principle. Closure implies that thinking has exhausted itself in its topic. Preparatory thinking is always on the way.

Heidegger experienced the major thinkers of the West in what they said in their texts, but also in what they left unsaid. This fore-reaching element of their thought he called their *Lehre* (teaching). In this chapter, I want to uncover Heidegger's own teaching and what he left unsaid, which guided what he said and was in turn renewed as the articulation of his thought stretched along to surpass it.

A teaching is the sayer's guiding thought, his "one unique thought."[1] "The "teaching" of a thinker is the unspoken in what he says, to which

---

[1] *What Is Called Thinking?* [1951/52] New York: Harper and Row, 1976, 50 [Part One, Lecture Six]. Heidegger reserved the term *sayer* for the writer of philosophical and poetic texts.

man is exposed in order to expend himself on behalf of it."[2] Heidegger explains that for every great thinker there is something unspoken, because the thinker "*thinks* always one jump more originally than he directly *speaks.*"[3] As a result, any interpretation of a thinker's thought "must therefore try to say what is unsaid in his [thought]." I will apply the same approach to Heidegger himself.

Heidegger's published texts will be our starting point. A thoughtful encounter with him, as with any great thinker, must begin with what he has said. Only then can it move into the open space of his thought. There we will look for what he has left unsaid. Though it may be expressible in a few words, the unspoken is an abundance of thought. It is not the result of the thinker's limited ability to express himself.[4] Thinking that is drawn on by the unspoken is preparatory thinking.

Heidegger's preparatory thought has three elements. The first two elements are formal: preparatory thought is *meditative* and *paratactic.* Paratactic discourse is the medium of saying [*Sagen*], the common expression of both primordial thinking and poetizing.[5] The third element of preparatory thinking is more difficult to characterize. It is related to Heidegger's conception of earth, of which there are hints in his interpretation of the fable "Cura" in *Being and Time* and in the *Prolegomena to the History of the Concept of Time*. This element of preparatory thought is discussed in Chapter Two of the present work, where Heidegger's interpretation of the fable is discussed.[6]

---

[2] "Plato's Doctrine of Truth" [1940], in William Barrett and Henry D. Aiken (eds.), *Philosophy in the Twentieth Century*, Vol. 3 (1962) New York: Harper and Row, 1982, 251.

[3] "The Will to Power as Art" [1936/37], in *Nietzsche*, Vol. I, *The Will to Power as Art*, New York: Harper and Row, 1979, 134. Cf. David Krell, "Art and Truth in Raging Discord: Heidegger and Nietzsche on the Will to Power," in *Boundary 1*, IV (2), 1976, 381.

[4] See Thomas Sheehan's "Preface" to *Heidegger: The Man and the Thinker*, Chicago: Precedent Publishing Company, 1981, xvi-xviii.

[5] *What Is Called Thinking?*, 182 ff. See also my article "Interpretation for Freud and Heidegger: Parataxis and Disclosure," in *The International Review of Psycho-Analysis*, IX (1), 1982, 67-74.

[6] On Heidegger's concept of earth, see "Moira" [1951/52], in *Early Greek Thinking*, New York: Harper and Row, 1985, 79-101.

What did Heidegger say about preparatory thinking? Division One of the first part of *Sein und Zeit* (Sections 9–44) bears the title "Preparatory Fundamental Analysis of *Dasein* [Existence]."[7] More than a third of the work's 83 sections are devoted to the preparational phase of the complete existential analytic of Existence. "The analytic of Existence, which is proceeding towards the phenomenon of *Sorge*, is to prepare the way for the problematic of fundamental ontology — the question of the meaning of be[ing] [*Sein*] in general."[8]

Be[ing] and Time was designed to unfold in three phases: first is the analysis of Existence, which prepares for "the disclosedness of the meaning of the be[ing] of *Sorge*." Regarding this phase, Heidegger writes that "every ontologically explicit question about the be[ing] of Existence has had the way already prepared for it by the kind of be[ing] which Existence has."[9] The second phase is the explication of *Sorge*, as preparatory for an understanding of temporality. The final phase is the disclosure of

---

[7] The convention in this study of rendering *Dasein* as "the *Dasein*" when it is not translated as 'Existence' follows Albert Hofstadter's lead in his translation of *Die Grundprobleme der Phänomenologie* [*The Fundamental Problems of Phenomenology*]. See Hofstadter's appendix, "A Note on the *Da* and the *Dasein*," in *The Basic Problems of Phenomenology* [1927], Bloomington: Indiana University Press, 1982, 333–337. There is no need to defer to the German term when one realizes that, for Heidegger, only human beings exist. This characteristic of human being, Existence, is reflected by Heidegger's technical use of the common German term *Dasein*.

[8] *Being and Time* [1927], London: Student Christian Movement Press, 1962, 360. *Sorge* is customarily translated as 'care'. This is not satisfactory, as Chapter Two will demonstrate. Like *Dasein*, it is a key term for Heidegger. For the time being, I leave it untranslated. See José Ortega y Gasset's comments on *Sorge*, in *What Is Philosophy?*, New York: W.W. Norton Company, 1960, 249. Ortega's comments are from lectures he gave in Buenos Aires and Madrid, in 1927–28, the year Heidegger published *Sein und Zeit*. Herbert Spiegelberg also considers 'care' to be an inappropriate translation of *Sorge*. See *The Phenomenological Movement*, Volume I, The Hague: Martinus Nijhoff, Second Edition, 1969, 333. As for the form my translation of *Sein* as 'be[ing]', see Chapter Four "Who Is Heidegger's Nietzsche?".

[9] *Being and Time*, 364

temporality as the horizon of the question of be[ing], which is itself preparatory for interrogating the meaning of be[ing].

Heidegger's procedure calls for making distinctions among ontic, ontological and preontological levels of fundamental ontology. Taken together, the phases of explication, which play themselves out in the three fundamental ontological dimensions, may be schematized as *four* preparational moments:

(A) The entire analysis of Existence is preparational for raising the question of be[ing].

(B) The purely ontic analysis of the everydayness of Existence (in Division One) is preparational for the ontological-temporal analysis of Existence (in Division Two).

(C) The ontico-ontological analysis of Existence is necessary as preparatory for revealing the fundamental structure of Existence, which is *Sorge*.

(D) A preontological disclosure of Existence, which determines the provenance of the entire course of the analysis, occurs in a form that is essentially different from the rest of the analysis.

In reporting this outline, I am not saying anything about what Heidegger wants to accomplish in his analysis. I merely want to bring to the reader's attention the preparatory nature of each moment of the analysis.

The outcome of Part One of *Being and Time* (of which, as we know, only two-thirds was published under that title) is designed to accomplish "the interpretation of Existence in terms of temporality, and the explication of time as the transcendental horizon for the question of be[ing]."[10] Heidegger himself summarizes the preparatory moments of his analysis in the concluding section of the published work, where he recalls that his

---

[10] *Being and Time*, 63.

task has been to interpret the *primordial whole* of factual Existence with regard to its possibilities of authentic and inauthentic existing [*Existierens*], and to do so in an existential-ontological manner *in terms of its very basis*. Temporality has manifested itself as this basis and accordingly as the meaning of the be[ing] of *Sorge*. So that which our preparatory existential analytic of Existence contributed *before* temporality was laid bare, has now been taken back into temporality as the primordial structure of the totality of be[ing] of Existence.[11]

The "structure of the totality of be[ing] of Existence" is revealed as *Sorge*, and since the meaning of *Sorge* is temporality, time and Existence are inseparable. Existence belongs to time. With this in mind, the decisive question of *Being and Time* for our theme therefore becomes the following: "How is this disclosive [*erschließendes*] understanding of be[ing] at all possible for Existence?"[12]

As we know, the projected Third Division of Part One of the work was identified by Heidegger as contained in the Marburg University lecture course published in 1975 as *Die Grundprobleme der Phänomenologie* [*The Fundamental Problems of Phenomenology*].[13] This text furthers the preparational work of *Being and Time*, concluding with a discussion of the difference between a being of some kind [*das Seiende*] and be[ing] [*das Sein*]. From the perspective of *Being and Time*, this difference, called the ontological difference, is a consequence of the exceptional place of Existence in the scheme of things in their entirety.

In *The Fundamental Problems of Phenomenology*, however, the ontological difference is clarified on the basis of the distinction between the time of Existence [*Zeitlichkeit*], to which Existence belongs, and time as "the condition of the possibility of all understanding of be[ing]"[14] or temporality [*Temporalität*].

---

[11] *Being and Time*, 468.
[12] *Being and Time*, 48
[13] *The Basic Problems of Phenomenology*, 1 (note 1).
[14] Ibid., 274.

The nature of the preparational work has changed between the two texts because of Heidegger's shift of emphasis to time as the grounding phenomenon of the understanding of be[ing] in general.

In "Nietzsche's Pronouncement: 'God Is Dead'," a work dating from the decade, 1936 to 1946, during which he concentrated to a great extent on Nietzsche, Heidegger explicitly discusses preparatory thinking.[15] The following passage from the essay is very important to our discussion:

> What matters to preparatory thinking is to light up [*lichten*] that play space [*Spielraum*] within which be[ing] itself (the event of enownment [*Ereignis*]) might again be able to take [*nehmen*] man into an originative tension [*anfänglichen Bezug*] (usage [*Brauch*]) with respect to his essence. The essence of such thinking is to be preparing.[16]

> This thinking, which is essential and therefore everywhere and in every respect preparatory, happens in the unapparent [*Unscheinbaren*]. Here all *commentatio* [*Mitdenken*], ungainly and groping though it may be, is an essential help. The *commentatio* turns out to be an inconspicuous sowing [*Aussaat*], not certifiable through its worth or utility, of sowers who perhaps see neither blade nor fruit and know no harvest. They serve the dissemination and, even before, the preparation of this.[17]

---

[15] "The Word of Nietzsche: 'God Is Dead'" [1943], in *The Question Concerning Technology and Other Essays*, New York: Harper and Row, 1982, 53–112. With the exception of this text, none of the results of Heidegger's conversation with Nietzsche were published until 1961.

[16] The words set apart, preceded by an *, are Heidegger's glosses, which the editor, at Heidegger's request, gleaned from the author's own copy of the 1950 imprint of *Holzwege*. I translate *Ereignis* as 'event of enownment' to emphasize that the event brings Existence *into its own*. *Brauch* is rendered 'usage' to hint at the fact that Existence is put to use by language in certain linguistic usages. Language has Existence entirely at its disposal. The relation of Existence and language is a feature of be[ing]. Cf. William J. Richardson's comments on this passage in *Heidegger: Through Phenomenology to Thought* (1963) The Hague: Martinus Nijhoff, 439, and Charles E. Scott on "Heidegger's Attempt to Communicate a Mystery," in *Philosophy Today*, 10, 1966, 133.

[17] "The Word of Nietzsche: 'God Is Dead'," 55.

In this passage, sowing seed is Heidegger's metaphor for conversation about the meaning of be[ing] with the great thinkers who preceded him. The second part of *Being and Time*, as we recall, was to have included inseminations of Kant, Descartes and Aristotle. Seeding the texts of ancient and modern philosophy with the question about the meaning of be[ing] will bear fruit in due course. The preparation for renewing that question with each major thinker in the Western tradition is carried out, in part, in *Being and Time*. Such questioning is genuine *commentatio* [*Mitdenken*], the root system of hermeneutics.

Heidegger identifies be[ing] with an event that brings together be[ing] and beings of one kind or another. He speaks here about *man* as one kind of being. In the text, 'man' refers to the "who" of human being, Existence. Be[ing] takes the *essence* of the "who" into "a primal relationship." Preparatory thinking "illuminates that play space" in which the relationship occurs. It is a deceptively simple event for which conversation [*commentatio*] with another thinker is "an essential help."

In recent years, the image of the sower has been capitalized upon and socialized in literary and philosophical circles. Here is its original appearance. Before disseminating, however, one readies the ground (existing texts) for planting with the necessary spade work (study). All texts are ultimately subject to dissemination, even though in a given season (historical era) only some seeding will take hold, root and grow.

The field that is to be cultivated is metaphysics. But how does the thinker work?

> It is a matter of first having a presentiment of, then of finding, then of cultivating, that field. It is a matter of taking a first walk to that field. Many are the ways, still unknown, that lead there.[18]

---

[18] See also Heidegger's brief, though illuminating reflection "Der Feldweg [The Fieldpath]" [1949], *Journal of Chinese Philosophy* 13 1986, 455–458, and my memorial paper "Messkirch: Martin Heidegger: June 1976," *Philosophy Today* 20, 1976, 259–261.

The first phase of preparatory thinking is a thus a kind of divining [*ahnen*] of the field that is to be cleared. Heidegger speaks of the one, singular way of divination given to each thinker, who proceeds in his own way, crossing and recrossing his territory throughout a lifetime of thinking. The way of each thinker is peculiar to him and him alone, and makes a loner [*Einzelgänger*] of every thinker.

Recalling his own path, Heidegger refers to his first, giant step toward that field: "Perhaps the title *Being and Time* is a road marker [*Wegzeichen*] belonging to such a way." These words — 'be[ing]', 'time' — mark the alpha and omega of Heidegger's sojourn through the Western metaphysical tradition.

"It is a matter of taking a first walk in that field," says Heidegger. But how is one prepared from the outset to undertake such a course?

In the memorial address, "Gelassenheit. Bodenständigkeit im Atomzeitalter [Releasement. Stability in the Atomic Age]," given in 1955, Heidegger said, by way of clarifying the relationship between the "who" of human being and ·*meditative* thinking:

> Yet anyone can follow the path of meditative thinking in his own manner and within his own limits. Why? Because man is a *thinking*, that is, a meditative essence [*besinnende Wesen*].[19]

Insofar as meditative thinking is a kind of preparatory thinking, the same can be said about preparatory thinking. The "who's" essence is thinking. Thinking is the essential way of being human, and in each case, one's thought is unique.

Heidegger called the disposition to think releasement [*Gelassenheit*], describing it as a playful serenity. Releasement is serene melancholy [*das*

---

[19] "Memorial Address" [1955], in *Discourse on Thinking*, New York: Harper and Row, 1970, 47.

Kuinzige],[20] a sense that "Yes, it will come to me." Even the waiting of releasement is active. It waits persistently.

Thinking that prepares the ground is not passive. It is laborious activity that engages the tradition of metaphysics, beginning with the fundamental question: What is at stake at this historical moment? Preparatory thinking is thoroughly critical in aim.[21]

Preparatory thinking reckons without closure or a final summing up. It begins with the question: What is happening in our age? What are we about, as historical Existence, in what we do? Preparatory thinking clarifies this "being about." In doing so, it attends to what we have not explicitly seen. Its aim is to bring into view and make discernible what has been overlooked, lost sight of and therefore taken for granted. Epistemological predominance is given to clarity, rather than to certainty.

Preparatory thinking brings into focus what has already gotten underway. To accomplish this, it must first have determined what the focus shall be. In accomplishing the latter, thinking orients itself and gets its bearings, places or positions itself. Preparatory thinking is both extensive, in covering the ground of the tradition, and intensive, in determining first what "considering something" amounts to. It is the "guidance system" of any subsequent manipulative (calculative) thinking.

Preparatory thinking remains incomplete. Its task is to keep open what matters for thinking. Is there merely an unjustifiable postponement at work here? Does such thinking deliberately avoid declaring anything for fear of being challenged?

What matters for thinking is always eventual. "Higher than actuality stands *possibility*."[22] Consider the question of be[ing]. For Heidegger,

---

[20] "The Fieldpath," 457.

[21] The meaning of 'critique' is "clarifying." See *What Is a Thing?* [1935/36] Chicago: Henry Regnery, 1985, 119–121 [Section B,II,1].

[22] *Being and Time*, 63.

what matters for thinking is the question of be[ing]. But can the *thinking of be[ing]* be accomplished in Existence? Surely, we cannot suppose (as some commentators have) that be[ing] "does the thinking" and that the entire problem for Heidegger is the result of the ambiguity of the objective and subjective genitive constructions. In that case, the thinking of be[ing] is really be[ing] thinking or not thinking on "our" behalf or in cooperation with "us," depending on "its" whim.

I do not see that this is Heidegger's understanding of the matter. Instead, he wants to remind us about something forgotten (be[ing]) that thinking, paradoxically, tends to obscure as it reveals beings of all kinds. Preparatory thinking reveals that paradox throughout the metaphysical tradition. We have come up short so far in thinking the meaning of be[ing] because of our immersion in be[ing] and because of the concealing nature of thinking.

I have used the phrase "way of thought" to characterize the unique path of thinking followed by each thinker: his *prospectus*. It is the way thinking takes him. Thinking also has the character of a movement. The way and the movement of thinking are closely related.

The way of thought refers to the topography over which a thinker's thinking ranges. We may call the thinking that follows its necessary course original thinking.[23] For Heidegger, the way of thought leads to the question about the meaning of be[ing]. Heidegger calls the peregrinations of thought *Holzwege*, a name for the trails through wooded areas used by foresters. The effort of Heidegger's radical hermeneutic phenomenology may be likened to felling great longstanding trees, thus opening a clearing in which their ground, metaphysics, is opened to view.

The movement of thought for any fundamental thinker arrives deep in that metaphysical forest. Unlike his predecessors, Heidegger determined to remain at the heart of the woods and open a clearing there, where the ground of metaphysics could be explored. The positivists among them

---

[23] Sometimes I will use the terms "genuine thinking" or "fundamental thinking" to express the same idea.

want to stay out of the woods altogether, while the deconstructivists mere-ly chop down the trees and leave, hoping to sell the pulp.

An original thinker's questions inevitably reach their own source in the Existence of the interrogator. This is one of the characteristics of the movement of thought. The movement of thought in every case traverses the tradition into which the thinker has been born and returns to the thinker's Existence. Along the way, every original thinker comes across certain basic questions and matters for thought that the tradition holds out for him. He must eventually reach the question of be[ing] as such.

Heidegger distinguished the work of a thinker from that of the profession-al philosophers, realizing that the latter are caught up in an unacknowl-edged metaphysics of some kind.[24] To think, however, is never to rest on a principle. The leading idea or principle of a philosophical school or system always hides something unarticulated which silently presides over the enunciated principle and its related ideas. These ideas, from the start and in the end, obscure the "one unique thought" of the thinker.

Heidegger also makes a decisive departure from the historians of philoso-phy — for example, Hegel, who determined the *logos* of the Absolute Idea in its unfolding as the *Leitmotif* of his account of the history of philoso-phy. For Heidegger, the history of philosophy is a series of revealing/concealing moments or epochs, in each of which be[ing] "takes to" the way of thought of a certain spokesman. In each instance, some-thing primordial is discovered but at once covered over by an underlying foundational principle and superstructure of concepts. Be[ing] is, in this way, admitted to thought as a theme in various guises.[25] Heidegger is sen-sitive to his own position in the tradition, and in order to avoid entrap-

---

[24] See Walter Biemel, *Martin Heidegger: An Illustrated Study* (1976) New York: Harcourt, Brace, Jovanovich, 147, and Chapter 9 *passim*.

[25] See William J. Richardson, "Heidegger's Way Through Phenomenology and the Thinking of Being," in Thomas Sheehan (ed.), *Heidegger: The Man and the Thinker* (1981) Chicago: Precedent Publishing Company, 80–84.

ment in a metaphysical position of his own, his thinking remains preparatory. He is always "on the way."[26]

Where does preparatory thinking take place? This question serves as the starting point for the next phase of our discussion. What is the site (locus) of thinking? The question is important, because psychologists, among others, claim that thinking is one of the human being's psychological faculties or functions. Heidegger claims that thinking is the essential event of Existence. Existence thinks. What is the *topos* of Existence? What is the relation of human being and Existence?

Like time, thinking eludes us when we try to grasp it.[27] Perhaps thinking is not "something" at all, and we would be on the wrong track in giving it entitative status. As bearers of the tradition, we are in correspondence with the movement of thought. Existence is that relation of openness between human being and be[ing]. That very relation persists in thinking. How may we grasp the meaning of the relation more precisely?

Heidegger says, in the essay "Releasement": "The nature of thinking (that indwelling releasement to that which regions [*Gegnet*]) ... is the essentially human relation to that which regions, something we presage as the nearness of distance."[28] Thinking is releasement to what situates or gives a framework to Existence in the first place. Thinking is the relation in which Existence first becomes evident, clearing the way in turn for identifying something like human being.

The distinction between human being (humanity) and Existence is central to an understanding of preparatory thinking, as we will see in greater

---

[26] See the essay, "The End of Philosophy and the Task of Thinking" [1964], in *On Time and Being*, New York: Harper and Row, 1978, 373–392.

[27] Augustine, *Confessions*, XI, Chapter 14 (William Watts, trans.): "What is time then? If nobody asks me, I know; but if I were desirous to explain it to one that should ask me, plainly I know not."

[28] "Conversation on a Country Path about Thinking" [1944/45], in *Discourse on Thinking*, New York: Harper and Row, 1970, 87.

detail in Chapter Two. In anticipation of that, a few remarks are now in order.

Existence is the place of an event. It is the site where thinking takes place as a correspondence with be[ing]. Existence is the relation between human being and be[ing]. As such, it is the occasion of the coming to pass of the ontological difference. Finally, Existence is the condition for the emergence of human being, the preontological interplay of Existence and thinking. Humanity is that "emergency" for the sake of which Existence arises.

The essential nature of Existence, then, lies in being the site of an event, the moment of a two-fold relation (to thinking and to be[ing]), and the critical condition for that "emergency" among beings known as humanity. Existence is in a critical position historically. Understood in this way, Existence is akin to the chthonic gods, which did not recognize a distinction between human beings and a *summum ens* (God). As the occasion for the emergence of mortals, Existence is that point of intersection where life [*anima*] and spirit [*Geist*] concur.

Thinking is the way of Existence. The relation of human being to be[ing] is mirrored in the relation between Existence and thinking. The movement of thought occurs in Existence, yet the distinction between human being and Existence occurs only in thought. Furthermore, only in language is the movement of thought articulated for the first time. There are many difficulties in these relationships, all of which are closely connected with Heidegger's notion of thinking as preparatory. In order of occurrence, thinking makes the distinction between human being and Existence, yet in order of knowing, the distinction is recognized only *after* the distinction has been made.

In Heidegger's last formal series of lectures, given in 1951–52, at the University of Freiburg before his retirement, Heidegger said: "Every way of thought from the very beginning *moves within* the entire relationship between be[ing] and the essence of humanity [*Menschenwesen*], otherwise it is not thought."[29]

The essence of humanity is what Heidegger had called Existence [*Dasein*] in *Being and Time* and elsewhere. The fulfilled relation of mutuality between be[ing] and human being is "in" Existence, that is, "in" thinking, since thinking is existing. Thinking is thus the disposition in which and from out of which what there is in the world makes a difference. World is where human beings dwell on this earth.

In questioning, the fundamental mode of preparatory thinking, language first comes to speech. The place of language in Existence is expressed by Heidegger in a puzzling way in his 1951 lecture in memory of Max Kommerell.[30] There he said: "Language speaks" — not human beings. Something crucial is being enunciated here. A recasting of the statement may make what Heidegger is saying here more accessible. Heidegger breaks with the long tradition that says thinking occurs in words. Instead, he insists that language is the companion of thinking. It brings thought to word. They are inseparable, like "yes" and "no" or *yang* and *yin*. One cannot be conceived without the other, but their relation allows for certain habits of usage in which one of the pair remains independent of the other.

Language articulates the difference between thinking and language itself. Likewise it makes the distinction between human being and Existence. Is thinking the source of this distinction or does language somehow speak it? It was despair of adequately working out the relation between language and thinking that made of *Being and Time* a torso. Heidegger's early efforts at working out a phenomenology of historical Existence could not be continued for want of adequate language in which to express himself.

---

[29] *What Is Called Thinking?*, 80.
[30] "Language" [1950], in *Poetry, Language, Thought*, New York: Harper and Row, 1975, 198.

We have seen so far that thinking originates in making the distinction between human being and Existence, while the distinction itself is necessary for there to be evidence of thinking. This must also be the case for the thinking of be[ing].

A further determination of the sense of preparatory thinking may be made on the basis of the preceding remarks. In making the distinction between human being and Existence, a thinker welcomes thought. Welcoming is the feature of thinking that marks it as preparatory. The primal relationship between be[ing] and human being spoken of earlier is one of usage [*Brauch*]. I understand this usage to being linguistic. Moments of preparatory thinking welcome thought. This welcoming of thought by thinking may signal to some a mystical element in Heidegger's thinking. There is passion in it, but nothing mystical.

As noted, in *Gelassenheit*, Heidegger had said that the distinguishing feature of meditative thinking [*besinnliche Denken*] is to be preparatory.[31] "Meditative thinking" is a formulation of the essence of welcoming thought. In such welcoming, there is waiting. How are we to understand the sense of waiting here?

Thinking that welcomes *lets it occur to oneself* to ask the question of be[ing], having first "taken a walk to that field" where the question can arise at all.[32] To welcome thought means both to greet and to receive with assurance what is greeted. The word welcome provides a hint about the meaning of welcoming thought as a feature of preparatory thinking. In welcoming, one is intimately related to what comes, whether it be a person or an event. The Indo-European root of welcome is **quem-**, which like all primal words has basic meanings that are antithetical. It means both "to come" and "to go": to arrive and depart in one movement. This double

---

[31] "Memorial Address," 46–47.

[32] The question of the meaning of be[ing] is the *terminus ad quem* that forever outdistances every thinker, because the truth of such questioning is that it is always "aletheic"; that is, it continues to conceal itself in each successive wave of thinking about be[ing], which in each case necessarily objectifies the sense of be[ing] as a metaphysical position, while revealing a determination of be[ing].

movement is reflected in the essence of truth as *alētheia*. Welcoming thought is being open to the revealing/veiling of truth. Welcoming thought, taken both as greeting actively and receiving with assurance that which is greeted corresponds to the appropriating/withdrawing event of be[ing] [*Ereignis*]. Finally, to welcome thought is to receive it with assurance. This assurance is extended to what is welcomed by greeting it in a particular way: engaging with it in repeated evocations of "what matters."

In its movement to Existence, thought reveals and obscures in one moment the essence of humanity, which is thus discovered as Existence welcoming thought. Existence, in thinking, identifies human being by disclosing it. In thinking, human being discovers itself as Existence. This serves as the prototype for all discovery of things. Insofar as Existence is the ontological place [*topos*] of such discovery, in thinking it is the source of the distinction that reveals human being for the first time. In the history of metaphysics, this step has been overlooked and philosophers in the tradition have taken human being as their starting point, rather than Existence. Heidegger's departure from the tradition is to take Existence as the starting point.

The discussion of preparatory thinking thus turns on the fundamental ontological connection between human being and Existence. The connection can be reconstructed only *a posteriori*, in the meditative activity of preparatory thinking. Paradoxically, the relation of human being to Existence is obscured precisely by that which reveals the distinction, the movement of thought. This is the way truth works, however, according to Heidegger.

I turn once more to the primary question posed earlier: What is the meaning of preparatory thinking for Heidegger?

In his essay entitled "The Thing," Heidegger writes:

> Thinking is perhaps the, after all, an unavoidable path, which refuses to be a path of salvation and brings no new wisdom. The path is at most a field-path [*Feldweg*], a path through fields, which does not just speak of renunciation but

already has renounced, namely, renounced the claim to a binding doctrine....[33]

In the passage cited, Heidegger once again calls up the metaphor of a field path. A *Feldweg* is known to German farmers as a walkway between tracts of farmland that separates the fields of acreage tended by different families. Like any border, a *Feldweg* at once divides and provides a means of access to different areas. On such a path, one is on a course, but for an explorer the path's destination is not known. It is thus a way that is unavoidable and without guarantees. It leads the sojourner on. The path of preparatory thinking has renounced [*versichtet*] from the outset any teaching or doctrine (destination) that might be followed. The renunciation to which Heidegger refers is another expression for releasement, the predisposition for preparatory thinking.

NOW TO RETURN TO THE STARTING POINT OF THIS DISCUSSION. In *Being and Time*, the projected complete preparatory existential ontological analysis is two-fold, beginning with Existence and then moving to time as the horizon for the question about the meaning of be[ing]. Time is finally characterized as the earthbound [*zeitlich*] dimension of Existence.[34] Within the perspective of Heidegger's fundamental ontology *bringing to an end* is also a form of preparation. It is the breaking out of life into inauthentic and, finally, authentic Existence as being in a world.[35]

Preparatory thinking brings an to end life without awareness that something is going on. It catches mere life "unawares." Existence becomes au-

---

[33] "The Thing" [1949], in *Poetry, Language, Thought*, New York: Harper and Row, 1975, 185.

[34] The adjective *zeitlich* is translated as 'earth-bound' in order to underscore the fact that Existence is bound over to the contingencies of the earth, first and foremost.

[35] *In der Welt sein* is translated as 'being in a world' in order to stress that the mathematically measured world of natural science is different for each of us at different times. "The world" varies historically. My world or yours is ontologically different from everyone else's.

thentic as its conditionality [*Befindlichkeit*] is made explicit. Awareness of being in a world is awareness of a concrete situation.

Heidegger sees the preparatory moment of Existence in what he calls the moment of vision [*Augenblick*], which occurs to one as the insight into his abandonment [*Geworfenheit*] to life on this earth. To be in a world is already to be on this earth. The thinking that brings such awareness is preparatory thinking.

In the moment of vision, being human and Existence emerge together. Whatever "I" was before this moment is gone forever when the double nature of being human — Existence *and* human being — originates. Existence is only on this earth. Even when Existence is aware of its fundamental being in a world, it remains inauthentic, as Heidegger made clear in *Being and Time*.

Preparatory thinking bridges the abyss between world and earth. Happening onto a world [*Verfallenheit*] and the abandonment of Existence to this earth [*Geworfenheit*] are complementary moments of being human. *Existence is in a world on this earth.* Preparatory thinking brings to an end the solely earth-bound way of being in which other living beings merely perdure. Being human finally precludes that status.

Preparatory thinking opens up the distinction between human being and Existence, which then becomes the site wherein preparatory thinking makes the very distinction between the source of thinking (Existence) and human being. The source eclipses itself at its site. This *ekleipsis* is the moment of truth — *alētheia*. Preparatory thinking must repeatedly welcome. It must also know how to wait. In reinitiating itself, it holds open the difference between human being and Existence. Once opened, no one can close the gap.

Two

The Fable "Cura" In *Being and Time*: The Sorrow of Existence

"Leap and vision require long, slow preparation, especially if we are to transpose ourselves to that utterance which is not yet one utterance among many."[36]

A NUMBER OF NEW TRANSLATIONS OF KEY TERMS in Heidegger's lexicon have already been introduced in Chapter One. They seem to bear Heidegger's sense well, even though they are sometimes hard on the ear: *zeitlich* (earth-bound); *Befindlichkeit* (conditionality [of an historical epoch]); *Geworfenheit* (abandonment [to this earth]); *Verfallenheit* (happening [onto this earth]). I have dared to translate *Dasein* as 'Existence' (always understood in contrast with human being). 'Existence' answers to the question "Who", while 'human being' answers to the question "What?". Finally, I have introduced a translation of *Sein* as 'be[ing]', stressing the sense of the bare root form 'be' to which Heidegger seems to be directing our attention without forgetting the active sense of the participle 'being'.

One term stands apart from all the rest: *Sorge*. An adequate understanding of Heidegger's analysis of Existence in *Being and Time* rests on understanding what he means by this term. I have always been dissatisfied by the translation of the term as 'care.' So far in this essay, the word *Sorge* has been left untouched.

---

[36] *What Is Called Thinking?*, 233. *Sprung und Blick bedürfen einer langen und langsamen Vorbereitung, zumal dann, wenn es sich auch um das Übersetzen in dasjenige Wort handelt, das nicht ein beliebiges Wort und anderen ist.*

Before looking at the term, I will suggest one further sense of preparatory thinking. It rests on the unspoken any original thinker harbors. In addition to the relation of preparatory ,thinking to Existence (the movement of thought), there is its relation to the content of thought (the way of thought of any single thinker). For Heidegger, *Sorge* is the ontological structure of Existence. The meaning of *Sorge* reveals the unspoken in Heidegger's thought, as I will try to show.

The epicenter of *Being and Time* is a *fabula* attributed to the first-century Latin author, bibliographer and scholar Gaius Hyginus.[37] I think that it contains more than Heidegger explicitly tells us he has found it; namely, "preontological evidence for the existential-ontological interpretation of Existence as *Sorge*."[38] On the basis of a fresh interpretation of the fable and in light of the discussion of Heidegger's notion of preparatory thinking in Chapter One, I will try to recover something of what Heidegger has left unsaid.

He tells us he "chanced upon" the text of Hyginus's fable in an article by Kondrad Burdach, "Faust und die Sorge," in an issue of the *German Quarterly for Literary Criticism and the History of Ideas*. Burdach had taken the Latin text from Franz Bücheler's transcription of the fable, which had appeared in 1886.[39]

---

[37] *Hygini Fabulae*, edited by H.J. Rose (1933) Leyden: Sythoff. Rose remarks (144) that among the fables in the anthology, the fable 'Cura' "alone is theoretical" in nature. This places it in that class of cultural literary works that Robert Graves termed "philosophical myths." Robert Graves, *Greek Mythology* (1955) London: Penguin Books, Volume I, 33.

[38] *Being and Time*, 242, n. v.

[39] Konrad Burdach (1859–1936) was co-editor of an edition (1891) of Goethe's works. Franz Bücheler (1837–1902) was also a classical philologist who had assisted in editing five volumes of the *Anthologica Latina* [1837–1926]. He taught at the University of Freiburg from 1858 to 1866. In his article, Burdach notes that the appearance of *Sorge* as one of the fates in Goethe's *Faust* (Part II, Act V, lines 11382 ff.) is of the greatest importance in the resolution of the drama. See also Part I, "Night" (lines 644 ff.) where *Sorge* is also mentioned. He also notes that the figure of *Sorge* was generally known among scholars as early as the 18th century from Benjamin Hederich's *Dictionary of Ancient Mythology* (1742).

The translators of the first English translation of *Sein une Zeit*, John Macquarrie and Edward Robinson, tell us that they have effected a "compromise" between the original Latin and Burdach's German translation in their rendering. Some textual variations can be found both in Heidegger's adjustment of Burdach's translation and in the English translators' version of the German text.[40]

In the fable, we are listening to an account of a little drama by an observer who is picking up the action midstream: "When crossing the river, *Sorge* sees some chalky mud ...." The episode is the conclusion of a series of preceding events we are in the dark about. The text of the fable as printed in *Sein und Zeit* is as follows:

1   *Cura cum fluvium transiret, vidit cretosum lutum*
     sustulitque cogitabunda atque coepit fingere
     dum deliberat quid iam fecisset, Jovis intervenit.
     rogat eum Cura ut det illi spiritum, et facile impetrat.
5   *cui cum vellet Cura nomen ex sese ipsa imponere,*
     Jovis prohibuit suumque nomen ei dandum esse dictitat.
     dum Cura et Jovis disceptant, Tellus surrexit simul
     suumque nomen esse volt cui corpus praebuerit suum.
     sumpserunt Saturnum iudicem, is sic aecus iudicat:
10   *"tu Jovis quia spiritum dedisti, in morte spiritum,*
     tuque Tellus, quia dedisti corpus, corpus recipito,

---

[40] There are ten variations from Burdach's German in Heidegger's transcription in *Sein und Zeit*. At line 2, after *Erdreich*, Heidegger replaces Burdach's semicolon with a colon. Burdach places *Sorge* between single quotation marks only at lines 1 and 4, but is not consistent in this practice at lines 9, 16 and 17. Heidegger is consistent in placing the word between single quotation marks. At line 9, Burdach has the word *miteinander* between 'Jupiter' and *stritten*. Heidegger omits the word. At line 10, Burdach had *Gebild*, which Heidegger reads *Gebilde*. Burdach does not enclose Saturn's speech beginning at line 14 between quotation marks, but Heidegger does. The full punctuation is omitted at least through the 12th Niemeyer edition of *Sein und Zeit*, though this is corrected in the *Gesamtausgabe* edition. Burdach capitalizes the *du* addressing Erde at line 15, but Heidegger does not. At line 17, Burdach had *so lange*, which Heidegger reads as *solange*. Evidently, then, Heidegger's source for the Latin is Bücheler's "Coniectanea."

Cura enim quia prima finxit, teneat quamdiu vixerit.
sed quae nunc de nomine eius vobis controversia est,
homo vocetur, quia videtur esse factus ex humo."

In my translation, I have tried to read the Latin *through* the German:

Once when *Sorge* was crossing a river, she saw some clay-rich earth. She thoughtfully took up a piece and began to shape it. While she was meditating on what she had made, Jupiter came by. *Sorge* asked him to give the piece of clay spirit, and this he gladly granted. But when she wanted her name bestowed upon her creation, he forbade this, and demanded that it be given his name instead. While *Sorge* and Jupiter were disputing thus, Earth (Tellus) arose and desired that her own name be conferred on the creation, since she had offered a piece of her own body for it. The disputants asked Saturn to be their arbiter, who judged favorably as follows: "Since thou, Jupiter, hast given it its spirit, thou shalt receive that spirit at its death, and since thou, Earth, hast given it its body, thou shalt receive its body. But since *Sorge* first created this being, *Sorge* may possess it as long as it lives. And because there is now a dispute as to its name, let it be called *homo*, since it is made out of *humus* (earth)."[41]

---

[41] Rose's critical edition runs as follows:

1   *Cura cum quendom fluvium transiret, vidit*
     cretosum lutum, sustulit cogitabunda et coepit
     fingere hominem. dum deliberat secum quidnam
     fecisset, intervenit Jovis; rogat eum Cura
5   *ut ei daret spiritum, quod facile ab Jove*
     impetravit, cui cum vellet Cura nomen suum
     imponere, Jovis prohibuit suumque nomen ei
     dandum esse dixit. dum de nomine Cura et
     Jovis disceptarent, surrexit et Tellus suumque
10   *nomen ei imponi debere dicebat, quandoquidem*
     corpus suum praebuisset. sumpserunt Saturnum
     judicem; quibus Saturnus [secus]* videtur
     judicasse: Tu Jovis quoniam spiritum dedisti
     [...]** corpus recipito. Cura quoniam prima
15   *eum finxit, quamdiu vixerit Cura eum possideat;*
     sed quoniam de nomine eius controversia est,
     homo vocetur quoniam ex humo videtur esse factus.

Heidegger places the word *Sorge* between quotations marks to remind the reader that the customary, everyday sense of the word is *not* intended. 'Care', as the translation of *Sorge*, denotes a constant state of attentiveness to things, but this is a secondary sense of the word and translating *Sorge* this way does little justice to the full richness of meaning of the word as Heidegger uses it. There are at least two other sense of the word, one more primary and the other also secondary. In the fable recorded by Hyginus, *Sorge* is a literary expression for a mythic being, while, for Heidegger, it is *terminus technicus* in his *analytique* of Existence.

The fable "Cura" is not a myth. Its primary significance is didactic. As such, it does not belong among the many narratives of the doings of the gods in the Roman pantheon. As indicated earlier, it is a philosophical allegory and, as a *fabula*, a dramatic episode meant to edify the reader. The early sense of a *fabula* is a brief dramatic piece or playlet.

There are five characters in the scene. The climax of the action is the assignment of a name to one of the characters. In Heidegger's reading of the fable, following Burdach, Cura's name is translated *Sorge* and Tellus is rendered *Erde*. By contrast, the names Jupiter and Saturn are retained unchanged. Finally, *das Gebild* is named *homo*.

Jupiter, whose name recalls his solar provenance, is usually associated with activity, movement, light. His father, Saturn, represents time. The name is derived from Saturn's role in agricultural myths as "the sower of seed."[42] The Indo-European root for Saturn is **se-**, which means to implant. In general, Saturn suggests time and dissemination. Tellus, who is identified

---

At (*) Rose interpolates: *sec[um contemplat]us*. At (**) there is a lacuna in the text into which Rose inserts *animam post mortem accipe; quoniam corpus praebuit*. He also substitutes *anima* for *spiritum* at line 14. The most notable philological variant for the present study is the appearance of the word *hominem* at line 3. Following Rose, the fable has it that Cura takes up a piece of earth explicitly "to fashion man." Finally, Rose believes that this *fabula* is not Greek because of Hyginus's derivation of *homo* from *humus*.

[42] We recall here Heidegger's characterization of the preparatory thinker as a sower of seed.

with Vesta (as maternal genetrix of all things, Tellus Mater, is Mother Earth), means ground or floor, that upon which everything takes its position and takes place. All things rest on and with her. She is the site of all activity, the ground on which there is an appropriate place for everything. In other myths, Tellus/Vesta is veiled.

But who is Cura? Where does she come from? Though found in Roman mythology, she does not have a Greek predecessor. According to one authority, her origins are most likely Babylonian. There she was known as Ceres.[43] Her name is derived from 'Cer' (variously, 'Car' and 'Q're'), which means fate or destiny. She is identified with darkness, Moira (or Moera), the "new moon child" of necessity (the "strong fate").[44] In the fable, she is *sorrow* personified.[45] I will explain why this seems evident to me.

The modern acceptation of sorrow does not adequately grasp the fundamental sense of the word as it is used in the fable. We tend to think only of sadness or grief in reaction to the death of a parent or friend. As the fable makes clear, however, the sorrow spoken of possesses the human being throughout his lifetime. It is not something occasional. Instead, the sorrow Heidegger is thinking of here resembles instead the melancholy of *Gelassenheit* or *das Kuinzige*. John Locke defined it in this way: "Sorrow is uneasiness in the mind, upon the thought of a good lost, a good which might have been enjoyed longer."[46] According to the fable, sorrow, which possesses every human being, is the human condition. In the 15th century, the verb sorrow still meant to look after, which reflects the sec-

---

[43] *The New Larousse Encyclopedia of Mythology* (1973) New York: Prometheus Press, 61 and 211. See also Robert Graves, op. cit., Section 82.6. Though Ceres' rites were known in Greece, her temple was found only in the Roman Empire.

[44] See Graves, Sections 10c and 90.8.

[45] See Julius Pokorny, *Indogermanisches etymologisches Wörterbuch* (1959–69) Bern: Francke, Volume 1, 611, the entry for *cura*. He derives the word from the root Indo-European root kois-, which is glossed *sorgen?*. In the entry, Pokorny glosses *cura* with *Sorge*.

[46] *An Essay Concerning Human Understanding*, Book II, Chapter XX, Section 8.

ondary meaning of *Sorge* as care. We must always keep in mind, however, that *Sorge* is, for Heidegger, the fundamental ontological structure of all of the existentials, the "categories" of Existence. It is the condition of there being any caretaking, solicitude or looking after, any caring for things or caring about people.

The Indo-European root of 'sorrow' is **swergh-**, which is also the root for *Sorge*.[47] Heidegger's reference to the fable makes it clear that he was sensitive to this basic sense of *Sorge* as 'sorrow.'

We return now to the action of the fable. Cura has been wandering about. We come upon her as she is about to cross a river. A river is rich in symbolic suggestions. It may divide two realm, belonging to neither. It suggests the flow of cosmic time, change, and the course of a lifetime. As a boundary, it may stand for the horizon of time, what Heidegger calls *Temporalität*. Cura herself stands for darkness, as we have seen.

Dark destiny abroad, Cura is at the threshold of time and change, where she meets Jupiter, the son of time (Saturn). She stops short of entering time, however, having spotted an outgrowth [*physis*] of clay on the bank beneath her. The clay-rich earth mentioned in the fable is the stuff out of which jugs and other durable things can be crafted. Such earth is also often a *talutatium*, an indication of valuable minerals within the soil, the most valuable part of Mother Earth.[48]

Thoughtfully, Cura picks up a piece of this earth. In the very act of being taken up, this matter takes on the form that Cura fatefully has to give it. The resulting form's own destiny is to have been made in conformity with Cura, the wistful Fate, and to belong to her. She works this fragment of earth in the same manner in which she had taken it up: thoughtfully. Cura is not blind fate.

---

[47] Pokorny, op. cit., Volume 1, 1051.
[48] For the relation between Tellus (earth) and homo (humanity), see Alois Walde, *Lateinisches etymologisches Wörterbuch* (1910) Heidelberg: Winter, 372–73.

Now Jupiter, whose name suggests what divides time,[49] appears as Cura is meditating on what she has just done. The god of great activity and light, Jupiter shines like the sun. His brightness interrupts her dark meditation, but suffuses her creation with spirit. This is Jupiter's gift. Cura now wants Jupiter to give it her name, but he declines. Why? Presumably, a creature invested with spirit should not bear the name of a twilight creature fashioned out of mud. Tellus, whose body had been robbed by Cura of some of its substance, now rears up to make her own case, that in all fairness, the creature should be given *her* name, considering the sacrifice she has made.

The creature thus emerges in the midst of strife. The verb used to name Cura's action is *sustellere*, which can mean to lift up and enhance or to destroy.[50] Burdach's translation of *sustellere* as *nehmen* preserves this ambiguity. *Nehmen* can mean to take up into safekeeping and to take to, manifesting an affinity for it. Or it can mean to seize, lay hold of or capture. Cura's action includes all of these elements. The uneasy relation between earth and sorrow determines the character of Cura's creature.

Still one more question may be raised about their relation. Is Cura, as destiny, more primordial than earth herself? Or can there be a question of precedence here? Stated otherwise, how are destiny and substance related? We may be able to shed a little light on this question in what follows.

---

[49] 'Jupiter' is derived from the Indo-European root **da-**, to divide, as the tide divides phases of the day. There is a further connection here between Cura, as Moira (the child of the new moon), and the lunar influences on the movement of the tides: Jupiter, the son of time, oversees the appearance of Cura.

[50] An interesting connection between Tellus and Cura lies hidden in the word used to describe Cura's creative gesture. Another German word for *sustellere* is *aufheben* (sublate). The name Tellus is derived from the same root as *sustellere*. In fact, earth also shares some of the antithetical sense of "taking up" that describes Cura's act. Earth is the source of life and death: it forms and destroys. In the fable, Cura elevates earth even as she wrests part of earth's body from her for Cura's purposes. Therefore it is earth's destiny that she (Cura) is "elevated" in the formation of man.

Saturn is asked to adjudicate the three-way dispute about what name the creature shall have. The creature of sorrow, made of earth but suffused with spirit, now stands under the judgment of time, though it still remains in the hands of sorrow. Saturn is the only character in the fable who speaks. He first addresses his son, Jupiter. Time first addresses *Geist*. Since spirit or mind was only loaned, so to speak, to the creature, it must be returned to the giver when the creature finally dies. Next, Saturn speaks to earth. She shall have back the part of her that had been borrowed by Cura when the creature fashioned by Cura dies.

Nothing is said about the life force of the creature that Cura brought to the creature. The fable clearly implies a creationist view of life, but we are not able to understand the meaning of the creature's death from what the fable says. The place of death in this philosophical allegory is puzzling. In Rose's reconstruction of the text, there is some mention of death in an interpolated line. Of course, when he was writing *Being and Time*, Heidegger could not have been familiar with Rose's work, which appeared only in 1933.

The creature's life [*anima*] is not returned to Cura. What becomes of it? It is evidently bound up with the creature's being possessed by sorrow throughout its life. *Knowing that it will die possesses the human being.* This essential feature of Existence figures at the heart of Heidegger's analysis. Knowing that it must die is the most fundamental possibility of Existence.

The creature is both a gift of the earth and something wrenched from it by Cura. Torn from his mother, Earth, his life is an ambivalent affair which is related to his awareness that he will die. Here emergence [*physis*] and creation are contrasted. Human life is portrayed in the fable as a consequence of creation, but somehow out of tune with nature. The fable "Cura" thus stands between the Greek conception of nature as *physis* and the Christian view of nature as created by God.

Saturn speaks directly to Tellus and Jupiter, but Cura is addressed indirectly. This may be an indication of her less-than-godly status. Saturn speaks about Cura only, as though she were unconscious or asleep. He say: "But since Sorrow first created this being, Sorrow may possess it as long as it lives."

Why did Heidegger choose this document, and not another creation allegory? I would suggest that it has to do with the naming of the creature. There is a three-way struggle over what it shall be named. Had it been named after Jupiter, its essence would have suggested its intelligence and spirituality. Yet, it is understandable that Saturn does not allow this, since he had been ejected from the heavens by Jupiter. The latter's importunate nature in wanting to override Cura's initial request that the creature be named after her offends him (Time). Tellus, the last character to request that the creature be her namesake is also denied the honor, though an indirect link remains to her in Saturn's choice of name: *homo*, from *humus* — earth, ground, soil.

It comes as a surprise that Saturn does not name the creature after its creatrix. Knowing Heidegger's care in distinguishing the human being from Existence, it is likely that the implied separation in the fable interested him. Already in this fable, the human being [*homo*] and its ontological structure or essence (sorrow) are also distinguished.

The creature is not named after its ontological structure, but rather for its material provenance. The human being is the material site of the occurrence of Existence. This distinction is evident in the fable and we may suppose that Heidegger's interest in the fable stems from this early "evidence" of the way of seeing matters that he himself was explicating.

The fable occupies a position in Heidegger's exposition that belongs neither to the ontic analysis of everyday life nor to the ontological analysis of the existentials. His introductory remarks to the presentation of the fable run as follows:

> In our foregoing interpretations [*Interpretationen*], which have finally led to exhibiting sorrow as the be[ing] of Existence, everything depended on our arriving at the right *ontological* foundations for that being which in each case we ourselves are, and which we call "man." To do this it was necessary from the outset to change the direction of our analysis from the approach which had not been clarified ontologically and is in principle questionable. In com-

parison with this definition, the existential-ontological interpretation may seem strange, especially if 'sorrow' is understood just ontologically as worry [*Besorgnis*] or grief [*Bekümmeris*]. Accordingly we shall now cite a document which is preontological in character, even though its demonstrative force is "merely historical."

We must bear in mind, however, that in this document Existence is expressing itself "primordially," unaffected by any theoretical interpretation [*Interpretation*] and without aiming to propose any. We must also note that the be[ing] of Existence is characterized by historicality [*Geschichtlichkeit*], though this must first be demonstrated ontologically. *If* Existence is historical [*ge-schichtlich*] in the very depths of its be[ing], then any expression [*Aussage*] which comes from its history and goes back to it, and which, moreover, is *prior* to any scientific knowledge, will have especial weight, even though its importance is never purely ontological. *That understanding of be[ing] which lies in Existence itself expresses itself preontologically* [emphasis added]. The document which we are about to cite should make plain that our existential interpretation [*Interpretation*] is not a mere fabrication, but that as an ontological construction [*Konstruktion*] it is well grounded and has been sketched out beforehand in elemental ways.

There is an ancient fable in which Existence's interpretation [*Auslegung*] of itself as "sorrow" has been embedded [*niedergelegt*] [:].

The meaning of the term 'preontological' is important. It signifies the realm of Existence prior to the emergence in thought of the ontological difference, that is, prior to metaphysics and the conceptual differentiation between the 'ontic' and the 'ontological' realms.

"That understanding of be[ing] which lies in Existence itself, expresses itself preontologically." The inherent understanding of be[ing] that is crucial for Heidegger's analysis of Existence thus expresses itself preontologically. The embeddedness of Existence in an historical situation makes Existence historical "in the very depths of its be[ing]," from out of which its understanding of be[ing] expresses itself. Anything that speaks out of this historicality must have special value. The fable is an example of such an expression [*Aussage*], which "comes from its history and goes back to it." The circular movement from and back to the history of Existence is the hermeneutic circle of genuine interpretation [*Auslegung*], which is distinguished from literary or philological exegesis [*Interpretation*].

Additional testimony to the important place of the fable "Cura" in *Being and Time*, is buried in footnote (cited above) a few paragraphs later:

> The way in which "sorrow" is viewed in the foregoing existential analytic of Existence is one that the author has awakened to [*erwuchs*] in connection with his attempts at an interpretation [*Interpretation*] of Augustinian (i.e. Helleno-Christian) anthropology with regard to the axiomatic foundations [*grundsätzlichen Fundamente*] arrived at in the ontology of Aristotle.

Heidegger's reading of Augustine's anthropology with a view to Aristotle's ontology of Existence lay at the source of his insight into the fundamental ontological structure of Existence. The view of Existence given in the fable, like its idea of nature, is from the borderland between the Greek and early Christian views of human being. The river Cura is about to cross may itself stand for this boundary. The view of Existence in the fable is unique in that it belongs to both worlds. Heidegger's distance from scientific anthropology could not be better marked than by his observation in the inconspicuous footnote just given and should put to rest any claims about what he was trying to do in the existential *analytique* in *Being and Time*.

The view to which he "awoke" following his efforts at interpreting Augustine is presented in *Being and Time*. It must have been reassuring to find a little-known fable that embodied the same effort of reading the early Church Father with the eyes of an Aristotle. The unknown author of the fable lived in the historical moment of Helleno-Christian encounter which Heidegger was now repeating in the early years of the 20th century.

We have now reached the point in our drama where the name of the creature is bestowed on it by Saturn. "And because there is now a dispute as to its name, let it be called *homo*, for it is made out of *humus* (earth). Since there is strife, time must adjudicate. Time has the only "say" in the fable. Time has the last word (*homo*). The creature's name is made out of the

Indo-European root **dhghem-**, from which the word 'chthonic' is also derived.

At this point, we look back to another detail of the language of the fable. The verb used by the author of the fable to describe the creation of homo is *fingere*, translated with *bilden*, to give shape to or form. By contrast, when referring to the making up of a name for the creature, the verb is *facere*, translated with *machen* (to make or compose). In the fable, the human being is formed, while its name, like the fable itself, is composed. While its body has been shaped using material on hand, its name has been created out of nothing. In the naming of the creature a more fundamental sense of origin is indicated. Cura's work had been mere transformation, but real creation *ex nihilo* is here the work of time. Saturn, not Jupiter, would figure, then, as the Roman precursor of the Christian God.

For Heidegger, the creature of the fable "Cura" is a preontological expression of Existence, that is, *by* historical Existence *about* its essence. The fate of Existence is to be held throughout its lifetime by sorrow. This sorrow is inseparable from the gift of its life. It determines the be[ing] of Existence, which is to attentively heed other beings, including human beings.

At this point in his interpretation of the fable Heidegger notes the meaning of Saturn as Time, and he cites a poem by Herder. The poem, "Das Kind der Sorge," shows that Saturn (Time) decides "wherein the 'primordial' be[ing] of this creature is to be seen":[51]

> Once by a murmuring river
> Sorrow sat down, and there,
> In a vision, thought to form with her touch
> A wavering figure.

---

[51] This poem of Johann Gottfried von Herder (1744–1803) appears in his *Eigene Gedichte*. Heidegger cites it in the 1889 edition of Herder's works by Bernhard Ludwig Suphan. The text given here is from Herder's *Sämmtliche Werke* (1821), edited by Johann von Müller, Volume XX, 7–8. Alternative readings are based on the edition of *Herders Poetisches Werke* (1889), edited by Carl Redlich, Berlin: Weidmannische Buchhandlung, Volume V, 75–76.

"What dost thou, pensive goddess?"
Asked Zeus, who drew quite close.
"I've formed a figure of clay;
Bring it to life, I pray thee, god."

"Well, then! Live! — It lives!
And let it be my creature!"
But then said Sorrow:
"No! To me. Give it to me, Lord!"

"My touch has formed it" —
"And *I* gave life to the clay!"
Said Jupiter. As he spoke thus,
There Tellus also passed by.

"It's mine! From my own
Womb she took the child."
"Well, then, wait!" said Jupiter.
"Here comes Saturn, the arbiter."

Saturn said: "Be still, all of you!"
Thus is the will of highest fate:
Thou who gave it life,
Take its spirit when it dies;

Thou, Tellus, its bones;
Since none of it's part of you,
To you, its mother, O Sorrow,
Will it be granted in life.

Yet as long as it breathes,
Never will you forsake your child.
Alike is it beholden to you,
Day after day, unto the grave.

The decree of destiny was fulfilled,
And this creature was called Man.
In life it belongs to Sorrow,
In death, to Earth and God.[52]

Herder refers to Tellus as the creature's mother, though he also says the creature's body was taken from Tellus' womb. He also substitutes 'God' for Zeus/Jupiter, in the poem's last line, emphasizing the Christian element in the myth. The highest authority of all, however, is fate [*das Geschick*] or destiny [*Schicksal*]!

---

[52]   *Einst sass am murmelnden Strome / Die Sorge nieder und sann: / Da bildet' im Traum der Gedanken / Ihr Finger ein leimernes Bild.*

"Was hast du, sinnende Göttin?" / Spricht Zeus, der eben ihr naht. / "Ein Bild von Thone gebildet, / Beleb's, ich bitte dich, Gott."

"Wohlan dann! Lebe! — Es lebet! / Und mein sey dieses Geschöpf!" — / Dagegen redet die Sorge: / "Nein, lass es, lass es mire, Herr.

Mein Finger hat es gebildet" — / "Und ich gab Lebe den Thon," / Sprach Jupiter. Als sie so sprachen, / Da trat auch Tellus hinan.

"Mein ists! Sie hat mire genommen / Von meinem Schoose das Kind." / "Wohlan, sprach Jupiter, wartet, / Dort kommt ein Entscheider, Saturn."

*Saturn sprach: "Habet es alle!" / So will's das hohe **Geschick**. / Du, der das Leben ihm schenkte, / Nimm, wenn es stirbet, den Geist.*

Du, Tellus, sein Gebeine: / Denn mehr gehöret dir nicht. / Dir, seiner Mutter, O Sorge, / Wird es im Leben geschenkt.

Du wirst, so lang' es nur ahmet, / Es nie verlassen, den Kind. / Dir ähnlich wird es von Tage / Zu Tage sich mühen ins Grab."

*Des **Schicksals** Spruch ist erfüllet / Und Mensch heißt dieses Geschöpf. / Im Leben gehört es der Sorge, / Der Erd' im Sterben und Gott.*

In the fifth stanza, Herder glosses 'Saturn' with *Zeit*.

Several details, which certainly did not escape Heidegger, are illuminated in Herder's treatment of the fable. Sorrow reaches into the water and takes up a clump of mud, from which she shapes a "wavering figure." This suggests the creature's evanescence. It is a reflected image on the surface of water. Herder implies that Sorrow conjures up the image of the figure *as* she fashions it. The creation itself is generated by Sorrow's imagination, which evokes the creature as her touch produces it.

The creation act has the quality of a vision or even a dream. Zeus/Jupiter refers to Sorrow as a "pensive goddess." She demonstrates something like meditative thinking, the originative thinking that Heidegger will characterize as preparatory thinking.

Yet another feature of preparatory thinking may be adduced at this point. It is akin to what Kant called the transcendental imagination. We recall Heidegger's interest in the initial centrality of the transcendental imagination in Kant's *Critique of Pure Reason* and his apparent subsequent retreat from giving it that position in the second edition of the work.[53]

Life and spirit come to the creature together as the result of Jupiter's exclamation: "Live!" In the fable, Sorrow had bestowed *anima* on the creature, while Jupiter brought *spiritus* to it. Herder characterizes what Sorrow fashioned as a creation [*Geschöpf*], likening her act to the work of a sculptor: a work of art, not of manufacture. Herder emphasizes the mutuality of obligation between man and sorrow. To say that sorrow may never give up its hold on man means that man is beholden to sorrow throughout his life. Man is in debt to sorrow in some way. At the same time, sorrow is paradoxically man's security during his lifetime.

The concluding stanza of the poem contains the only explicit reference to the Christian *Weltanschauung*. The fate of Existence is to belong to sorrow. At death, it belongs equally to heaven and earth. Fate is related here to time and not to sorrow, as in the fable.

---

[53] *Kant and the Problem of Metaphysics* [1927/28], Bloomington: Indiana University Press, 1991 [especially Part III].

Heidegger had been led to the poem by Burdach, who had cited it in his article. His decision to include it as additional evidence of a preontological expression of the fundamental structure of Existence as sorrow was likely based on Herder's having highlighted the place and meaning of time in the naming of the creature.

The chthonic provenance of Existence, which is expressed in the fable, means that it remains earthbound. Earth's contribution comes as an ambivalent gift. Thanks to Zeus/Jupiter/God, it gleams with spirit, but this shining is withdrawn at the moment its *anima* leaves it. Sorrow, not spirit, is the singular feature of Existence, according to the fable "Cura". I think this is the twist that gave the fable its centrality in *Being and Time*. It marks Heidegger's departure from other accounts of human nature, which have always made spirit or consciousness the central feature of human nature. Heidegger sees that Existence is endowed with and beholden to sorrow before consciousness can figure at all in the picture.

The conditionality of Existence is a consequence of this precedence of life over spirit. Whatever feline life, for example, is beholden to, human life is beholden to sorrow. It follows that each form of life has its own ontological "character."

According to the fable, the Existence of man is the condition of its being a creature that is earthbound yet endowed with spirit. This turns upside down the naturalistic explanation, to which we have become accustomed, that the human being is first a creature of the earth that has subsequently acquired spirit (mind, consciousness) whether by a genetic fluke or by grace. The Helleno-Christian interpretation given in the fable is preontological, but is it a full-blown Christian interpretation, although it still carries with it the deep tendency of Greek thinking.

Heidegger's fundamental ontology puts the relation of Existence and time on a new footing. The ontological structure of Existence is sorrow. Again, this has nothing to do with a chronic psychological state that would give the picture of someone in a perpetual state of mourning.

The sense of this ontological sorrow, as felt by a child, is beautifully captured in the lines of the American writer James Agee (1909–1955), in his posthumously published novel *A Death in the Family* (1915): "By some chance, here they are, all on this earth; and who shall ever tell the sorrow of being on this earth."[54] There is no unhappiness here.

> They are not talking much, and the talk is quiet, of nothing in particular, of nothing at all in particular, of nothing at all. The stars are wide and alive, they seem each like a smile of great sweetness, and they seem very near.

As the unifying fundamental ontological structure of Existence, sorrow holds together the existentials, including attunement or conditionality, the capacity for moods such as grief. Sorrow, according to the fable, dispenses its destiny to the creature. Existence is, as the German idiomatic expression has it, earth's *Sorgenkind* (problem child). As a consequence of having spirit or mind, it knows its status. As a living being, that means, above all, knowing it will not always be alive — that it must die. Animal beings lack spirit in this sense. Here, again, the Christian notion of spirit dominates the picture.

Existence is mortal, unlike the gods, who are deathless, and animals, who lack knowledge of their coming death. Mortal means both about to die and knowledgeable of that impending death. Animals, though they have *anima*, lack *spiritus*, which implies knowledge. They carry on their lives without any awareness of the future, which is when death will occur. Existence is that *place* on earth, among things, living and inanimate, where destiny has meaning. Destiny has meaning only for Existence. In terms of the fable, Cura, who is also understood as destiny, bestows herself only on the human being. Meanwhile, Existence is the temporary harbor of spirit.

Sorrow possesses Existence. She holds on to Existence, which is beholden to her in turn. We may characterize the beholdenness of Existence more accurately as heed, which is, like care, a secondary meaning of *Sorge*. Only on the basis of the securing hold sorrow has on Existence can Existence

---

[54] New York: Avon Books, 14.

attend to other beings, especially human beings, and, of course, to itself. Sorrow, heed and care about and for beings is the full meaning of *Sorge*, in its primary and two secondary senses.

The word 'heed' comes from the Indo-European root **kadh-**, to cover, shelter and protect. The fundamental sense of heed is to protect. For Heidegger, Existence, as the site which occasions and situates the event of enownment [*Ereignis*] to be[ing], participates in the play of hiding and revealing that is called truth. It is, as Heidegger says, "in the truth" in so participating in be[ing]. Heeding is the sense of the fundamental structure of Existence that reflects most clearly its relation to be[ing]. But in heeding be[ing], Existence hides itself. Therefore, it can never be fully transparent to itself.[55] Like *homo* of the fable, Existence is also neither animal nor god, neither merely alive nor free of destiny. We may call *homo* a chthonic god, *der letzte Gott*.

Existence is that *condicio* or divine agreement in which it is discovered that human being is mortal. Existence heeds its own implicit death, but in so doing hides itself. This is one of the features of heeding, as we have seen. Existence is the way of being that tends to its life (as animals also do) but also attends its always imminent death. This makes human being unique among beings. Being on this earth, but no longer entirely a part of it — its finite transcendence — is the way the fable "Cura" portrays Existence. Its ontic commitments tend to distract it from its ontological being towards death. As the fable shows, this is not a mistake that human beings make, but it part of their essence, which is Existence. In sum, Existence is the site of its very own be[ing] as sorrow, heed and care.[56]

---

[55] Though Heidegger does not say this, it would follow from the nature of its relation to one's be[ing], that Existence precisely does not have access to itself. Others do, just as, conversely, one has access to their Existence, while they do not. This is a feature of *Mitdasein* (coexistence) that Heidegger seems not have worked out in *Being and Time*.

[56] The Taoist *Weltanschauung* characterizes the relation of heaven (Jupiter) and earth (Tellus) with respect to man, the boundary creature, with the figure of *yang* and *yin* bordering at a wavering line called *jen*.

Heidegger covers some of the same ground in his lecture course, *Prolegomena to the History of the Concept of Time*, which was given around the same time that *Being and Time* was in its germinal stage, in the summer of 1925. The lectures, in fact, serves as an introduction to the book. Following is the passage from that course in which he discusses the fable "Cura":[57]

THE FABLE "CURA" AS EVIDENCE FOR A PRIMORDIAL SELF-INTERPRETATION OF EXISTENCE

The assertion that the structure of the be[ing] of Existence is sorrow is a phenomenological one, not a prescientific self-interpretation, like the assertion: "Life is sorrow and pain." A ground structure is encountered in the former assertion which the second assertion reproduces only in one of its immediate everyday aspects. But the first assertion can and must at the same time be taken as the definition of man, if Existence is our theme. Also, this interpretation of Existence based on the phenomenon of sorrow is not something I have merely thought up. Neither has it grown out of a definite philosophical position — I have no philosophy as such. Rather, it is suggested simply by the analysis of the matter itself. Nothing is being read into the matter (in this case, Existence); instead, everything is drawn from it. Existence itself is the self-interpreting, self-articulating being. Seven years ago, while I was investigating these structures in connection with my attempt to reach the ontological foundations of Augustinian anthropology, I came across the phenomenon of sorrow. Of course, Augustine and ancient Christian anthropology in general did not know the phenomenon explicitly, nor even directly as a term, although *cura* (sorrow) [as care] had played a part in Seneca, as well as in the New Testament, as is well known. Later, however, I later came across a self-interpretation of Existence in an old fable, in which *Existence sees itself as sorrow* [emphasis added]. Such interpretations have the primary advantage that they are drawn from an originally naïve glimpse of Existence itself, and, on that account, play an exceptionally important role in all interpretation, as Aristotle already knew.

---

[57] *History of the Concept of Time* [1925], Bloomington: Indiana University Press, 301 ff. The text should be read in connection with the only recently published lecture, "Der Begriff der Zeit," given in 1924. See *The Concept of Time*, London: Blackwell, 1992.

After reading the fable, he goes on:

> In this naïve interpretation of Existence we observe the astonishing fact that
> here the sight is set on Existence, and that along with body and spirit, some-
> thing like "sorrow" is seen as that phenomenon which is to be imparted to
> [*zugesprochen wird*] this being as long as it lives, that is, as Existence, which
> we have regarded here [in the prolegomena] as to be in a world [*In-der-Welt-
> sein*]. Kondrad Burdach, through whom I came across this fable, has now
> worked out the details. Burdach shows here that Goethe got the fable of
> Hyginus from Herder and adapted it in the second part of his *Faust*. Burdach
> then gives, as always in a very reliable and scholarly way, a large amount of
> material relating to the history of this concept. He says that the word in the
> New testament for *Sorge* (*sollicitudo* in the Vulgate), μέριμνα (or as it proba-
> bly was originally called, φροντίς) was already a technical term in the moral
> philosophy of the Stoics. It was used in Seneca's 90th letter, which was also
> known to Goethe, for the description of primitive man [*primitiven Menschen*].
> The *double sense of cura* [emphasis added] refers to care [*Sorge*] for something
> as caring about [*Besorgen*], being absorbed by things [*Aufgehen in der Welt*],
> but also in the sense of resignation [*Hingabe*]. This occurs with the [existen-
> tial] structures we have exposed. But does this not mean that in a certain way
> *cura* is already seen in the natural interpretation of Existence, although not in
> the form of an explicit question regarding the very structure of the be[ing] of
> Existence?

This is the penultimate paragraph of Heidegger's handwritten manuscript
of the text of the course. It is significant that the course should end here.
The fable is the climax of the course as originally conceived, which is
further attestation to its importance for Heidegger.

Heidegger speaks openly of the double sense of *cura* in the fable, as caring
about [*Besorgen*] and resignation [*Hingabe*]. What he here calls *Hingabe*
later becomes *Gelassenheit*. In connection with this, Existence is the way
of the being *who* protects or guards be[ing]. Heidegger hints making explicit the sense of *cura* in the *Prolegomena*, since *Hingabe* also means devo-
tion that watches over and protects. But the primordial sense of *Sorge*, as
sorrow, is not revealed here.

To be in a world means to be distanced from the earth in a fundamental
way. Considering the fable as we have, the place of earth in Heidegger's

conception of Existence gains in importance. In a sense, earth is an even more elusive notion than sorrow.

In the fable, there are two meanings of earth, which continue to appear in Heidegger's thought. It is plausible that the ambiguity of this usage was not new to Heidegger when he came across the fable and that he found confirmation of it in the text preserved by Hyginus. For Heidegger, there are two senses of earth, one cosmic and the other ontological.

First, there is the earth of man as a natural creature, which is the object of study by the natural sciences. However, there is also the earth of Existence, the creation of a chthonic goddess. As a site [topos], Existence is intimately a part of this earth, which the gods have never really abandoned.

How shall we, finally, understand the ontological meaning of Existence from the preontological account given in the fable "Cura"? The "existential condition for the possibility" of all of the "categories" of Existence is expressed in the fable. This condition is termed sorrow. "To be in a world has the stamp [Prägung] of 'sorrow', which accords with its be[ing]." This, its ontological nature, has been determined by time (Saturn). "Thus the pre-ontological characterization of man's essence expressed in this fable has brought to view in advance the kind of be[ing] which dominates his temporal sojourn in the world [zeitlichen Wandel in der Welt].[58]

The position of the fable at the heart of Being and Time and at the climax of his Prolegomena to the book suggests that it was a crucial text to have "come across." It evidently reassured Heidegger that his fundamental ontology had been anticipated. There could be no more suitable and fitting term than 'sorrow' to characterize humanity's curious position between heaven and earth, life and death, nature and art. Care and heed, the secondary senses of the ontological structure of the existentialia, further deepen the meaning of Sorge in Heidegger's analytique of Existence.

---

[58] Being and Time, 243.

I have tried to uncover the primary sense of *Sorge* in the preceding look at Heidegger's interpretation of the fable "Cura". The effort arose from a dissatisfaction about the translation of *Sorge* as 'care', believing as I do that the English word does not do justice to the unspoken underlying primary sense of the term in Heidegger's usage. I have wanted to recover that sense of the term.

Further hints about what remains unsaid in Heidegger's teaching still need to be brought to light, but I do not for a moment think Heidegger was unwilling to be more explicit, nor do I believe he wanted to be obscure in order to seem profound.

Three

The Telling Word

I

ON JANUARY 26, 1964, AS PART OF A SERIES of broadcast programs of Radio Zurich entitled "Wirkendes Wort [The Telling Word]," Martin Heidegger read excerpts from *Die Mappe meines Urgroßvaters [My Great-grandfather's Notebook]*, an unfinished novel by the Austrian writer Adalbert Stifter.[59] The excerpts and the text of the commentary were published later that year and have been reprinted in Volume 13 of the Heidegger *Gesamtausgabe, Aus der Erfahrung des Denkens [From the Experience of Thinking]*. In the brief remarks that accompanied his reading, Heidegger touched on several elements of his theory of "poetic speech," but his comments there also have bearing on Heidegger's understanding of actuality [*Wirklichkeit*] and the nature of the real.

The remarks Heidegger made about Stifter's "Eisgeschichte [Ice Tale]" are part of his broader study of language. Since he usually chose his examples from poetry, having singled out Stifter's *prose* for an examination of the essence of poetic speech at work seems high praise indeed.

Adalbert Stifter was born in Oberplan (Bohemia), in 1805, and died in Linz, in 1868. Heidegger refers to the *Studienmappe* (Working 'Notebook') (1844) version of the novel, which was the second version to appear during Stifter's lifetime. Another version of the novel was in the works at the

---

[59]   See the Appendix following this chapter.

time of Stifter's death. The episode called the "Ice Tale" appears only in the *Studien* version, in chapter 4, entitled "Margarita".

II

Heidegger's comments begin with a reference to a letter from Stifter to his publisher, in which the writer predicts that the "Ice Tale" *muß tief wirken*: it is bound to have a profound effect on the reader. Heidegger then asks: "What might the poet have meant by the effect [*Wirkung*] of his words [*Wort*]?"[60]

Heidegger attempts to understand how poetic speech comes to work its unique magic on the listener. He does this, in part, with the help of an exploration of the transformations of the German verb *wirken*, (to do or effect).[61]

In the "Ice Tale," a feeling for the great mystery that lies at the heart of experience is occasioned by freezing conditions that have all but paralyzed a region of the Black Forest and its inhabitants. Stifter calls the iciness that grips everything *das Ding* (the thing). "It" has frozen people in their tracks and threatens their homes and lives, as well as the natural environment on which they depend. The "thing" holds everything, in totality, in thrall.

Heidegger inquires whether the effect of the episode lies in the strangeness of the "thing" in and of itself, in Stifter's art as a gifted stylist, or in a combination of these or other elements. "Or does the affecting [*das Wirk-*

---

[60] *Das Wort* has variously the sense of "[the] words," "expression," "writing," "poetic utterance or speech," and "the poetic word," "pronouncement."

[61] In German, the verb *wirken* has a broad range of applications, from kneading dough (perhaps the most ancient), knitting and weaving, and working the land, to the operation of tools and machinery. The adjective and adverb form, *wirklich*, like the noun *Wirklichkeit*, connotes a sense of the true. *Wirken* is derived from the Indo-European root **werg-**, from which the Greek words *ergon* (and *organon*) and *orgia*, and the English words 'work' and 'wrought' are also derived.

en] in words have yet an entirely different sense?" He answers: "[The affecting] works [*wirkt*] in what it evokes in the reader, namely, the very attending [*Hören*] to the Said [*das Gesagte*], i.e. what is pointed to by the words. The affecting in words is a calling and pointing to."

The affecting in words "does not cause effects [*Wirkungen*] of the kind produced by pressure and force in the field of mechanical operations." The effect in question is not the effect of a cause. Nor is the affecting in words something like the consequence or conclusion of a logical "if → then" deduction. That is to say, such an effect does not occur in the realm of creation metaphysics or natural science. For this reason, Stifter's tale also does not portray the powers of nature as forces unleashed on man. For him, as for Heidegger, man and nature are not embattled in opposition. They are, together, part of a great unity and an even greater mystery.

The effect of the telling word is indistinguishable from what it evokes in the listener: "an attending to the Said." The affecting in the telling word is "a calling and pointing to" the Said. The Said is what is spoken *of*, not the words themselves, whether spoken or written. Of course, language can also objectify things by naming and describing them, but this would be to speak *about* them, not *of* them. For Heidegger, speaking about things is a degraded use of language, even though it is the standard form of scientific discourse and everyday conversation. The telling word, by contrast, is poetic. It makes real [*wirklich*] what it expresses. It is the kind of utterance that lets beings be.

In the "Ice Tale," the Said is marked by the word 'thing'. Stifter's words are telling because they effect actualities and summon the listener to what they point to. Poetic speech does not capture in words what summons the listener. It summons the listener to the unspeakable and unutterable. " ... [T]he pointing to the invisible ... through the letting be heard of the un- spoken — this Saying is what is telling in the words of Adalbert Stifter." The telling word in Stifter's tale takes the writer and listener to the limit of expression with the soft ring of the word *Ding*.

Heidegger probes further: "Yet to what do the words [*das Wort*] of the 'Ice Tale' point?" Not to the powers [*Kräfte*] of nature. These are "only a sign [*Zeichen*]. For they point to what is wholly invisible, yet all-determining, above all, for all that to which man must correspond [*entsprechen*] out of the very ground of his Existence if he is to be able to dwell on this earth."

What is it, that the telling word points to? Heidegger notes that, in the preface to *Bunte Steine [Colored Stones]*, a collection of Stifter's stories, the writer names it *das Größe* (the great), while in the "Ice Tale," he had tagged it merely "the thing." Had Stifter's literary powers failed him while writing the "Ice Tale"? Not at all, Heidegger thinks. In fact, he praises Stifter precisely for what he has done with this harmless little word 'thing'. Through its use, Stifter has been able to evoke something without explicitly naming it. But the reader is brought up short at the end of Stifter's eloquence. The word 'thing' is an empty word. It fails to make explicit anything in particular, but for that very reason it contains within it the greatest amount of possibility.[62]

The ice storm is an occasion that reveals the ineffable. The meteorological conditions of an ice-locked alpine forest are only signs indicating the presence of something invisible which the poet cannot put into words. This failure of expression is what interests Heidegger. Stifter is, for Heidegger, a poet because poets are those who try to find words to invoke the unnameable, whether in prose or verse.

Stifter himself finally decided that *My Great-grandfather's Notebook* "didn't work," and did not include the "Ice Tale" in the final version of the novel. It is unclear how he would have taken to the irony of Heidegger's praise for what he considered to be a failure.

---

[62]   This is the "thing" buried in the word 'nothing'.

III

In conclusion, building on Heidegger's comments, I will reflect a bit further on Heidegger's understanding of how the telling word works.

The thinker and poet have in common their search for the telling word. Both face the unnameable and both speak the telling word at the height of their powers. Heidegger had written, in 1943, in his postscript to "What Is Metaphysics?": "The thinker utters be[ing] [*sagt das Sein*]. The poet [*der Dichter*] names the Holy."[63] One of the points of Heidegger's comments on the "Ice Tale" broadens this pronouncement: the poet *announces* the unspeakable. The genuine or originative thinker, by comparison, enunciates hints that point to the unspoken in the thought of other thinkers. Heidegger himself was such a thinker, what one might call a "thinker of the thinker," as Hölderlin was, for him, "the poet of the poet."[64]

The telling word, we recall, points "to what is wholly invisible, yet all-determining, above all, for all that to which man must correspond [*entsprechen*] out of the very ground of his Existence." Man's Existence originates in answering to, literally, speaking out of that to which the telling word points. Is this the primary way or even the only way man's Existence originates?

Both the poet, who "names the holy," and the thinker, who "utters be[ing]," announce the unspoken, whether the unspoken remain unspoken because it is unspeakable (because beyond us as human beings), or whether it be the unarticulated "one singular thought" of all that a thinker actually articulates. The telling word is a nod to either what is destined never to be spoken or what has not yet been revealed.

---

[63] "Postscript" (1943) to "What Is Metaphysics?, in *Existence and Being* (1949), edited by Werner Brock (Chicago: Henry Regnery), 360. The original text is in the *Gesamtausgabe Wegmarken*, Volume 9 (Frankfurt: Klostermann, 1976), 312.

[64] "Hölderlin and the Essence of Poetry," in *Existence and Being*, edited by Werner Brock (Washington: Regnery Gateway, 1988), 271.

For Heidegger, the thinker's course begins with something unspoken. This, his guiding thought, remains the silent source of his utterances. The poet's efforts end at the verge of the unspeakable. A dumb abyss leaves him speechless, perhaps for days or even years, as with Hölderlin. For Heidegger, the poet is familiar with the unspeakable. By contrast, the unspoken thought that lies at the beginning of a thinker's work eludes him throughout the course of his thought. We may ask the thinker: Why write another article or give another conference paper? Heidegger's answer is that the thinker, in speaking or writing, nears that "one singular thought" that incites his thinking. The thinker is drawn out of his silence to speak by the unenunciated of his thought. Speaking is the asymptotic approach to a point that will never be reached.

The poet's approach to Parnassus, by contrast, is a self-regenerating quest for the expression of what, by definition, cannot be expressed: the finally unnameable, for which there is even "a want of holy names" that might "work" for a given historical moment. The unspeakable draws the poet on. Poetic speech always falls short of its absurd goal, yet the poet strives again and again for expressions that will name the invisible mystery lying at the heart of actuality.

Human Existence corresponds to what the telling word announces. The correspondence does not, however, originate with the speaker, but rather with the unspoken. This much is clear. Yet it is difficult to conceptualize the unspoken. Elsewhere, Heidegger writes: "Language speaks."[65] How may we understand the correspondence between the unspeakable and poetic speech in light of this statement that "language speaks." Following the Heideggerian principle that "the essence of something (x) is not anything x-like," we may say that the essence of language is not anything linguistic. Its origin and truth are, in fact, as we have seen, the unspeakable. The least language-like is silence, which is the origin of language.

---

[65]   See the essay "Language" (1950), in *Poetry, Language, Thought* (1971) New York: Harper and Row, 189–210.

The correspondence of man's Existence and the unspeakable originates with the unspeakable, as we have seen. Language, in turn, speaks out of the unspeakable and, thereby, originates the correspondence between the unspeakable and man's Existence. The speaking out of language effects this correspondence, as the complementary meanings of *entsprechen* tell us.

IV

Finally, let us look in on a writer, whether Stifter or Heidegger, Hölderlin or Heraclitus, whether thinker or poet, or the thinker as poet. We want to understand what happens. According to Heidegger, when the telling word is enunciated, it is not a consequence of literary skill or even the greatness of the speaker's theme. Instead, we understand that the speaker of the telling word is first of all a listener, who announces what he hears. Does he hear voices then? Is the speaker of the telling word merely sensitive to what is in the air? No. He is in correspondence with silence, not with language. Language speaks out of that silence. The problem of the telling word is a question about silence, not about language.

Appendix to Chapter 3

A Translation of the "Ice Tale"

When we finally got close to the mountain valley and the forest that ranges across the heights began to loom over our path, suddenly from the dark wood that stands on beautiful jutting rocks we heard a noise that was very peculiar, which neither of us had ever heard before, as though many thousands or even millions of glass tubes were rattling against one another. And in this confusion it withdrew into the distance. The dark wood, however, was too far off to our right for us to have been able to discern very clearly any sound coming from it, and in the silence that pervaded the sky and everything around us, it seemed very odd to us. We had continued a bit farther on before we could stop the horse, which was now underway on its homeward run, hoping to reach its stall sometime that day. We finally stopped though and heard something like a vague rushing sound in the air, and then ... nothing more. The rushing sound, however, had no resemblance to the distant noise we had heard before above even the hoof-beats of our horse. We drove farther on, drawing nearer still the forest below and at last saw the dark opening where the road entered the woods. Although it was still early afternoon and the gray sky shone so brightly that it looked like the shimmer over a setting sun, still it was a winter afternoon and so dreary that the white field ahead of us was already beginning to grow pale, and twilight seemed to hold sway in the mountains. Yet, once again, it only seemed so, for the darkness of the tree trunks stood out markedly against the glimmer of the snowy ground.

As soon as we came to the place where we could go in under the canopy of the forest, Thomas stopped us. We saw standing before us a very slender fir tree bent down by the frosty ice, forming an arch over the route such as people used to make for an imperial visitor. The splendor and weight of ice hanging from the trees was — ineffable! There stood the pines, like candelabra from which innumerable inverted tapers projected in wondrous immensity. The silverning tapers shimmered, the candlesticks themselves were silver, but not all of them stood upright. Many were bent down every which way. We now recognized the rushing sound we had heard in the air earlier. Now it was not in the air — it was with us. Unremitting, it dominated the depths of the forest as boughs and branches cracked and fell to the ground. It was all the more frightening since everything was motionless. In all the glittering and shining, not a twig, not a single pine needle stirred save when, after a while, we noticed a tree bent further down than it had been from the weight of a slowly moving icicle. We waited and just stared, at a loss about whether to go into the thing, not knowing whether it was out of wonderment or fear. Our horse must have wanted to share feelings of the same kind, since the poor animal, lightly drawing up its hooves, eased the sleigh back a bit.

As we stood there and stared — we had not yet said a word — we again heard something fall, a sound we had been aware of twice before today. But now it was quite familiar to us: a loud intense crash. Something like a shriek came first, then followed a short wail, a rushing or scraping sound, and then the dull resounding fall when a mighty tree hits the ground. The clap roared like a storm through the forest and its density of branches, and around us everywhere was a ringing and shimmering as though an infinitude of shattered glass had been thrown together and shaken tumultuously. Then it was as it had been before. The tree trunks stood towering up together, nothing stirred, and the motionless rushing sound continued. It was remarkable when even a branch or twig or piece of ice fell nearby. We did not see where it had come from, only a quick flash of light as it came down, perhaps heard its impact, but saw nothing of the upward swing of the abandoned disburdened twig. And our staring continued as before.

It became clear to us that we could go no farther into the forest. Somewhere a tree and all its branches might be lying across the road, something we could not get over or even get around because the trees were so close together, their needles meshed, with snow pushing up through all the branches and undergrowth. If, however, we were to turn around and head back the way we had wanted to follow, the one we had set out on, a tree might in the meantime have fallen across it, and there we would be, in the middle! The rain continued to pour down unabated. We were once again so bundled up that we could not even move without breaking the blanket. The sleigh was heavy and glazed and the chestnut carried its own extra burden. If perhaps just an ounce more weight accumulated in a tree, it would collapse. In truth, the tree trunks themselves were about to break and the icicles, with tips like sharp wedges, seemed about to rain down on us. We saw them strewn all over the path that lay ahead of us, and while we were standing there, several thudding falls had been heard in the distance. When we looked back whence we had come, neither a single human being nor any other living creature was to be seen anywhere in the entire area around us. There we were — the chestnut, Thomas and I — alone in open nature.

I told Thomas that we should turn back. We set out, brushed off our clothing as much as we could, and removed the clinging ice from the chestnut's hair. It seemed to us that the ice was forming more quickly now than it had in the forenoon. Was it merely that we had observed the event at that time, while in hindsight its progress seemed slower than in the afternoon, when we had other things to do, and only after a while first noticed how much more ice had accumulated? Or was it just colder and raining harder? We did not know. Thomas then turned the horse and sleigh around and we drove back as quickly as we could to the nearest houses in Eidun. [...]

By the time we were finally out of there and stood in the pasture looking down into the valley where my house is, it had become quite dark. By then, however, we were already close enough and no longer worried. Through the uniformly thick grayish air all around us we saw my house and deep blue smoke, most certainly coming from a fire started by our housekeeper, Maria, as she prepared our meal, rising directly up from it. Here we once again let down the scaling ladders and slowly climbed down until we had reached bottom and the level ground and could once again put them aside.

Groups of people in my neighborhood stood by the doors of their houses and looked at the sky.

"O, Doctor!" they shouted. "Doctor! Where have you been on such a frightful day?"

"I've come from Dubs and Eidun," I said. "I left behind the horse and sleigh and came across Meierbach's fields and the pasture because I couldn't get through the forest."

I stayed with these people for a while. The day was truly frightening. Even there we could hear all around us the rushing sound of the forest, interspersed with the sounds of trees falling, sounds that followed ever closer upon one another. Even there, where we could see nothing because of the thickness of the fog, we heard the cracking and crashing sounds from the lofty forest above us. The sky was still as white as it had been all day, and now, as evening approached, its shimmering grew paler yet. The sky was completely still and a steady fine rain fell.

"God have mercy on anyone out there, especially in the forest," said one of the bystanders.

"No fear!" said another. "Nobody's going to stay out there."

Thomas and I were carrying a considerable amount of extra weight we could no longer support, and for that reason we took leave of the people and went into the house. Every tree had a black area around it where a great many branches had been pulled down when a more severe hailstorm had struck. The timber railing I used to separate the yard from the as yet unfinished garden was silver like the screen standing in front of a church altar. Nearby, an old plum tree which was still growing from its original cutting had been bowed over. To keep the fir tree beside my small summer bench from being damaged, someone had knocked down the ice from it with long poles as far as he could reach, and when the top of the tree seemed about to tilt, my other servant, Kajetan, had climbed up to it, carefully knocked down the ice, and then tied around the highest branches two barn ropes which he let down and shook from time to time. They knew this tree was dear to me and also very beautiful, with green branches so thickly bunched together that an enormous weight of ice had been clinging to it which might easily split the tree or at least break its boughs.

I went into my room which was good and warm, laid all the things I had taken from the sleigh on the table, and took off my clothes, knocked the ice from them, and hung them up in the kitchen since they were very damp.

After I had changed my clothes, I learned that Gottlieb had gone into the forest deep in the valley, thinking I would have to pass through the valley by sleigh on my way back, but he had not yet returned. I told Kajetan to go and get him, but to take someone else with him (if he could find anybody who would go), and also take along a lantern, put crampons on their shoes, and take staff in hand. Later, when they brought him back, he looked as though he were encased in rings of armor, since he had been unable to keep the ice from covering him completely.

I ate a little of the meal that had been put aside for me. Twilight had already passed and by now night had set in. I could hear the whirring noise even in my room as the servants, filled with anxiety, walked about the house.

After a while, Thomas, who had also eaten and changed his clothes, came in to see me and said that the people in the neighborhood had gathered and were in a turmoil. I put on a heavy coat and with the aid of a staff crossed over the ice toward their houses. It was already completely dark, yet the ice on the ground gave off a vague sheen and snowy lustre. I could feel the rain on my face, which was damp all over, as well as on my hand which was holding the mountain staff. The din, like the rushing sound of a distant waterfall, was amplified by the darkness all around in places where no eye could penetrate. The breaking sound became much more distinct, as though a powerful army or raging battle were approaching. As I got closer to their houses, I saw some people standing out in the snow rather than near their doors or close to a wall.

"O, Doctor! Help us! O, Doctor! Help!" some of them cried out when they saw me coming, recognizing my gait.

"I can't help you. God is ever great and wondrous. He will help us and save us," I said as I walked up to them.

We stood together a while and listened to the sound. I soon became aware of their conversations and their fear that during the night their houses might be crushed. I told them that especially near us, where evergreens are so prevalent, on every branch and between the tiniest twigs and needles, the indescribable downward flowing water collects as a peculiar frosty glaze that wins out over everything, congeals, and through a steady unceasing accumulation on the boughs, drags down with it the needles, twigs, branches and boughs, and finally bends and breaks the tree. But on the roofs, where a smooth covering of snow lies, the layer of ice underneath is made even smoother and the running water moves right along. They merely had to break off pieces of ice with their hook irons to see that only a meager thickness of ice could stick to the sloping surfaces. In the trees, it was as though a profusion of hands grew down from innumerable arms through an immensity of hair, while on the houses everything slid toward the edge of the roofs and hung down in icicles, which weakened and fell off or could be safely and easily loosened and knocked down. I consoled them in this way and now they understood an event that had only bewildered them before, since they had never before lived through a thing of such great force and intensity.

I then walked back home. I was not all that calm myself and trembled inside because, what should happen to the vegetation if the rain continued in this way and the thundering increased and occurred in even more rapid succession than now when everything was already in a state of direst extremity. The weight had piled up. A fraction of an ounce, a dram, a drop could destroy a hundred year old tree. I turned up the light in my room and did not want to sleep. Also, during my long stay and delay down in the valley, the Gottlieb boy had run a slight fever, so I had a look at him and prescribed something for him.

An hour later, Thomas came in and said that the people had met and prayed, the noise was so terrifying. I told him that it had to change soon, and with that he left me.

I went into my room where the din penetrated with the sound of thousands of waves crashing one after another, and finally stretched out on the leather couch I have and fell asleep from exhaustion.

When I awoke again, I heard a howling sound high above my roof that I could not adequately account for. But when I stood up, pulled myself together, and walked over to the window and opened the shutter, I realized that it was the wind and saw that a storm was moving across the sky. I wanted to satisfy myself that it was still raining and know whether the wind was colder or warmer, so I threw a jacket over my shoulders and walked past the front room where I saw light coming through the partially open doorway leading to where Thomas sleeps. Of course, he is in a place close to my room so that I can call for him with my bell if I need something or something happens to me. I went into his room and saw him sitting at his table. He had not even lain down, he confessed, because he was too frightened. I told him I was going down to check on the weather. He stood right up, took his lamp and came down the stairs behind me. When we had reached the front of the house downstairs, I placed my light in a niche by the stairs where he also put his lamp. I then unlocked the door leading out into the courtyard, and as we stepped onto the cold porch outside, we were hit by a gust of warm mild air. The uncommon condition of things that had prevailed all day long had let up. The warmth that had been coming on since afternoon and until now had prevailed only at higher elevations was now descending, as usually happens, and the air currents which, of course, were already pressing down from aloft had turned into a full-blown storm. As far as I could tell, the sky had also become different. The solitary gray color had broken up, and dark and black patches were scattered here and there. The rain was now no longer as intense and struck our faces in large, more scattered, heavier drops. While I was standing there some men who must have been in the vicinity of my house came up to me. Now my courtyard is not at all like most and not as well taken care of now as it used to be. Two of its sides, which are set in a rectangle, are formed by walls of my house. The third one once consisted of a board fence behind which the garden, already equipped with a timber rail gate, extended. Finally, the fourth side was also a fence (not very well put together), which had a wrought iron gate that was usually open. In the middle of the garden there was to have been a well, which, at that time, also had not even been begun. And so it was that people could readily walk into the courtyard. They were standing out in the open and, feeling great anxiety, wanted to see how things were. When they saw the light in the window of my room disappear and saw it get dark in there immediately afterwards, and noticed the light moving down along the staircase inside the house, they thought I would be coming out into the courtyard and therefore came up closer to my house. At first they feared that there had been real devastation and unheard-of horrors and that the storm would now even add to it. It told them, however, that everything was all right, that the worst now lay behind us. It was to be expected that the cold, now below us and no longer aloft, would soon disappear. And now that the wind was so warm, no new ice would be formed and the old ice would certainly diminish. Nor, as they feared and believed, could the wind topple more trees than had fallen when it was calm. For when it rose it surely could not have as much strength as had been behind the force that burdened so many a tree trunk that the trees had broken down.

But it would certainly be strong enough to shake down the half-congealed water that was suspended on the pine needles and the pieces of ice that barely adhered to them. The next stronger wind would find already lightened trees and disburden them even more. Thus the calm is frightening where all that is secret gathers and may burden us, and the storm which violently shakes all that has been gathered together is our deliverance. And even though many a tree might be broken and brought to ruin by the wind, nevertheless a great many more must surely be saved by it, and the trees that had not withstood the worst of it would have fallen all the same if the calm had lasted much longer. And the wind had not merely shaken down the ice but with its warm breath had also eaten away at it, first the more delicate and then the more robust of its textures, and in that way did not allow the resulting water or even that which fell from the heavens to remain on its branches as a merely warm but gentle breeze would have. And, indeed, although we could not hear the rushing sound of the forest above the howling of the storm, nevertheless, for that very reason the heavy falls that we were certainly still aware of were hardly noticed.

After a while, when the wind had become more and more violent and, as we thought, warmer, we wished each other a good night and went home. I went to my room, undressed, lay down on my bed and slept very soundly until morning when broad daylight was at long last in the sky.

Four

Who Is Heidegger's Nietzsche?

I

BETWEEN 1973 AND 1987 ENGLISH TRANSLATIONS of all ten parts of
Martin Heidegger's two-volume *Nietzsche* (1961) [= *N*] were published by
Harper and Row. The first to be published were parts VIII–X, which
appeared with "Overcoming Metaphysics [*Überwindung der Metaphysik*]"
(a set of twenty-eight notes on Nietzsche Heidegger wrote between 1936
and 1946) as *The End of Philosophy* (1973), translated by Joan
Stambaugh.[66] Parts VIII–X are three essays written in 1941: "Metaphysics
as History of Being [*Die Metaphysik als Geschichte des Seins*]," "Sketches for
a History of Being as Metaphysics [*Entwürfe zur Geschichte des Seins als
Metaphysik*]," and "Recollection in Metaphysics [*Die Erinnerung in die
Metaphysik*]."

Heidegger's "Foreword *Vorwort*" to both volumes of *N* and the remaining
parts of the work were next published in English in four volumes under
the overall title *Nietzsche* in the following order: Volume I (1979) [= *Ne/I*],

---

[66] At that time, the translator wrote: "The remainder of *Nietzsche* [1961] will
be published in two volumes, one volume containing the material on nihilism and
a final volume containing the material on Nietzsche proper. This present book
contains little on Nietzsche as such; but, rather, it represents the fruit of the two
German volumes entitled *Nietzsche*. It is published first because it contains
Heidegger's most comprehensive treatment of the history of Being as metaphysics...." *The End of Philosophy* (1973) New York: Harper and Row, vii. The editorial
plan evidently changed in crossing the continent: the two volumes referred to
became *four*, all of which were published by Harper and Row, San Francisco.

The Will to Power as Art (the "Foreword" written in 1961 [in *Ne*/I= "Author's Foreword to All Volumes"] and Part I of *N*: Heidegger's *first* lecture course on Nietzsche, given during the winter semester of 1936/37 at the University of Freiburg [*Nietzsche: Der Wille zur Macht als Kunst*, in *Ne*/I= "The Will to Power as Art"]); Volume IV (1982) [= *Ne*/IV], *Nihilism* (Parts V and VII of *N*): the *fourth* and last lecture course on Nietzsche Heidegger gave at Freiburg, offered during the second trimester of 1940 [*Nietzsche: Der europäische Nihilismus* in *Ne*/IV= "European Nihilism"], and an essay written during the years 1944–46 but published for the first time in *N* [*Die seinsgeschichtliche Bestimmung des Nihilismus* in *Ne*/IV= "Nihilism as Determined by the History of Being"⁶⁷]); Volume II (1984) [= *Ne*/II], *The Eternal Recurrence of the Same* (Part II of *N*: Heidegger's *second* lecture course on Nietzsche, given during the summer semester of 1937 at Freiburg. [*Nietzsches metaphysische Grundstellung im abendländischen Denken. Die ewige Wiederkehr des Gleichen* in *Ne*/II= "The Eternal Recurrence of the Same"]), and the 1953 lecture *Wer ist Nietzsches Zarathustra?*, not included in *N* in *Ne*/II= "Who Is Nietzsche's Zarathustra?"]⁶⁸; and Volume III (1987) [= *Ne*/III], *The Will to Power as Knowledge and as Metaphysics* (Parts III, IV and VI of *N*: Heidegger's *third* lecture course on Nietzsche, given during the summer semester of 1939 at Freiburg [*Nietzsches Lehre vom Willen zur Macht als Erkenntnis* in *Ne*/III= "The Will to Power as Knowledge"; a two-lecture conclusion to the first three courses on Nietzsche [parts I–III of *N*], written in 1939 but not presented [*Die ewige Wiederkehr des Gleichens und der Wille zur Macht* in *Ne*/III= "The Eternal Recurrence of the Same and the Will to Power"); and a lecture course prepared for the winter semester of 1941/42 at Freiburg but not given [*Nietzsches Metaphysik* in *Ne*/III= "Nietzsche's Metaphysics"]).

---

⁶⁷ This part was originally announced in the "Plan of the English Edition" as "The Determination of Nihilism in the History of Being," *Ne*/I, xii. The title was changed for *Ne*/IV and in subsequent volumes to its present version.

⁶⁸ The lecture, first published in Heidegger's *Vorträge und Aufsätze* (1954), 101–126, had been translated by Bernd Magnus in 1967 for *The Review of Metaphysics*, 20, 411–431.

Volume I of *N* has been reissued as volumes 6.1 (1996) in Division One of the *Gesamtausgabe* [= *GA*]. Volume II is due as *GA* 6.2. In the meantime, however, the handwritten manuscripts Heidegger prepared for the five lecture courses (which comprise the bulk of *N*) have been compared with various typescripts of Heidegger's handwritten manuscripts, the printed text, and Heidegger's marginal notes to his copies of *N*. These texts, which restore and supplement the courses as Heidegger gave them (with the exception of *Nietzsches Metaphysik*, which was not given), have been published in five volumes of Division Two of the *GA*, which bear the titles Heidegger gave to his courses: Volume 43 (1985), *Nietzsche: Der Wille zur Macht als Kunst* [*The Will to Power as Art*]; Volume 44 (1986), *Nietzsches metaphysische Grundstellung im abendländischen Denken. Die ewige Wiederkehr des Gleichen* [*Nietzsche's Fundamental Metaphysical Position in Western Thought. The Eternal Recurrence of the Equivalent*]; Volume 48 (1986), *Nietzsche: Der europäische Nihilismus* [*Nietzsche. European Nihilism*]; and Volume 47 (1989), *Nietzsches Lehre vom Willen zur Macht als Erkenntnis* [*Nietzsche's Teaching on the Will to Power as Knowledge*]. (Volume 47 includes the three-lecture conclusion to the first three course: *Die ewige Wiederkehr des Gleichens und der Wille zur Macht* ["The Eternal Recurrence of the Equivalent and the Will to Power].") Volume 50 (1–87) contains *Nietzsches Metaphysik*, the course announced for the winter semester of 1941/42 for which Heidegger substituted a course on *Hölderlins Hymne 'Andenken'* (Volume 52 in Division Two of the *GA*). One other course on Nietzsche's thought, prepared for the winter semester of 1938/39 at Freiburg but also not given, is due as Volume 48 in Division Two of the *GA*: *Nietzsches II. Unzeitgemässe Betrachtung Vom Nutzen und Nachteil der Historie für das Leben*] ("Nietzsche's Second Untimely Reflection On the Use and Liability of History for Life").[69]

---

[69] Heidegger's other writings on Nietzsche include "Nietzsches Wort 'Gott ist tot'," an address delivered by Heidegger in 1943, which was, Heidegger notes in *Holzwege* (*GA* 5, 375), "based upon the Nietzsche lectures that were given between 1936 and 1940 during five semesters at the University of Freiburg." The essay was translated by William Lovitt as "Nietzsche's Word: 'God Is Dead'" in a selection of Heidegger's lectures published as *The Question Concerning Technology and Other Essays* (1977). Heidegger's note is misleading insofar as it suggests that he gave five courses of lectures on Nietzsche between 1936 and 1940. Five courses

Volumes 43, 44, 47 and 48 and the first part of Volume 50 amount to a
very different text from the one Heidegger published in 1961, which forms
the basis of the English translations. This is suggested by the fact that the
editors of the *GA* have chosen to reissue *N* as a separate work. Whatever
the reasons for Heidegger's decision in 1961 to publish an abridged version
of his courses on Nietzsche (and the related material included in *N*), the
more complete *GA* text must now be considered on its own. It reflects
Heidegger's changing interpretation of Nietzsche's thought in the years
following 1961.

The *GA* volumes containing the four courses Heidegger actually gave
include Heidegger's periodic recapitulations given prior to beginning new
topics during the courses. This follows his practice familiar to readers of
the two-semester lecture series *Was heisst Denken?* [*What Is Called Thinking?*] (1954)[70], which Heidegger gave at Freiburg in 1951–52. Occasional
notes related to the four lecture courses are also included at appropriate
points in the *GA* text and material omitted from *N* has been restored.
More important, paragraphs and even whole sections have been completely
rewritten, reflecting Heidegger's ongoing *Gespräch* with Nietzsche, which
clearly did not end with the publication of *N*.

A translation of the *GA* texts corresponding to *N* would have been an
important addition to Heidegger in English. Instead, the four volumes
published under the general title *Nietzsche* have been reprinted "with a
minimum of changes."[71] This reprint, published exactly thirty years after

---

were announced but only four were given, not including the course prepared for
1938/39.

[70]   Due as *GA* 8, *Was heisst Denken?* was translated in 1968 by Fred D. Wieck
and J. Glenn Gray. Professor Gray was at the time of the publication of the last
three parts of *N* in English (1973) the co-editor with Joan Stambaugh of Harper
and Row's planned edition of Heidegger's *Works*. He was the original dedicatee of
all four volumes of the English *Nietzsche* (*Ne*/III, x.).

[71]   "In order to keep the cost of the paperback edition as low as possible, the
volumes have been reprinted with a minimum of changes" (*Nep*1/I, "Editor's
Preface," xxix). The "Preface" to each volume has been modified; otherwise, all
four volumes have been reprinted, page for page. A few mechanical errors remain.

the appearance of *N*, prints together volumes I–II and III–IV of the original clothbound edition in two paperbound volumes. Perhaps interest in the successful marketing of a paperback edition of *Nietzsche* (1979–87) took precedence over the more important objective of translating the original text of Heidegger's discussion with Nietzsche as it is now available in the *GA*.

The original pagination of the paired volumes is preserved within each paperbound volume. Like the clothbound volumes, this edition does not contain indexes. (This, unfortunately, is also a limitation of the *GA* edition so far, with the exception of *Frühe Schriften*.) The editor has supplied a number of notes throughout the translations, many of them devoted to problems of translation. The "Introduction to the Paperback Edition" is a timely essay entitled "Heidegger Nietzsche Nazism" by the editor, David Farrell Krell, whose analyses of the four volumes have also been retained along with his glossaries of key terms, one for each of the reprinted volumes. The editor translated all of parts I, II and IV, and "to ensure a modicum of consistency,"[72] revised the translations of parts III and VI by Joan Stambaugh and Frank A. Capuzzi, respectively. The translations of Parts V and VII are nonetheless attributed to Dr. Capuzzi.

Apart from a number of important limitations of the translations themselves, the appearance of the *GA* text of Heidegger's conversation with Nietzsche surely called for a new translation. Failing that, given the opportunity to at least make available in English all ten parts of *N* in a complete edition, the editor and publisher might have devoted the approximately 150 pages now allotted to the editor's analyses and new introduction to reprinting with suitable revisions the contents of *The End of Philosophy*. The glossaries might have been consolidated to afford additional space.

For example, in the nine years since its appearance, no one seems to have noticed the repetition of three lines of type on page 191 of *Ne/IV*, which were not corrected for the reprint.

[72] *Nep2*, "Editor's Preface," Volume 3, x.

II

These translations of *N* sometimes introduce avoidable ambiguities into Heidegger's text, while also perpetuating prevailing "standard" mistranslations of a number of Heidegger's key terms.

The complete title of Heidegger's second lecture course on Nietzsche is "Nietzsches metaphysische Grundstellung im abendländischen Denken. Die ewige Wiederkehr des Gleichen." The first part of the title has been eliminated in the translation. But of greater importance, the noun *das Gleiche* is translated 'the same,' as it is in the title of the two-lecture conclusion to Heidegger's first three Nietzsche courses, "Die ewige Wiederkehr des Gleichens und der Wille zur Macht," even though in *The Will to Power as Art*, 'the same' translates the noun *das Selbe* and, in *Nihilism, das Selbe* is translated 'the selfsame,' which in passages of *The Eternal Recurrence of the Same* is hyphenated 'the self-same.' This inconsistency follows from uncertainties about the translation of *das Gleiche*.

Das Selbe and *das Gleiche* clearly mean very different things. In fact, Heidegger uses the term *das Selbe* (same) to clarify the meaning of *das Gleiche* (equivalent). The text in which this occurs is found in the two-lecture finale just cited.[73] In the *GA* edition of this passage, Heidegger writes: *Was "wird," ist selbst "das Gleiche," will heissen: das Selbe in der Jeweiligkeit des Anderen.*[74] Compare this to the version in *N*, which is the basis of the English translation: *Was wird, ist das Gleiche selbst, will heissen: das Eine und Selbe (Identische) in der jeweiligen Verschiedenheit des Anderen,*[75] which has been translated as follows: "What becomes is the same itself, and that means the one and selfsame (the identical) that in each case is within the difference of the other."[76]

---

[73] The passage has been revised for the *GA* and thus also stands as an example of the important differences between the text there and in *N*.

[74] *GA* 47, 279.

[75] *N* II, 11.

[76] *Nep2/*III, 165.

Let us look first at the passage in *N*. It is on the thought of *das Werden* (what becomes) in Nietzsche. What has Heidegger actually written there? "What becomes" is the "equivalent itself" [*das Gleiche selbst*], which means, the 'one and the same' [*das Selbe*] the identical in the fleeting distinctiveness of what is other. Equivalent is the appropriate translation here because of its allusion to equal power. More on this shortly. However, in the *GA* text, we now find the following sentence in its place: "What becomes is itself the equivalent, which means, the *same* in the fleetingness of what is other."

It is evident that when he rewrote this passage, Heidegger had in mind a very different grasp of Nietzsche's notion of what becomes than he gave in *N*. Whether this is to be traced to a restoration of his original text from 1939 or to a revision made sometime after 1961, I do not know. In either case, in *Nep2* the reader misses the sense of Heidegger's gloss on the term *das Gleiche* because of its mistranslation as the same. Moreover, in the *GA* edition, the term 'equivalent' is placed between double quotation marks, indicating the problematic nature of the term itself as a suitable expression for what is being thought. Heidegger's gloss then becomes even more noteworthy.

References to "the one" and to identity (two important terms from the history of metaphysics which Heidegger studies with great care here and elsewhere) are eliminated, and the phrase "fleeting distinction" [*der jeweiligen Verschiedenheit*] (a term still harboring allusions to formal logic) is replaced by 'fleetingness' [*Jeweiligkeit*] (a term referring to temporality). This is not the place for a full elucidation of this important passage, though a few related comments are in order.

We note that, in his lectures, Heidegger expands Nietzsche's phrase "eternal recurrence" to "eternal recurrence of the equivalent." This is in itself already an interpretation of Nietzsche's thought of eternal recurrence, and a disclosure of further riches in it.[77] And "the equivalent"? What is it? It is "the *same* [now emphasized by Heidegger] in the fleetingness of what is other." It is what all apparent otherness or disparity has in common: evanescence. What was seemingly other turns out not to have been novel, unexpected or different after all. What was thought to be new is what has already recurred; more than that, it is and has been endlessly recurring. These cyclic (circulatory) repetitions have equivalent power in history. (The allusion to the body's circulatory system is not unexpected in Nietzsche's "physiology.") The "sameness" of the equivalent recurrences lies in their evanescence as seemingly different.

In the sentence that immediately follows in the *GA* text, Heidegger completes his gloss on "the equivalent": *Im Gleichen ist die Anwesung des Selben gedacht.* In translation: "The coming to presence [*die Anwesung*] of the same [*des Selben*] is thought in the equivalent [*das Gleiche.*]" Finally, we note that the short paragraph on *das Selbe* (translated as "the self-same" in *Ne*/III) that follows in *N* is eliminated in the *GA* edition.[78]

III

I also want to bring forward the translators' adoption of the mistranslation of what is surely the fundamental term in Heidegger's vocabulary. It is

---

[77]   Here, Heidegger attempts to articulate the unspoken in Nietzsche's thought. Nietzsche does not use the phrase "the eternal recurrence of the equivalent" in any of the notes collected in the book *Der Wille zur Macht*. However, in one of the notes (#1041), he writes the following — which may have been the hint Heidegger caught sight of that served him in his interpretative expansion of Nietzsche's expression *die ewige Wiederkehr*: "Such an experimental philosophy as I live...wants the eternal circulation [*den ewige Kreislauf*]: — the same things [*dieselben Dinge*], the same logic [*dieselbe Logik*] and illogic of entanglements." From the notebooks (1883–88) of Friedrich Nietzsche, published as *The Will to Power*, New York: Random House, 1967, translated by Walter Kaufmann and R.J. Hollingdale, 536.

[78]   The importance of the term *das Selbe* throughout Heidegger's writings is well known. Above all, it names the characteristic that all the terms for *das Sein*, in the history of metaphysics share. These terms are the *same*, in that they bespeak the same matter, *das Sein*.

especially important to discuss this here, since Heidegger's texts on Nietzsche bring into focus his critique of all metaphysics, and in particular, Nietzsche's metaphysics, as the history of — *Sein*.

Das Sein is neither the gerund or the present participle of the verb *sein*. It is the nominalized infinitive and, therefore, should not be rendered 'Existence,' 'essence,' or 'being' (whether or not capitalized). This custom began with Werner Brock's edition of four essays by Heidegger in 1949[79] and was adopted by subsequent translators. It is important to see that Heidegger does not ask the question about being, but about 'be', as used, for example, by Wallace Stevens: "Let be be finale of seem."[80]

Accustomed to the grammatical conventions of English, we always include the prepositional word 'to' when giving the infinitive form of a verb.[81] We say "to run" when giving the infinitive form of the verb 'run' and we say "to be" when giving the infinitive form of the verb 'be'. But there is no such prepositional word with a German infinitive. In German one says only "*sein*" when giving the infinitive form of the verb *sein*. For us, however, the particle 'to' is always given with the name of the verb. When asked for the infinitive form of the German verb *sein*, we say "to be." But the infinitive is not heard that way in German.

---

[79] *Existence and Being*, four essays by Martin Heidegger, edited by Werner Brock, translated by R.F.C. Hull, Alan Crick and Douglas Scott, Chicago: Henry Regnery, 1949. The precedent was set by Gilbert Ryle in his review in 1929 of *Sein und Zeit* in *Mind*, 38, 355–370.

[80] Wallace Stevens, "The Emperor of Ice Cream," in *The Collected Poems*, New York: Random House, 1982, 64. Interestingly enough, the line might stand as an expression of the metaphysical position against which Nietzsche struggled. The poem was first published in 1923 in *Harmonium*.

[81] The prepositional word "to" is the descendent of a dative construction in Old and Middle English. See the second edition of *The Oxford English Dictionary* (1989), the entry for the word 'to', Section B [Compact edition, 2071].

The term *Sein*, as Heidegger uses it, is the nominalized "bare infinitive" (or root form)[82] of the verb *sein*. Heidegger's construction of the noun from the root form allows him to formulate the root form as a matter for thought, since only in this form can it function as the subject or object of a sentence. In fact, Heidegger calls what this construction names *the* matter for thought, *die Sache des Denkens* (what matters for thinking).

This *be* is implicated everywhere in what we experience, says Heidegger, yet we rarely ever hear it alone (without modals) in speaking. Nor do we see the word alone except in dictionaries and grammar textbooks. The daunting peculiarity of the *Seinsfrage*, the question about be, originates in hearing the root form in all its austerity. The *Seinsfrage* is the question about the meaning that the root form 'be' bears. We are expected to be brought up short by the sound and sense of the nominalized "bare infinitive" 'be'. We are supposed to pause out of perplexity about its meaning, though not because we feel we must guess what Heidegger means.

The word 'be' stands out in the preceding sentences and, indeed, throughout Heidegger's early writings. It calls out to us unlike any other word in the language. Heidegger's attention to and usage of the word jars the ear and sensibility of the highly literate as well as the everyday speaker of German. This effect should not be lost on the English speaking reader of Heidegger's texts, but it *is* lost if *das Sein* is translated as the gerund 'being'. In that case, the reader misses the entirely unusual sense and sound of the word 'be' as Heidegger hears and pronounces it. The reader finds nothing questionable about it and continues to think of it as traditional ontology has for a very long time, as something substantive. "Being" is inevitably thought of in that case as an entity of some kind, even if it is elevated to the position of being the highest entity of all.

---

[82] We may recall here Heidegger's *Habilitationsschrift* (1915) on the *Grammatica Speculativa* of Thomas of Erfurt (still ascribed to Duns Scotus when Heidegger studied the text). All of the modes of expression are said to "resolve [auflösen] into" the infinitive. *Die Kategorien- und Bedeutungslehre des Duns Scotus*, in *GA* 1, 388.

Heidegger is fond of nominalizing verbals (and verbalizing adjectives) to make them express what has been left unthought. He begins this practice with the nominalized infinitive *Sein*.[83] The unaccustomed formulation sets thinking in the direction of what heretofore has not been thought and rarely formulated.[84] For Heidegger, without an understanding of what *be* means, philosophical investigations are groundless. Like the word itself, *be* seems to have no meaning of its own, and even when seemingly having been recovered through analysis, its meaning is inevitably passed over and covered up. Of course, word formations themselves do not automatically reveal what has been left unthought. But they provide hints [*Winke*].

The traditional mistranslation of Heidegger's basic term *Sein* as 'Being' has sent the reader unfamiliar with Heidegger's German text down a blind alley. This is the case in the version of *N* under discussion. I suspect that native German speaking teachers of Heidegger's texts have overlooked this difficulty because they hear Heidegger in German while speaking the standardized English vocabulary of his words in order not to be misunder-

---

[83] Heidegger's *Einführung in die Metaphysik [Introduction into Metaphysics]* (especially sections 2 and 4(1) confirms this. This book is the text of a course of lectures given in the spring semester of 1935 at Freiburg. The work, as Heidegger notes in the preface to *Sein und Zeit* (beginning in 1953 with the 7th edition), constitutes an elucidation [*Erläuterung*] of the question about the meaning of *be* (GA 2, vii). As fine a translator of German into English as Ralph Manheim misses what is at stake in these lectures in his translation entitled *An Introduction to Metaphysics* (1959) (New Haven: Yale University Press). Manheim's title makes the volume sound like a textbook, instead of the formal education in the problematic of Western metaphysics that it is.

[84] Recall the first page of *Sein und Zeit*. It begins with a few lines from Plato's dialogue *The Sophist* (244a), which Heidegger translates: *Denn offenbar seid ihr doch schon lange mit dem vertraut, was ihr eigentlich meint, wenn ihr den Ausdruck* [*seiend* [the present participle] *gebraucht, wir jedoch glaubten es einst zwar zu verstehen, jetzt aber sind wir in Verlegenheit gekommen.* He then notes that we do not know what we mean by the present participle "being." Why? Because we do not know the meaning of "be" (the root form). The first aim of *Be[ing] and Time* is to awaken [*wecken*] an understanding of the great importance of the question, What is the meaning of "be"?

stood by their native English speaking colleagues familiar with the authorized translations.

In *The Will to Power as Art* Heidegger articulates the step from Nietzsche's thought to the task of thinking. But the translation in *Ne*/I precludes the required recognition of this step by the reader: "Thinking Being, will to power, as eternal return, thinking the most difficult thought of philosophy, means thinking Be[ing] as Time."[85] Here are Heidegger's words: *Das Sein, den Willen zur Macht, als ewige Wiederkunft denken, den schwerster Gedanken der Philosophie, heisst, das Sein als Zeit denken.*[86]

What does Heidegger's sentence about Nietzsche say? We have in it a summary formulation of Heidegger's reading of Nietzsche and a statement of his own enduring problematic: "To think be, [which for Nietzsche is] the will to power as eternal return, [that is,] to think the most difficult thought of philosophy, is [*heißt*] to think be as time." For Nietzsche, *be* is understood as will to power (as eternal return); but to think *be*, the most difficult of thoughts, calls for [*heißt*] thinking *be* as time. Heidegger adds: "Nietzsche thinks this thought, but he does not yet think it as a question of be and time."[87] Nietzsche, too, passes over what his predecessors in the tradition of metaphysics took for granted: the meaning of *be*.

The history of bespeaking *be* (metaphysics) culminates with Nietzsche, the final and most fundamental spokesman of metaphysics. Nietzsche thinks *be* as will to power (as eternal return of the equivalent), but in doing so he fails to meditate on the meaning of *be* as such. Yet Heidegger's Nietzsche is nonetheless the philosopher who comes *closest* to thinking the meaning of *be*.

---

[85] *Nep*1/I, 20. Why capitalize 'time?'
[86] *GA* 43, 22.
[87] *Nietzsche dachte diesen Gedanken, aber er dachte ihn noch nicht als Frage von Sein und Zeit. GA* 43, 22–23.

IV

Heidegger's lecture courses on Nietzsche are a coming to terms [*Aus-ein-ander-setzung*][88] with Nietzsche; that is, an immersion in the terms of Nietzsche's thought, beginning with what is for Heidegger the fundamental term of Nietzsche's metaphysics: will to power. Unfortunately, in the translations at hand, Heidegger's terms are often misspoken.

A full appreciation of Heidegger's *Nietzsche-Gespräch* must wait for a translation of the *GA* Nietzsche. In the meantime, *caveat lector*.

Heidegger calls for a serious encounter with one's own language, not only with German and Greek. For Heidegger this often occurs in the translation of thought between another so-called "natural language" and one's own. Only a little of that work will be aided by the English version of Heidegger's *Nietzsche*.

---

[88] Certainly not a "confrontation," as this word is translated throughout *Nep*. There is nothing argumentative or oppositional about Heidegger's discussion with Nietzsche or for that matter with any of the figures in the Western metaphysical tradition. He does not wish to debate Nietzsche, to prove himself "correct" about what is in Nietzsche's philosophy. He wants to reveal the unspoken in Nietzsche's text by coming to terms with it. Nietzsche, on the other hand, certainly confronts *das Sein* in the form of the Christian God in order to bring it up to tempo with will to power.

Five

The Experience Of Voice in Language

Auditory Experience

IN ENGLISH WE COMMONLY SPEAK OF A CONTRAST between listening and hearing. Hearing refers to the sensation of sounds, while listening refers to the higher level of attending to what is heard. We say that listening follows hearing. Physiological psychologists recognize hearing without any subsequent paying attention to what the inner ear has transformed into electromagnetic impulses. Listening, which occurs at the level of perception, involves bestowing meaning on what has been sensed by the receptor organs of the ears. It is well known that only a small fraction of what is heard is attended to or listened to.

Ordinarily, this distinction between "sensory hearing" and "perceptual listening" comes into view only when there is a failure to make sense of what has been sensed, when there has been a lapse in understanding auditory sensations. Thus, for example, the perceptual disorder known as auditory aphasia, which is evidently the consequence of dysfunction at the cerebral level, is the inability to make sense of what has been heard. It is a functional failure of the auditory sense at a higher level of neurological organization.[89]

In the preceding account, which psychology gives, of auditory experience (hearing and listening), no attention is given, however, to what makes

---

[89] The several usages of the word 'sense' have contributed to confusion about the distinction.

auditory experience possible in the first place. The present essay is on the trail of just that.[90]

The auditory sense is probably the first of the so-called "higher senses" to develop in the organism. It is equiprimordial with the tactile and kinaesthetic senses in embryonic development. After the sense of hearing is functional, it is impossible to entirely shut out sounds. By contrast, it is easy enough to close one's eyes to prevent fresh access of light into the chambers of the eyes. Even while asleep, the ears are open for business. Certain general anesthetics render the patient senseless in all but the auditory field, with the result that the patient is a frightened listener to the surgeon's words and operations on the patient's body. Hearing is also evidently the sense that is most reluctant to give up its realm. The very ill, for example, some who have been in a coma, later report having heard the voices of people conversing. It is common lore that those who are ostensibly unconscious and otherwise unresponsive should be considered to be nonetheless auditorially competent.

The auditory sense, as a result, is the more vulnerable of the two higher sensory spheres, sight and hearing. This much psychology has to tell us. Since psychology is founded on empiricism and the strict distinction between things physical and things psychological, it cannot tell us anything about experience understood as neither psychological nor physical nor as a combination of both. Yet we must admit, from a phenomenological point of view, that auditory experience cannot be reduced to any of the points of view just enumerated. The following study of *hearkening* is part of a broader clarification of acoustic experience that is not reducible to physical or psychological terms. Everyday usage suggests that listening is hearing with greater effort or application. Listening is thus straining to hear better, a physical intensification of the hearing process, in an attempt

---

[90]   I will use the term "auditory experience" when referring to psychology's account of sensory hearing and perceptual listening (the "auditory sense") and will reserve the term "acoustic" for the condition or ground of auditory "experience" or "hearkening."

to somehow "turn up" the hearing apparatus.[91] Listening is defined as making a conscious effort to hear, attending closely to what is heard. Thus we listen in order to hear more keenly. I suggest, however, that we leave the ordinary usages of hearing (a physiological term) and listening (a psychological term) in tact and, in order to avoid an entangled confusion of the connotations these two terms bear, restore to the vocabulary a word not much heard these days, 'hearkening', to refer to what makes hearing and listening possible in the first place. The term 'hearkening' refers to a feature of human Existence. We hearken to the grammatical voice. In this essay, I am interested in the primacy of hearkening.[92]

Hearing, Listening and Hearkening

To say that I am always hearkening to what surrounds me suggests that I am fundamentally sensitive and attuned to a world which in a primary way can be heard. Only in reflection will I be in a position to distinguish between hearing and listening, between the physical and the psychological. In reflection, I will, first of all, note the listening: sounds are meaningful to me as calls, warnings, namings, language. Next, I will identify the function of hearing, locate the ears as the sensory organs of hearing, and attribute the function of hearing to the ears. Listening, in this way, requires effective hearing.[93]

---

[91] This is an attempt to understand the ear as a kind of microphone. Radio and television technicians thus "turn up the pot" on their microphone when a speaker is talking softly. The ear, by contrast, functions at one level, in order to be able to distinguish louder from softer sounds.

[92] 'Hearken' derives from the Indo-European root qeu-: to watch, pay attention to.

[93] The delimitation of the sense of hearing to the ears may have been a late development. Who is to say that, when first conceptualized, hearing was attributed to the ears at all or only to the ears, especially since covering the ears did not eliminate the sounds but only muffled them? Listening would more likely have been closely coordinated with seeing and perhaps not distinguished from it.

On the account given by psychology, the physiologically deaf are deprived of both the ability to hear and the capacity to listening. But are they not, all the same, attuned to the world as a world that fundamentally *can* be heard, though for them in a deficient mode? This is the key to the meaning of hearkening. Before a sound is heard, that is, before vibrating air is translated into neuroelectric current by the organ of Corti in the inner ear, and before auditory sensations are given meaning, that is, before a sound is defined as a dog's bark, a bird's tweet, a cricket's clicks, or a word, I hearken to the voice of *be*[ing]. The deaf as much as the auditorially competent hearken to it, just as the blind and sighted equally relate to the face of the world, that is, to the beheld world.

Hearken and *Hören*

It seems to me that hearkening is what Heidegger points to in his paronomasia on the words *hören* and *gehören*, meaning 'to hear' and 'to belong to,' respectively. He says that to have heard the poetic word is to belong to the world in a fundamental and unique way, in a experience of language that reveals its full compass for thinking and writing [*Dichten*]. The Greek word ἀκουάζομαι, to hearken to, also means to be called to, summoned. Ἀκούειν means to hear. Both verbs are formed from the α-privative and the Indo-European root (s)keu or (s)qeu, meaning to cover or hide. A-(s)-keu-yo (→ ἀκούειν) means to hearken to that which is uncovered or unhidden. The relationship of hearkening, so understood, and Heidegger's meditations on ἀλήθεια is striking. What is unconcealed in ἀλήθεια (a visual image) may have a deeper sense of ἀκούειν (being hearkened to). If acoustic unhiddenness is more primordial than the visual, hearkening would then be the unhiddenness that lies "before" the unhiddenness of truth.

Hearkening is in by-play with silence, not the absence of sound (such as the deaf person experiences), but the silence of the world itself before it speaks its meanings mediated by the human senses. There is evidence from a genetic psychological perspective that the world begins to speak to the infant (meaning "one who does not speak") at a certain point during the early months of its life and it answers back.[94] Out of the blue, the world speaks to the infant, it comes to the infant and the infant "comes to" in a primary way. At that point, the infant speaks and becomes a child.[95]

We are reminded here of Heidegger's fondness for acoustic images: the *Stimmung* (attunement) of *Dasein* (Existence) to the world; the call of *Sein* (*be*[ing]); the eminently still and silent ambience of *Gelassenheit* (releasement).

Before going on to the discussion of the voice of *be*[ing], a few further comments on the relationship between ἀλήθεια and ἀκούειν are in order. It is in the nature of ἀλήθεια to obscure or cover over and hide as it discloses and reveals. Thomas Sheehan coins the term 'pres-ab-sence' to name this making present by means of absence of ἀλήθεια.[96] Truth involves obscuring, making less clear and even confusing while revealing what has heretofore been obscure. There is a trade-off of some clarity for more obscurity in truth as ἀλήθεια. These are the confounding moments of truth construed in this way by Heidegger. Does ἀκούειν (hearkening) precede ἀλήθεια (truth)?

What is articulated by language and thus heard (and perhaps listened to) can occur to one only because what is hearkened to is itself not heard.[97] A corollary to this follows: at least one thought (the thought of *be*[ing]) is kept in abeyance and in hiding while another is articulated.

What is hearkened to is overheard. It is thus superseded by sound (speech) and the meaning that listening accomplishes. There is then a phenomen-

---

[94]   René Spitz (1965), *The First Year of Life*, New York: International Universities Press.

[95]   The case of Helen Keller is exemplary of how the world can speak acoustically through another sense modality.

[96]   "Introduction: Heidegger, the Project and the Fulfillment," to Sheehan's anthology *Heidegger: The Man and the Thinker* (1981) Chicago: Precedent Publishing Company, xviii.

[97]   I leave aside for the moment the problem of writing, which can be either read "to oneself" or read aloud.

ology of the word as it is present silently in hearkening and grounds any hearing and listening.⁹⁸ To what do we hearken? The voice of be[ing].

For Heidegger the ontology of Existence is immersed in everyday ontic affairs. Hearkening, however, is preontological. It is prelimary to auditory experience (hearing and listening). Hearkening (ἀκούειν) provides Existence with the attuned sense of the world, which Heidegger early in 1924 termed "the real ἀισθησις."⁹⁹ I relate this primordial sense (ἀισθησις) of the world to what occurs in hearkening and to what Heidegger much later, in 1972, indentified to the Chinese philosopher Chung-yuan Chang as the "the identity of aesthetic feeling with pre-ontological experience."¹⁰⁰ It also seems likely that hearkening is the preontological source of the basic structure of Existence, which, in *Being and Time*, Heidegger calls *Sorge* (sorrow).¹⁰¹

Hearkening and Voice

The experience of the voice of be[ing] is fundamental to language. What happens in hearkening to the voice of be[ing]? I become receptive to meanings, including those embodied in words. This receptivity is the preparatory moment of auditory experience. The preparatory moment is active and receptive. I am overtaken by the voice of be[ing] before I even hear a word

---

⁹⁸ There are different phenomenologies of the word, as the word is heard, listened to, spoken, or written.

⁹⁹ The text from May 30, 1924 is cited by P. Christopher Smith in his paper "On the Uses and Abuses of Aristotle's Rhetoric in Heidegger's Fundamental Ontology: The Lecture Course, Summer, 1924," which was presented at the 27th annual American Heidegger Conference, Stony Brook, New York (*Proceedings*, 245). It is quoted from the manuscript for Heidegger's course on the "Grundbegriffe der Aristotelischen Philosophie [Fundamental Concepts of Aristotelian Philosophy]" given during the summer semester of 1924 at the University of Marburg.

¹⁰⁰ See Chang's "Reflections" in Günther Neske (ed.), *Erinnerung an Martin Heidegger* (1970) Pfullingen: Neske, 69–70.

¹⁰¹ See Chapter Two for my translation of *Sorge* as 'sorrow'.

any interlocutor has spoken. It is the same when I myself speak. I have uttered the first words before I realize just what I have said. I never know quite what I will have said until the sentence comes to a stop.

The voice of *be*[ing] passes through me, in the way music passes through the performer of a musical score. Its voice grasps me before I grasp what I have heard or said. Its activity engages me in hearing and listening. To one of Heidegger's students, Walter Strolz, one of the outstanding characteristics of Heidegger's *Dasein* was that the great teacher "hearkened with great intensity."[102] Heidegger's "conversations" with great poets and thinkers of his tradition were special occasions of hearkening, which underlies any discerning listening to what is said in a writer's texts.

Hearkening is not a mere passive vulnerability to whatever is floating about "in the air." The voice of *be*[ing] overtakes me, brings me to a stop. The initial moment of acoustic engagement initiates the sequence of auditory experience. In extreme instances, I may feel that what will follow is entirely new, "unheard of" before. The grasp of hearkening is full-bodied. Hearkening comes upon me, unexpectedly and without warning or precedent, as something new and evocative.

When I try to listen to my own speech, it is always somehow "outside of me" in the acoustic realm. The experience is uncanny. For the writer, the dimensions of author and listener coincide. Without an other-interlocutor, the writer must wait for language to begin the conversation. The poet experiences this *in extremis* when he or she uses a word in a new way, as does the thinker when he discovers a buried sense of a word. But what is the origin of a new usage for either the poet or the thinker? Why did the

---

[102] My interview in 1976 with Professor Walter Strolz in Freiburg. See "Messkirch: Martin Heidegger: June 1976," in *Philosophy Today* XX (4), Winter 1976, 259–61. It seems to me that what Freud, in his "Ratschläge für den Artz bei der psychoanalytischen Behandlung [Recommendations to Physicians Practising Psycho-Analysis]," (1912) called the psychoanalyst's "gleichschwebende Aufmerksamkeit [evenly-suspended attention]" also refers to hearkening. Cf. Sigmund Freud, *Studienausgabe Ergänzungsband. Schriften zur Behandlungstechnik*, Frankfurt: Fischer, 171; *Standard Edition*, XII, 111 (translated by Joan Riviere).

buried sense come to light just then for the thinker? For the poet [*Dichter*] the word is brand new. For the thinker, a key word is disclosed. The poet cannot tell the source of his word, even the most familiar word. He only knows that he was committed to saying *that* word.

The Voice of *Be*[ing]

In 1943, in his "Postscript" to "What Is Metaphysics?" Heidegger spoke about the "the silent voice of *be*[ing]," the voice to which Existence hearkens. There is nothing mysterious in this notion of the voice of *be*[ing].[103] In my view, Heidegger is referring to a grammatical voice, though one without a name in German.

There are only two grammatical voices [*Aktionsart*] in German, the *Aktiv* and the *Passiv [die Leideform]*. There is no μεσότης (middle voice) as found in Sanskrit or Greek, for example, to indicate what happens before reflection occurs and thought intervenes, before the split is established between agent and object, subject and predicate.

But the verb *sein* (*be*[ing]) can be said to speak in the "middle voice," which may be spoken of as what is both self-effecting and self-affecting, in this case: *be*[ing] [*das Sein*] originates any and all meaning, but only with respect to *be*[ing] itself, to which any and all meaning returns, but not without having had an effect on *be*[ing] itself. Just as the Greek μεσότης is not easily differentiated from the παθητικός (passive voice) and from reflexive forms of usage, the "middle voice" of German (and English) verbs remains hidden in the so-called "infinitive" of the verb *sein*. The "middle voice" is the voice of *be*[ing] [*Sein*], no matter what the verb. It is my conviction that this is s formulation toward which Heidegger only slowly felt his way from his earliest interest in the *grammatica speculativa* to his

---

[103] See *Wegmarken* (1976) *GA* 9, Frankfurt: Klostermann, 306–307, 310–311, and the marginal note to Heidegger's 1949 edition of the lecture, 306. The "Postscript" was revised for this edition.

latest meditations on language. For me, this is one intelligible way of understanding the meaning of be[ing].

The "middle voice" of be[ing] resonates with what Richard Wisser has called *la voix qui pense*.[104] "The voice that thinks" has two meanings: (a) it is the voice of the grammatical structures that we may say unfold (*Aktiv*) or, alternatively, are played out (*Passiv*) from the "bare infinitive"; but (b) it also refers to what we call the "voice" of a writer. We speak of someone "finding" this voice or failing to find it as a writer.

In conclusion, we can now better understand two of the more puzzling of Heidegger's utterances: *Wir kommen nie zu Gedanken. / Sie kommen zu uns* and *Die Sprache spricht*.[105] I conclude with a few preliminary thoughts about these two texts, beginning with the second of them.

"Language speaks." This now famous utterance makes sense if the word 'speaks' refers to the grammatical "voice" and not only the human being's organs of speech. I think this is what Heidegger has in mind. "We never go to thoughts. They come to us." How could it be otherwise? A little reflection makes it clear that one never knows where a thought will end, just how it will "come out."

---

[104] Richard Wisser, "La Voix qui Pense et sa Pensée. Martin Heidegger," in *Les Études Philosophiques*, October-December, 1958, 495–500.

[105] (1) *Aus der Erfahrung des Denkens* (1947), in *GA* 13, 78, translated by Albert Hofstadter in 1971 as "The Thinker as Poet," in *Poetry, Language, Thought*, New York: Harper and Row, 6. (2) "Die Sprache" (1950), in *Unterwegs zur Sprache*, *GA* 12, 30. Translated in 1971 by Albert Hofstadter as "Language" (1950), in *Poetry, Language, Thought* (1971) New York: Harper and Row, 210.

At best one has "an idea" (of what) to say. This "idea to say" is made
determinate or realized only by speaking, whether the speech is sub-
vocalized, enunciated or written. How this works when reading is another
matter.[106]

---

[106] See Heidegger little reflection "Was heißt Lesen?" (1954), in *Aus der Er-
fahrung des Denkens*, GA 13, 111. *Was heißt Lesen? Das Tragende und Leitende im
Lesen ist die Sammlung. Worauf sammelt sie? Auf das Geschriebene, auf das in der
Schrift Gesagte. Das eigentliche Lesen ist die Sammlung auf das, was ohne unser
Wissen einst schon unser Wesen in den Anspruch genommen hat, mögen wir dabei
ihm entsprechen oder versagen.*

*Ohne das eigentliche Lesen vermögen wir auch nicht das uns Anblickende zu
sehen und das Erscheinende und Scheinende zu schauen.*

Six

Geometry And Memory

On the Phenomenology of Place

WHAT IS MEMORY? I had been steadily drawn to the question for some time. Mine was, of course, an ancient preoccupation. It happened one late afternoon in the summer of 1985 that I was on the car ferry from Orient Point, at the end of Long Island, to New London, Connecticut. Sailing along, I recalled what I knew about memory.

According to the standard account, memory stands in a unique relation with the past. It concerns what has happened, and the past is a container for what has happened. The present marks where the past ends and meets the subject in the present. The future makes the present something more than an end point for the past and allows the past to accrue. It also gives time its forward-moving direction. All three temporal aspects are implicated by any one of them.

This is the generally accepted explanation of time on which the psychological concept of memory is based. The term memory refers to two processes: (1) *retention*, which memorializes experience and relegates it as representational content to a past of its own making. Memory thus contains the past. Memory also means (2) *retrieval*, recalling the past from where it continues to be memorialized.[107]

---

[107] How this is accomplished at the level of cortical functioning does not affect the discussion here. While it is of great interest to know how what I have called memorializing occurs in the physical environment of the brain, an explanation of how cells are organized does not address the meaning of memorialization. For a recent survey of the most important findings of neuroscience on memory

Thanks to memory the subject comes to *have* what it has *done*. A memory is thought of as a possession. Yet it seems the subject does not have that *much* of what it has done. Evidently, most of the details have not been retained since the subject cannot recall them.

I assumed this much as I continued across Long Island Sound. It was a very clear day, so I pursued a bit further what I knew about memory. What does it retain, I wondered? What is its purpose? How are memories retrieved? How has experience come to require memory to supplement what one does? What is the meaning of memory for the future? How are memory and the future connected? Considering these questions, I soon left behind much of what I had accepted about memory.

The concept of memory used by psychologists is unsatisfactory, above all, because the rememberer is understood to be an animal creature blessed with a variety of mental functions or faculties, including memory, all of which work like mechanisms which are put to use by the subject. But is memory a mental faculty or function, after all? Is it a component of a natural thing, which operates like a device, or an organ, such as my hand, which I use to manipulate things? Or is it perhaps something that uses *me* to my benefit, a spiritual organ that allows me to carry out certain works for the sake of a higher intelligence? Surely not.

Staring straight ahead, I felt uneasy, even disoriented. I seemed to have gotten nowhere. Then I considered how much this sense of uneasiness resembled the experience so many others had reported of a sense of timeless immobility while on the water, where experience is somehow frozen and fixed, at a standstill, yet still moving along, albeit imperceptibly. That feeling suggested the famous Now in discussions about temporality: the nunc stans.

Many things converged at that point and, out of the blue, it occurred to me to ask: How are memory and the concept of a point of view related? What is the relation of memory to the present? What is the present? What is the place of memory in the relation between the past and the future?

---

and an hypothesis about how memorializing might work, see Charles M. Fair, *Memory and Central Nervous Organization* (1988) New York: Paragon House.

*Then I felt sure that remembering and the notion of a point of view somehow origi-
nated together. I wondered whether remembering is possible only by imagining a point
of view which is projected into a future of experience as already completed, expressed
by the future perfect tense ("will have ..."). Yes, the perfect tense expresses what memory
is said to accomplish, and if experience is what the subject does, memory is the
perfecting of experience by continuing it in some form after it has occurred.*

*I wondered further if the very possibility of taking a point of view is based on a wish
to be remembered in such a specified, conditional future? It occurred to me that the
notion of a point of view is uniquely western. Geometry, I thought, transforms our
way of seeing by requiring us to take such a fixed point of view or point of reference
with respect to things. Geometry and the point of view are conceived together. Both
imply memory. What is memory?*

*How had I gotten to this point? On the water, I was having the not uncommon
experience of a change in orientation which provided me with the occasion for these
reflections. I felt as though I were repeating the experience of an ancient event and
making a fresh beginning, and I wanted to work out the implications of these intu-
itions.*

Geometry and the Sea

Human beings have always gone into the water. Beyond the surf, their
floating bodies were drawn back to shore by the tide. On occasion, a
swimmer might go out too far and never return. Sailing, though, going
deliberately out to sea, was another matter. This was a venture requiring
the kind of confidence that eventually led to the discovery of continents,
commercial trade routes, and geometry.[108]

Certain everyday activities — for example, hunting — required taking
chances, but the voyage out to sea was a self-imposed risky kind of play.
At first, sailing usually meant going where one would or could not stay
indefinitely. Who knew whether there was anything far out to sea? Later,
after the discovery of other lands, going to sea might mean staying away

---

[108]   Plane geometry, the geometry of a uniform surface, is the geometry in
question. Its possibility is my interest here.

forever, but in the beginning, the voyage out, like contemplation or reflection, could not continue forever. Just as it was necessary to return to everyday concerns from reflecting on life, one would have to return home from a sea voyage. The journey out to sea was therefore expected to be limited.

Sea travel, contemplation and reflection have this in common: they begin by making a fateful turn away from everyday life. I would like to suggest that *geometry*, which prescribes a world constructed according to necessary principles, is founded on an experience on the water, and not from an experience on land. That experience transforms the earth and Existence. Such a transformation is not the necessary consequence of going to sea, of course. Other cultures do not see the world in this way even though they have also gone to sea.

Our first geometrician was probably a sailor who lived on a western shore facing seaward. Starting out in the morning, he watched the sun rising and sailed with his mates against the earth's spin. But returning home in the evening, with the sun behind him, instead of facing land and home with the others, our first geometrician turned his back on the approaching shore, lingering awhile to observe the sun approach the horizon. He turned around to face the past, to recollect.

While the others gazed longingly toward their home port, our first geometrician alone looked back, temporarily abandoning the lure of communal experience, and watched the line of the setting sun's reflected light stretching across the water toward him. Solitary, he faced the sun, the primary single. His gaze and the sun comprised the two *termini* of a long reflection. The origin of the point of view and with it geometry likely occurred then at the end of the day, when the sun had nearly set on the western horizon and its reflection reached eastward across a darkening body of water.

The sun appears to rise, move across the sky, set and reappear with regularity in a familiar place. Our notion of a next "anything whatsoever" is modeled on that of the next reappearance of the sun or its companion moon. A fundamental expression of nature is given in such recurrences. We design our lives on such patterns of cyclical regularity.

As the sun reached the horizon, our first geometrician saw it as a fixed point of reference, casting a steady line of reflected light towards him, the observer — *wherever he might be* on the water. For if he moved even a few feet, a perfect line of pure reflection followed him, its source point remaining unchanged. He saw a line of light radiating from where the sun touched the horizon's perfect circumference: a perfectly smooth horizon and a perfectly rectilinear line. Whether at anchor or sailing along, the horizon, sun-point and line of reflection remain constant, fixed and unchanging for the observer. Here were images of steadiness and maybe even the idea of certainty!

Then, in a momentous step, the mythical figure described here as "our first geometrician" tried to bring onto land that line leading toward him from the apparently fixed point of the setting sun. What is the meaning of these points and this line and the circumlinear horizon?

The fixed points and straight lines elaborated by geometry are ideal, imagined, as illusory as the even line of reflected light that I suspect our first geometrician believed was aimed directly at him from the center of the sun fixed on the horizon. That fixed point and its radiating line could not be used to measure things, however. Such a line does not survive where *things* are. We will soon see where he saw its counterpart on land.

When on the water, we must first estimate our own position by means of a system of coordinates and only then can we infer distances. By contrast, on land we estimate and measure in one act, since our position is fixed by where we stand. Here on land, something is attainable because it is first at a remove, *placed* at a distance. Only what is thus set apart can then be approached. It is fixed at a distance in order to be brought near. A thing's attainability is set up in this way and we measure just that attainability. At sea, however, the remotive step requires a prior step to establish where we are in the first place. At sea and against its open horizon with no other object in sight, these relationships cannot be established. The open sea lacks distinctive topography. We are truly "at sea" until land is sighted.

Our first geometrician throws an illusory grid of *loci* over things that does touch the things. Geometry prescribes spaces, but it cannot conceive places. In fact, things "disappear" when fixed *loci* are applied to them. They become objects in space.

The part of the earth we inhabit is, of course, solid land. What mapping and surveying, architectural design and physics have accomplished here on land in transforming the original reality of the earth has been possible only on the basis of the leveling of its topography to conform to the requirements of rectilinear measurement which geometry accomplishes.

The account geometry gives of its prospective world begins by defining the *geometric point*, in order then to be able to define its *line*, and so on. It is likely, however, that the order of discovery of these elements was different than the order of their formal presentation in Euclid's famous book. I will try to show why shortly. Euclid is not our first geometrician, of course. He or his students only summarized the consequences of the geometric transformation of the earth in the text we have received called the Στοιχεῖα (*Elements*.)

The world that originates within the spaces created by the geometric transformation is a world of realities that challenge the things to which our bodies have long been accustomed. It is the technological world that plays with time. There are still cultures on the earth, of course, whose members see the world in a "pregeometric" way, but we who live under the spell of the *point of view* are permanently excluded from again seeing the earth as they do.

The Earth Measurer

Our first geometrician sets his sights along what appears to be a fixed and unchanging span running from his own gaze to where the sun meets the horizon. When the point of observation (the position of the observer) shifts, the sun's point of rest (the observed point of reference) remains constant. Our first geometrician forgets that he, therefore, is not a frozen and fixed point of *observation* like the sun, since the line running between the sun and him seems to be unchanging. Our first geometrician concludes that both of its *termini* are fixed. He begins his constructions using an image of the line running between the observed point of reference, the sun, and his position as an observer.

The word γεωμετρία (geometry) literally means "earth measure." A literal translation, however, fails to capture the sense of the act carried out by the geometrician. Let us look more closely at what our first γεωμέτρης (geometrician) does.

Using himself as an instrument and thereby changing his ontological status, the geometrician is henceforth the measure of earth. What does the geometrician measure? Spaces, of course. In everyday life, by contrast, each of us *estimates* the *places* we inhabit, which include the things we use (both already extant things of nature and the things we have fabricated) and other human beings. But such estimating of things has nothing in common with the measuring of the geometrician. He measures the objects that occupy space. For the geometer, the spaces occupied by a desk, a galaxy or an imagined subatomic particle are equally readily rendered in a drawing. Homogeneous space accommodates objects of every order. The physicist, astronomer and school child map out a common space.

The objects of geometry are drawn on the illustrative screen of the geometric plane which, like a shadow, lies flat. Its boundaries are drawn for convenience, but like the line, it goes on forever.

What is once moved onto the geometric plane is laid down to rest once and for all. The drawn lines now "stand for" things, including the geometrician, who is represented by the point where every geometric illustration begins. Geometry's powerful claim is to show that things will be a certain way in a preconceived and thereby fixed, spatialized future (a future perfect). It is known in advance what and how things will have turned out to be. Geometry's prescience is, in this way, the source of the ambition of the natural sciences to predict.

After the geometric transformation of the earth places disappear and are transformed into spaces. Things become objects which are eventually implicated in a spatio-temporal manifold. Movement is brought to a halt, however, when things are laid down and fixed on a bi-dimensional, homogeneous, spatial surface. So is time.

Geometry invents objects, things that have been dis-placed and brought to a standstill. Metaphysics is then required to explain movement and time. The concept of temporality, the basic concept and problem of metaphysics, is required in order to compensate for the immobilization of things imposed by the geometric transformation and to restore moveability to objects and motion in the world. The concept of dimensionality is introduced in order to simulate the solidity things once had. The trinality of objects (volume, solids) has to be reconstructed by solid geometry.

The world represented in the geometrician's drawings occurs in the future perfect tense, which we may call the geometric tense, the tense of what will have been: geometry projects and draws what will have been.[109]

Perhaps the most far-reaching consequence of the geometric transformation is the pervasive system of networks of artificial lines along which we *are moved*: highways, railroads, air routes, telecommunication routings, military deployments, lines of command, channels of authority, rounds in hospitals, management flow charts, and computer programs, to name but a few. Networks are flat and atemporal. They link objects in geometric space according to principles of mechanical association.

Networks have abandoned the sun as the point of reference and transferred it to man at the observer's point of view. Objects thus appear in a twilight of artificial illumination. The perfect future lies ahead in the darkness of a day that has not yet dawned. Having overcome homesickness, our first geometrician, like the Judeo-Christian god, creates a new world.

---

[109]   The geometrician's project and its evident impossibility is beautifully presented in M.C. Escher's drawing of the geometrician's hand, the hand that draws itself drawing itself. [Fig. 1, "Drawing Hands," January 1948.]

Geometry also initiates reflection. *Our geometrician is also the first speculative thinker (metaphysician) whose way of thinking is a paradoxical recollection of the future perfect, the articulation of what will have taken place.* Even when trying to explain the meaning of the present, metaphysics speaks in the future perfect tense. It systematizes the consequences of the world's objects constructed by geometry. The primary topic of metaphysics becomes being and its moments: movement and change, time and making a beginning (occasion). Its aim is to reconstitute what geometry has unmade. From the start, however, the new world *ordo geometrica* is on trial. Evidence must be assembled to account for and justify it. Metaphysics, which builds a case for the world transformed by geometry, is itself built on geometry's recollection of a perfect conditional future. As such, metaphysics is a system of memories.

The Elements of Geometry

Our first geometrician's ship has been secured at the harbor landing and his mates have disembarked and gone home. His thinking is now confined by the dimensions of what he can measure. Soon he will draw himself into a corner with his illustrative proofs and then go underground, into Plato's cave. Once inside this realm, however, it will be necessary for him to find an explanation of why he must but cannot leave that realm.

To our first geometrician, experience is suggested by a circle, the perfect circle of the horizon seen at sea. It encompasses all he can see, the perspective of θεωρία (a certain way of looking). Our first geometrician *is* the point of view, the center of the circle of experience. The line connecting him, the point of observation, to the point of reference, the sun resting at the limit of experience, radiates *from* the horizon to him. The Greeks did not have a word for this line, the radius.[110]

---

[110] Sir Thomas L. Heath's commentary on his edition of *Euclid. The Elements* [Second Edition (1925)] New York: Dover Books, Volume I, 155. It was left up to the Romans to characterize this line as streaming (radiating) from the sun to the observer.

What has happened in the transformation he effected? We see its results in the definitions of Euclid's Στοιχεῖα. These definitions, postulates and axioms methodically spell out the consequences of our first geometrician's outlook. The drawings illustrate the forms of the representational world. Each διορισμός (definition) surely counts among the most important Greek texts we have inherited.

A στοιχεῖον (element) is a not further reducible component of a substance, an audible utterance, or a proof. It is also a fundamental principle [*Grundbegriff*]. And it is the name of the shadow cast by the γνώμων (indicator) on the face of a sundial. The γνώμων is the upright stake or rod of a certain kind of sundial that points out the time of day by casting a shadow of varying length across the sundial's face.[111]

Σημεῖόν. The Point of View

The definition of the point is given first. It is the representation of the geometrician as point of view. The text of the definition reads: Σημεῖόν ἐστιν, οὗ μήρος οὐθέν. **An indication is that which surely does not have a μήρος.** (I will leave the word μήρος untranslated for the time being.) The system of geometric revision of things in their totality begins with this definition, though undoubtedly the elements were not derived in the same order as they are presented.

Euclid's word σημεῖόν is traditionally translated by the Latin word *punctum*, a term which also corresponds to the Greek word στίγμα, originally meaning a puncture caused by a insect's sting or a tattoo incision. But a σημεῖόν is not, in the first place, a *punctum*.

---

[111]   It is but one step further to preserve this shadow as the memory trace, which is somehow retained on an imaginary mental *tabula rasa*. Modern versions of the memory trace are patterns in the circuitry of the cerebral cortex and adjacent structures. All such traces, like the elements of geometry, are shadows.

The several senses of σημεῖόν include the following: (1) an announcement of a performance of some kind, including a theatrical performance; (2) a mark of the appearance of an event, an omen or sign of the event; and, of course, (3) a linguistic sign in the form of either (a) an utterance, the audible indication of a verbal formulation, (b) an inscription or visible mark (hand-made or mechanically produced) on a physical medium of some sort, for example, stone or paper or even an opaque screen or electromagnetic surface, or (c) a visible configuration of a gestural sign language. In a certain way, an inscription is an indication much like an omen, since a written sign is the forebearer of its audible enunciation.

The σημεῖόν as defined by Euclid has features of all three of the senses of the term. It heralds a performance; namely, the drawing of the objects of the representational world which is initiated by starting at a certain point of view. The point at which a beginning is made is the first mark or sign of the representational world and is an omen of what is to come. The geometric σημεῖόν stands as the point of view of an observer, in fact, any observer. A σημεῖόν is the announcement and indication of "the *subject*" and the representational world he configures. Finally, the σημεῖόν is a στίγμα or physical *punctum*.

"An indication is that which surely does not have a μέρος." What does this indication "surely lack"? A μέρος is a share or turn someone takes in an activity requiring more than one person, such as standing guard. A μέρος is therefore someone's own specific orientation and place with respect to a situation, one's singular and unique place *vis-à-vis* the situation. This is precisely what the σημεῖόν is said to "surely lack." It is "point of view" as such, no determinate point of view. The σημεῖόν is nowhere, ἀτόπος. The representational world of the geometric transformation is in this way the forerunner of every utopia.

The geometric point is defined as a *bare indication, without orientation, placeless*. It marks a mere terminus, any beginning *or* end. But as merely possible mark, it lacks context and meaning.

Euclid's text implies that the bare indication, the point of view, lacks dimension, since dimensionality is one of the qualities of a place (τόπος).

It cannot be turned nor can it adjust itself to reveal other sides or views of itself to what is nearby. It is invisible, inaudible, impalpable. It cannot be sensed in any way. The first appearance of the geometric σημεῖόν marks the first step in the transformation of things to objects. It is the point of observation through which the thing disappears, only to reappear, transposed, *inside* the observing subject and, reflexively, outside of it on the geometric representational surface. It is illustrated in optics by the focal point. At that point and beginning from it, an ideal space is created in which things are represented as objects.

Geometry's bare indication is a species of μονάς, a singularity, something unto itself, like our first geometrician.[112] It marks the setting up of an entirely new situation. The geometrically transformed earth no longer has the sun as its point of reference. The human being, in the person of the geometrician, has replaced the sun. The sun has set.

Subsequently, the geometrician takes the place of a god every time he touches stylus to surface. His acts accomplish the transformation of a universe of infinitely changing meaning — the center of which is everywhere, its circumference nowhere — to a circumscribed, conditionally perfect world of fixed characteristics, a world whose meanings are once and for all determined. The events in such a world can be predicted, measured, manipulated and managed. The inscription of the first geometric point thus marks a new center of things outside the natural universe with its cycles, seasons and solar center.

In the geometric transformation of the earth the center of things moves along the first straight line our first geometrician sees, *away from* the sun and toward the observer, and enters the observer. In order of discovery of the elements of geometry, the line must precede the point. For purposes of geometric construction, however, the order is the reverse.

A great responsibility, then, falls to our first geometrician. The geometric world, apart from nature, yet not outside of it, has to be illustrated. Had

---

112   As such it is the model of Leibniz's monad.

our first geometrician merely told his friends what he had seen, he would have been ignored. His point of view had to be demonstrated, and that meant visualized and recorded. Only the totality of the geometrician's demonstrations provides a complete picture of what he has envisaged.

He is in a privileged albeit uninhabitable position. The geometrician's companions are the objects of the sciences and solitude. His most memorable embodiment is Faustus: scientist, metaphysician, scholar, loner. Other people, now also viewed as objects, cannot reach him as they once did. The things of everyday life become inaccessible to him and to each other. Transformed into objects, things lose their intimacy and become ontologically problematic. Philosophy must then invent ways for things to make contact with each other.

To our first geometrician the visual horizon seems to be ready-made for him as its center. It is no longer his horizon, however, but rather the encircling boundary of a fixed world. Claiming that the horizon is fixed, like the position of the observing geometrician himself, is the fiction of geometry and its representational world. Unlike things, the objects of this world cannot change.[113]

Γραμμή. The Line of Sight

In the order of their presentation by Euclid, the next of the elements to be defined is the line. Γραμμὴ δὲ μῆκος ἀπλατές. **A line is breadthless length.** This is the radiant line our first geometrician sees running from the sun to himself.

---

[113] See Jan van den Berg's studies of the changing nature of reality in *Things. Four Metabletic Reflections* (1970) Pittsburgh: Duquesne University Press, and *Humanitas* (Pittsburgh) VII (3), Winter 1971, for a bibliography of works by van den Berg.

A γραμμή is a boundary or limit. In the notion of the γραμμή, Euclid's definition of the line coincides with his concept of a *definition*. A definition delimits an idea the way a boundary line delimits an area of surface.

There is significant ambiguity in Euclid's definition of the line. The γραμμή as defined here is not a line segment, which stops at two *termini*, both of which may be construed as a beginning and end. Line segments, though they are the material of the illustrations of plane geometry, are not instances of what Euclid's text defines as the γραμμή. Instead, Euclid is defining the concept of boundary, which he will need later on.

A line *segment* may be construed as (1) a stretch between two *termini*, running *from* one end *to* the other in a particular direction, or (2) an elongated point extended away from itself in a certain direction (like the arrow of time). *Termini* are not points in the way Euclid has defined a point. In fact, Euclid's text does not say how such a segment is to be demarcated. It is concerned only with the definition of the line as boundary.

Yet the line running from the sun to the observer that inspires the geometric transformation is just such a segment, with the sun and observer occupying its two termini. When transferred from that setting to the bidimensional illustrative surface the line loses infinity. Before being drawn or otherwise inscribed, the line may be said to go on forever in either direction. In the sand or on paper, however, it appears that it must have been limited, segmented, cut in two places. How was this effected? Were two points first established and then connected? Or has the infinite line been intersected by two other lines, or by two terminal points? How can we understand the meaning of the line segment?

Boundary and Limit

Euclid's third definition — Γραμμῆς δὲ πέρατα σημεῖα — will explain this. This definition has to be understood differently than we have up to this point.[114] **The perfections of a line segment are *indications*.** The solution to the puzzle of the definition of the line segment is to be found here. In this definition, σημεῖόν again means bare indication. The key word here is πέρας, which means both limit and *perfection*. The perfections of the line are bare indications. Of what?

The drawn line of the third definition is conceived as a kind of living thing, the limits of which are nowhere to be found. But this is also the line's perfection. The πέρας of something is the point at which the thing has reached its fulfillment. The limits are dead ends. In order to make the line something manageable, the line has been drawn as in an already completed (perfected) and, in this way, limited future.

The other element of the second definition of a γραμμή, whether as boundary or limit, is that it lacks πλάτος (thickness, width). It is sheer μῆκος (length). We will return in a moment to consider the meaning of γραμμή as boundary.

A line segment lacks thickness in order to limit its dimensions to one,[115] so that the other two dimensions (width and depth) can be added in turn. The first dimension (length) is defined in terms of what it lacks, namely, the next dimension (breadth). Length is thereby conceived geometrically as deficient to planarity. Again the order of presentation belies the order of conception of the whole scheme.

The Straight Line

A serious problem remains. How is the γραμμή generated? That is, how is it elongated? Euclid's fourth definition — Εὐθεῖα γραμμή ἐστιν, ἥτις ἐξ

---

[114] Aristotle noted this difficulty in *Metaphysics*, 1060 b.
[115] Things do not have dimensions. Passing through the focal point of the geometric transformation, things disappear. The μέτρα (dimensions) required to reconstitute objects, the simulacra of things, are human inventions: length, width and depth are human measures. They are features of geometry, not properties of things.

ἴσου τοῖς ἐφ᾽ ἑαυτῆς σημείοις κεῖται — does not clarify matters, though it presumably is intended to do so.[116] **A straight line is a line which lies evenly with the points on itself.**

The definition makes sense at least with regard to when it appears in the order of the definitions when we realize that *the straight line must play the part of the self-evident given of geometry.* What is straight in this sense — εὐθύ(ς) — can only be the unimpeded, straightforward line that runs between the seer and the source of visibility. It is the element with which the geometric transformation begins: the radiant line already in place between the sun and our first geometrician. The geometric *point* is not the first element. In fact, it is defined only in the fourth definition. For the first time the σημεῖόν as location with respect to geometric line segments is then determined. A point makes sense only as a point on a line. It cannot be defined without the definition of a line segment already in place.

The original element of geometry — the γραμμή — is neither horizontal nor vertical. The line of sight leading from the sun to the observer's eyes is sagittal. We recall that it is always the same line no matter where one is positioned with the respect to the source of light. Horizontality and verticality are established with respect to the sagittal radiant line, the line for which the Greeks did not have a word.

Perhaps the obscurity of the fourth definition is due to the difficulty of trying to use the notion of the point as an indication *after* it has been distinguished as a limit in the third definition. The further sense of the fourth definition is that any point along the line of sight appears to be isometric with respect to any other point.

---

[116]   Heath speaks of the language of the definition as "hopelessly obscure," ibid., 167.

Horizon, Movement and Place

So far, then, the elements of the geometric transformation consist of the σημεῖόν — *the bare indication of the position of an observer* — and the γραμμή — both *boundary* and limit (πέρας). With these geometry can begin its work of establishing spaces. Abstract geometric space as such has been invented. The spaces it creates are not, however, the places in which human life takes place.

The point of view of disembodied observation is now projected onto a two-dimensional ἐπίπεδον (plane surface)[117], where objects occupying geometric space are illustrated. The illusion of timelessness and permanent presence is given with the portrayal and representation of *objects*. What is its source? Clearly, the water's smooth and stable surface is the prototype for the geometric plane. Moving through the water, I experience a smooth, even path. This homogeneous surface is the inspiration for the geometric plane.

The point *drawn* on the geometric plane is a στίγμα. There the bare indication leaves a visible trace. The systematic mapping of the objective spatial world begins at that point where the first στίγμα begins the drawing of the first geometric figure.

Let us survey in summary the bare mark Euclid speaks about in *Elements*. As already noted, it is a sign or omen and therefore prospective. Its predecessors were most likely astronomical and meteorological signs; for example, the appearance or disappearance and configurations of stars, meteors, regularly recurring daily and seasonal changes, and changes in the weather.[118]

---

[117] The word ἐπιφάνεια refers to surface as such; that is, what is open to view, "on the surface."

[118] Dawn is thus a sign of the imminent appearance of the sun. Darkening daytime skies portend an approaching storm. The luminescence of twilight indicates oncoming night. Certain subtle differences in temperature, moisture, air and light are the first signs of a change of season. Each event is heralded by a more or less dramatic change of environmental or atmospheric conditions which are the indications or signs on the basis of which a prognosis about an event in the *imme-*

But what is the referent of a *bare* indication, a sign or mark without content? This is something new under the sun. What meaning can an empty sign have? The geometrician's first visible inscription marks *nothing*. *Our first geometrician is the first to illustrate nothingness.*

As an object is drawn, the thing it represents is brought to a standstill, and the thing disappear. A thing is a place χώρα. The thing collapses through the loss of all dimensions into one empty point (the focal point), which passes through the eye of the geometrician, and emerges on the geometrician's bidimensional representational display as an object. The fateful move that initiates all this is the laying down of the first bare indication, the mark of nothingness.

Geometry is the real mysticism of the West. The geometrician draws objects, which are the ghosts of things.[119] The world he constructs is one of an already accomplished, already completed (perfected) future, a world missing two dimensions, depth and movement, which it must then reconstruct.

The point does not have anything to it and therefore cannot lack anything; yet it is a singularity [μονάς] that marks the initiation of a new world. Having temporarily abandoned his place in the real world of men's affairs, our first geometrician indicates a world in which already completely determined events must happen.

The projected geometric point is the starting point and first record of that future perfect entirety, a world that *will have turned out* (and therefore must turn out) a certain way. Designed by the geometrician, the world is described in terms of a closed future. The geometrician's illustrations are a record of the shapes this conditional perfect future must assume. Science comes to see objects the way geometry portrays them.

---

diate future can be made. The bare indication has this futural significance.

[119]   So-called memory traces (engrams), photographic images, and video and holographic displays are replicas of the illustrations of the geometrician.

Our first geometrician thus removes himself from the center of his visual horizon through the observing point of view which he himself is and reappears on the geometric surface that he has invented, where he is represented by the first point inscribed on the illustrative surface, there where "the objective world" begins.

Horizon

By the time the sun had disappeared below the horizon that day, our first geometrician had moved the earth inside his own skull (Plato's cavern), having replaced the changing openness of the horizon with the fixed perimeter of his observational world, which maps out the geometric field. In Plato's *Republic* (Πολιτεία) this field is depicted by the wall on which the shadows of things are projected. The sun, the fixed point of reference for all things human, is gone. It is replaced by a fire of human creation. But the geometrician's own real horizon has also disappeared. He no longer lives entirely *on the earth*. He and the rest of us who have grown up in the geometrically transformed realm of objects live *in a world*.

The sun had already set as we approached New London. My thoughts had changed course. What happens to things, I wondered, things nearby or "out there": the ship's rail, the man standing next to me, the small craft crossing our prow. How had these things been changed by the geometric transformation of the earth? How had the geometric transformation irretrievably obscured what I was looking at? Surely the place that each thing is could be rediscovered and recovered, couldn't it? I looked back at the horizon.

In order to grasp the objects geometry has invented, it is necessary to invent *perception*, which works by sending out mysterious rays to surround and apprehend the objects, capture them, and somehow bring them inside the viewer. The camera does this especially well, but it does not replicate seeing. A fundamental difference between sensing and perceiving is also introduced. What is the single act of seeing must now be described as a two-step affair: objects are sensed by the eye's neuro-receptors, and the brain interprets the meaning of the sensations. The second step is termed perception. But these processes are only required for the visual apprehension of objects. But so it also goes for the other senses. In fact, the distinguishing of separate senses is necessary to account for all of the properties an object has. Things are experienced in a unitary way, however, so that it makes sense, for example, to taste with the eyes, as Pierre Franey describes the way people experience food. After the creation of an object, its properties have to be restored and reassembled piecemeal.

A thing, by contrast, has its own ὅρος (horizon) which delimits the place is takes and makes. What a thing calls out as, how it speaks to me, reaches me from the place it takes in front of its horizon. Unlike objects, things are always changing and becoming newly delimited and redefined.[120] The multitude of horizons corresponding to the many things in life give one's life its ambiguities, irony and wit.

The planet on which I stand is a sphere. The way we live with things on the earth is based on a little recognized feature of our bodies: we are spherical creatures, though our extended appendages disguise this basic fact.[121] The sphere symbolizes bodiliness, which is formed [στερεός]. There are no straight lines in a living body. The very cells that make up our bodies are spherical. Our field of vision is ovaloid. We are oriented to cycles of light and temperature, recurring events, circles of friends, spheres of influence. Existence takes place within an exquisite hermeneutic circle of anticipation and interpretation, its changing center corresponding to the changing whole of "what e'er there be," which determines the place [χώρα] of my Existence.

No matter how quickly I move toward it, my horizon always outpaces me as it ever nears, while never reaching, me. But things are within my grasp only because my horizon is not. Things change in front of me. If the horizon of each sense did not change, things would remain the same. I am therefore always reorienting myself with respect to things. Things meet me

---

[120]   This is also true of the personal past each of us claims. We revise it and it changes as we change.

[121]   In truth, the body is a *torus*, so that talking in one sense about the body in terms of inside and outside really make no sense.

in various modes of encounter, while I approach objects, grasp them, work on them, manipulate them.

The fixed horizon of objectivity, which geometry assumes, applies to any and everyone. The horizons of experience, however, are singular: the horizon of any sense in front of which I experience a thing is always *my* horizon, mine alone. It is involved in my Existence.

Moving, Seeing, Listening

We have seen that movement has to be restored to the objects produced by the geometric transformation. Stasis, not movement, is exceptional and what is in need of being explained. We now know from Physics that in all realms — microcosmic (subatomic), mesocosmic (human), macrocosmic — nothing is at rest. It did not require physics to inform us of that, however. Everyday experience shows us the changing nature of all things.

Movement is restored in relation to the horizon. Posture and gait are the primary accommodations I make to the horizon.[122] In reaching toward me, the horizon draws me up to the standing position. It presents itself differently depending on my body's stature. This is most evident during early childhood, when an individual first attains the upright posture, and at certain other times in life when the upright posture is abandoned or lost (lying down at night or falling). I am not trained to walk. The horizon pulls me up and forward. When I am strong enough, I support this stand. The by-play between gravity and drawing forward is repeated with rhythmic regularity when I walk. The most open by-play with the horizon is dancing.

Following the geometric transformation of the earth and Existence, however, the neurophysiologist, Charles S. Sherrington, *invents* the isolated

---

[122]   See Erwin Straus's "Lived Movement" (1935), "The Upright Posture" (1948) and other essays included in his collected papers *Phenomenological Psychology* (1966) New York: Basic Books.

reflex which in combination with other reflexes is said to account for the postural model of the living body.[123] A number of partial neurological moments in complex combination come to comprise a movement. Yet in order to isolate and elicit any single reflex moment, the integrity of the organism must be disrupted.[124] The workings of an isolated reflex may tell us something about the nervous system but it cannot tell us about the Existence that gives meaning to that system. The science of neurology, like the other biological (natural) sciences, is based on the geometric transformation of Existence.

Only my relation to the horizon can account for bodiliness and movement. By horizon I mean, of course, the combined horizons of the several senses, if it is possible to divide them up in the first place. My body's upright integrity is maintained against a horizon of adjustments to the places in which I am implicated. I stand toward the approaching horizon by which I am encompassed and in that posture reflect the tension that maintains my posture.

Upright posture provides the context and structure of all my peculiarly human acts. Having stood to walk, my hands are thus freed for the manipulation of things. Mutual encounter, face to face, gaze to gaze, is also significantly manual, hand to hand. I greet another person with outstretched hands, wave or beckon to him with a hand.[125] With both hands open, I am the equivalent of every other person. My outstretched hand does not assure the other person that I do not conceal a weapon in my fist, as some anthropologists have suggested. I become inequivalent to the other when I close one or both of my hands to him, or hide my hands. Equivalence means parity of openness with respect to things, including especially others.

---

[123]   *The Integrative Action of the Nervous System* (1906) New Haven: Yale University Press.
[124]   It has been demonstrated that spinal reflexes are not fixed. They can be modified by experience. See Erwin Straus, *The Primary World of the Senses. A Vindication of Sensory Experience* (1963 1935), New York: Macmillan/The Free Press of Glencoe.
[125]   The hand becomes the symbol of imagination.

In spite of the unity of the ὅρος, the horizon of each sense can be described. Though the *visual* horizon is fully encircling, I always face it only partially. I see where I *am*, in the active sense of the verb '[to] be'. Walking, my gaze scans along its convex, upward curving arc. The upright posture first lifts my gaze upward. To estimate the distance that reaches toward me and to maintain my footing, I lower my gaze, which I soon do more easily than raise it.

Walking is the prototypical free act. It demonstrates the equilibrium I have achieved with respect to the visual horizon after having assumed the upright posture. To be free is to walk the human gait. One does not *run* free. I run in pursuit or escape. I walk freely.

Though I am often diverted from the horizon, I am always drawn back to it. And so, if I turn my head upward to look into the sky, my eyes begin to close in a gesture of return to the horizon. If I try to keep my eyes fully open while moving my head back further yet, I experience vertigo as the equilibrium is disturbed which during childhood was established only with great difficulty. With my head thrown back and the visual field above the horizon, my eyes' scanning function is temporarily suspended. As I lift my gaze above the horizon, I lose orientation as an earthbound creature. If I then try to walk, I may teeter and fall off balance. If I turn my gaze downward below the horizon, I lower my expectations, lose momentum and, facing the ground, limit what is likely to meet me.

Facing the circumambient *acoustic* horizon, I am oriented and directed in a different way. The acoustic horizon is the fully encompassing *spherical* surround of hearkening. This acoustic *atmosphaera* cannot be fully appreciated visually. For this reason it has been neglected by philosophy and science, which takes its metaphors from geometry, which is fundamentally visual.

The acoustic horizon is the horizon of language. With the advent of writing, the horizon of language is narrowed down and contained by the visual horizon. On account of its acoustic horizonality, my bodily relation to the visual horizon is never fixed in one direction. My body senses as a whole as I accommodate the changes my body actualizes when it moves.

Perceiving occurs through the unity of my several sensory horizons. The theoretical isolation of the various sensory horizons, as already noted, is a fundamental consequence of the geometric transformation of Existence.

While awake, my body moves continuously (like my eyes) in order to maintain orientation to the horizon. In maintaining balance, I retain my freedom. At night when I want to sleep or when I am ill, I lie down in order to abandon the visual horizon. Lying down, I effectively raise the horizon and allow myself to fall asleep under it. I also lie down to die. When the last horizon (probably the acoustic horizon) reaches me and overtakes me, things and the horizon become congruent, and I die.

I am in every instance already oriented. I move in order to maintain my orientation, not to establish it. I can, of course, allow myself to be pushed along, but to be treated in that way disturbs my balance with respect to the horizon and my freedom is undermined. When being passively moved at speeds that exceed the few miles per hour I might be able to attain in walking, I am unable to reorient myself apace quickly enough to the horizon to maintain orientation. Being moved along, eventually I resign myself to constricting the world and limit it to the interior of my conveyance. The rest of the world from which I am by then disoriented becomes mere background.

Acting is precisely *not* being moved by something, as it were, from behind, but being engaged by being drawing into the horizon. The emphasis on motivation by modern psychologists is in line with a passive interpretation of movement. We recognize the space of the psychologist's world as geometric space. In it the subject has become an object motivated by personal and cultural objects.

The consequences of being moved from one position to another are far-reaching, whether one is moved by an automobile, train or airplane. Being moved through space from one position to another has transformed the places of life to positions in experience, all of which are increasingly interchangeable. In the geometrically transformed world, uniform spaces become the surrogates for particular places.

Sitting, like standing, is an action. Sitting, my gaze moves upward more easily than when I am standing and I do not lose my equilibrium as quickly.[126] My gaze sweeps across the horizon and I have occasion to reflect on the arc of the horizon as though I were independent of it. Sitting encourages reflection, which implies a certain independence from everyday experience.

The full visual horizon can be inspected only above the earth. At that distance, however, the earth has already become something different from the earth we inhabit. It is no longer anything any of its inhabitants can really understand.[127] For the many hours of an intercontinental flight, for example, I am not in any particular geographic place. I am inside the cramped metal cave of the airplane with its contours and noise. The extraordinary removal from the ground that occurs under such circumstances reveals a limitless visual expanse below me which is, however, nothing by which I can orient myself.

Geometric space encompasses light years and ångstroms with the same ease as it does inches, meters and yards. Its measurements confound the events that take place on the scale of the everyday (insects, books, trees, buildings, mountains, people) with events on a cosmic or subatomic scale, which can be only mathematically imagined and represented. Thus the real and the imaginable occupy one unreal illustrated world of geometric representations, whose scale is adjusted to fit a piece of paper, the page of a book, a chalkboard, or a movie or video screen.

A confusion of places follows our attempts to accommodate ourselves to the spaces measured by mechanical and electronic instruments which are alien to the body and its means of moving and encompassing distances. Such disorientation characterizes life in the technological (that is, geometri-

---

[126]   Being seated means having been provided with something to sit upon, while sitting names the active posture described here.

[127]   Perhaps the Ascension episode in the Christian myth expresses the human desire to rise to such a complete view of the human horizon which symbolizes life on this earth.

cally transformed) world. But to return to earth. The standing position best supports conversation and the rhythm of walking sets its pace, which changes to accommodate the topic.

Orientations to the Other

We may consider two basic modes of being oriented with respect to someone else: face to face and side by side. In either mode, talking while sitting establishes greater emotional commitment which is suited for counsel, guidance, admonition and certain kinds of instruction. Lying down (as is the custom, for example, in psychoanalysis) focuses interest on what is said by the one reclining. The disembodying effect of psychoanalysis is both one of its unique traits and its great disadvantage. Psychoanalysis, however, is clearly an outgrowth of discourse while walking. It is in the tradition of philosophical discussion, rather than clinical medicine. In effect, the participants in psychoanalysis attempt to take a walk while one is lying down and the other is sitting. The psychoanalytic situation directs attention to the hypothetical inner world (Platonic Cave) of the analysand, a private version of the geometrized object world. Of course, we often find it easier to talk with someone about something we do not want to face when we are walking together.

The stage of a theater presents an artificial horizon in front of which the confusions of geometrically transformed Existence are voiced and portrayed. In fact the theater presents two visual horizons, the upstage horizon of the set and the downstage proscenium frame with its often outwardly curved front. The action takes place between these two horizons. This peculiarity sets off the theatrical performance from cinema, where images of the inner representational world are projected onto a luminescent screen. Video images are similar.[128]

---

[128]   We recall that Freud likened the dream world to a theater. It is clearly more a cinema than a stage theater, however.

When someone approaches me where I am sitting, I must look up to meet his voice and gaze. Otherwise, in that position I remain his inferior, child-like.[129] I confirm our parity and equivalence by standing up to meet the other face to face. In legal and other institutional settings,[130] one is interrogated while sitting. Open questioning is precluded between one who is seated and one who is standing (for example, an examining attorney or professor). Tutelage and training of any kind, regardless of the intentions of those who provide it, will have the effect of subjection since they are carried out within this positional arrangement. Genuine teaching, by contrast, occurs only when both student and teacher walk side by side or meet face to face, as in the Socratic and peripatetic traditions.[131]

Professional relationships of all kinds are based on the situation in which one person (the authoritarian though not necessarily authoritative figure) stands while the other sits. Teacher and student, physician and patient, legal counselor and client, employer and employee, are in all professional relations determined by this arrangement. It is the prototype for all situations in which an evaluating judgement is offered and dispensed.[132] This arrangement only continues what began in early childhood when the difference in physical stature between youngster and adult parents required two corresponding levels of status. Later in life, the standing one aspires to in the community depends to a great extent upon the status he has been accorded earlier when passing from childhood to adulthood.

---

[129]   This is the customary position of the student.

[130]   A case can be made for understanding all institutions as basically legal. A monarch's court (or any legislative or executive body) and the court of justice have a common source in legal proceedings: a presiding judge, competing interests, evidence, the exercise and distribution of power, and so on. The courtroom is the prototype for all institutions in which "professional relationships" are set up. The legal language of philosophy (law, evidence, argument) has its source here, too.

[131]   Basic reform of schooling will begin by replacing the typical classroom arrangement with one suitable for questioning, not interrogating.

[132]   Were teaching not concerned with evaluation of the student, it would lose its professional cast. Medical, including psychiatric, diagnosis is also a judgment, not primarily an assessment of facts.

The practice of medicine requires that the agent (physician) stand and the patient lie down. When I, as a patient, abrogate my status willingly and temporarily — for example, to undergo a surgical procedure — I permit its relinquishment without at the same time suffering a diminution in my status.

Language, Speaking and Writing

We usually also read in the sitting position. The priest, legislator, statesman, or teacher who reads a text while standing performs an unusual variation of the act of reading. His pronouncements speak from a position that possesses the power proceeding from law, whether it be a law of nature represented by the physician, divine law promulgated by a priest, or human law declared by a judge.

A written text is a fixed visible form given to verbal expressions. Its unique hermeneutic characteristics have been exposed recently by literary critics.[133] What is writing from the perspective of the geometric transformation? Writing is an act which silences speech in the way the drawings of geometry silence things. Objects are to things as writing is to speech. What might have occasioned the act of writing? Writing may have been first prompted when the expression on another person's face turned out to have been dissimulated, when what I had "read" there turned out to be wrong. Writing was perhaps then instituted as a way of preserving a record of the expression observed for use later as evidence of what had been expressed and observed. Writing would then be a form of representation that is a response to misrepresentation or dissimulation. The force of the text would lie in the fact that it cannot be altered without visible evidence of change. Thus, a face might have lied, but not a text.

An alternative account of its origin is that writing silently speaks the unspeakable, what I will not or cannot bring myself to express in audible

---

[133] See, for example, Jacques Derrida, *Of Grammatology* (1967) Baltimore: Johns Hopkins Press, 1976.

speech. Since in speaking we make our presence known, we may write in order to remain unnoticed at the time we are expressing ourselves.[134] A written text allows what has been committed to the "memory" of the retaining surface or circuit to be repeated, but again without requiring the speaker's presence or disclosing the reader's presence. The concept of memory as inscription of images (mnemic traces) is likely a metaphor of writing.[135] In writing, finally, the spoken word is divorced from its speaker and becomes an artifact. At the same time, in this way the darkness and invisibility of the origin of speech are forgotten and overcome.

Place, Time and Experience

With the recollection of a conditional future, *our first geometrician initiates time*. Time carves out "experiences" in the way space allocates objects. Time becomes the container of experience and we say that human beings are "in" time. Experience is the name for Existence aware of this kind of temporality.[136] The future perfect tense, which becomes the fundamental tense of language after the geometric transformation, expresses the predom-

---

[134] Perhaps *speaking* articulate sounds begins at night when we can not see one another. In daylight, we can read the other's face and gestures, but at night, when we cannot see the expression on his face or his gestures, we do not have a clear idea of what he is doing unless what he does has direct impact on us or he tells us about it. The impulse to speak might then first have occurred at night. Speech would then be a nocturnal manifestation that reinvents what cannot be seen. In the act of speaking, we would be expressing a primary wish, that it not be night and that there be light instead, so that we might see. To be heard at night is to be acknowledged as present, though not seen. To be heard speaking is to disclose what we mean but are unable to show. Telephone conversations, during which the person spoken to and I cannot see each other, institutionalizes the nighttime origin of speech.

[135] We may assume that theories of memory, which see it as incisions in wax or creases in paper, originate from reflections on the meaning of writing.

[136] See my paper "Human Being and Existence. A Problem in Phenomenological Psychology," *Review of Existential Psychology and Psychiatry* 22, 1990, 116–140.

inance of *experience* in our view of Existence. Existence *temporalized* in the future perfect tense is termed *experience*. Such temporalization of Existence and our first geometrician's new awareness occur together.[137] The "present" which he subsequently invents is designed on the model of the "future perfect."

The present is, therefore, an afterthought of the future perfect. Our first geometrician can say "I do this" only because he has already determined how "I will have done it." Awareness is divided into a tense structure which language articulates. Nowhere is the complexity of this seen more vividly than in the tense structure of Greek. As a consequence of dividing up awareness in this way, waking awareness (consciousness) and oneiric awareness become for the first time discontinuous, and consciousness takes precedence over the dream life.

Existence

Our first geometrician's Existence is confined to experiences in the world of objects. Western languages describe experiences in this world predominantly in visual metaphors. The other sensory dimensions with their own horizons are in turn interpreted in visual terms.

Within the geometric view of the world, the return to Existence is seen as an escape from experience. The primacy of experience is ensured by the elaboration of the representational world to include the invisible realm of ideas. But for this to have occurred, what was once the continuity of Existence had first to be incised.

The discontinuities of the world of experience our first geometrician introduced into Existence have become the legacy of every infant who grows up in the western world. In the beginning of its life, it does not have awareness of its Existence. The child accustoms itself to the world of

---

[137]   The history of metaphysics is the record of this dominance of experience over Existence.

experience by means of language, the major feature of which is its tense structure. Language thus always refers to experience — not to Existence, which is tenseless.

A correlate of the point of view, which of our first geometrician forces upon us, is history: the collective, public past which is construed as the conditional future's occasion and cause. The occidental world is only now attempting to understand the meaning of history. We are all characters in the metaphysical dream of the geometrically transformed earth which we call history. So far, though, only rarely has someone in that dream (Hegel, for example) suspected that he is dreaming. Earlier I suggested that an excess of awareness precipitated our first geometrician's dream. Perhaps a similar excess of imagination within that dream will help rouse us from it.

Music

The concluding thoughts of this essay are about music. Why music? When music emerges from silence, it leaves things alone. By contrast, the other formal systems of signs, including mathematics and the natural languages, transform things into objects. Perhaps music is the φάρμακον for the ailments the geometrician's science has created. The rhythmic structure of music in no way resembles the regularity of calculated time (the μέτρον of geometry). It expresses thought in a symbolism that is direct and concrete. Nietzsche says somewhere that without music, life would be a mistake. It may be that the situation is even more critical and that, without a recovered sense of μουσική in the primary sense (beginning with a deepened appreciation for music), we in the *Abendland* will fall into a deeper, dreamless sleep in which we will be so dead to the nightime geometrized world that we will not even be able sense the danger and know that it is possible to wake up.

Postscript: One More Fanciful Genesis

The empirical natural sciences that have arisen and taken their place since the geometric transformation of the earth may be imagined to have appeared in the course of a single "day," during which each of the sciences took its place within a fixed horizon at whose center was the observational point of view. Many new sciences are only now being named during the closing hours of that day.

Meteorology thus may be thought to have originated soon after dawn. The prototype of the empirical natural sciences, meteorology is the very model of that to which any nearly perfect science aspires. Not surprisingly, its claims are most relevant to the inhabitants of densely populated urban areas of a few square miles, but even so the great patterns of change that affect climate locally are wonderfully unpredictable. The successes of meteorology are limited because the conditions of the earth's atmosphere and its surface are very *local*. Meteorology wants to tell in advance what *will have been*, to predict how things will have turned out, so that there are no surprises. Above all else, it wants to predict events in the interest of successful control of the conditions of everyday life and work. Business travel and vacations can then be profitably scheduled. Options can be ordered in the market place. News can be timed for optimal effect on the public. Even though meteorology has become known as among the least successful sciences in this respect, it provides a model for what the other natural sciences can expect to achieve in the application of their findings.

Physics and the *life sciences* based on it (*chemistry, biology* and *physiology*) appear soon after meteorology early in the day heralded by the geometric transformation. Recently, the applications of these sciences to disease and distress have been extensive when applied to the practice of *medicine*. The physician was traditionally the individual's counsel on pain and dying. Originally, as a shaman, his role was combined with that of judge and priest. Only recently has the physician been thought of as a scientist as the natural sciences were enlisted to aid the physician in the practice of his healing arts. Medicine as an art, however, must have arisen one night long before the geometrician's sunset vision, long before the dawn of the geometrically transmuted day, while medical science is a product of the early hours of the geometrically transformed day. *Metaphysics*, the twilight science, surely originated late in the day.

Heidegger Bibliography,
1949 to 2015

Preface

I. Bibliography of English Translations of the Writings of Martin Heidegger (1949-2015)

      A. The Heidegger *Gesamtausgabe*
      B. Master Bibliography
      C. Supplemental Bibliography: Heidegger and Politics
      D. Letters
      E. Unpublished Translations
      F. Translators by Alphanumeric Code of Item
      G. Translators by Title of Item

II. German Texts Translated into English (1949-2015): Alphabetical

III. German Texts Translated into English (1949-2015): Date of Composition

IV. Contents of the Heidegger *Gesamtausgabe* (1975-2015) by Volume Number

V. Lecture Courses (1919-1955) and Seminars (1927-1973): Date of Composition

VI. Lecture Courses (1919-1955) and Seminars (1927-1973): Date of First Publication in German

VII. Video and Audio Recordings (1955-2009)

PREFACE
for DFJ

Begun in 1977, the year after the death of Martin Heidegger, the following bibliography is for the use of students of his thought whose first language is English. This *Bibliography of English Translations of the Writings of Martin Heidegger* details the history of translations into English of Heidegger's books, essays, lecture courses, book reviews, poetry and letters (1949-2011). It begins with a list of the volumes of the Heidegger *Gesamtausgabe* (= *GA* [1975-]) published to date, to which the entries are keyed. The "Master Bibliography" is followed by a "Supplemental Bibliography: Heidegger and Politics" and a bibliography of "Unpublished Translations" available online. It concludes with two lists of the translators, the first keyed to an alphanumeric code at the end of each entry {} and the other giving the titles of the translators' contributions.

For the scholar's convenience, several other bibliographies have been created. Two give the original German titles of the translated texts: the first (II) arranged alphabetically by title, the other (III) given by date of composition of the text. Bibliography IV gives the table of contents for each of the published volumes of the *Gesamtausgabe*. Since Heidegger's lecture courses (1915-1955) and seminars (1927-1973) occupy a significant portion of Heidegger's published works, two further bibliographies have been prepared, one (V) listing the courses and seminars in chronological order of having been offered, the other (VI) listing them by date of first publication in German. A bibliography of video and audio materials (VII) is given last. Apart from some audio books in English, all but one are audio recordings.

An earlier version of this bibligography appeared in my study of Heidegger's philosophy of translation, *Translating Heidegger* (Amherst: Humanity Books, 2004), in my books *The Voice that Thinks: Heidegger* Studies (Greensburg: Eadmer Press, 1997) and *Preparatory Thinking in Heidegger's Teaching* (New York: Philosophical Library, 1987), and in manuscripts held by the New York Public Library (1993) and the library of St. Vincent College and Archabbey (1978).

> Miles Groth
> March 1, 2016
> New York

I. BIBLIOGRAPHY OF ENGLISH TRANSLATIONS (1949-2014)

Each entry presents four kinds of information about books, essays, lecture courses, book reviews and poems by Martin Heidegger that have been translated into English:

[A]   Title and translator(s): Here are given the title(s) of English translation(s) (A,B,C etc.), date of first appearance of the translation (...), and translator(s) [...].

[B]   History of the text: Occasion of composition. Texts in [B] preceded by ^ are available in an audio or video version, listed in bibliography VII, "Video and Audio Recordings."

[C]   German source(s): Given here are a reference to the first publication in German and the current German source(s), usually a volume in *GA*.

[D]   English source(s): Publication references corresponding to the listing(s) in [A] (A,B,C etc.), including the most current edition of the source(s). Titles in [D] preceded by * are bilingual.

Entries in the bibliography are alphabetized by title of the *first* appearance of the text or *a portion* of it. This may not be the best way to proceed, but it preserves the history of the translations. On occasion, when a text has become best known by a title published later (B5 and Q3), that title is given in brackets before the first translation to provide the reader with help locating the text. In one case (Z1), excerpts published earlier but now available in the first item are included within the entry as separate items. Finally, there is the case of *Nietzsche* (N2). The various texts contained in the original German two-volume text (1961) are all referenced separately but the four-volume set corresponding to the 1961 set is given its own entry. Apart from the "Letter on Humanism" and the "Letter to William J Richardson," which are philosophical texts unto themselves, letters comprise a category of their own (Part E, below). Translations of exerpts from letters and other documents relating to Heidegger's interest in Asian philosophy can be found in Lin Ma and Jaap van Brakel, "Heidegger's Comportment toward East-West Dialogue, in *Philosophy East and West* 56(4), 2006, pp. 519-566 (esp. pp. 536,539, 541 542, 547). Finally, many passages from Heidegger's early dissertations and papers, reprinted in *GA* 1, are translated in John van

Buren's *The Young Heidegger. Rumor of the Hidden King* (Bloomington: Indiana University Press, 1994). References are made to Theodore Kisiel and Thomas Sheehan (eds.), *Becoming Heidegger. On the Trail of His Early Occasional Wrirings, 1910-1927* (Evanston: Northwestern University Press, 2007), which was withdrawn after publication, in the event it should become available.

A. THE HEIDEGGER *GESAMTAUSGABE* [1975-2014]

References in the bibliography to *GA* are based on the following list of volumes published to date (Spring 2012). The title of the volume and the date of its *first* publication (in a number of instances before *GA*) are given. If the text first appeared as a lecture course, the date and place of the course are given (usually SS [= Summer Semester] or WS [= Winter Semester]). The volumes marked ~ have been translated in whole or in part.

1975

GA 24~   *Die Grundprobleme der Phänomenologie* [1975]
             SS 1927, University of Marburg
             (Friedrich-Wilhelm von Herrmann)

1976

GA 9~   *Wegmarken* [1967]
             (Friedrich-Wilhelm von Herrmann)

GA 21~   *Logik. Die Frage nach der Wahrheit* [1976]
             WS 1925/26, University of Marburg
             (Walter Biemel)

1977

GA 2~   *Sein und Zeit* [1927]
             (Friedrich-Wilhelm von Herrmann)

GA 5~   *Holzwege* [1950]
             (Friedrich-Wilhelm von Herrmann)

GA 25~   *Phänomenologische Interpretation von Kants Kritik der reinen Vernunft* [1977]
             WS 1927/28, University of Freiburg
             (Ingtraud Görland)

1978

GA 1~   *Frühe Schriften* [1972]
             (Friedrich-Wilhelm von Herrmann)

GA 26~   *Metaphysische Anfangsgründe der Logik im Ausgang der*
                Leibniz [1978]
                SS 1928, Marburg University
                (Klaus Held)

1979
GA 20~   *Prolegomena zur Geschichte des Zeitbegriffs* [1979]
                SS 1925, Freiburg University
                (Petra Jaeger)

GA 55~   *Heraklit.* 1. Der Anfang des abendländischen Denkens. 2.
                Logik. Heraklits Lehre zum Logos [1979]
                1. SS 1943, University of Freiburg. 2. SS 1944, University of
                Freiburg
                (Manfred S. Frings)

1980
GA 32~   *Hegels Phänomenologie des Geistes* [1980]
                WS 1930/31, University of Freiburg
                (Ingtraud Görland)

GA 39   *Hölderlins Hymnen "Germanien" und "Der Rhein"* [1980]
                WS 1934/35, University of Freiburg
                (Susanne Ziegler)

1981
GA 4~   *Erläuterungen zu Hölderlins Dichtung* [1944]
                (Friedrich-Wilhelm von Herrmann)

GA 33~   *Aristoteles, Metaphysik Θ 1-3. Von Wesen und Wirklichkeit*
                der Kraft [1981]
                WS 1931, University of Freiburg
                (Heinrich Hüni)

GA 51~   *Grundbegriffe* [1981]
                SS 1941, University of Freiburg
                (Petra Jaeger)

1982

GA 31~   *Vom Wesen der menschlichen Freiheit. Einleitung in die*
              Philosophie [1982]
              SS 1930, University of Freiburg
              (Hartmut Tietjen)

GA 52   *Hölderlins Hymne "Andenken"* [1982]
              WS 1941/42, University of Freiburg
              (Curd Ochwadt)

GA 54~   *Parmenides* [1982]
              WS 1942/43, University of Freiburg
              (Manfred S. Frings)

1983

GA 13~   *Aus der Erfahrung des Denkens (1910-1976)* [1954]
              (Friedrich-Wilhelm von Herrmann)

GA 29/30~   *Die Grundbegriffe der Metaphysik. Welt—Endlichkeit—*
              Einsamkeit [1983]
              WS 1929/30, University of Freiburg
              (Friedrich-Wilhelm von Herrmann)

GA 40~   *Einführung in die Metaphysik* [1953]
              SS 1935, University of Freiburg
              (Petra Jaeger)

1984

GA 41~   *Die Frage nach dem Ding. Zu Kants Lehre von den*
              transzendentalen Grundsätzen [1962]
              WS 1935/36, University of Freiburg
              (Petra Jaeger)

GA 45~   *Grundfragen der Philosophie. Ausgewählte "Probleme" der*
              "Logik" [1984]
              WS 1937/38, University of Freiburg
              (Friedrich-Wilhelm von Herrmann)

GA 53~   *Hölderlins Hymne "Der Ister"* [1984]
             SS 1942, University of Freiburg
             (Walter Biemel)

1985
GA 12~   *Unterwegs zur Sprache* [1959]
             (Friedrich-Wilhelm von Herrmann)

GA 43~   *Nietzsche: Der Wilfle zur Macht als Kunst* [1961 (earlier
             version)]
             WS 1936/37, University of Freiburg
             (Bernd Heimbüchel)

GA 61~   *Phänomenologische Interpretationen zu Aristoteles.*
             Einführung in die phänomenologische Forschung [1985]
             WS 1921/22, University of Freiburg
             (Walter Bröcker and Käte Bröcker-Oltmanns)

1986
GA 15~   *Seminare* [1986]
             1. "Heraklit" WS 1966/67, University of Freiburg (with Eugen
             Fink)
             2. "Vier Seminare" 1966, 1967, 1968 (Le Thor), 1973
             (Zähringen)
             3. "Aussprache mit Martin Heidegger" 1951, 1952 (Zürich)
             (Curd Ochwadt)

GA 44~   *Nietzsches metaphysische Grundstellung im abendländischen*
             Denken: Die ewige Wiederkehr des Gleichen [1961 (earlier
             version)]
             SS 1937, University of Freiburg
             (Marion Heinz)

GA 48~   *Nietzsche: Der europäische Nihilismus* [1961 (earlier
             version)]
             Second Trimester 1940, University of Freiburg
             (Petra Jaeger)

1987

GA 56/57~   *Zur Bestimmung der Philosophie* [1987; rev. ed. 1999]
                1. Die Idee der Philosophie und das
                Weltanschauungsproblem.
                2. Phänomenologie und transzendentale Wertphilosophie [mit
                einer Nachschrift der Vorlesung; Über das Wesen der
                Universität und des akademischen Studiums]

                1. Kriegsnotsemester [War Emergency Semester] 1919,
                University of Freiburg
                2. SS 1919, University of Freiburg
                (Bernd Heimbüchel)

1988

GA 34~   *Vom Wesen der Wahrheit. Zu Platons Höhlengleichnis und
                Theätet* [1988]
                WS 1931/32, University of Freiburg
                (Hermann Mörchen)

GA 42~   *Schelling: Vom Wesen der menschlichen Freiheit (1809)*
                [1971]
                SS 1936, University of Freiburg
                (Ingrid Schüßler)

GA 63~   *Ontologie (Hermeneutik der Faktizität)* [1988]
                SS 1923, University of Freiburg
                (Käte Bröcker-Oltmanns)

1989

GA 47~   *Nietzsches Lehre vom Willen zur Macht als Erkenntnis* [1961
                (earlier version)]
                SS 1939, University of Freiburg
                (Eberhard Hanser)

GA 65~   *Beiträge zur Philosophie (Vom Ereignis)* [1989]
                (Friedrich-Wilhelm von Herrmann)

GA 50~   1. *Nietzsches Metaphysik.*
          2. *Einleitung in die Philosophie. Denken und Dichten* [1991]

          1. WS 1941/42 [not given]
          2. WS 1944/45, University of Freiburg
          (Petra Jaeger)

1991
GA 3~   *Kant und das Problem der Metaphysik* [1929]
          WS 1925-26, University of Marburg
          (Friedrich-Wilhelm von Herrmann)

GA 49   *Die Metaphysik des deutschen Idealismus (Schelling)* [1991]
          First Trimester 1941 and Seminar SS 1941, University of
          Freiburg
          (Günther Seibold)

1992
GA 19~   *Platon: Sophistes* [1992]
          WS 1924/25, University of Marburg
          (Ingeborg Schüßler)

GA 58   *Grundprobleme der Phänomenologie (1919/20)* [1992]
          WS 1919/20, University of Freiburg
          (Hans-Helmuth Gander)

1993
GA 68   *Hegel.*
          1. Die Negativität. Eine Auseinandersetzung mit Hegel aus
          dem Ansatz in der Negativität (1938/39, 1941).
          2. Erläuterung der "Einleitung" zu Hegels "Phänomenologie
          des Geistes" (1942) [1993]
          (Ingrid Schüßler)

GA 59~   *Phänomenologie der Anschauung und des Ausdrucks.*
                Theorie der philosophischen Begriffsbildung [1993]
                SS 1920, University of Freiburg
                (Claudius Strube)

GA 22~   *Die Grundbegriffe der antiken Philosophie* [1993]
                SS 1926, University of Marburg
                (Franz-Karl Blust)

GA 58~   *Grundprobleme der Phänomenologie (1919/20)*
                [1993; rev. ed. 2010]
                WS 1919/20, University of Freiburg
                (Hans-Helmuth Gander)

1994
GA 17~   *Einführung in die phänomenologische Forschung* [1994]
                WS 1923/24, University of Marburg
                (Friedrich-Wilhelm von Herrmann)

GA 79~   *Bremer und Freiburger Vorträge* [1994]
                1. Einblick in das was ist (1949)
                2. Grundsätze des Denkens (1957)
                (Petra Jaeger)

1995
GA 77~   *Feldweg-Gespräche* [1995]
                (Ingrid Schüßler)

GA 60~   *Phänomenologie des religiösen Lebens* [1995]
                1. Einleitung in die Phänomenologie der Religion (1920/21)
                2. Augustinus und der Neuplatonismus (1921)
                3. Die philosophischen Grundlagen der mittelalterischen
                Mystik (1918/1919)

                (1. Matthias Jung and Thomas Reghely
                2. Claudius Strube
                3. Claudius Strube)

1996

GA 6.1~   *Nietzsche I* [1996]
                (Brigitte Schillebach)

GA 27   *Einleitung in die Philosophie* [1996]
                WS 1928/29, University of Freiburg
                (Otto Saame and Ina Saame-Speidel)

1997

GA 28   *Der deutsche Idealismus (Fichte, Schelling, Hegel) und die
                philosophische Problemlage der Gegenwart ("Einführung in
                das akademische Studium")* [1997]
                SS 1929, University of Freiburg
                (Claudius Strube)

GA 10~   *Der Satz vom Grund* [1997]
                WS 1955/56, University of Freiburg
                (Petra Jaeger)

GA 6.2~   *Nietzsche II* [1997]
                (Brigitte Schillibach)

GA 66~   *Besinnung* [1997]
                (Friedrich-Wilhelm von Herrmann)

1998

GA 69   *Die Geschichte des Seyns* [1998]
                1. Die Geschichte des Seyns (1938-40)
                2. Κοινόν. Aus der Geschichte des Seyns (1939-40)
                (Peter Trawny)

GA 38~   *Logik als die Frage nach dem Wesen der Sprache* [1998]
                SS 1934, University of Freiburg
                (Günther Seubold)

1999

GA 67   *Metaphysik und Nihilismus* [1999]
                1. Die Überwindung der Metaphysik
                2. Das Wesen des Nihilismus
                (Hans-Joachim Friedrich)

GA 85~   *Vom Wesen der Sprache. Zu Herders Abhandlung "Uber den*
                Ursprung der Sprache" [1999]
                (Ingrid Schüßler)

2000

GA 75   *Zu Hölderlin. Griechenlandreisen* [2000]
                (Curt Ochwadt)

GA 7~   *Vorträge und Aufsätze* [2000]
                (Friedrich Wilhelm von Herrmann)

GA 16~   *Reden und andere Zeugnisse eines Lebensweges* [2000]
                (Hermann Heidegger)

2001

GA 36/37~   *Sein und Wahrheit* [2001]
                (Hartmut Tietjen)

2002

GA 18~   *Grundbegriffe der aristotelischen Philosophie* [2002]
                SS 1924, University of Marburg
                (Mark Michalski)

GA 8~   *Was heißt Denken?* [2002]
                WS 1951-52 and SS 1952, University of Freiburg
                (Paola-Ludovika Coriando)

2003

GA 46   *Zur Auslegung von Nietzsches II. Unzeitgemäßer Betrachtung*
               "Vom Nutzen und Nachteil der Historie für das Leben" [2003]
               WS 1938/39, University of Freiburg
               (Hans-Joachim Friedrich)

2004

GA 87   *Nietzsche. Seminare 1937 und 1944* [2004]
               (Peter von Ruckteschell)

GA 90~   *Zu Ernst Jünger* [2004]
               (Peter Trawny)

GA 64~   *Der Begriff der Zeit* [2004]
               (Friedrich-Wilhelm von Herrmann)

2005

GA 70   *Über den Anfang* [2005]
               (Paola-Ludovica Coriando)

GA 62~   *Phänomenologische Interpretationen ausgewählte*
               Abhandlungen des Aristoteles zur Ontologie und Logik [2005]
               SS 1922, University of Freiburg
               Phänomenologische Interpretationen zu Aristoteles (Anzeige
               der hermeneutischen Situation) Ausarbeitung für die
               Marburger und die Göttinger Philosophische Fakultät
               (Autumn 1922)
               (Günther Neumann)

2006

GA 11~   *Identität und Differenz* [2006]
               (Friedrich-Wilhlm von Herrmann)

GA 23   *Geschichte der Philosophie von Thomas von Aquin bis Kant*
               [2006]
               SS 1926/27, University of Marburg
               (Helmut Vetter)

2007

GA 14~   *Zur Sache des Denkens* [2007]
                (Friedrich-Wilhelm von Herrmann)

GA 81~   *Gedachtes* [2007]
                (Paola-Ludovika Coriando)

2008

GA 88   *Seminare (Übungen) 1937/38 und 1941/42* [2008]
                1. Die metaphysischen Grundstellungden des abendländischen
                Denkens
                2. Einübung in das philosophische Denken
                (Alfred Denker)

2009

GA 76   *Leitgedanken zur Entstehung der Metaphysik, der
                neuzeitlichen Wissenschaft under modernen Technik* [2009]
                (Claudius Strube)

GA 71~   *Das Ereignis* [2009]
                (Friedrich-Wilhelm von Herrmann)

2010

GA 78   *Der Spruch des Anaximander* [2010]
                (Ingebord Schüßler)

GA 74   *Zum Wesen der Sprache und Zur Frage nach der Kunst*
                [2010]
                (Thomas Regehly)

2011

GA 86   *Seminare. Hegel – Schelling* [2011]
                (Peter Trawny)

2012

GA 35   *Der Anfang der abendländischen Philosophie.*
               Auslegung des Anaximander und Parmenides.[2012]
               (Peter Trawny)

GA 83   *Seminare*
               Platon – Aristoteles – Augustinus [2012]
               (Mark Michalski)

2013

GA 84.1   *Seminare*
               Kant—Leibniz—Schiller (2013)
               (Günther Neumann)

GA 73.1   *Zum Ereignis—Denken* (2013)
               I-V
               (Peter Trawny)

GA 73.2   *Zum Ereignis* (2013)
               VI
               (Peter Trawny)

2014

GA 94   *Überlegungen II-VI*
               (Schwarze Hefte 1931-1938)
               Peter Trawny

GA 95   *Überlegungen VII-XI*
               (Schwarze Hefte 1938/39) (2014)
               Peter Trawny

GA 96   *Überlegungen XII-XV*
               (Scharze Hefte 1939-1941) (2014)
               Peter Trawny

2015   *Anmerkungen I-IV*
                  (Schwarze Hefte 1942-1948) (2015)
                  Peter Trawny

B. MASTER BIBLIOGRAPHY

1. [A]   "Acknowledgment on the Conferment of the National Hebel
          Memorial Prize" (1997) [Miles Groth].

    [B]   "Dank bei der Verleihung des staatlichen
          Hebelgedenkenpreises": Address given May 10, 1960, on the
          occasion of the 200th anniversary of the birth of Johann Peter
          Hebel when Heidegger was awarded the Hebel Prize.

    [C]   *Hebel-Feier. Reden zum 200.Geburtstag des Dichters* (1960)
          Karlsruhe: C.F. Müller, pp. 27-29. *GA* 16 (2000), pp. 565-567.

    [D]   "Acknowledgement on the Conferment of the National Hebel
          Memorial Prize," in *Delos* 19/20, April 1997 (Summer-Winter
          1994), pp. 30-34. {A1}

2. [A]   "Adalbert Stifter's `Ice Tale'" (1993) [Miles Groth].

    [B]   "Adalbert Stifters `Eisgeschichte'": Lecture broadcast on
          Radio Zürich, January 26, 1964.

    [C]   Daniel Bodmer (ed.), *Wirkendes Wort* (1964) Zürich:
          Schweizerische Bibliophilen-Gesellschaft, pp. 23-38. *GA* 13
          (1983), pp. 185-198.

    [D]   Published in part in Robert Crease (ed.), *Proceedings. 27th
          Annual Heidegger Conference* (1993) Stony Brook:
          SUNY/Stony Brook, pp. 21-23, and Appendix A. See also the
          translator's "The Telling Word," in *The Voice that Thinks:
          Heidegger Studies* (1997) Greensburg: Eadmer Press, pp. 43-
          58. {A2}

3. [A]   (A)   "The Age of the World View" (1951) [Marjorie
                Grene].

          (B)   "The Age of the World Picture" (1977) [William
                Lovitt].

          (C)   "The Age of the World Picture" (2002) [Julian
                Young].

          (D)   "The Age of the World Picture" (2009) [Jerome
                Veith].

    [B]   "Die Begründung des neuzeitlichen Weltbildes durch die
          Metaphysik": Lecture given June 9, 1938, Freiburg. Revised
          title (1950): "Die Zeit des Weltbildes."

[C]   *Holzwege* (1950): *GA* 5 (1977), pp. 75-113.

[D]   (A)   *Measure* (Chicago) 2, 1951, pp. 269-284. Reprinted in *boundary 2* (Binghamton) IV (2), 1976, pp. 1-15, and William V. Spanos (ed.), *Martin Heidegger and the Question of Literature: Toward a Postmodern Literary Hermeneutics* (1979) Bloomington: Indiana University Press, pp. 1-15 (a reissue of the journal).

      (B)   *The Question Concerning Technology and Other Essays* (1977) New York: Garland, 1982, pp. 115-154.

      (C)   *Off the Beaten Track* (2002) Cambridge: Cambridge University Press, pp. 57-85.

      (D)   Günther Figal (ed.), *The Heidegger Reader* (2009) New Haven: Yale University Press, pp. 207-223. Based on *GA* 5 (1977), pp. 75-96. {A3}

4.   [A]   "Aletheia (Heraclitus, Fragment B 16)" (1975) [Frank Capuzzi].

    [B]   "Heraklit": Text written in 1954 for a *Festschrift* based on material from the lecture course "Der Anfang des abendländischen Denkens," prepared for the Summer Semester 1943, University of Freiburg. Cf. *Heraklit: GA* 55 (1979), pp. 1-181. Revised title (1954): "Aletheia (Heraklit, Fragment 16)."

    [C]   *Festschrift zur Feier des 350jährigen Bestehens des Heinrich-Suso-Gymnasiums in Konstanz* (1954) Konstanz: Heinrich-Suso-Gymnasium, pp. 60-76. Reprinted in *Vorträge und Aufsätze* III (1954) Pfullingen: Neske, 1978, pp. 53-78. *GA* 7 (2000), pp. 263-288.

    [D]   *Early Greek Thinking* (1975) New York: Harper and Row, 1985, pp. 102-123. {A4}

5.   [A]   (A)   "The Anaximander Fragment" (1975) [David Farrell Krell].

      (B)   "Anaximander's Saying" (2002) [Julian Young].

    [B]   "Der Spruch des Anaximander": Essay written in 1946, Todtnauberg.

[C]   *Holzwege* (1950) Frankfurt: Klostermann, pp. 296-343. *GA 5*
        (1977), pp. 321-373.

[D]   (A)   *Arion* (Boston) 4, 1974, pp. 576-626. Reprinted in
                Early Greek Thinking (1975)
                New York: Harper and Row, 1985, pp. 13-58.

        (B)   *Off the Beaten Track* (2002) Cambridge: Cambridge
                University Press, pp. 242-281. {A5}

6. [A]   "Αγχιβασιν: A Triadic Conversation on a Country Path
            between a Scientist, a Scholar and a Guide" (2010) [Bret W.
            Davis].

    [B]   "Αγχιβασιν. Ein Gespräch selbstdritt auf einem Feldweg
            zwischen einem Forscher, einem Gelehrten und einem
            Weisen": Dialogue dated April 7, 1945.

    [C]   An excerpt was published as "Zur Erörterung der
            Gelassenheit. Aus einem Feldweggespräch über das Denken"
            in *Gelassenheit* (1959), Pfullingen: Neske (8ᵗʰ ed., 1985), pp.
            29-73, reprinted in *GA*13 (1983), pp. 37-74, translated in 1966
            as "Conversation on a Country Path about Thinking" (see C8).
            Only the last pages of the 1959 version (in *GA* 13 [1983], pp.
            58-74) correspond exactly to the *GA* 77 (1995) version (pp.
            138-157). *GA* 77 (1995), pp. 1-159.

    [D]   *Country Path Conversations* (2010) Bloomington: Indiana
            University Press, pp. 1-104. {A11}

7. [A]   "Appendix to *Nietzsche's Metaphysics*" (2011) [Phillip
            Jacques Braunstein].

    [B]   "Aufzeichnungen zu Nietzsches Metaphysik": Notes to the
            text "Nietzsches Metaphysik" (1940) {N3}.

    [C]   *GA* 50 (1990), pp. 83-87.

    [D]   *Introduction to Philosophy—Thinking and Poetizing* (2011)
            Bloomington: Indiana University Press, pp. 63-67. {A12}

8. [A]   *Aristotle's* Metaphysics Θ *1-3. On the Essence and Actuality
            of Force* (1995) [Walter Brogan and Peter Warnek].

    [B]   "Interpretationen zur antiken Philosophie / Aristoteles,
            Metaphysik Θ": Lecture course given Summer Semester 1931,
            University of Freiburg.

[C]   *GA* 33 (1981).

[D]   *Aristotle's* Metaphysics Θ *1-3. On the Essence and Actuality
        of Force* (1995) Bloomington: Indiana University Press. {A6}

9.   [A]   (A)   "Art and Space" (1973) [Charles Seibert].
            (B)   "Art and Space" (2009) [Jerome Veith].
     [B]   "Raum, Mensch und Sprache": Lecture given October 3, 1964,
            at the Galerie im Erker, St. Gallen, Switzerland.
     [C]   *Die Kunst und der Raum* (1969) St. Gallen: Erker-Verlag.
            Appears with a French translation. The first edition of 150
            copies included 25 that contained Chillida's paper cutouts. *GA*
            13 (1983), pp. 203-210. Heidegger reads the text on a
            recording (St. Gallen: Erker, 1969).
     [D]   (A)   *Man and World* (Dordrecht) 6, 1973, pp. 3-8.
            (B)   Günther Figal (ed.), *The Heidegger Reader* (2009)
                   New Haven: Yale University Press, pp. 305-309.
                   {A7}

10. [A]   "Art and Thinking" (1963) [Hannah Arendt].
     [B]   "Die Kunst und das Denken": Colloquy with Hoseki Shin'ichi
            Hisamatsu held on May 18, 1958, University of Freiburg,
            transcribed by Alfredo Guzzoni.
     [C]   Alfred L. Copley, *Heidegger und Hisamatsu und ein
            Zuhörender* (1963) Kyoto: Bokubi Verlag, pp. 43-80 (includes
            a Japanese text of the colloquy). *GA* 16 (2000), pp. 552-557.
     [D]   Alfred L. Copley, *Listening to Heidegger and Hisamatsu*
            (1963) Kyoto: Bokubi Press, pp. 48-78. {A8}

11. [A]   (A)   "As When on a Holiday . . ." (2000) [Keith Hoeller].
            (B)   "As When on a Holiday . . ." (2009) [Jerome Veith].
     [B]   "Wie wenn am Feiertage . . .": Lecture presented often in
            1939-40.
     [C]   *Hölderlins Hymne "Wie wenn am Feiertage"*(1941) Halle:
            Niemeyer. *GA* 4 (1981), pp. 47-77.
     [D]   (A)   "As When on a Holiday," in *Elucidations of
                   Hölderlin's Poetry* (2000) Amherst: Humanity
                   Books, pp. 67-99.

(B)   Günther Figal (ed.), *The Heidegger Reader* (2009)
New Haven: Yale University Press, pp. 151-176.
{A9}

12.   [A]   "Augustine and Neo-Platonism" (2004) [Matthias Fritsch and
Jennifer Anna Gosetti-Ferencei].
[B]   "Augustinus und der Neuplatonismus": Lecture course given
during the Summer Semester 1920, University of Freiburg.
[C]   *GA* 60 (1995), pp. 157-299.
[D]   *The Phenomenology of Religious Life* (2004) Bloomington:
Indiana University Press, pp. 113-227. {A13}

13.   [A]   (A)   "Author's Book Notice" (2002) [John van Buren].
(B)   "Author's Notice" (2007) [Aaron Bunch].
[B]   "Selbstanzeige" [*Die Kategorien- und Bedeutungslehre des
Duns Scotus*]: Book notice from 1917 of the author's
Habilitationsschrift.
[C]   *Kant-Studien* (Berlin) 21, 1917, pp. 467-468. *GA* 1 (1978), p.
412.
[D]   (A)   *Supplements. From the Earliest Essays to* Being and
Time *and Beyond*
(2002) Albany: SUNY Press, pp. 61-62.
(B)   Theodore Kisiel and Thomas Sheehan (eds.),
*Becoming Heidegger. On the Trail of His Early
Occasional Wrirings, 1910-1927* (2007) Evanston:
Northwestern University Press, pp. 77-78. {A10}

14.   [A]   *Basic Concepts* (1993) [Gary E. Aylesworth].
[B]   "Grundbegriffe": Lecture course given during the Winter
Semester 1941, University of Freiburg.
[C]   *GA* 51 (1981).
[D]   *Basic Concepts* (1993) Bloomington: Indiana University
Press. {B1}

15.   [A]   *Basic Concepts of Ancient Philosophy* (2008) [Richard
Rojcewicz].

[B]   "Grundbegriffe der antiken Philosophie": Lecture course given during the Summer Semester 1926, University of Marburg.

[C]   *GA* 22 (1993).

[D]   *Basic Concepts of Ancient Philosophy* (2008) Bloomington: Indiana University Press. {B9}

16.   [A]   *Basic Concepts of Aristotelian Philosophy* (2009) [Robert D. Metcalf and Mark B. Tanzer].

[B]   "Grundbegriffe der aristotelischen Philosophie": Lecture course given during the Summer Senester 1924, University of Marburg.

[C]   *GA* 18 (1993).

[D]   *Basic Concepts of Aristotelian Philosophy* (2009) Bloomington: Indiana University Press. {B10}

17.   [A]   *Basic Principles of Thinking* (2012) [Andrew W. Mitchell].

[B]   Five lectures given SS 1957, University of Freiburg (*studium generale*). Two lectures were published separately as "Principles of Thinking" {P21} (Lecture I) and "The Principle of Identity" {P20} (Lecture III). Lecture II includes a review of Lecture I.

[C]   *GA* 79 (1994), pp. 79-176.

[D]   *Bremen and Freiburg Lectures* (2012) Bloomington: Indiana University Press, pp. 75-166. {B11}

18.   [A]   ^*The Basic Problems of Phenomenology* (1982) [Albert Hofstadter].

[B]   "Die Grundprobleme der Phänomenologie": Lecture course given during the Spring Semester 1927, University of Marburg.

[C]   *GA* 24 (1975).

[D]   *The Basic Problems of Phenomenology* (1982; rev. ed., 1988) Bloomington: Indiana University Press. A sound version (2005) for the blind is available. {B3}

19.   [A]   *Basic Problems of Phenomenology (1919/1920)* (2013) [Scott M. Campbell].

[B] "Grundprobleme der Phänomenologie": Lecture course given during the Winter Semester 1919-20, University of Freiburg.
[C] *GA* 58 (1993; rev. ed. 2010).
[D] *Basic Problem of Phenomenology (1919/1920)* (2013) London: Bloomsbury. {B8}

20. [A] "The Basic Question of Being as Such" (1986) [Parvis Emad and Kenneth Maly].
[B] Text dictated to Jean Beaufret in September 1946.
[C] A French translation is included in [D].
[D] *Heidegger Studies* (Berlin) 2, 1986, pp. 4-5. {B4}

21. [A] *Basic Questions of Philosophy* (1994) [Richard Rojcewicz and André Schuwer].
[B] "Grundfragen der Philosophie: Vom Wesen der Wahrheit (*aletheia* und *poiesis*)": Lecture course given during the Winter Semester 1937-38, University of Freiburg.
[C] *GA* 45 (1984).
[D] *Basic Questions of Philosophy. Selected "Problems" of "Logic"* (1994) Bloomington: Indiana University Press. {B2}

22. [A] *The Beginning of Western Philosophy. Interpretation of Anaximander and Parmenides* (2015) [Richard Rojcewicz].
[B] "Der Anfang der abendländischen Philosophie, Auslegung des Anaximander und Parmenides": Lecture course given during the Summer Semester 1932, University of Freiburg.
[C] *GA* 35 (2012).
[D] *The Beginning of Western Philosophy. Interpretation of Anaximander and Parmenides* (2015) Bloomington: Indiana University Press. {B12}

23. [A] (A) [*Being and Time*]. *Sein und Zeit. An Informal Paraphrase of Sections 1-53, with Certain Omissions as Noted* (1955) [Robert J. Trahern, John Wild, Hubert Dreyfus and Cornelis de Deugd].
(B) *Being and Time* (1962) [John Macquarrie and Edward Robinson].

    (C) "Being and Time: Introduction" (1977) [Joan
        Stambaugh, in collaboration with J. Glenn Gray and
        David Farrell Krell].

    (D) *Being and Time* (1996) [Joan Stambaugh].

[B] *Sein und Zeit* (Erste Hälfte [First Half]): Text dedicated April
   8, 1926, Todtnauberg.

[C] *Jahrbuch für Phänomenologie und phänomenologische
   Forschung* (Halle) 8, 1927, pp. 1-438. Published as a separate
   volume, *Sein und Zeit* (1927) Tübingen: Niemeyer. *GA* 2
   (1977, based on the 7th ed., 1953).

[D] (A) *Sein und Zeit. An Informal Paraphrase of Sections
        1-53* (1955) Cambridge: Harvard Divinity School.

    (B) *Being and Time* (1962) New York: SCM (Student
        Christian Movement) Press. §§ 31-34 reprinted in
        Kurt Mueller-Vollmer (ed.), *The Hermeneutics
        Reader* (1990) New York: Continuum, pp. 214-240.
        §§ 2-7 and an excerpt from § 40 reprinted in Richard
        Kearney and Mara Rainwater (eds.), *The
        Contemporary Philosophy Reader* (1996) New York:
        Routledge, pp. 27-52. First paperback edition in
        2008, New York: HarperCollins, with a "Foreword"
        by Taylor Carman, pp. xiii-xxi.

    (C) *Basic Writings* (1977; rev. ed., 1993) San Francisco:
        HarperSanFrancisco, pp. 41-87 (rev. ed.).

    (D) *Being and Time. A Translation of* Sein und Zeit
        (1996) Albany: SUNY Press. §§ 6-8, 15-18, 25-27,
        35-38, 39-42, 46-53, 62, and 31-34 reprinted in
        Manfred Stassen (ed.), *Martin Heidegger.
        Philosophical and Political Essays* (2003) New
        York: Continuum, pp. 49-69, 97-119, 152-235, and
        236-64. Revised edition by Dennis Schmidt (2010).
        {B5}

24. [A] "Being-There and Being True According to Aristotle" (2007)
       [Brian Hansford Bowles].

   [B] Lecture given in December 1924.

[C]   Typescript (Franz Josef Brecht): "Dasein und Wahrsein nach
        Aristoteles (Interpretation von Buch VI [der] *Nikomachischen
        Ethik*)."
[D]   Theodore Kisiel and Thomas Sheehan (eds.), *Becoming
        Heidegger. On the Trail of His Early Occasional Writings,
        1910-1927* (2007) Evanston: Northwestern University Press,
        pp. 218-237. {B6}

25.   [A]   "Building Dwelling Thinking" (1971) [Albert Hofstadter].
      [B]   ^"Bauen Wohnen Denken": Lecture given August 5, 1951,
              Darmstadt.
      [C]   *Darmstädter Gespräch* II ["Mensch und Raum"] (1952)
              Darmstadt: Neue Darmstädter Verlagsanstalt, pp. 72-84.
              Reprinted in *Vorträge und Aufsätze* II (1954) Pfullingen:
              Neske, 1978, pp. 19-36. *GA* 7 (2000), pp. 145-164. A CD
              recording of the lecture, broadcast in 1951 on Westduetschen
              Rundfunks Köln, is available in the book Eduard Führ (ed.),
              *Bauen und Wohnen: Martin Heideggers Grundlegung einer
              Phänomenologie der Architektur* (2000) Munich: Waxmann
              Verlag.
      [D]   *Poetry, Language, Thought* (1971) New York: Harper and
              Row, 1975, pp. 145-161. Reprinted in *Basic Writings* (1977;
              rev. ed., 1993) San Francisco: HarperSanFrancisco, pp. 347-
              363 (rev. ed.). A CD version (2005) for the blind is available.
              {B7}

26.   [A]   (A)   "A Cassirer-Heidegger Seminar" (1964) [Carl H.
                      Hamburg].
              (B)   "A Discussion Between Ernst Cassirer and Martin
                      Heidegger" (1971) [Francis Slade].
              (C)   "Davos Disputation Between Ernst Cassirer and
                      Martin Heidegger" (1990) [Richard Taft].
      [B]   "Davoser Disputation zwischen Ernst Cassirer und Martin
              Heidegger [Protokoll der 'Arbeitsgemeinschaft Cassirer-
              Heidegger']": Summary of seminar discussions held March
              17-April 4, 1929, Davos Academy, prepared by Otto Bollnow
              and Joachim Ritter.

[C]   Guido Schneeberger, *Ergänzungen zu einer Heidegger-*
         Bibliographie (1960) Bern: Suhr, pp. 17-27. *GA* 3 (1991), pp.
         274-296.

[D]   (A)   *Philosophy and Phenomenological Research*
                  (Providence) 25, 1964-65, pp. 208-222.

         (B)   Nino Langiulli (ed.), *The Existentialist Tradition.*
                  Selected Writings (1971) Garden City: Doubleday,
                  1981, pp. 192-203. Reprinted in Nino Langiulli (ed.),
                  European Existentialism (1997) New Brunswick:
                  Transaction Publishers, pp. 192-203.

         (C)   *Kant and the Problem of Metaphysics* (1990)
                  Bloomington: Indiana University Press, pp. 171-185
                  (in the 5th edition [1997], pp. 193-207). {C1}

27.   [A]   "Cézanne" [from the series *Gedachtes* for René Char, last
               version 1974) (2009) [Jerome Veith].

      [B]   Poem, last version. See {T3}.

      [C]   *Cézanne: Aus der Reihe "Gedachtes" für René Char, L'Herne*
               1971, spätere Fassung 1974. Jahresgabe der Heidegger-
               Gesellschaft (Meßkirch) 6, 1991. *GA* 81 (2007), pp. 347-348.

      [D]   Günther Figal (ed.), *The Heidegger Reader* (2009) New
               Haven: Yale University Press, pp. 310-311. {C12}

28.   [A]   (A)   "Comments on Karl Jaspers's *Psychology of*
                        Worldviews (1998) [John van Buren].

               (B)   "Critical Comments on Karl Jaspers's *Psychology of*
                        Worldviews (2007) [Theodore Kisiel].

      [B]   "Anmerkungen zu Karl Jaspers *Psychologie der*
               Weltanschauungen": Review article, 1920.

      [C]   Hans Saner (ed.), *Karl Jaspers in der Diskussion* (1973)
               Munich: Pieper, pp. 70-100. *Wegmarken* (1967): *GA* 9 (1976),
               pp. 1-44.

      [D]   (A)   *Pathmarks* (1998) Cambridge: Cambridge University
                        Press, pp. 1-38.   Revised version published in John
                        van Buren (ed.), *Supplements. From the Earliest*
                        Essays to Being and Time *and Beyond* (John van
                        Buren, ed.) (2002) Albany: SUNY Press, pp. 71-103.

(B)   Theodore Kisiel and Thomas Sheehan (eds.), *Becoming Heidegger. On the Trail of His Early Occasional Writings, 1910-1927* (2007) Evanston: Northwestern University Press, pp. 116-149. {C2}

29.   [A]   (A) "The Concept of Time" (1992) [William McNeill].
           (B) "The Concept of Time" (2007) [Theodore Kisiel].

    [B]   "Der Begriff der Zeit": Lecture delivered to the Marburg Theological Society on July 25, 1924.

    [C]   *Der Begriff der Zeit: Vortrag vor der Marburger Theologenschaft Juli 1924* (1989) Tübingen: Niemeyer. *GA* 64 (2004), pp. 107-125.

    [D]   (A)   * *The Concept of Time* (1992) London: Blackwell.
           (B)   Theodore Kisiel and Thomas Sheehan (eds.), *Becoming Heidegger. On the Trail of His Early Occasional Writings, 1910-1927* (2007) Evanston: Northwestern University Press, pp. 200-213. {C3}

30.   [A]   *The Concept of Time [The First Draft of Being and Time]* (2011) [Ingo Farin and Alex Skinner].

    [B]   "Der Begriff der Zeit": Text of unpublished review article written in 1924 for the *Deutsche Vierteljahrsheft für Literaturwissenschaft und Geistesgeschichte.*

    [C]   *GA* 64 (2004), pp. 1-103.

    [D]   *The Concept of Time* (2011) London: Continuum. {C13}

31.   [A]   (A)   "The Concept of Time in the Science of History" (1978) [Harry S. Taylor and Hans W. Uffelmann].
           (B)   "The Concept of Time in the Science of History" (2002) [Harry S. Taylor, Hans W. Uffelmann and John van Buren].
           (C)   "The Concept of Time in the Science of History" (2007) [Theodore Kisiel].

    [B]   "Der Zeitbegriff in der Geschichtswissenschaft": Trial lecture for the *venia legendi* at the University of Freiburg im Breisgau, presented to the philosophy faculty on July 27, 1915.

[C]   *Zeitschrift für Philosophie und philosophische Kritik* (Leipzig) 161, 1916, pp. 173-188. *Frühe Schriften* (1972): GA 1 (1978), pp. 413-433.

[D]   (A)   *Journal of the British Society for Phenomenology* (Manchester) 9 (1)January 1978, pp. 3-10.

        (B)   *Supplements. From the Earliest Essays to* Being and Time *and Beyond* (2002) Albany: SUNY Press, pp. 49-60.

        (C)   Theodore Kisiel and Thomas Sheehan (eds.), *Becoming Heidegger. On the Trail of His Early Occasional Writings, 1910-1927)* (2007) Evanston: Northwestern University Press, pp. 61-72. {C4}

32.   [A]   "Consolation" (1993) [Allan Blunden].

     [B]   "Trost": Poem written in early 1915.

     [C]   *Heliand* (Berlin) 6, 1915, p. 161. Reprinted in Hugo Ott, *Martin Heidegger. Unterwegs zu seiner Biographie* (1988) Frankfurt: Campus, p. 89. *GA* 16 (2000), p. 36.

     [D]   Hugo Ott, *Martin Heidegger. A Political Life* (1993) London: Basic Books, pp. 88-89. {C5}

33.   [A]   (A)   *Contributions to Philosophy: From Enowning* (1999) [Parvis Emad and Kenneth Maly].

        (B)   *"Ereignis"* (2009) [Jerome Veith].

        (C)   *Contributions to Philosophy (Of the Event)* (2012) [Richard Rojcewicz and Daniela Vallega-Neu].

     [B]   Texts from 1936-1938.

     [C]   *GA* 65 (1989).

     [D]   (A)   *Contributions to Philosophy: From Enowning* (1999) Bloomington: Indiana University Press.

        (B)   Günther Figal (ed.), *The Heidegger Reader* (2009) New Haven: Yale University Press, pp. 177-188 (excerpt from *GA* 65 [1989], pp. 4-20).

        (C)   *Contributions to Philosophy (Of the Event)* (2012) Bloomington: Indiana University Press. {C6}

34.   [A]   "Conversation on a Country Path about Thinking" (1966) [John M. Anderson and E. Hans Freund].

[B]   "Zur Erörterung der Gelassenheit. Aus einem
        Feldweggespräch über das Denken": Text from the years
        1944-45.
[C]   *Gelassenheit* (1959) Pfullingen: Neske (8th ed., 1985), pp. 27-
        71. *GA* 13 (1983), pp. 37-74. A Japanese translation appeared
        in 1958.
[D]   *Discourse on Thinking* (1966) New York: Harper and Row,
        1970, pp. 58-90. {C8}

35. [A]   "Conversation with Martin Heidegger" (1976) [James G. Hart
             and John C. Maraldo].
     [B]   "Gespräch mit Martin Heidegger": Protocol of informal
             discussions at the Protestant Academy of Hofgeismar, held in
             early December, 1953, recorded by Hermann Noack,
             corrected and completed by Heidegger in 1973.
     [C]   *Anstösse. Berichte aus der Arbeit der Evangelischen
             Akademie Hofgeismar* (Hofgeismar) 1, 1954, pp. 31-37.
     [D]   *The Piety of Thinking* (1976) Bloomington: Indiana University
             Press, pp. 59-71. {C7}

36. [A]   "Cüppers, Ad. Jos. *Sealed Lips: The Story of the Irish Folk
             Life in the 19th Century*" (1991) [John Protevi].
     [B]   "Cüppers, Ad. Jos. *Versiegelte Lippen. Erzählung aus den
             irishcen Volkleben des 19. Jahrhunderts*": Book review from
             December 1910.
     [C]   *Der Akademiker* (Munich) 3(2), December 1910, p. 29. *GA* 16
             (2000), p. 9.
     [D]   * *Graduate Faculty Philosophy Journal* (New York) 14-15,
             1991, p. 495. {C9}

37. [A]   (A)   "*Curriculum vitae*" (1965) [Therese Schrynemakers].
             (B)   "*Curriculum vitae* 1913" (1988, 2007) [Thomas
                     Sheehan].
     [B]   "Lebenslauf": Text appended to Heidegger's doctoral
             dissertation (1914), University of Freiburg.
     [C]   *Die Lehre vom Urteil im Psychologismus. Ein kritisch-
             positiver Beitrag zur Logik* (1914) Leipzig: Barth, p. 111. GA
             16 (2000), p. 32 (as "Lebenslauf [Zur Promotion 1913])."

[D]   (A)   Joseph J. Kockelmans, *Martin Heidegger: A First
                Introduction to His Philosophy* (1965) Pittsburgh:
                Duquesne University Press, pp. 1-2. Reprinted in
                Listening (Dubuque) 12 (3), 1977, p. 110.

        (B)   Thomas Sheehan, "Heidegger's *Lehrjahre*," in John
                Sallis, Giuseppina Moneta and Jacques Taminiaux
                (eds.), *The Collegium Phaenomenologicum: The
                First Ten Years* [*Phaenomenologica* 105] (1988)
                Dordrecht: Kluwer, p. 106. Reprinted in Theodore
                Kisiel and Thomas Sheehan (eds.), *Becoming
                Heidegger. On the Trail of His Early Occasional
                Writings, 1910-1927* (2007) Evanston: Northwestern
                University Press, pp. 6-7. {C10}

38.   [A]   (A)   "Curriculum vitae 1915" (1988, 2007) [Thomas
                        Sheehan].
                (B)   "Résumé" (1993) [Allan Blunden].

        [B]   "Lebenslauf": Document written to accompany Heidegger's
                qualifying dissertation *Die Kategorien- und Bedeutungslehre
                des Duns Scotus* (1915). Reprinted *GA* 16 (2000), pp. 37-39.

        [C]   Hugo Ott, "Der junge Martin Heidegger. Gymnasial-
                Konviktszeit und Studium," in *Freiburger Diözesan-Archiv*
                (Freiburg) 104, 1984, pp. 323-325. Reprinted in *Martin
                Heidegger. Unterwegs zu seiner Biographie* (1988) Frankfurt:
                Campus, pp. 85-87. *GA* 16 (2000), pp. 37-39 (as "Lebenslauf
                [Zur Habilitation 1915])."

        [D]   (A)   Thomas Sheehan, "Heidegger's *Lehrjahre*," in John
                        Sallis, G. Moneta and Jacques Taminiaux (eds.) *The
                        Collegium Phaenomenologicum: The First Ten Years*
                        [*Phaenomenologica* 105] (1988) Dordrecht: Kluwer,
                        pp. 78-80 (German text 116-117). Reprinted in
                        Theodore Kisiel and Thomas Sheehan (eds.),
                        *Becoming Heidegger. On the Trail of His Early
                        Occasional Writings, 1910-1927* (2007) Evanston:
                        Northwestern University Press, pp. 7-9.

                (B)   Hugo Ott, *Martin Heidegger. A Political Life* (1993)
                        London: Basic Books, pp. 84-86. {C11}

39.   [A]   "The Danger" (2012) [Andrew W. Mitchell].
       [B]   "Die Gefahr": The third of four lectures first presented in the
              series "Einblick in das was ist," given December 1, 1949 at
              the Bremen Club.
       [C]   *GA* 79 (1994), pp. 46-67.
       [D]   *Bremen and Freiburg Lectures* (2012) Bloomington: Indiana
              University Press, pp. 43-63. Contains marginalia from *GA* 79
              (1994). {D3}

40.   [A]   "A Dialogue on Language" (1971) [Peter D. Hertz].
       [B]   "Aus einem Gespräch von der Sprache. Zwischen einem
              Japaner und einem Fragenden": Dialogue from the years
              1953-54.
       [C]   *Unterwegs zur Sprache* (1959): *GA* 12 (1985), pp. 79-146.
       [D]   *On the Way to Language* (1971) New York: Harper and Row,
              1982, pp. 1-54. {D1}

41.   [A]   (A)   *Duns Scotus' Theory of the Categories and of*
                     Meaning (1978) [Harold J. Robbins].
              (B)   "Signification and Radical Subjectivity in
                     Heidegger's Habilitationsschrift" (1979) [Roderick
                     M. Stewart].
              (C)   "Supplements to *The Doctrine of Categories and*
                     Meaning in Duns Scotus ["Author's Notice" and
                     "Conclusion: The Problem of Categoies"] (2007)
                     [Aaron Bunch].
       [B]   *Die Kategorien- und Bedeutungslehre des Duns Scotus*:
              Habilitationsschrift, University of Freiburg, 1915.
       [C]   *Die Kategorien- und Bedeutungslehre des Duns Scotus* (1916)
              Tübingen: Mohr. *GA* 1 (1978), pp. 189-411.
       [D]   (A)   *Duns Scotus' Theory of the Categories and of*
                     Meaning (1978) Ann Arbor: University Microfilms
                     International. Dissertation reprint (DePaul
                     University, 1978).
              (B)   Roderick M. Stewart, "Signification and Radical
                     Subjectivity in Heidegger's Habilitationsschrift," in
                     Man and World (Dordrecht) 12, 1979, pp. 378-386
                     (= (A) pp. 242-257 and LVI-LVIII).

(C)   Theodore Kisiel and Thomas Sheehan (eds.),
         *Becoming Heidegger. On the Trail of His Early
         Occasional Writings, 1910-1927* (2007) Evanston:
         Northwestern University Press, pp. 78-85. {D2}

42.   [A]   "Editor's Foreword" to Edmund Husserl, *The Phenomenology
              of Inner Time-Consciousness [1905]*" (1964) [James D.
              Churchill].
       [B]   "Vorbemerkungen des Herausgebers ("Einleitung")":
              Introduction written in 1928 to Heidegger's edition of
              Husserl's lectures on inner time consciousness.
       [C]   *Jahrbuch für Phänomenologie und phänomenologische
              Forschung* (Halle) 9, 1928, pp. 367-368. Reprinted in Edmund
              Husserl, *Zur Phänomenologie des inneren Zeitbewusstseins
              (1893-1917)* [Husserliana 9, Rudolf Boehm, ed.] (1966) The
              Hague: Martinus Nijhoff, pp. XXIV-XXV. *GA* 14 (2007), pp.
              133-136.
       [D]   Edmund Husserl, *The Phenomenology of Inner Time-
              Consciousness* (1964) Bloomington: Indiana University Press,
              1966, pp. 15-16. {E9}

43.   [A]   (A)   "The End of Philosophy and the Task of Thinking"
                     (1972) [Joan Stambaugh].
              (B)   "The End of Philosophy and the Task of Thinking"
                     (1977) [David Farrell Krell].
       [B]   "Das Ende der Philosophie und die Aufgabe des Denkens":
              Lecture read by Jean Beaufret in a French translation during a
              colloquium on Kierkegaard in Paris, April 21-23, 1964.
       [C]   Jean Beaufret and François Fédier (eds.), *Kierkegaard vivant*
              (1966) Paris: Gallimard, pp. 165-204. This French translation
              by the editors was followed by the first German edition, in *Zur
              Sache des Denkens* (1969) Tübingen: Niemeyer, pp. 61-80.
              GA 14 (2007), pp. 67-90.
       [D]   (A)   *On Time and Being* (1972) New York: Harper and
                     Row, 1978, pp. 55-73.
              (B)   *Basic Writings* (1977; rev. ed., 1993) San Francisco:
                     HarperSanFrancisco, pp. 431-449 (rev. ed.)
                     (modified version of (A)). {E1}

44.   [A]   *The Essence of Human Freedom. An Introduction to
                Philosophy* (2002) [Ted Sadler].
        [B]   "Einleitung in die Philosophie (*Über des Wesen der
                menschlichen Freiheit*)": Lecture course given during the
                Summer Semester of 1930, University of Freiburg.
        [C]   *GA* 31(1982).
        [D]   *The Essence of Human Freedom. An Introduction to
                Philosophy* (2002) New York: Continuum. {E2}

45.   [A]   (A)   *The Essence of Truth. On Plato's Cave Allegory and
                        Theaetetus* (2002) [TedSadler].
                (B)   "The Projection of Being in Science and Art" (2009)
                        [Jerome Veith].
        [B]   "Vom Wesen der Wahrheit. Zu Platons Höhlengleichnis und
                Theätet": Lecture course given during the Winter Semester of
                1931-32, University of Freiburg.
        [C]   *GA* 34 (1988).
        [D]   (A)   *The Essence of Truth. On Plato's Cave Allegory and
                        Theaetetus* (2002) New York: Continuum.
                (B)   Günther Figal (ed.), *The Heidegger Reader* (2009)
                        New Haven: Yale University Press, pp. 104-107
                        (excerpt from *GA* 34 [1988], pp. 60-64). {E3}

46.   [A]   "The Eternal Recurrence of the Same" (1984) [David Farrell
                Krell].
        [B]   "Nietzsches metaphysische Grundstellung im abendländischen
                Denken. Die ewige Wiederkehr des Gleichen": Heidegger's
                second lecture course on Nietzsche, given during the Summer
                Semester 1937, University of Freiburg.
        [C]   *Nietzsche I* (1961) Pfullingen: Neske, pp. 255-472 [Part II].
                Heidegger's substantially revised text of the lectures appears
                as *Nietzsches metaphysische Grundstellung im
                abendländischen Denken. Die ewige Wiederkehr des
                Gleichen: GA* 44 (1986). *Nietzsche* I and II (1961) reprinted
                as *GA* 6.1 (1996) and *GA* 6.2 (1997).
        [D]   *Nietzsche*, Volume II: *The Eternal Recurrence of the Same*
                (1984) New York: Harper and Row, pp. 3-208 [Part One].
                Excerpts of an earlier version of the translation were published

in *boundary 2* (Binghamton) IX (3) - X (1), 1981, pp. 25-39, under the title "Tragedy, Satyr-Play, and Telling Silence in Nietzsche's Thought of Eternal Recurrence." The excerpts include the epigraph to the lecture series, Section 4 ("`Incipit tragoedia'"), all but the last four paragraphs of Section 8 ("The Convalescent"), and the last two paragraphs of the concluding section ("Nietzsche's Fundamental Metaphysical Position") [= *Nietzsche* I (1961) pp. 255, 278-283, 302-316, 471-472].]. The HarperCollins paperback reprint [2 vols.] (1991) of all four volumes of the translations (see {N2}) combines volumes I and II and volumes III and IV. An audio (CD) version of all volumes of *Nietzsche* in this translation series is available. {E4}

47.   [A]   "The Eternal Recurrence of the Same and the Will to Power" (1987) [David Farrell Krell].

        [B]   "Die ewige Wiederkehr des Gleichen und der Wille zur Macht": A two-lecture conclusion to the first three courses on Nietzsche given at the University of Freiburg. These lectures, written in 1939, were never presented.

        [C]   *Nietzsche* II (1961) Pfullingen: Neske, pp. 7-29 [Part IV]. This appears as Part Three of *Nietzsches Lehre vom Willen zur Macht als Erkenntnis*: *GA* 47 (1989), pp. 275-295. *Nietzsche* I and II (1961) reprinted as *GA* 6.1 (1996) and *GA* 6.2 (1997).

        [D]   *Nietzsche*, Volume III: *The Will to Power as Knowledge and as Metaphysics* (1987) New York: Harper and Row, pp. 159-183 [Part Two]. The HarperCollins paperback reprint [2 vols.] (1991) of all four volumes of the translation of *Nietzsche* (see {N2}) combines volumes I and II and volumes III and IV. An audio (CD) version of all volumes of *Nietzsche* in this translation series is available. {E5}

48.   [A]   "European Nihilism" (1982) [Frank A. Capuzzi].

        [B]   "Nietzsche: Der europäische Nihilismus": Heidegger's fourth and last course on Nietzsche, given during the Second Trimester 1940 at the University of Freiburg.

        [C]   *Nietzsche* II (1961) Pfullingen: Neske, pp. 31-256 [Part V]. A substantially revised text of this lecture course has been published as *Nietzsche: Der europäische Nihilismus*: *GA* 48 (1986). *Nietzsche* I and II (1961) reprinted as *GA* 6.1 (1996) and *GA* 6.2 (1997).

[D]   *Nietzsche*, Volume IV: *Nihilism* (1982) New York: Harper and Row, pp. 3-196 [Part One]. The translation has been revised by the editor, David Farrell Krell (p. viii). The HarperCollins paperback reprint [2 vols.] (1991) of all four volumes of the translation of *Nietzsche* (see {N2}) combines volumes I and II and volumes III and IV. An audio (CD) version of all volumes of *Nietzsche* in this translation series is available. {E6}

49.   [A]   "Evening Conversation: In a Prisoner of War Camp in Russia, between a Younger and an Older Man" (2010) [Bret W. Davis].

        [B]   "Abendgespräch in einem Kriegsgefangenenlager in Rußland zwischen einem Jüngeren und einem Älteren": Dialogue dated May 8, 1945.

        [C]   *GA* 77 (1995), pp. 203-245.

        [D]   *Country Path Conversations* (2010) Bloomington: Indiana University Press, pp. 132-160. {E8}

50.   [A]   *The Event* (2013) [Richard Rojcewicz].

        [B]   "Das Ereignis": Text from 1941-42.

        [C]   *GA* 71 (2009).

        [D]   *The Event* (2013) Bloomington: Indiana Univrsity Press. {E10}

51.   [A]   (A)   "Eventide on Reichenau" (1963) [William J. Richardson].

                (B)   "Evening on the Reichenau" (1970) [John Peck].

                (C)   "Evening Walk on Reichenau" (1998) [Ewald Osers].

        [B]   "Abendgang auf der Reichenau": Poem written in 1916.

        [C]   *Das Bodenseebuch* (Konstanz) 4, 1917, p. 15. *GA* 13 (1983), p. 7.

        [D]   (A)   * William J. Richardson, *Heidegger. Through Phenomenology to Thought* [Phaenomenologica 13] (1963) The Hague: Martinus Nijhoff, p. 1.

(B)　　*Delos* (College Park) 3, 1970, pp. 60-61.

(C)　　Rüdiger Safranski, *Martin Heidegger. Between Good and Evil* (1998) Cambridge: Harvard University Press, p. 69. {E7}

52.　[A]　"Förster, Fr. W. *Authority and Freedom: Observations on the Cultural Problem of the Church*" (1991) [John Protevi].

　　[B]　"Förster, Fr. W. *Autorität und Freiheit. Betrachtungen zum Kulturproblem der Kirche*": Book review from May 1910.

　　[C]　*Der Akademiker* (Munich) 2, May 1910, pp. 109-110. *GA* 16 (2000), pp. 7-8.

　　[D]　* *Graduate Faculty Philosophy Journal* (New York) 14-15, 1991, pp. 491-493. Reprinted (edited) in Theodore Kisiel and Thomas Sheehan (eds.), *Becoming Heidegger. On the Trail of His Early Occasional Writings, 1910-1927* (2007) Evanston: Northwestern University Press, pp. 13-14. {F1}

53.　[A]　"For Edmund Husserl on His Seventieth Birthday" (1997, 2007) [Thomas Sheehan].

　　[B]　"Edmund Husserl zum 70. Geburtstag": Speech given on April 8, 1929, on the occasion of the presentation to Husserl of a *Festschrift* in his honor.

　　[C]　*Akademische Mitteilungen* (Freiburg), May 14, 1929, pp. 46-47. *GA* 16 (2000), pp. 56-60.

　　[D]　Thomas Sheehan and Richard E. Palmer (eds.), *Psychological and Transcendental Phenomenology and the Confrontation with Heidegger (1927-1931)* (Dordrecht: Kluwer, 1997), pp. 475-477. Revised translated in Theodore Kisiel and Thomas Sheehan (eds.), *Becoming Heidegger. On the Trail of His Early Occasional Writings, 1910-1927* (2007) Evanston: Northwestern University Press, pp. 417-420. {F2}

54.　[A]　*Four Seminars* (2003) [Andrew Mitchell and François Raffoul].

　　[B]　Protocols prepared and edited by various individuals Jean Beaufret, Roger Munier, François Fédier, François Vezin, Henri Mongis, and Jacques Taminiaux of several series of seminars given in 1966, 1968 and 1969 in Le Thor, Provence, and in 1973, at Heidegger's home in Zähringen (Freiburg im Breisgau), first published together as Martin Heidegger, *Questions IV* (Paris: Gallimard, 1976), translated from the French by Curd Ochwadt, the editor of the German edition, in collaboration with Beaufret, Fédier and Vezin.

[C]   *Vier Seminare. Le Thor 1966, 1968, 1969–Zähringen,* Frankfurt: Klostermann, 1973). *GA* 15 (1986), pp. 271-407. In the *GA* edition, two brief texts were appended by the editor: "Die Herkunft des Denkens" and "Parmenides: *aletheies eukyleos atremos etor.*"

[D]   *Four Seminars* (2003) Bloomington: Indiana University Press. {F3}

55.   [A]   (A)   "From the Last Marburg Lecture Course" (1971) [John Macquarrie].

      (B)   "From the Last Marburg Lecture Course" (1998) [William McNeill and Michael Heim].

      [B]   "Aus der letzten Marburger Vorlesung": Text based on §5 of the lecture course "Logik," given during the Summer Semester 1928 at the University of Marburg, published as *Metaphysische Anfangsgründe der Logik im Ausgang von Leibniz*: *GA* 26 (1978).

      [C]   Erich Dinkler and Hartwig Thyen (eds.), *Zeit und Geschichte. Dankesgabe an Rudolf Bultmann zum 80. Geburtstag im Auftrag der Alten Marburger* (1964) Tübingen: Mohr, pp. 491-507. *Wegmarken* (1967): *GA* 9 (1976), pp. 79-101.

      [D]   (A)   Edward Robinson (ed.), *The Future of Our Religious Past. Essays in Honor of Rudolf Bultmann* (1971) London: SCM [Student Christian Movement] Press, pp. 312-332.

      (B)   *Pathmarks* (1998) Cambridge: Cambridge University Press, pp. 63-81. Cf. §5 of *The Metaphysical Foundations of Logic* (1984) Bloomington: Indiana University Press, pp. 82-99. {F4}

56.   [A]   (A)   *The Fundamental Concepts of Metaphysics. World, Finitude, Solitude* (1995) [William McNeill and Nicholas Walker].

               (B)   "Description of the Situation. *Fundemental Attunement*" (2009) [Jerome Veith].

[B]   "Die Grundbegriffe der Metaphysik. Welt - Endlichkiet - Einsamkeit": Lecture course given during the Winter Semester 1929-30, University of Freiburg.

[C]   *GA* 29/30 (1983).

[D]   (A)   *The Fundamental Concepts of Metaphysics. World, Finitude, Solitude* (1995) Bloomington: Indiana University Press.

           (B)   Günther Figal (ed.), *The Heidegger Reader* (2009) New Haven: Yale University Press, pp. 79-103 (excerpt from *GA* 29/30 [1983], pp. 89-123). {F5}

57.   [A]   "The Fundamental Question of Philosophy" (2010) [Gregory Fried and Richard Polt].

       [B]   "Die Grundfrage der Philosophie": Lecture courses given Summer Semester 1933 at the University of Freiburg.

       [C]   *GA* 36/37 (2001), pp. 3-80 and 267-281 (notes and drafts for the course).

       [D]   *Being and Truth* (2010) Bloomington: Indiana University Press, pp. 3-63 and 202-213. {F6}

58.   [A]   (A)   "The *Ge-Stell*" (2009) [Jerome Veith].

               (B)   "Positionality" (2012) [Andrew W. Mitchell].

       [B]   "Das Ge-Stell": The second of four lectures first presented in the series "Einblick in das was ist," given December 1, 1949 at the Bremen Club. Revised as "Die Frage nach der Technik" [1953]. See {Q3}).

       [C]   *GA* 79 (1994), pp. 24-45.

       [D]   (A)   Günther Figal (ed.), *The Heidegger Reader* (2009) New Haven: Yale University Press, pp. 267-283.

               (B)   *Bremen and Freiburg Lectures* (2012) Bloomington: Indiana University Press, pp. 23-43 (includes marginalia from *GA* 79 [1994]). {G5}

59.   [A]   (A)   "Gethsemane Hours" (1993) [Allan Blunden].

               (B)   "Gethsemane Hours" (1998) [Ewald Osers].

       [B]   "Oelbergstunden": Poem written in early 1911.

[C]   *Allgemeine Rundschau* (Munich) April 8, 1911. Reprinted in
        Hugo Ott, *Martin Heidegger. Unterwegs zu seiner Biographie*
        (1988) Frankfurt: Campus, p. 71.
[D]   (A)   Hugo Ott, *Martin Heidegger. A Political Life* (1993)
                London: Basic Books, p. 68.
        (B)   Rüdiger Safranski, *Martin Heidegger. Between Good
                and Evil* (1998) Cambridge: Harvard University
                Press, p. 41. {G1}

60.   [A]   "A Glimpse into Heidegger's Study" (2000) [Keith Hoeller].
        [B]   "Ein Blick in die Werkstatt": Facsimile of Heidegger's
                marginal notes (c. 1959) to the texts of the second and third
                versions of Hölderlin's "Griechenland" in the *Grosse
                Stuttgarter Ausgabe* of Hölderlin's works, edited by Friedrich
                Beissner (Vol. 2, pp. 257-258).
        [C]   *GA* 4 (1981), pp. 199-202.
        [D]   *Elucidations of Hölderlin's Poetry* (2000) Amherst: Humanity
                Books, pp. 227-230. {G2}

61.   [A]   "Gredt, Jos. O.S.B. *Elements of Aristotelian-Thomistic
                Philosophy*, Vol. 1: *Logic*, Philos. Nat. Edit. II" (1991) [John
                Protevi].
        [B]   "Gredt, Jos. O.S.B. *Elementa Philosophiae Aristotelico-
                Thomisticae: Logica, Philos. Nat. Edit. II.*": Book review
                from 1912.
        [C]   *Der Akademiker* (Munich) 4(5), March 1912, pp. 76-77. *GA*
                16 (2000), p. 29-30.
        [D]   * *Graduate Faculty Philosophy Journal* (New York) 14-15,
                1991, pp. 517-519. {G3}

62.   [A]   "A Greeting to the Symposium in Beirut in November 1974"
                (1990) [Lisa Harries].
        [B]   "Ein Grußwort für das Symposion in Beirut November 1974":
                Note written in 1974 to participants in a conference at the
                Goethe Institute in Beirut, Lebanon.
        [C]   *Ekstasis* (Beirut) 8, 1981, pp. 1-2. Reprinted in Günther Neske
                and Emil Kettering (eds.), *Antwort: Heidegger im Gespräch*

(1988) Pfullingen: Neske, pp. 275-76. *GA* 16 (2000), pp. 742-743.

[D]   Günther Neske and Emil Kettering (eds.), *Martin Heidegger and National Socialism* (1990) New York: Paragon House, pp. 253-54. {G4}

63.   [A]   "Hebel—Friend of the House" (1983) [Bruce V. Foltz and Michael Heim].

[B]   ^"Hebel—der Hausfreund": Expanded version of "Gespräch mit Hebel beim 'Schatz-kästlein' zum Hebeltag," an address given in in 1956, in Lörrach.

[C]   *Hebel—der Hausfreund* (1957) Pfullingen: Neske (5th ed., 1985). *GA* 13 (1983), pp. 133-150. A CD version (2003) is available.

[D]   Darrel E. Christensen *et al.* (eds.), *Contemporary German Philosophy* (1983) University Park: The Pennsylvania State University Press, Vol. 3, pp. 89-101. {H1}

64.   [A]   *Hegel* (2015) [Joseph Arel and Niels Feuerhahn].

[B]   "Die Negativität. Eine Auseinandersetzung mit Hegel aus dem Ansatz in der Negativität (1938/39, 1941)" and "Erläuterung der 'Einleitung' zu Hegels 'Phänomenologie des Geistes (1942)'": Two treatises prepared for presentation to a small group of scholars.

[C]   *Hegel. GA* 68 (1993). Translation based on 2nd edition (2009).

[D]   *Hegel* (2015) Bloomington: Indiana University Press. {H15}

65.   [A]   "Hegel and the Greeks" (1998) [Robert Metcalf, John Sallis and William McNeill].

[B]   "Hegel und die Griechen": Lecture given at the Heidelberg Academy of Sciences, July 26, 1958. An earlier version presented in Aix-en-Provence on March 20, 1958, was published in a French translation by Jean Beaufret and Pierre-Paul Sagave in *Cahiers du Sud* (Paris) 47 (No. 349), January 1959, pp. 355-368.

[C]   *Wegmarken* (1967): *GA* 9 (1976), pp 427-444.

[D]   *Pathmarks* (1998) Cambridge: Cambridge University Press, pp. 323-336. {H2}

66. [A]   (A)   *Hegel's Concept of Experience* (1970) [J. Glenn Gray and Fred
            (B)   "Hegel's Concept of Experience" (2002) [Kenneth
                   Haynes].
     [B]   "Hegels Begriff der Erfahrung": Text written in 1942-43,
            based on a series of seminars devoted to Hegel's
            Phänomenologie des Geistes given at the University of
            Freiburg. Cf. *GA* 86 (2011), pp. 263-433.
     [C]   *Holzwege* (1950): *GA* 5 (1977), pp. 115-208.
     [D]   (A)   *Hegel's Concept of Experience* (1970) New York:
                   Harper and Row, 1989.
            (B)   *Off the Beaten Track* (2002) Cambridge: Cambridge
                   University Press, pp. 86-156. {H3}

67. [A]   *Hegel's Phenomenology of Spirit* (1988) [Parvis Emad and
            Kenneth Maly].
     [B]   "Hegels Phänomenologie des Geistes": Lecture course given
            during the Winter Semester 1930-31, University of Freiburg.
     [C]   *GA* 32 (1980).
     [D]   *Hegel's Phenomenology of Spirit* (1988) Bloomington:
            Indiana University Press. {H4}

68. [A]   "'Heidegger, Martin': Lexicon Article Attributed to Rudolf
            Bultmann" (2007) [Theodore Kisiel].
     [B]   Text of a lexicon entry prepared at the request of Rudolf
            Bultmann at the end of 1927.
     [C]   Hermann Gunkel and Leopold Zscharnak (eds.), *Die Religion
            in Geschichte und Gegnwart. Handwörterbuch für Theologie
            und Religionswissenschaft* (1928) Tübingen: Mohr, Vol. 2,
            column 1687-88. The entry was initially attributed to
            Bultmann.
     [D]   Theodore Kisiel and Thomas Sheehan (eds.), *Becoming
            Heidegger. On the Trail of His Early Occasional Wrirings,
            1910-1927* (2007) Evanston: Northwestern University Press,
            p. 331. {H5}

69. [A]   "A Heidegger Seminar on Hegel's *Differenzschrift*" [Seminar
            at Le Thor, 1968] (1980) [William Lovitt].

	[B]	"Seminar in Le Thor 1968": Protocols of the eight sessions of the second seminar, held August 30 - September 8, 1968, in Provence. Translated from the French text, *Questions* IV (1976) Paris: Gallimard, 1990 (*Questions III et IV*), pp. 372-414.
	[C]	Cf. *Vier Seminare* (1977) Frankfurt: Klostermann, pp. 24-63. *GA* 15 (1986), pp. 286-325. These are German translations by Curd Ochwadt of the French texts. See {F3}.
	[D]	*The Southwestern Journal of Philosophy* (Norman) XI (3), 1980, pp. 9-45. {H7}
70.	[A]	*Heraclitus Seminar 1966/67* (1979) [Charles H. Seibert].
	[B]	*Heraklit. Martin Heidegger-Eugen Fink. Seminar 1966/67*: Seminar on Heraclitus given with Eugen Fink during the Winter Semester 1966-67, University of Freiburg.
	[C]	*Heraklit. Martin Heidegger-Eugen Fink. Seminar 1966/67* (1970) Frankfurt: Klostermann. *GA* 15 (1986), pp. 9-263.
	[D]	*Heraclitus Seminar 1966/67* (1979) University (Alabama): Alabama University Press, 1979. {H9}
71.	[A]	*The History of Beyng* (2015) [William McNeill and Jeffrey Powell].
	[B]	1. "Die Geschichte des Seyns (1938/40)": Text from 1938-40. 2. "Κοινόν. Aus der Geschichte des Seyns (1939/40)": Text from 1939-40.
	[C]	*GA 69* (1998; rev. ed., 2012).
	[D]	*The History of Beyng* (2015) Bloomington: Indiana University Press, 2015. Contains "The History of Beyny (1938-40" and "Κοινόν. Out of the History of Beyng (1939-40)". {H16}
72.	[A]	^*History of the Concept of Time* (1985) [Theodore Kisiel].
	[B]	"Geschichte des Zeitbegriffs. Prolegomena zur Phänomenologie von Geschichte und Natur": Lecture course given during the Summer Semester 1925, University of Marburg.
	[C]	*GA* 20 (1988).

[D] *History of the Concept of Time: Prolegomena* (1985) Bloomington: Indiana University Press. A sound version (2005) for the blind is available. {H10}

73. [A] (A) "Hölderlin and the Essence of Poetry" (1949) [Douglas Scott].
      (B) "Hölderlin and the Essence of Poetry" (1959) [Paul de Man].
      (C) "Hölderlin and the Essence of Poetry" (2000) [Keith Hoeller].
      (D) "Hölderlin and the Essence of Poetry" (2009) [Jerome Veith].
  [B] "Hölderlin und das Wesen der Dichtung": Lecture given April 2, 1936, Rome.
  [C] *Das innere Reich* (Munich) 3, 1936, pp. 1065-1078. Reprinted in *Erläuterungen zu Hölderlins Dichtung* (1944): *GA* 4 (1981), pp. 33-48.
  [D] (A) *Existence and Being* (1949) Washington: Regnery Gateway, 1988, pp. 270-291.
      (B) *Quarterly Review of Literature* (Chapel Hill) 10, 1959, pp. 79-94.
      (C) *Elucidations of Hölderlin's Poetry* (2000) Amherst: Humanity Books, pp. 51-65.
      (D) Günther Figal (ed.), *The Heidegger Reader* (2009) New Haven: Yale University Press, pp. 117-129 (based on *GA* 4 [1981], pp. 33-48). {H11}

74. [A] "Hölderlin's Heaven and Earth" (2000) [Keith Hoeller].
  [B] ^"Hölderlins Erde und Himmel": Lecture given June 6, 1959, for the Munich Hölderlin Society.
  [C] *Hölderlin-Jahrbuch* (Tübingen) 11 (1958-60), pp. 17-39. *GA* 4 (1981), pp. 152-181. Heidegger recorded the lecture on January 18, 1960 at the University of Heidelberg. A CD version is available (Stuttgardt: Klett-Cotta, 1997).
  [D] *Elucidations of Hölderlin's Poetry* (2000) Amherst: Humanity Books, pp. 175-207. {H13}

75.   [A]   *Hölderlin's Hymn "The Ister"* (1996) [William McNeill and
                [Julia Davis].
        [B]   "Hölderlins Hymnen": Lecture course given during the
                Summer Semester 1942, University of Freiburg.
        [C]   *GA* 53 (1984).
        [D]   *Hölderlin's Hymn "The Ister"* (1996) Bloomington: Indiana
                University Press. {H12}

76.   [A]   *Hölderlins Hyms 'Germania' and 'The Rhine'* (2014)
                [William McNeill and Julia Ireland].
        [B]   *Hölderlins Hymnen "Germanien" und "Der Rhein"*: Lecture
                course given during the Winter Semester 1934-35, University
                of Freiburg.
        [C]   *GA* 39 (1980; rev. ed., 1989).
        [D]   *Hölderlins Hyms "Germania" and "The Rhine"* (2014)
                Bloomington: Indiana University Press {H14}

77.   [A]   (A)   "Homeland. Festival Address at a Centennial
                        Celebration" (1971) [Thomas F. O'Meara].
                (B)   "Meßkirch's Seventh Centennial" (1973) [Thomas J.
                        Sheehan].
        [B]   "700 Jahre Meßkirch (Ansprache zum Heimatabend)": Speech
                given July 22, 1961, Meßkirch.
        [C]   *700 Jahre Stadt* Meßkirch (1962) Meßkirch: Aker, pp. 7-16.
                GA 16 (2000), pp. 574-582.
        [D]   (A)   *Listening* (Dubuque) 6, 1971, pp. 231-238.
                (B)   * *Listening* (Dubuque) 8, 1973, pp. 41-57. {H14}

78.   [A]   (A)   "The Idea of Phenomenology" (1970) [John N. Deely
                        and Joseph A. Novak].
                (B)   "The Idea of Phenomenology" (1977) [Thomas
                        Sheehan].
                (C)   "'Phenomenology'. The *Encyclopaedia Britannica*
                        Article. Draft B ('Attempt at a Second Draft')" (1997,
                        2007) [Thomas Sheehan].
        [B]   "Versuch einer zweiten Bearbeitung. Einleitung. Die Idee der
                Phänomenologie und der Rückgang auf das Bewusstsein":

Article written for Husserl in 1927 for the Fourteenth Edition of the *EncyclopÆdia Britannica*.

[C]   Edmund Husserl, *Phänomenologische Psychologie* [Husserliana 9; Walter Biemel, ed.) (1962) The Hague: Martinus Nijhoff, 1968, pp. 256-263.

[D]   (A)   *The New Scholasticism* (Washington) 44, 1970, pp. 325-344.

          (B)   *Listening* (Dubuque) 12 (3), 1977, pp. 111-117. Includes a letter of October 22, 1927, to Edmund Husserl (cf. {L9}).

          (C)   Thomas Sheehan and Richard E. Palmer (eds.), *Psychological and Transcendental Phenomenology and the Confrontation with Heidegger (1927-1931)* Dordrecht: Kluwer, 1997, pp. 107-116. Reprinted in Theodore Kisiel and Thomas Sheehan (eds.), *Becoming Heidegger. On the Trail of His Early Occasional Writings, 1910-1927* (2007) Evanston: Northwestern University Press, pp. 306-328 (see also p. 383). See Sheehan's revised translation: http://www.stanford.edu/dept/relstud/Sheehan/pdf/5_ husserls_texts_online/8- %201927%20PHENOMENOLOGY%20DRAFT%2 0B.pdf {I1}

79.   [A]   (A)   "The idea of Philosophy and the Problem of Worldview" (2000) [Ted Sadler].

                 (B)   "The Environmental Experience" (2009) [Jerome Veith].

       [B]   "Die Idee der Philosophie und das Weltanschauungsproblem": Lecture course given during the Wartime Semester 1919, University of Freiburg. Includes "Wissenschaft und Universitätsreform" (pp. 1-6). Heidegger's first lecture course.

       [C]   *GA* 56/57 (1987), pp. 1-117. The 2nd, revised and enlarged edition of *GA* 56/57 (1999) includes additional material from a transcription of the course by Franz-Josef Brecht (pp. 215-220).

       [D]   (A)   *Towards the Definition of Philosophy* (2000) London: Athlone, pp. 1-99 and 183-188. Includes

<table>
<tr><td></td><td></td><td></td><td>preliminary remarks on "Science and University Reform" (pp. 3-5).</td></tr>
<tr><td></td><td></td><td>(B)</td><td>Günther Figal (ed.), The Heidegger Reader (2009) New Haven: Yale University Press, pp. 33-37 (excerpt from GA 56/57 [1987], pp. 70-74). {17}</td></tr>
<tr><td>80.</td><td>[A]</td><td>(A)</td><td>"In Memory of Max Scheler" (1981) [Thomas Sheehan].</td></tr>
<tr><td></td><td></td><td>(B)</td><td>"Max Scheler: In Memoriam" (1984) [Michael Heim].</td></tr>
<tr><td></td><td>[B]</td><td></td><td>"In memoriam Max Scheler": Eulogy on the death of Max Scheler, given on May 21, during the Summer Semester 1928, University of Marburg.</td></tr>
<tr><td></td><td>[C]</td><td></td><td>Paul Good (ed.), Max Scheler im Gegenwartsgeschehen der Philosophie (1975) Bern: Francke, pp. 9-10. Reprinted GA 26 (1978), pp. 62-64.</td></tr>
<tr><td></td><td>[D]</td><td>(A)</td><td>Thomas Sheehan (ed.), Heidegger. The Man and the Thinker (1981) Chicago: Precedent Publishing, pp. 159-160.</td></tr>
<tr><td></td><td></td><td>(B)</td><td>The Metaphysical Foundations of Logic (1984) Bloomington: Indiana University Press, pp. 50-52. {12}</td></tr>
<tr><td>81.</td><td>[A]</td><td>(A)</td><td>An Introduction to Metaphysics (1959) [Ralph Manheim].</td></tr>
<tr><td></td><td></td><td>(B)</td><td>^Introduction to Metaphysics (2000; rev. and expanded ed., 2014) [Gregory Fried and Richard Polt]</td></tr>
<tr><td></td><td>[B]</td><td></td><td>"Einführung in die Metaphysik": Lecture course given during the Summer Semester 1935, University of Freiburg.</td></tr>
<tr><td></td><td>[C]</td><td></td><td>GA 40 (1983). Contains extra material (pp. 217-230) not found in the Niemeyer edition (see [D] (B)).</td></tr>
<tr><td></td><td>[D]</td><td>(A)</td><td>An Introduction to Metaphysics (1959) New Haven: Yale University Press, 1974. Chapter 1, "The Fundamental Question of Metaphysics," was reprinted in William Barrett and Henry D. Aiken (eds.), Philosophy in the Twentieth Century. An Anthology (1962) New York: Random House, 1982,</td></tr>
</table>

Vol. 3, pp. 219-250. A sound version (2005) for the blind is available.

(B)   *Introduction to Metaphysics* (2000) New Haven: Yale University Press. Based on the edition published by Niemeyer (Tübingen) 4ᵗʰ ed., 1976; rev. and expanded ed. 2014, is based on *GA* 40, contains material from pp. 217-233, "For a Critique of the Lecture Course" and "First Version of Manuscript Pages 31-36," and the editor's "Afterword."{I3}

82.   [A]   *Introduction to Phenomenological Research* (2005) [David Dahlstrom].

[B]   "Einführung in die phänomenologische Forschung": Lecture course given during the Winter Semester 1923-24, University of Marburg.

[C]   *GA* 17 (1994).

[D]   *Introduction to Phenomenological* Research (2005) Bloomington: Indiana University Press. {I4}

83.   [A]   "Introduction to the Phenomenology of Religion" (2004) [Matthias Fritsch and Jennifer Anna Gosetti-Ferencei].

[B]   "Einleitung in die Phänomenologie der Religion: Lecture course given during the Winter Semester 1920-21, University of Freiburg.

[C]   *GA* 60 (1995), pp. 1-156.

[D]   *The Phenomenology of Religious Life* (2004) Bloomington: Indiana University Press, pp. 1-111. {I5}

84.   [A]   *Introduction to Philosophy—Thinking and Poetizing* (2011) [Phillip Jacques Braunstein].

[B]   "Einleitung in die Philosophie. Denken und Dichten": Fragment of a lecture course scheduled for the Winter Semester 1944-45, University of Freibug. The course was cancelled after the second session whn Heidegger was stripped of tenure and forbidden to teach.

[C]   *GA* 50 (1990), pp. 89-160.

[D]   *Introduction to Philosdophy—Thinking and Poetizing* (2011) Bloomington: Indiana University Press, pp. 1-62. {I6}

85. [A]   "Jörgensen, Joh. *Travelogue: Light and Dark Nature and Spirit* (1991) [John Protevi].

     [B]   "Jörgensen, Joh. *Das Reisebuch. Licht und dunke Natur und Geist*": Book review from July 1911.

     [C]   *Der Akademiker* (Munich) 3(3), January 1911, p. 45. *GA* 16 (2000), p. 10.

     [D]   • *Graduate Faculty Philosophy Journal* (New York) 14-15, 1991, p. 495. {J2}

86. [A]   "July Night" (1993) [Allan Blunden].

     [B]   "Julinacht": Poem written during the summer of 1911.

     [C]   Hugo Ott, *Martin Heidegger. Unterwegs zu seiner Biographie* (1988) Frankfurt: Campus, p. 72. *GA* 16 (2000), p.17.

     [D]   Hugo Ott, *Martin Heidegger. A Political Life* (1993) London: Basic Books, p. 69. {J3}

87. [A]   (A)   *Kant and the Problem of Metaphysics* (1962) [James S. Churchill].

            (B)   *Kant and the Problem of Metaphysics* [Richard Taft].
                   (I)   4th edition text (1990)
                   (II)   5th edition text (1997) [Appendix II: C (b), below: Peter Warnek]

     [B]   "Kant und das Problem der Metaphysik": Lecture course given during the Winter Semester 1925-26, University of Marburg.

     [C]   *Kant und das Problem der Metaphysik* (1929) Frankfurt: Klostermann (4th ed., 1973): *GA* 3 (1991). The 4th German edition includes (a) "Aufzeichnungen zum Kantbuch" (notes, from the 1930s or 1940s, in Heidegger's copy of the 1st edition of his book); (b) "Ernst Cassirer. Philosophie der symbolischen Formern. 2. Teil: Das mythische Denken. Berlin 1925" (a review of Cassirer's book, published in 1928) (see {R6}); (c) "Davoser Vorträge: Kants *Kritik der reinen Vernunft* und die Aufgabe einer Grundlegung der Metaphysik" (1929) (Heidegger's summary of three lectures given in March 1929 at the Davos Academy) (see {K2}); (d) "Davoser Disputation zwischen Ernst Cassirer und Martin Heidegger" (1929) (the transcript of a discussion between Heidegger and

Cassirer at the Davos Academy) (see {C1}); (e) "Zu Odebrechts und Cassirers Kritik des Kantbuches" (reactions to reviews from 1930-31, found in Heidegger's 1st edition copy of the book) (see {O17}); and (f) "Zur Geschichte des philosophischen Lehrstuhles seit 1866" (a *Festschrift* contribution originally published in 1927 in *Die Philipps-Universität zu Marburg 1527-1927*) (see {O18}).

[D]   (A)   *Kant and the Problem of Metaphysics* (1962) Bloomington: Indiana University Press. Based on the 2nd edition (1950) of the German text, it does not contain any of the supplementary texts. This was the translator's doctoral dissertation (Indiana University, 1960).

      (B)   *Kant and the Problem of Metaphysics* (1990) Bloomington: Indiana University Press). Taft translation (I) is of the 4th edition (1973) and contains only [C] (c) and (d). Taft translation (II) is of the 5th edition (1991) [= *GA* 3] and also contains [C] (a) "Notes on the Kantbook" (pp. 175-179), (b)"Ernst Cassirer: Philosophy of Symbolic Forms. Part Two: Mythical Thought. Berlin, 1925" (pp.180-190, translated by Peter Warnek), (e) "On Odebrecht's and Cassirer's Critiques of the Kantbook" (pp. 208-212), and (f) "On the History of the Philosophical Chair [at Marburg University] Since 1866" (pp. 213-217). {K1}

88.   [A]   "Kant's *Critique of Pure Reason* and the Task of a Laying of the Ground of Metaphysics" (1990) [Richard Taft].
      (I)   4th edition text (1990)
      (II)   5th edition text (1997): "Davos Lectures: Kant's *Critique of Pure Reason* and the Task of a Laying of the Ground for Metaphysics"
  [B]   "Davoser Vorträge: Kants *Kritik der reinen Vernunft* und die Aufgabe einer Grundlegung der Metaphysik": Summary of three lectures given in March 1929, at the Davos Academy.

[C]   *Davoser Revue* (Davos) 4 (7), 1929, pp. 194-196. Reprinted in *Kant und das Problem der Metaphysik* (4th ed., 1973): *GA* (1991), pp. 271-273.

[D]   *Kant and the Problem of Metaphysics* (1991) Bloomington: Indiana University Press, pp. 169-171 (in the 5th edition [1997], pp. 191-192) (cf. {K1}). {K2}

89.   [A]   (A)   "Kant's Thesis about Being" (1973) [Ted E. Klein, Jr. and William E. Pohl].

(B)   "Kant's Thesis about Being" (1998) [William McNeill, Ted E. Klein, Jr. and William E. Pohl].

[B]   "Kants These über das Sein": Lecture given May 17, 1961, in Kiel.

[C]   Thomas Würtenberger, Werner Maihofer, Alexander Hollerback and Erik Wolf (eds.), *Existenz und Ordnung. Festschrift für Erik Wolf zum 60. Geburtstag* (1962) Frankfurt: Klostermann, pp. 217-245. Reprinted in *Wegmarken* (1967): *GA* 9 (1976), pp. 445-480.

[D]   (A)   *The Southwestern Journal of Philosophy* (Norman) 4, 1973, pp. 7-33. Reprinted in Robert W. Shahan and J.N. Mohanty (eds.), *Thinking about Being* (1984) Norman: University of Oklahoma Press, pp. 7-33.

(B)   *Pathmarks* (1998) Cambridge: Cambridge University Press, pp. 337-363. {K3}

90.   [A]   ^"Language" (1971) [Albert Hofstadter].

[B]   ^"Die Sprache": Lecture given October 7, 1950, in Bühlerhöhe. Available on CD: *Von der Sache des Denkens. Vorträge, Reden und Gespräche* (Munich: Der Hörverlag, 2000), 4(6).

[C]   *Unterwegs zur Sprache* (1959): *GA* 12 (1985), pp. 7-30.

[D]   *Poetry, Language, Thought* (1971) New York: Harper and Row, 1975, pp. 189-210. A CD version (2005) for the blind is available. {L1}

91.   [A]   "Language" (1976) [Thomas Sheehan].
       [B]   "Sprache": Poem written in 1972, sent to Raymond Panikkar,
              University of California, Santa Barbara, in March 1976 (and
              to others).
       [C]   *Argile* (Paris) I, Winter 1973, pp. 4-5, 158 (with a French
              translation by Roger Munier). Reprinted in *GA* 13 (1983), p.
              229.
       [D]   * *Philosophy Today* (Celina) 20 (4), 1976, p. 291. {L2}

92.   [A]   "Language in the Poem. A Discussion on Georg Trakl's Poetic
              Work" (1971) [Peter D. Hertz].
       [B]   "Die Sprache im Gedicht. Eine Erörterung von Georg Trakls
              Gedicht" (1959): Revised version of "Georg Trakl. Eine
              Erörterung seines Gedichtes" (1953).
       [C]   *Merkur* (Munich) No. 61, 1953, pp. 226-258. Revised version
              in *Unterwegs zur Sprache* (1959): *GA* 12 (1985), pp. 31-78.
       [D]   *On the Way to Language* (1971) New York: Harper and Row,
              1982, pp. 159-198. {L3}

93.   [A]   "The Language of Johann Peter Hebel" (2009) [Jerome
              Veith].
       [B]   "Die Sprache Johann Peter Hebels": Essay from 1955.
       [C]   *Der Lichtgang* (Freiburg) 5(7), 1955, pp. 3-4. Reprinted in
              Rudolf K. Goldschmit Jentner and Otto Heuschele (eds.),
              Heimat Baden-Württemberg (1955) Heidelberg: Pfeffer, pp.
              324-326. *GA* 13, pp. 123-125.
       [D]   Günther Figal (ed.), *The Heidegger Reader* (2009) New
              Haven: Yale University Press, pp. 295-297. {L27}

94.   [A]   (A)   [Letter on Humanism:] "The Meaning of
                     `Humanism'" (1949) [no translator named].
              (B)   "Letter on Humanism" (1962) [Edgar Lohner].
              (C)   "Letter on Humanism" (1977) [Frank A. Capuzzi and
                     J. Glenn Gray].
              (D)   "Letter on `Humanism'" (1998) [William McNeill,
                     David Farrell Krell].
       [B]   "Brief über den Humanismus": Text based on a letter to Jean
              Beaufret written in 1946.

[C]   *Platons Lehre von der Wahrheit. Mit einem Brief über den Humanismus* (1947) Bern: Francke, pp. 53-119. *Wegmarken* (1967): *GA* 9 (1976), pp. 313-364.

[D]   (A)   *World Review* (London) #2 [New Series], April 1949, pp. 29-33. *This appears to be the first translation into English of something by Heidegger.*

        (B)   William Barrett and Henry D. Aiken (eds.), *Philosophy in the Twentieth Century. An Anthology* (1962) New York: Random House, 1982, Vol. 3, pp. 270-302. Reprinted in Nino Langiulli (ed.), *The Existentialist Tradition* (1971) Garden City: Doubleday, 1981, pp. 204-245 and Nino Langiulli (ed.), *European Existentialism* (1997) New Brunswick: Transaction Publishers, pp. 204-245.

        (C)   *Basic Writings* (1977; rev. ed., 1993) San Francisco: HarperSanFrancisco, pp. 217-265 (rev. ed.).

        (D)   *Pathmarks* (1998) Cambridge: Cambridge University Press, pp. 239-276. {L4}

95.   [A]   (A)   Letter to William J. Richardson ["Preface"] (1963) [William J. Richardson].

                (B)   "Letter to Father William J. Richardson" (2009) [Jerome Veith].

        [B]   "Ein Vorwort. Brief an Pater William J. Richardson:" Letter written in early April, 1962, Freiburg.

        [C]   "Preface," William J. Richardson, *Heidegger. Through Phenomenology to Thought* [Phaenomenologica 13] (1963) The Hague: Martinus Nijhoff, 1974, pp. IX-XXIII. *GA* 11 (2006), pp. 143-152.

        [D]   (A)   * [C] pp. VIII-XXII. Reprinted as "Preface" in *Filosofia Unisinos* (Sao Leopaldo) 5(8), 2004, pp. 11-18.

                (B)   Günther Figal (ed.), *The Heidegger Reader* (2009) New Haven: Yale University Press, pp. 298-304. {L16}

96.   [A]   *"Library of Valuable Novellas and Stories,* vol. 9, O. Hellinghaus, ed." (1991) [John Protevi].

[B]   "*Bibliothek vertvoller Novellen und Erzählungen.*
       Herausgegeben von Prof. Dr. O. Hellinghaus. Bd. IX": Book
       review from 1913.

[C]   *Der Akademiker* (Munich) 4(3), January 1913, p. 45. *GA* 16
       (2000), p. 31.

[D]   * *Graduate Faculty Philosophy Journal* (New York) 14-15,
       1991, p. 519. {L24}

97.   [A]   *Logic. The Question of Truth* (2010) [Thomas Sheehan].

       [B]   "Logik: Die Frage nach der Wahrheit": Lecture course given
              Winter Semester 1925-26, University of Marburg.

       [C]   *GA* 21 (1976).

       [D]   *Logic: The Question of Truth* (2010) Bloomington: Indiana
              University Press. {L30}

98.   [A]   *Logic as the Question Concerning the Essence of Language*
              (2009) [Wanda Torres Gregory and Yvonne Unna].

       [B]   "Logik als die Frage nach dem Wesen der Sprache": Lecture
              course given Summer Semester 1934, University of Freiburg.

       [C]   *GA* 38 (1998).

       [D]   *Logic as the Question Concerning the Essence of Language*
              (2009) Albany: SUNY Press. {L31}

99.   [A]   "Logos (Heraclitus, Fragment B 50" (1975) [David Farrell
              Krell and Frank Capuzzi].

       [B]   "Logos (Heraklit, Fragment 50)": Essay written for a
              Festschrift.

       [C]   Kurt Bauch (ed.), *Festschrift für Hans Jantzen* (1951) Berlin:
              Mann, pp. 7-18. Reprinted in *Vorträge und Aufsätze* III
              (1954) Pfullingen: Neske, 1978, pp. 3-25. *GA* (2000), pp. 211-
              234.

       [D]   *Early Greek Thinking* (1975) New York: Harper and Row,
              1985, pp. 59-78. {L25}

100.   [A]   "*Logos* and Langauge" (2009) [Jerome Veith].

       [B]   Recapitulation and one lecture session from "Logik. Heraklits
              Lehre vom Logos," lecture course given Summer Semester
              1944, University of Freiburg.

[C]   *GA* 55 (1979), pp. 251-260.

[D[Günther Figal (ed.), *The Heidegger Reader* (2009) New
        Haven: Yale UP, pp. 239-252. {L26}

101.   [A]   (A)   "Martin Heidegger: An Interview" (1971) [Vincent
                        Gualiardo and Robert Pambrun].

                (B)   "Martin Heidegger in Conversation" (1977) [B.
                        Srinirasa Murthy].

                (C)   "Martin Heidegger in Conversation with Richard
                        Wisser" (1990) [Lisa Harries].

        [B]   ^"Martin Heidegger im Gespräch:" Transcript of a
                conversation between Martin Heidegger and Richard Wisser
                on September 17, 1969, filmed for broadcast on television
                [ZDF].

        [C]   Richard Wisser (ed.), *Martin Heidegger im Gespräch* (1970)
                Freiburg: K. Alber, pp. 67-77. Reprinted in Günther Neske
                and Emil Kettering (eds.), *Antwort. Martin Heidegger im
                Gespräch* (1988) Pfullingen: Neske, pp. 21-28. Available on
                CD: *Von der Sache des Denkens. Vorträge, Reden und
                Gespräche*, Munich: Der Hörverlag, 2000. A DVD of the
                documentary is available: "Martin Heidegger im Denken
                Unterwegs" (Baden-Baden: Südwestfunk VHS 1975; DVD
                2004)

        [D]   (A)   *Listening* (Dubuque) 6, 1971, pp. 34-40.

                (B)   Richard Wisser (ed.), *Martin Heidegger in
                        Conversation* (1977) New Delhi: Arnold-
                        Heinemann/Rakesh Press, pp. 38-47.

                (C)   Günther Neske and Emil Kettering (eds.), *Martin
                        Heidegger and National Socialism* (1990) New York:
                        Paragon House, pp. 81-87. {M1}

102.   [A]   "Memorial Address" (1966) [John M. Anderson and E. Hans
                Freund].

        [B]   ^"Gelassenheit. Bodenständigkeit im Atomzeitalter": Address
                given October 30, 1955, on the 175th anniversary of the birth
                of the composer Conradin Kreuzer, Meßkirch. An LP
                recording of the address was issued by Telefunken in 1955.

Available on CD: *Von der Sache des Denkens. Vorträge, Reden und Gespräche*, Munich: Der Hörverlag, 2000.

[C] *Gelassenheit* (1959) Pfullingen: Neske, pp. 9-28. *GA* 16 (2000), pp. 517-529. A Japanese edition appeared in 1958.

[D] *Discourse on Thinking* (1966) New York: Harper and Row, 1970, pp. 43-57. Reprinted in Manfred Stassen (ed.), *Martin Heidegger. Philosophical and Political Essays* (2003) New York: Continuum, pp. 87-96. {M3}

103. [A] (A) ^*The Metaphysical Foundations of Logic* (1984) [Michael Heim].

(B) "The Problem of *Being and Time*" and "Transcendence" (2009) [Jerome Veith].

[B] "Logik": Lecture course given during the Spring Semester 1928, University of Marburg.

[C] *GA* 26 (1978).

[D] (A) *The Metaphysical Foundations of Logic* (1984) Bloomington: Indiana University Press. A sound version (2005) for the blind is available.

(B) Günther Figal (ed.), *The Heidegger Reader* (2009) New Haven: Yale University Press, pp. 33-37 and 68-78 (excerpts from *GA* 26 [1978], pp. 170-177 and 239-252). {M5}

104. [A] "Metaphysics as History of Being" (1973) [Joan Stambaugh].

[B] "Die Metaphysik als Geschichte des Seins": Essay written in 1941, Freiburg.

[C] *Nietzsche* II (1961) Pfullingen: Neske, pp. 399-457 [Part VIII].

[D] *The End of Philosophy* (1973) New York: Harper and Row, pp. 1-54. {M6}

105. [A] *Mindfulness* (2006) [Parvis Emad and Thomas Kalary].

[B] Text from 1938-39.

[C] *GA* 66 (1997).

[D] *Mindfulness* (2006) London: Continuum. {M7}

106. [A]   "Modern Natural Science and Technology" (1977) [John
            Sallis].
      [B]   "Neuzeitliche Naturwissenschaft und moderne Technik":
            Letter written April 11, 1976, to the participants of 10th
            American Heidegger Conference, held May 14-16, 1976,
            DePaul University, Chicago, Illinois.
      [C]   *Research in Phenomenology* (Pittsburgh) 7, 1977, pp. 1-2.
            Reprinted in John Sallis (ed.), *Radical Phenomenology* (1978)
            Englewood Cliffs: Humanities Press). *GA* 16 (2000), pp. 747-
            748.
      [D]   * [C] pp. 3-4. {M8}

107. [A]   "Moira (Parmenides VIII, 34-41)" (1975) [Frank Capuzzi].
      [B]   "Moira (Parmenides VIII, 34-41)": Undelivered portion of the
            lecture course "Was heißt Denken?," given during Winter
            Semester 1951-52 and Summer Semester 1952, University of
            Freiburg.
      [C]   *Vorträge und Aufsätze* III (1954) Pfullingen: Neske, 1978, pp.
            27-52. Reprinted in *GA* 7 (2000), pp. 235-261.
      [D]   *Early Greek Thinking* (1975) New York: Harper and Row,
            1985, pp. 79-101. It is a supplement to *What Is Called
            Thinking?* (1968) New York: Harper and Row, 1976, p. 240
            ff. [Part II, Lecture XI] (see {W5}). {M9}

108. [A]   "More founding than poetry . . ." (1977) [J. Glenn Gray].
      [B]   Untitled poem, addressed to those who commemorated
            Heidegger's 85th birthday, September 26, 1974.
      [C]   Walter Strolz, "Ein Gedächtniswort," in *Zum Gedenken an
            Martin Heidegger 1889-1976* (1977) Meßkirch: Stadt
            Meßkirch, p. 22. *GA* 16 (2000), p. 741.
      [D]   * J. Glenn Gray, "Heidegger on Remembering and
            Remembering Heidegger," in *Man and World* 10(1), 1977, p.
            78. {M11}

109. [A]   "My Way to Phenomenology" (1972) [Joan Stambaugh].
      [B]   "Mein Weg in die Phänomenologie": Essay written in 1963 in
            honor of the publisher Hermann Niemeyer. Supplement added
            in 1969.

[C]   *Hermann Niemeyer zum 80. Geburtstag am 16. April 1963*
       (1963) Tübingen: [privately published]. Reprinted in *Zur
       Sache des Denkens* (1969) Tübingen: Niemeyer, pp. 81-90.
       GA 14 (2007), pp. 91-102.

[D]   *On Time and Being* (1972) New York: Harper and Row, 1978,
       pp. 74-82. Reprinted in Walter Kaufmann (ed.), *Existentialism
       from Dostoevsky to Sartre* (1956; rev. ed., 1975) New York:
       New American Library, 1984, pp. 234-241 (beginning with
       the revised edition). Reprinted in Manfred Stassen (ed.),
       Martin Heidegger. Philosophical and Political Essays (2003)
       New York: Continuum, pp. 70-76. {M10}

110.   [A]   "The Nature of Language" (1971) [Peter D. Hertz].

       [B]   "Das Wesen der Sprache": Text from a lecture series given
              December 4 and 18, 1957 and February 5, 1958, University of
              Freiburg.

       [C]   *Unterwegs zur Sprache* (1959): *GA* 12 (1985), pp. 147-204.

       [D]   *On the Way to Language* (1971) New York: Harper and Row,
              1982, pp. 57-108. Translated as "The Essence of Language"
              by (1964), translator's master's dissertation, Columbia
              University. {N1}

111.   [A]   *Nietzsche* (1979-1987) [Frank A. Capuzzi, David Farrell
              Krell, Joan Stambaugh].

              (1)   Volume I: *The Will to Power as Art* (1979). See "The
                     Will to Power as Art" for details ({W12}).

              (2)   Volume II: *The Eternal Recurrence of the Same*
                     (1984). See "The Eternal Recurrence of the Same"
                     and "Who Is Nietzsche's Zarathustra?" for details
                     ({E5} and {W9}).

              (3)   Volume III: *The Will to Power as Knowledge* and as
                     Metaphysics (1987). See "The Will to Power as
                     Knowledge," "The Eternal Recurrence of the Same"
                     and "Nietzsche's Metaphysics" for details ({E4},
                     {N3} and {W13}).

              (4)   Volume IV: *Nihilism* (1982). See "European
                     Nihilism" and "Nihilism as Determined by the
                     History of Being" for details ({E6} and {N4}).

All four volumes were reprinted in the two-volume paperback edition *Nietzsche* (1991) San Francisco: HarperCollins, which combines volumes I and II, III and IV, respectively. Three parts of the original two-volume *Nietzsche*, published in 1961 (Pfullingen: Neske), were not included in this translation. They had been previously translated by Joan Stambaugh and published in *The End of Philosophy* (1973) New York: Harper and Row, pp. 1-83. See "Metaphysics as History of Being" {M6}, "Sketches for a History of Being as Metaphysics" {S3}, and "Recollection in Metaphysics" {R3} for details. An audio (CD) version of all volumes of *Nietzsche* in this translation series is available. {N2)

112. [A] (A)   "Nietzsche's Metaphysics" (1987) [Frank A. Capuzzi].

            (B)   "On Nietzsche" (2009) [Jerome Veith)].

      [B] "Nietzsches Metaphysik": Originally thought to be a lecture course prepared in 1940 for the Winter Semester of 1941-42 at the University of Freiburg but not given, the text is an essay unto itself (see "Editor's Afterword" to *GA* 50 and "Editor's Preface" to the translation, p. viii). The text in *GA* 6.2 (1997), pp. 231-300, follows that of *GA* 50. The notes to this text appear only in *GA* 50 (pp. 83-87). See "Appendix to *Nietzsche's Metaphysics*" {A12}.

      [C] *Nietzsche* II (1961) Pfullingen: Neske, pp. 257-333 [Part VI]. A substantially revised text has been published in *Nietzsches Metaphysik*: *GA* 50 (1990), pp. 1-87. *Nietzsche* I and II (1961) reprinted as *GA* 6.1 (1996) and *GA* 6.2 (1997).

      [D] (A)   *Nietzsche, Volume III: The Will to Power as Knowledge and as Metaphysics* (1987) New York: Harper and Row, pp. 185-251 [Part Three]. The translation has been somewhat modified by the editor of *Nietzsche*, David Farrel Krell (p. viii). The HarperCollins paperback reprint [2 vols.] (1991) of all four volumes of the translation of *Nietzsche* (see {N2}) combines volumes I and II and volumes III and IV. An audio (CD) version of all volumes of *Nietzsche* in this translation series is available.

      (B)   Günther Figal (ed.), *The Heidegger Reader* (2009)
                New Haven: Yale University Press, pp. 224-238
                (excerpt of *GA* 50 [1990], pp. 3-9, 11-20 and 21-25).
                {N3}

113.   [A]   "Nihilism as Determined by the History of Being" (1982)
             [Frank A. Capuzzi].
       [B]   "Die seinsgeschichtliche Bestimmung des Nihilismus": Essay
             written during the years 1944-46 in conjunction with the
             author's study of Nietzsche.
       [C]   *Nietzsche* II (1961) Pfullingen: Neske, pp. 335-398 [Part VII].
             Nietzsche I and II (1961) reprinted as *GA* 6.1 (1996) and *GA*
             6.2 (1997).
       [D]   *Nietzsche*, Volume IV: *Nihilism* (1982) New York: Harper
             and Row, pp. 197-250 [Part Two]. The HarperCollins
             paperback reprint [2 vols.] (1991) of all four volumes of the
             translation of *Nietzsche* (see {N2}) combines volumes I and II
             and volumes III and IV. An audio (CD) version of all volumes
             of *Nietzsche* in this translation series is available. {N4}

114.   [A]   "Notes on the Kantbook" (1997) [Richard Taft].
       [B]   "Aufzeichnungen zum Kantbuch": Notes found in
             Heidegger's copy of the first
       [C]   *Kant und das Problem der Metaphysik* (1929): *GA* 3, pp. 249-
             254.
       [D]   *Kant and the Problem of Metaohysics* [5th ed.] (1997)
             Bloomington: Indiana University Press, pp. 175-179. {N5}

115.   [A]   (A)   "Of the Origin of the Work of Art (first elaboration)"
                     (2008) [Markus Zisselsberger].
             (B)   "On the Origin of the Work of Art. *First Version*"
                     (2009) [Jerome Veith].
       [B]   First version (1935) of a lecture subsequently given to the
             Kunstwissenschaftliche Gesellschaft at the University of
             Freiburg on Noveber 13, 1935.
       [C]   "Vom Ursprung des Kunstwerkes: Erste Ausarbeitung," in
             Heidegger Studies (Berlin), 1989, pp. 5-22.

[D]   (A)   *Epoché. A Journal for the History of Philosophy*
                (Charlottesvile) 12(2), 2008, pp. 329-347.
        (B)   Günther Figal (ed.), *The Heidegger Reader* (2009)
                New Haven: Yale University Press, pp. 130-150.
                {O15}

116.   [A]   (A)   "On the Being and Concept of Φύσις in Aristotle's
                        Physics B, 1" (1976) [Thomas Sheehan].
                (B)   "On the Essence and Concept of Φύσις in Aristotle's
                        Physics B, 1" (1998) [Thomas Sheehan and William
                        McNeill].
        [B]   "Vom Wesen und Begriff der Φύσις. Aristoteles *Physik* B,1":
                Essay written in 1939 for a seminar entitled "Über die Φύσις
                bei Aristoteles," given the First Trimester 1940, University of
                Freiburg.
        [C]   *Il Pensiero* (Milan) 3(2) and 3(3), 1958, pp. 131-156, 265-
                290. Reprinted in *Wegmarken* (1967): *GA* 9 (1976), pp. 239-
                301.
        [D]   (A)   *Man and World* (Dordrecht) 9, 1976, pp. 219-270.
                (B)   *Pathmarks* (1998) Cambridge: Cambridge University
                        Press, pp. 183-230. {O4}

117.   [A]   "On Ernst Jünger [(1) and (2)]" (2009) [Jerome Veith].
        [B]   Two texts on Ernst Jünger from 1939-40.
        [C]   *GA* 90 (2004): [III, "Von Ernst Jünger 1939/40" and IV,
                "Ernst Jünger 1939/40"], pp. 233-260.
        [D]   Günther Figal (ed.), *The Heidegger Reader* (2009) New
                Haven: Yale University Press, pp. 189-200, 201-206. {O16}

118.   [A]   (A)   "On the Essence of the Ground" (1962) [Jean T.
                        Wilde and William Kimmel].
                (B)   *The Essence of Reasons* (1969) [Terrence Malick].
                (C)   "On the Essence of Ground" (1998) [William
                        McNeill].
        [B]   "Vom Wesen des Grundes": Essay for a *Festschrift*
                celebrating the 70th birthday of Edmund Husserl. The third
                edition (1949) of the book was supplemented with a
                "Vorwort."

[C]   *Festschrift. Edmund Husserl zum 70. Geburtstag. Ergänzungsband zum Jahrbuch für Philosophie und phänomenologische Forschung* (1929) Halle: Niemeyer, pp. 71-100. Published with a "Vorwort" as *Vom Wesen des Grundes* (1949) Frankfurt: Klostermann. Reprinted in *Wegmarken* (1967): *GA* 9 (1976), pp. 123-175.

[D]   (A)   Jean T. Wilde and William Kimmel (eds.), *The Search for Being* (1962) New York: Twayne, pp. 507-520. Includes the "Preface" (1949) and the text of the essay only through the end of Part One ["The Problem of the Ground"].

        (B)   * *The Essence of Reasons* (1969) Evanston: Northwestern University Press.

        (C)   *Pathmarks* (1998) Cambridge: Cambridge University Press, pp. 97-135. {O6}

119.   [A]   *On the Essence of Language. The Metaphysics of Language and the Essencing of the Word. Concerning Herder's Treatise* On the Origin of Language (2004) [Wanda Torres Gregory and Yvonne Unna].

        [B]   "Vom Wesen der Sprache. Die Metaphysik der Sprache und die Wesung des Wortes. Zu Herders Abhandlung "'Über den Ursprung der Sprache'": Notes for a graduate seminar given during Summer Semester 1939, University of Freiburg.

        [C]   *GA* 85 (1999).

        [D]   *On the Essence of Language. The Metaphysics of Language and the Essencing of the Word. Concerning Herder's Treatise* On the Origin of Language (Albany: SUNY Press, 2004). {O5}

120.   [A]   (A)   "On the Essence of Truth" (1949) [R.F.C. Hull and Alan Crick].

        (B)   "On the Essence of Truth" (1977) [John Sallis].

        (C)   "On the Essence of Truth" (1998) [John Sallis and William McNeill].

        [B]   "Vom Wesen der Wahrheit": Lecture written in 1930.

[C]   *Vom Wesen der Wahrheit* (1943) Frankfurt: Klostermann. A concluding note (§9) was added for the second edition (1949). Reprinted in *Wegmarken* (1967): *GA* 9 (1976), pp. 177-202.

[D]   (A)   *Existence and Being* (1949) Washington: Regnery Gateway, 1988, pp. 292-324.

(B)   *Basic Writings* (1977; rev. ed., 1993) San Francisco: HarperSanFrancisco, pp. 115-138 (rev. ed.).

(C)   *Pathmarks* (1998) Cambridge: Cambridge University Press, pp. 136-154. {O7}

121.   [A]   "On the Essence of Truth" (2010) [Gregory Fried and Richard Polt].

[B]   "Vom Wesen der Wahrheit," Notes and drafts for the lecture course given Winter Semester 19933-34, University of Freiburg.

[C]   *GA* 36/37 (2001), pp. 83-264 and 285-298.

[D]   *Being and Truth* (2010) Bloomington: Indiana University Press, pp. 67-201 and 214-224. {O20}

122.   [A]   "On the Essence of Truth [Pentecost Monday, 1926]" (2007) [Theodore Kisiel].

[B]   "Vortrag gehalten von Prof. Martin Heidegger am Pfingstmontag 1926 in Marburg vor der Akademischen Vereinigung."Lecture for Pentecost Monday, 1926, given at the Marburg Academic Association.

[C]   Manuscript, Helene Weiss Archive (Stanford University). No German text.

[D]   Theodore Kisiel and Thomas Sheehan (eds.*)*, *Becoming Heidegger. On the Trail of His Early Occasional Writings, 1910-1927* (2007) Evanston: Northwestern University Press, pp. 277-288. {O8}

123.   [A]   "On the History of the Philosophical Chair Since 1866" (1997) [Richard Taft].

[B]   "Zur Geschichte des philosophischen Lehrstules seit 1866": An account of the development of the Marburg School of Kant studies

[C]   *Die Philipps-Universität zu Marburg 1527-1927* (1927)
        Marburg: N.G. Elwert'sche Verlagsbuchhandlung, pp. 681-
        687. *GA* 3 (1991), pp. 304-311
[D]   *Kant and the Problem of Metaphysics* [5ᵗʰ ed.] (1997)
        Bloomington: Indiana University Press, pp. 213-217. {O18}

124.   [A]   "On the Nature of the University and Academic Study" (2000)
                [Ted Sadler].
        [B]   "Über das Wesen der Universität und das akademischen
                Studiums": Lecture course given during the Summer Semester
                1919, University of Freiburg
        [C]   *GA* 56/57 (1987), pp. 205-214
        [D]   *Towards the Definition of Philosophy* (2000) London:
                Athlone, pp. 173-181. {O1}

125.   [A]   "On Odebrecht's and Cassirer's Critiques of the Kantbook"
                (1997) [Richard Taft].
        [B]   "Zu Odebrechts und Cassirers Kritik des Kantbuches": Notes
                found in Heidegger's copy of the first edition of *Kant und das
                Problem der Meatphysik* on reviews of the book published by
                Ernst Cassirer (in *Kantstudien* [Berlin] 1-2, 1931, pp. 1-26)
                and Rudolf Odebrecht (in *Blätter für deutsche Philosophie*
                [Heidelberg] 6(1), 1931-32, pp. 132-135).
        [C]   *Kant und das Problem der Metaphysik* (1929): *GA* 3 (1991),
                pp. 297-303.
        [D]   *Kant ant the Problemm of Metaphysics* [5ᵗʰ ed.] (1997)
                Bloomington: Indiana University Press, pp. 208-212. {O17}

126.   [A]   (A)   "On a Philosophical Orientation for Academics"
                        (1991, 2007) [John Protevi].
                (B)   "On a Philosophical Orientation for Academics"
                        (2007) [John Protevi and Theodore Kisiel].
        [B]   "Zur philosophischen Orientierung für Akademiker (März
                1911)": Essay written in 1911.
        [C]   *Der Akademiker* (Munich) 3(5), March 1911, pp. 66-67.
                Reprinted in *GA* 16 (2000), pp. 11-14.
        [D]   (A)   * *Graduate Faculty Philosophy Journal* (New York)
                        14-15, 1991, pp. 497-50

(B)   Theodore Kisiel and Thomas Sheehan (eds.),
*Becoming Heidegger. On the Trail of His Early
Occasional Writings, 1910-1927* (2007) Evanston:
Northwestern University Press, pp. 14-16. {O2}

127.   [A]   "On the Question Concerning the Determination of the Matter
for Thinking" (2010) [Richard Capobianco and Marie Göbel].
       [B]   "Zur Frage nach der Bestimmung der Sache des Denkens":
Expanded version of a lecture given October 30, 1965, in
Amriswil, in honor of Ludwig Binswanger.
       [C]   Franz Larese and Jürg Janett (eds.), *Zur Frage nach der
Bestimmung der Sache des Denkens* (1984) St. Gallen. *GA* 16
(2000), pp. 620-633. First published in a Japanese translation
in 1968 by Koichi Tsujimura, including a *Vorwort* by
Heidegger. The *Vorwort* was first published in Hartmut
Buchner (ed.), *Japan und Heidegger* (1989) Sigmaringen:
Thorbecker, pp. 230-231. *GA* 16 (2000), p. 695.
       [D]   *Epoché: A Journal for the History of Philosophy* 14(2), 2010,
pp. 213-223. {O19}

128.   [A]   "On Still Paths" (1993) [Allan Blunden].
       [B]   "Auf stillen Pfaden": Poem written in early 1911.
       [C]   *Der Akademiker* (Munich), July 1911. Reprinted in Hugo Ott,
Martin Heidegger. Unterwegs zu seiner Biographie (1988)
Frankfurt: Campus, p. 71. *GA* 16 (2000), p. 16.
       [D]   Hugo Ott, *Martin Heidegger. A Political Life* (1993) London:
Basic Books, p. 68. {O3}

129.   [A]   "On the Way to Being. Reflecting on Conversations with
Martin Heidegger" (1970) [Zygmunt Adamczewski].
       [B]   Record by Zygmunt Adamczewski of conversations with
Heidegger in Freiburg and Todtnauberg, October 1968.
       [C]   German text unpublished.
       [D]   John Sallis (ed.), *Heidegger and the Path of Thinking* (1970)
Pittsburgh: Duquesne University Press, pp. 12-36. {O9}

130. [A] (A) "Only a God Can Save Us: *Der Spiegel's* Interview with Martin Heidegger" (1976) [Maria P. Alter and John D. Caputo].

(B) "Only a God Can Save Us Now" (1977) [David Schendler].

(C) "'Only a God Can Save Us': The *Spiegel* Interview with Martin Heidegger" (1981) [William J. Richardson].

(D) "*Der Spiegel* Interview with Martin Heidegger" (1990) [Lisa Harries].

(E) "*Der Spiegel* Interview with Martin Heidegger" (2009) [Jerome Vieth].

[B] "Nur noch ein Gott kann uns retten": Transcript of an interview with Heidegger audiotaped on September 23, 1966, published in 1976.

[C] *Der Spiegel* (Hamburg) May 31, 1976, pp. 193-219. Reprinted in Günther Neske and Emil Kettering (eds.), *Antwort. Martin Heidegger im Gespräch* (1988) Pfullingen: Neske, pp. 81-114. *GA* 16 (2000), pp. 652-683 (version not edited for publication in the magazine; see editor's note in *GA* 16 [2000], pp. 815-818).

[D] (A) *Philosophy Today* (Celina) 20 (4), 1976, pp. 267-284. Reprinted in Richard Wolin (ed.), *The Heidegger Controversy. A Critical Reader* (1991) Cambridge: MIT Press, 1993, pp. 91-116, and in Manfred Stassen (ed.), *Martin Heidegger. Philosophical and Political Essays* (2003) New York: Continuum, pp. 24-48.

(B) *Graduate Faculty Philosophy Journal* (New York) 6 (1), 1977, pp. 5-27.

(C) Thomas Sheehan (ed.), *Heidegger. The Man and the Thinker* (1981) Chicago: Precedent Publishing Company, pp. 45-67.

(D) Günther Neske and Emil Kettering (eds.), *Martin Heidegger and National Socialism* (1990) New York: Paragon House, pp. 41-66.

(E) Günther Figal (ed.), *The Heidegger Reader* (2009) New Haven: Yale University Press, pp. 313-333. Based on *GA* 16 (2000), pp. 107-117, this is said to be based on "the complete version" of the interview, "rather than the edited version ultimately published in *Der Spiegel*" (p. 313). {O10}

131. [A]   *Ontology--The Hermeneutics of Facticity* (1999) [John van Buren].

       [B]   "Ontologie (Hermeneutik der Faktizität)": Lecture course given during the Summer Semester of 1923, University of Freiburg.

       [C]   *GA* 63 (1988).

       [D]   *Ontology--The Hermeneutics of Facticity* (Bloomington: Indiana University Press, 1999). {O11}

132. [A]   (A)   "The Onto-theo-logical Nature of Metaphysics" (1960) [Kurt F. Leidecker].

              (B)   "The Onto-theo-logical Constitution of Metaphysics" (1969) [Joan Stambaugh].

       [B]   "Die onto-theo-logische Verfassung der Metaphysik": Concluding lecture for a seminar during the winter semester 1956-57 on Hegel's *Science of Logic*, given on February 24, 1957, in Todtnauberg.

       [C]   *Identität und Differenz* (1957) Pfullingen: Neske, pp. 35-73. *GA* 11 (2006), pp. 51-79

       [D]   (A)   *Essays in Metaphysics. Identity and Difference* (1960) New York: Philosophical Library, pp. 33-67.

              (B)   * *Identity and Difference* (1969) New York: Harper and Row, pp. 42-74. A CD version (2005) for the blind is available. {O12}

133. [A]   (A)   "The Origin of the Work of Art" (1965) [Albert Hofstadter]

              (B)   "The Origin of the Work of Art" (2002) [Julian Young]

       [B]   ^"Der Ursprung des Kunstwerkes": Lecture given November 13, 1935, in Freiburg. Expanded to a series of three lectures given November 17 and 24, 1936, and December 1, 1936, in Frankfurt. A *Zusatz* was added in 1956. The first version of the lecture appears in this bibliography as {O15}.

[C]   *Holzwege* (1950): *GA* 5 (1977), pp. 1-74. A sound-book audio
        version (1977) is available (Reclam 1977).

[D]   (A)   Albert Hofstadter (ed.) *Philosophies of Art and
                Beauty (1965) New York:Random House, pp. 647-
                701 (without "Addendum"). Reprinted in
                Poetry,Language, Thought (1971) New York: Harper
                and Row, 1975, pp. 17-87,with "Addendum."
                Complete version reprinted in revised edition of
                Basic Writings (1993) San Francisco:
                HarperSanFrancisco, pp. 139-212.

        (B)   *Off the Beaten Track* (2002) Cambridge: Cambridge
                University Press, pp. 1-56. {O13}

134.   [A]   "Overcoming Metaphysics" (1973) [Joan Stambaugh].

        [B]   "Seinsverlassenheit und Irrnis": Notes on Nietzsche from the
                years 1936-46.

        [C]   Section XVI, in Egon Fritz and Erich Wiese (eds.), *Ernst
                Barlach. Dramatiker, Bildhauer, Zeichner* (1951) Darmstadt:
                Kulturverwaltung der Stadt Darmstadt, pp. 5-12; Sections I-
                XXV and XXVII-XXVIII, in Fritz Hollwich (ed.), *Im
                Umkreis der Kunst. Festschrift für Emil Preetorius* (1954)
                Wiesbaden: Insel-Verlag, pp. 117-136. The complete text first
                appeared as "Überwindung der Metaphysik" in *Vorträge und
                Aufsätze* I (1954) Pfullingen: Neske, 1978, pp. 63-91. *GA* 7
                (2000): pp. 67-98.

        [D]   *The End of Philosophy* (1973) New York: Harper and Row,
                pp. 84-110. Reprinted in Richard Wolin (ed.), *The Heidegger
                Controversy. A Critical Reader* (1991) Cambridge: MIT
                Press, 1993, pp. 67-90. {O14}

135.   [A]   *Parmenides* (1992) [André Schuwer and Richard Rojcewicz].

        [B]   "Parmenides": Lecture course given during the Winter
                Semester 1942-43, University of Freiburg.

        [C]   *GA* 54 (1982).

        [D]   *Parmenides* (1992) Bloomington: Indiana University Press.
                {P1}

136. [A] (A) [The Pathway] "The Field Path. A Meditation"
                 (1950) [NN].
            (B) "The Pathway" (1967) [Thomas F. O'Meara].
            (C) "The Pathway" (1973) [Thomas Sheehan].
            (D) "The Fieldpath" (1986) [Berit Mexia].
      [B] ^"Zur Zuspruch des Feldweges": Essay written in 1949.
           Revised title: "Der Feldweg" (1950).
      [C] *Hamburg Sontagsblatt* (Hamburg) 2 (43), October 23, 1949,
           5-23, and earlier in the year in several privately published
           editions. Published under the revised title in *Wort und
           Wahrheit* (Vienna) 5, 1950, pp. 267-69. *GA* 13 (1983), pp. 87-
           90. Available on CD: *Von der Sache des Denkens. Vorträge,
           Reden und Gespräche* (Munich: Der Hörverlag, 2000).
      [D] (A) *World Review* (London) #11 [New Series], January
                 1950, pp. 5-6.
            (B) *Listening* (Dubuque) 2, 1967, pp. 88-91. Reprinted in
                 Manfred Stassen (ed.), *Martin Heidegger.
                 Philosophical and Political Essays* (2003) New
                 York: Continuum, pp. 77-79.
            (C) * *Listening* (Dubuque) 8, 1973, pp. 32-39. Reprinted
                 in Thomas Sheehan (ed.), *Heidegger. The Man and
                 the Thinker* (1981) Chicago: Precedent Publishing
                 Company, pp. 69-72, and in Thomas Frick (ed.), *The
                 Sacred Theory of the Earth* (1986) Berkeley: North
                 Atlantic Books, pp. 45-48 (English only).
            (D) *Journal of Chinese Philosophy* (Dordrecht) 13, 1986,
                 pp. 455-457. {P2}

137. [A] (A) "*Per mortem ad vitam* (Thoughts on Johannes
                 Jörgensen's *Lies of Life and Truth of Life*)" (1991)
                 [John Protevi].
            (B) "*Per mortem ad vitam* (Thoughts on Johannes
                 Jörgensen's *Lies of Life and Truth of Life*)" (1991)
                 [John Protevi and John van Buren].
      [B] "Per mortem ad vitam (Gedanken über Jörgensens *Lebenslüge
           und Lebenswahrheit*)": Book review essay written in March
           1910.

[C] *Der Akademiker* (Munich) 2(5), March 1910, pp. 72-73. *GA*
     16 (2000), pp. 3-6.

[D] (A) * *Graduate Faculty Philosophy Journal* (New York)
          14-15, 1991, pp. 487-491.

     (B) *Supplements. From the Earliest Essays to* Being and
          Time *and Beyond* (2002) Albany: SUNY Press, pp.
          35-37. {P3}

138. [A] *Phenomenological Interpretation of Kant's* Critique of Pure
          Reason (1997) [Parvis Emad and Kenneth Maly].

     [B] "Phänomenologische Interpretation von Kants Kritik der
          reinen Vernunft": Lecture course given during the Winter
          Semester 1927-28, University of Marburg.

     [C] *GA* 25 (1977).

     [D] *Phenomenological Interpretation of Kant's* Critique of Pure
          Reason (1997) Bloomington: Indiana University Press. {P4}

139. [A] *Phenomenological Interpretations of Aristotle: Initiation into
          Phenomenological Research* (2001) [Richard Rojcewicz].

     [B] "Phänomenologische Interpretationen zu Aristoteles.
          Einführung in die phänomenologische Forschung": Lecture
          course given during the Winter Semester 1921-22, University
          of Freiburg.

     [C] *GA* 61 (1985).

     [D] *Phenomenological Interpretations of Aristotle: Initiation into
          Phenomenological Research* (2001) Bloomington: Indiana
          University Press, 2001. {P5}

140. [A] (A) "Phenomenological Interpretations with Respect to
               Aristotle: Indication of the Hermeneutical Situation"
               (1992) [Michael Baur].

          (B) "Phenomenological Interpretations in Connection
               with Aristotle: An Indication of the Hermeneutical
               Situation" (2002) [John van Buren].

          (C) "Phenomenological Interpretations with Respect to
               Aristotle: Indication of the Hermeneutical Situation"
               (2007) [Theodore Kisiel].

         (D)   "Indication of the Hermeneutical Situation" (2009)
                   [Jerome Veith].

[B]   "Phänomenologische Interpretationen zu Aristoteles (Anzeige der hermeneutischen Situation)": Text written in the fall of 1922 outlining Heidegger's current and future research, submitted as part his application for a full-time teaching position.

[C]   *Dilthey-Jahrbuch für Philosophie und Geschichte der Gesisteswissenschaften* (Göttingen), 6, 1989, pp. 235-269. Text edited by Hans-Ulrich Lessing. GA 62 (2005), pp. 346-384.

[D]   (A)   *Man and World*, 25 (3/4), 1992, pp. 355-393.

         (B)   *Supplements. From the Earliest Essays to* Being and Time *and Beyond* (2002) Albany: SUNY Press, pp. 111-145.

         (C)   Theodore Kisiel and Thomas Sheehan (eds.), *Becoming Heidegger. On the Trail of His Early Occasional Writings, 1910-1927* (2007) Evanston: Northwestern University Press, pp. 155-184.

         (D)   Günther Figal (ed.), *The Heidegger Reader* (2009) New Haven: Yale University Press, pp. 38-61 (excerpt based on *GA* 62 [2005], pp. 346-384). {P6}

141.   [A]   (A)   "Phenomenology and Theology" (1976) [James G. Hart and John C. Maraldo].

         (B)   "Phenomenology and Theology" (1998) [William McNeill, James G. Hart and John C. Maraldo].

     [B]   "Phänomenologie und Theologie": Lecture given March 9, 1927, in Tübingen. A "Vorwort" was added in 1970 for the first German publication of the lecture.

     [C]   *Archives de Philosophie* (Paris) 32, 1969, pp. 356-395 (with a French translation by the editors of the journal and Marcel Méry). Published in *Phänomenologie und Theologie. Rudolf Bultmann gewidmet in freundschaftlichem Gedenken an die Marburger Jahre 1923 bis 1928* (1970) Frankfurt: Klostermann, pp. 9-10, 13-33. Reprinted in *Wegmarken* (1967): *GA* 9 (1976), pp. 45-67.

[D]   (A)   *The Piety of Thinking* (1976) Bloomington: Indiana
University Press, pp. 3-21.

(B)   *Pathmarks* (1998) Cambridge: Cambridge University
Press, pp. 39-54. {P7}

142.   [A]   "Phenomenology and Transcendental Philosophy of Value"
(2000) [Ted Sadler].

[B]   "Phänomenologie und tranzendentale Wertphilosophie":
Lecture course given during the Summer Semester 1919,
University of Freiburg

[C]   *GA* 56/57 (1987), pp. 119-203

[D]   *Towards the Definition of Philosophy* (2000) London:
Athlone, pp. 103-171. {P28}

143.   [A]   *Phenomenology of Intuition and Expression* (2010) [Tracy
Colony].

[B]   *Phänomenologie der Anschauung und des Ausdrucks*: Lecture
course given during the Summer Semester1920, University of
Freiburg

[C]   *GA* 59 (1993)

[D]   *Phenomenology of Intuition and Expression* (2010). New
York: Continuum. {P8}.

144.   [A]   (A)   "The Philosophical Foundations of Medieval
Mysticism" (2004) [Matthias Fritsch and Jennifer
Gosetti-Ferencei].

(B)   "On Schleiermacher's Second Speech, 'On the
Essence of Religion'" (2007) [Theodore Kisiel].

[B]   "Die philosophischen Grundfragen der mittelalterischen
Mystik": Lecture course announced for the Winter Semester
1918-19, University of Freiburg, but not given.

[C]   *GA* 60 (1995), pp. 301-337.

[D]   (A)   *The Phenomenology of Religious Life* (2004)
Bloomington: Indiana University Press, pp. 229-254.

(B)   Theodore Kisiel and Thomas Sheehan (eds.),
*Becoming Heidegger. On the Trail of His Early
Occasional Writing, 1910-1927)* (2007) Evanston:

Northwestern University Press, pp. 86-91 (excerpt, *GA* 60 [1995], pp. 319-322). {P27}

145. [A] (A) "Plato's Doctrine of Truth" (1962) [John Barlow].
   (B) "Plato's Doctrine of Truth" (1998) [William McNeill and Thomas Sheehan].
   [B] "Platons Lehre von der Wahrheit": Essay written in 1940 for a private lecture, related to the lecture course "Vom Wesen der Wahrheit" given during the Winter Semester 1930-31, University of Freiburg. See *Vom Wesen der Wahrheit. Zu Platons Höhlengleichnis und Theätet*: *GA* 34 (1988) {E3}.
   [C] *Geistige Überlieferung* (Berlin) 2, 1942, pp. 96-124. Printed as a separate work *Platons Lehre von der Wahrheit. Mit einem Brief über den Humanismus* (1947) Bern: Francke, pp. 5-52. Reprinted in *Wegmarken* (1967): *GA* 9 (1976), pp. 203-238.
   [D] (A) William Barrett and Henry D. Aiken (eds.), *Philosophy in the Twentieth Century. An Anthology* (1962) New York: Random House, 1982, Vol. 3, pp. 251-270.
   (B) *Pathmarks* (1998) Cambridge: Cambridge University Press, pp. 155-182. {P9}

146. [A] *Plato's* Sophist (1997) [Richard Rojcewicz and André Schuwer].
   [B] "Interpretation Platonischer Dialoge (*Sophistes, Philebus*)": Lecture course given during the Winter Semester 1924-25, University of Marburg.
   [C] *GA* 19 (1992).
   [D] *Plato's* Sophist (1997) Bloomington: Indiana University Press. {P10}

147. [A] "The Poem" (2000) [Keith Hoeller].
   [B] "Das Gedicht": Revised version of a lecture given on August 25, 1968, in Amriswil in honor of Ernst Jünger's 70th birthday.
   [C] *Erläuterungen zu Hölderlins Dichtung* (4th ed., 1971) Frankfurt: Klostermann, pp. 182-192. Reprinted in *GA* 4 (1981), pp. 182-192.

[D]   *Elucidations of Hölderlin's Poetry* (2000) Amherst: Humanity
        Books, pp. 209-219. {P11}

148.   [A]   ^"... Poetically Man Dwells ..." (1971) [Albert Hofstadter].
        [B]   "... dichterisch wohnet der Mensch ...": Lecture given on
                October 6, 1951, in Bühlerhöhe.
        [C]   *Akzente. Zeitschrift für Dichtung* (Munich) 1, 1954, pp. 57-71.
                Reprinted in *Vorträge und Aufsätze* II (1954) Pfullingen:
                Neske, 1978, pp. 61-78. *GA* 7 (2000), pp. 189-208.
        [D]   *Poetry, Language, Thought* (1971) New York: Harper and
                Row, 1975, pp. 213-229. Reprinted in Manfred Stassen (ed.),
                Martin Heidegger. Philosophical and Political Essays (2003)
                New York: Continuum, pp. 265-78. Excerpts (pp. 213-216
                and 227-227 of 1971) published in *Canadian Journal of
                Psychoanalysis* (Montreal) 10(2), 2002, pp. 233-236. A CD
                version (2005) for the blind is available. {P12}

149.   [A]   (A)   "Postscript" to "What Is Metaphysics?" (1949)
                        [R.F.C. Hull and Alan Crick].
                (B)   "Postscript" to "What Is Metaphysics?" (1998)
                        [William McNeill].
        [B]   "Nachwort zu `Was ist Metaphysik?'": Postscript to the
                inaugural lecture (1929), added in 1943 for the 4th edition of
                the lecture. Revised in 1949 for the 5th edition. See {W6}.
        [C]   *Was ist Metaphysik?* (1929) Frankfurt: Klostermann, 1949,
                pp. 43-52. Reprinted in *Wegmarken* (1967): *GA* 9 (1976), pp.
                303-312.
        [D]   (A)   *Existence and Being* (1949) Washington: Regnery
                        Gateway, 1988, pp. 349-361 (revised version).
                        Reprinted in Walter Kaufmann (ed.), *Existentialism
                        from Dostoevsky to Sartre* (1956, rev. ed., 1975) New
                        York: New American Library, 1984, pp. 257-264
                        (beginning with revised edition).
                (B)   *Pathmarks* (1998) Cambridge: Cambridge University
                        Press, pp. 231-238. {P13}

150.   [A]   "Poverty" (2011) [Thomas Kalary and Frank Schalow].

[B]   "Die Armut": Address given June 27, 1945, in Hausen, near
        the Beuron Archabbey.
[C]   *Heidegger Studies* (Berline) 10, 1994, pp. 5-11. *GA* 73
        (forthcoming).
[D]   Frank Schalow (ed.), *Heidegger, Translation and the Task of
        Thinking* (2011) New York: Springer, pp. 3-10. {P29}

151. [A]   "Prefaces to *Elucidations of Hölderlin's Poetry* (2000) [Keith
            Hoeller].
      [B]   "Vorwort" to 2ⁿᵈ Edition (1951) and "Vorwort" to 4ᵗʰ Edition
            (1971) of *Erläuterungen zu Hölderlins Dichtung.* The 1951
            preface includes the concluding part of the "Preface to the
            Repetition of the Address 'Homecoming'," of June 21, 1943.
            The 1971 preface is an abbreviated version of the 1ˢᵗ Edition
            introductory note.
      [C]   *Erläuterungen zu Hölderlins Dichtung* (1951, 1971): *GA* 4
            (1981), pp. 7-8.
      [D]   *Elucidations of Hölderlin's Poetry* (2000) Amherst: Humanity
            Books, pp. 21-22. {P16}

152. [A]   "Preface" [to *Pathmarks*] (1998) [William McNeill].
      [B]   "Vorbemerkung": Prefatory note to the first edition of
            Wegmarken, Freiburg im Breisgau, early summer 1967.
      [C]   *Wegmarken* (1967): *GA* 9 (1976), pp. IX-X.
      [D]   *Pathmarks* (1998) Cambridge: Cambridge University Press, p.
            XIII. {P14}

153. [A]   (A)   "Preface to a Reading of Hölderlin's Poems" (2000)
                  [Keith Hoeller].
            (B)   "A Word on Hölderlin's Poetry" (2001) [Franz Mayr
                  and Richard Askay].
      [B]   ^"Vorwort zur Lesung von Hölderlins Gedichten": Text of
            introductory comments on the recording *Martin Heidegger
            ließt Hölderlin* (1963) Pfullingen: Neske.
      [C]   *Erläuterungen zu Hölderlins Dichtung, GA* 4 (1981): pp. 195-
            197. Available on the CD *Heidegger ließt Hölderlin* (Klett-
            Cotta, 1997)

[D]   (A)   *Elucidations of Hölderlin's Poetry* (2000) Amherst:
               Humanity Books, pp. 224-226.
       (B)   *Zollikon Seminars. Protocols–Conversations–Letters*
               (2001) Evanston Northwestern University Press, pp.
               265-267. (Cf. {Z1}. The text was sent toMedard
               Boss in a letter of October 2, 1963.) {P15}

154.   [A]   (A)   "Prefatory Remark to a Repetition of the Address"
               (1949) [Douglas Scott].
       (B)   "Preface to a Repetition of the Address
               'Homecoming'" (2000] [Keith Hoeller].
       [B]   "Vorbemerkung zur Wiederholung der Rede": Introductory
               remarks to the lecture given on June 21, 1943, University of
               Freiburg. The text consists of two paragraphs followed by
               what was published as the Preface to the 1st Edition (1944) of
               Erläuterungen zu Hölderlins Dichtung. It appeared following
               the text of the address "'Heimkunft / An die Verwandten."
       [C]   *Erläuterungen zu Hölderlins Dichtung* (1944) Frankfurt:
               Klostermann, pp. 31-32. The text was omitted beginning with
               the 2nd Edition (1951) and restored in the 4th edition (1971).
               GA 4 (1981), pp. 193-194.
       [D]   (A)   *Existence and Being* (1949) Washington: Regnery
               Gateway, 1988, pp. 233-235
       (B)   *Elucidations of Hölderlin's Poetry* (2000) Amherst:
               Humanity Books, pp. 221-223. {P17}

155.   [A]   (A)   "The Principle of Ground" (1974) [Keith Hoeller].
       (B)   "The Principle of Reason" (1991) [Reginald Lilly].
       [B]   "Der Satz vom Grund": Lecture given May 25, 1956, at the
               Bremen Club and October 24, 1956, at the University of
               Vienna. Included with the publication of Heidegger's course
               of the same name given during the Winter Semester 1955-56,
               University of Freiburg (*GA* 10 [1997]). See {P19}.
       [C]   *Wissenschaft und Wahrheit* (Vienna) 9, 1956, pp. 241-250.
               Reprinted in *Der Satz vom Grund* (1957) Pfullingen: Neske,
               1986, pp. 191-211. *GA* 10 (1997), pp. 171-189.
       [D]   (A)   *Man and World* (Dordrecht) 7, 1974, pp. 207-222.

(B)   *The Principle of Reason* (1991) Bloomington:
         Indiana University Press, pp. 117-129. {P18}

156.   [A]   (A)   "The Principle of Identity" (1960) [Kurt F.
                       Leidecker].
              (B)   "The Principle of Identity" (1969) [Joan Stambaugh].
              (C)   "The Principle of Identity" (2009) [Jerome Veith].
              (D)   "The Principle of Identity" [*Principles of Thinking*:
                       Lecture III] (2012) [Andrew J. Mitchell].
       [B]   ^"Der Satz der Identität": Lecture given June 27, 1957, at the
              University of Freiburg, on the occasion of the 500th
              anniversary of the founding of the university as one of a series
              of five lectures in the *stadium generale*. See {B11}.
       [C]   *Die Albert-Ludwigs-Universität Freiburg 1457-1957. Die
              Festvorträge bei der Jubiläumsfeier* (1957) Freiburg: F.K.
              Schulz, pp. 69-79. Reprinted in *Identität und Differenz* (1957)
              Pfullingen: Neske, pp. 11-34, *Bremeer und Freiburger*
              Vorträge (1994): *GA* 79, pp. 115-129. Heidegger recorded the
              lecture on June 27, 1957, at the University of Freiburg. A CD
              of the recording is available as *Martin Heidegger. Der Satz
              der Identität* (Stuttgardt: Klett-Cotta, 1997) and in *Von der
              Sache des Denkens. Vorträge, Reden und Gespräche* (Munich:
              Der Hörverlag, 2000).
       [D]   (A)   *Essays in Metaphysics. Identity and Difference*
                       (1960) New York: Philosophical Library, pp. 13-32.
              (B)   * *Identity and Difference* (1969) New York: Harper
                       and Row, pp. 23-41.
              (C)   Günther Figal (ed.), *The Heidegger Reader* (2009)
                       New Haven: Yale University Press, pp. 284-294.
       (D)   *Bremen and Freiburg Lectures* (2012) Bloomington: Indiana
              University Press, pp. 108-121. {P20}

157.   [A]   *The Principle of Reason* (1991) [Reginald Lilly].
       [B]   "Der Satz vom Grund": Lecture course given during the
              Winter Semester 1955-56, University of Freiburg.
       [C]   *Der Satz vom Grund* (1957) Pfullingen: Neske, pp. 13-188.
              GA 10 (1997), pp. 1-169.

[D]   *The Principle of Reason* (1991) Bloomington: Indiana University Press, pp. 3-113. {P19}

158.   [A]   (A)   "Principles of Thinking" (1976) [James G. Hart and John C. Maraldo].

(B)   Lecture I, *The Principles of Thinking* (2012) [Andrew W. Mitchell].

[B]   "Grundsätze des Denkens": Revised version of the first of five lectures given at the Univesity of Freiburg, SS 1957. Published in 1958 in honor of the 75th birthday of Viktor Emil von Gebsattel (see {B11}).

[C]   *Jahrbuch für Psychologie und Psychotherapie* (Freiburg) 6, 1958, pp. 33-41. *GA* 79 (1997), pp. 81-96.

[D]   (A)   *The Piety of Thinking* (1976) Bloomington: Indiana University Press, pp. 46-58.

(B)   *Bremen and Freiburg Lectures* (2012) Bloomington: Indiana University Press, pp. 77-91. {P21}

159.   [A]   (A)   "The Problem of the Categories" (1979) [Roderick M. Stewart]

(B)   "Conclusion: The Problem of Categories" (2002) [Roderick M. Stewart and John van Buren].

[B]   "Schluss: Das Kategorienproblem": Conclusion to *Die Kategorien- und Bedeutungslehre des Duns Scotus* (see {D2}).

[C]   *Die Kategorien- und Bedeutungslehre des Duns Scotus* (1916) Tübingen: Mohr, pp. 341-353. *Frühe Schriften* (1972): *GA* 1 (1978), pp. 399-411.

[D]   (A)   "The Problem of Categories," in *Man and World* (Dordrecht) 12, 1979, pp. 378-386.

(B)   *Supplements. From the Earliest Essays to* Being and Time *and Beyond* (John van Buren, ed.) (2002) Albany: SUNY Press, pp. 62-68. {P22}

160.   [A]   (A)   "The Problem of a Non-objectifying Thinking and Speaking in Contemporary Theology" (1968) [Gerry Gill].

(B)   "The Theological Discussion of 'The Problem of a
           Non-objectifying Thinking and Speaking in
           Contemporary Theology'--Some Pointers to Its Major
           Aspects" (1976) [James G. Hart and John C.
           Maraldo].

(C)   "The Theological Discussion of 'The Problem of a
           Non-objectifying Thinking and Speaking in
           Contemporary Theology'--Some Pointers to Its Major
           Aspects" (1998) [William McNeill, James G. Hart
           and John C. Maraldo].

[B]   "Einige Hinweise auf Hauptgesichtspunkte für das
           theologische Gespräch über 'Das Problem eines
           nichtobjectivierenden Denkens und Sprechens in der heutigen
           Theologie'": Letter written March 11, 1964, to participants of
           a conference held April 9-11, 1964, at Drew University.

[C]   *Archives de Philosophie* (Paris) 32, 1969, pp. 396-415.
           Reprinted in *Phänomenologie und Theologie. Rudolf
           Bultmann gewidmet in freundschaftlichem Gedenken an die
           Marburger Jahre 1923 bis 1928* (1970) Frankfurt:
           Klostermann, pp. 37-46. *Wegmarken* (1967): *GA* 9 (1976), pp.
           68-77.

[D]   (A)   Jerry Gill (ed.), *Philosophy and Religion. Some
                      Contemporary Perspectives* (1968) Minneapolis:
                      Burgess, pp. 59-65.

           (B)   *The Piety of Thinking* (1976) Bloomington: Indiana
                      University Press, pp. 22-31.

           (C)   *Pathmarks* (1998) Cambridge: Cambridge University
                      Press, pp. 54-62. {P23}

161.   [A]   (A)   "The Problem of Reality in Modern Philosophy"
                      (1973) [Phillip J. Bossert].

           (B)   "The Problem of Reality in Modern Philosophy"
                      (2002) [Phillip J. Bossert and John van Buren].

           (C)   "The Problem of Reality in Modern Philosophy"
                      (2007) [Aaron Bunch].

        [B]   "Das Realitätsproblem in der modernen Philosophie":
                   Heidegger's first published paper.

[C]   *Philosophisches Jahrbuch der Görresgesellschaft* (Fulda) 25, 1912, pp. 353-363. *Frühe Schriften* (1972): *GA* 1 (1978), pp. 1-15.

[D]   (A)   *Journal of the British Society for Phenomenology* (Manchester) 4, 1973, pp. 64-71.

        (B)   *Supplements. From the Earliest Essays to* Being and Time *and Beyond* (2002) Albany: SUNY Press, pp. 39-48.

        (C)   Theodore Kisiel and Thomas Sheehan (eds.), *Becoming Heidegger. On the Trail of His Early Occasional Writings, 1910-1927* (2007) Evanston: Northwestern University Press, pp. 20-29. {P24}

162.   [A]   (A)   "The Problem of Sin in Luther" (2002) [John van Buren].

        (B)   "The Problem of Sin in Luther" (2007) [Brian Handsford Bowles and Theodore Kisiel].

        [B]   "Das Problem der Sünde bei Luther": Student transcript of a two-part talk given in Rudolf Bultmann's seminar on "The Ethics of St. Paul," on February 14 and 21, 1924.

        [C]   Bernd Jaspert (ed.), *Sachgemäße Exegese: Die Protokolle aus Rudolf Bultmanns Neutestamentlichen Seminaren 1921-1951* (1996) Marburg: Elwert, pp. 28-33.

        [D]   (A)   *Supplements. From the Earliest Essays to* Being and Time *and Beyond* (2002) Albany: SUNY Press, pp. 105-110.

        (B)   Theodore Kisiel and Thomas Sheehan (eds.), *Becoming Heidegger. On the Trail of His Early Occasional Writings, 1910-1927* (2007) Evanston: Northwestern University Press, pp. 189-195 (translation edited by Theodore Kisiel). {P25}

163.   [A]   "Psychology of Religion and the Subconscious" (1991) [John Protevi].

        [B]   "Religionspsychologie und Unterbewusstsein": Essay from 1912.

        [C]   *Der Akademiker* (Munich) 4(5), March 1912, pp. 66-68. Reprinted in *GA* 16 (2000), pp. 18-28.

[D]   * *Graduate Faculty Philosophy Journal* (New York) 14-15,
         1991, pp. 503-517. {P26}

164. [A]   "Question and Judgment" (2007) [Theodore Kisiel].
      [B]   "Frage und Urteil": Lecture, July 10, 1915.
      [C]   *Martin Heidegger and Heinrich Rickert, Briefe 1912 bis 1933
               und andere Dokumente aus den Nachlässen* (2002) Frankfurt:
               Klostermann, pp. 80-90. *GA* 80 (forthcoming).
      [D]   Theodore Kisiel and Thomas Sheehan (eds.), *Becoming
               Heidegger. On the Trail of His Early Occasional Writings,
               1910-1927* (2007) Evanston: Northwestern University Press,
               pp. 52-59. {Q1}

165. [A]   (A)   *The Question of Being* (1958) [William Kluback and
                     Jean T. Wilde].
               (B)   "On the Question of Being" (1998) [William
                     McNeill].
      [B]   "Zur Seinsfrage": Essay written in 1955 for a volume
               dedicated to Ernst Jünger. Original title "Über `die Linie'."
               Jünger's paper "Die Linie" had been published d in a
               Festschrift for Heidegger, *Anteile. Martin Heidegger zum 60.
               Geburtstag* (1950) Frankfurt: Klostermann, pp. 245-284.
      [C]   *Freundschaftliche Begegnungen. Festschrift für Ernst Jünger
               zum 60. Geburtstag* (1955) Frankfurt: Klostermann, pp. 9-45.
               Published as a separate voume, *Zur Seinsfrage* (1956)
               Frankfurt: Klostermann. Reprinted in *Wegmarken* (1967): *GA*
               9 (1976), pp. 385-426.
      [D]   (A)   * *The Question of Being* (1958) New York: Twayne.
                     Reprinted in Manfred Stassen (ed.), *Martin
                     Heidegger. Philosophical and Political Essays*
                     (2003) New York: Continuum, pp. 120-151 (English
                     translation only).
               (B)   *Pathmarks* (1998) Cambridge: Cambridge University
                     Press, pp. 291-322. {Q2}

166. [A]   (A)   [The Question Concerning Technology] "Martin
                     Heidegger's *The Question about Technic*. A

Translation and Commentary" (1973) [Edwin Michael Alexander].

(B) "The Question Concerning Technology" (1977) [William Lovitt].

[B] Revised and expanded version of "Das Ge-Stell," the second of four lectures first presented in the series "Einblick in das was ist," given December 1, 1949, at the Bremen Club. Subsequenbtly given as "Die Frage nach der Technik" on November 18, 1953, at the Bavarian Academy of Fine Arts, Munich.

[C] *Gestalt und Gedanke* (Munich) 3, 1954, pp. 70-108. Reprinted in *Vorträge und Aufsätze* I (1954) Pfullingen: Neske, 1978, pp. 5-36. *GA* 7 (2000), pp. 5-36.

[D] (A) *Martin Heidegger's* The Question about Technic. *A Translation and Commentary* (1973) Ann Arbor: University Microfilms. Translator's dissertation (McMaster University, 1973).

(B) *The Question Concerning Technology and Other Essays* (1977) New York: Harper and Row, 1982, pp. 3-35. Reprinted in *Basic Writings* (1977; rev. ed., 1993) San Francisco: HarperSanFrancisco, pp. 311-341 (rev. ed.), and in Manfred Stassen (ed.), *Martin Heidegger. Philosophical and Political Essays* (2003) New York: Continuum, pp. 279-303. {Q3}

167. [A] "Recent Research in Logic" (2007) [Theodore Kisiel]

[B] "Neuere Forschungen über Logik": Review essay

[C] *Literarische Rundschau für das katholische Deutschland* (Freiburg) 38 (10-11-12), October-November-December 1912, cols 465-472, 517-524 and 565-570. *GA* 1 (1978), pp. 17-43.

[D] Theodore Kisiel and Thomas Sheehan (eds.), *Becoming Heidegger. On the Trail of His Early Occasional Writings, 1910-1927* (2007) Evanston: NorthwesternUniversity Press, pp. 31-44 (paraphrase of parts 1-2 and summary of a portion of part 3). {R1}

168. [A] "A Recollection" (1970) [Hans Seigfried].

[B]   "Antrittsrede": Inaugural address at the Heidelberg Academy of Sciences, Fall 1957, on being admitted to the Academy.

[C]   *Jahresheft der Heidelberger Akademie der Wissenschaften* (Heidelberg) 48, 1957/58, pp. 20-21. Reprinted in the "Vorwort" to the first edition of *Frühe Schriften* (1972). *GA* 1 (1978), pp. 55-57.

[D]   *Man and World* (Dordrecht) 3 (1), 1970, pp. 3-4. Reprinted in Thomas Sheehan (ed.), *Heidegger. The Man and the Thinker* (1981) Chicago: Precedent Publishing, pp. 21-22, and in Theodore Kisiel and Thomas Sheehan (eds.), *Becoming Heidegger. On the Trail of His Early Occasional Writings, 1910-1927* (2007) Evanston: Northwestern University Press, pp. 9-10 (as "A Recollective 'Vita' 1957"). {R2}

169.   [A]   "Recollection in Metaphysics" (1973) [Joan Stambaugh].

        [B]   "Die Erinnerung in die Metaphysik": Essay written in 1941.

        [C]   *Nietzsche* II (1961) Pfullingen: Neske, pp. 481-490 [Part X]. *GA* 6.2 (1997), pp. 439-448.

        [D]   *The End of Philosophy* (1973) New York: Harper and Row, pp. 75-83. {R3}

170.   [A]   "Remembrance" (2000) [Keith Hoeller].

        [B]   "Andenken": Contribution to a Hölderlin 100th anniversary memorial volume.

        [C]   Paul Kluckholm (ed.), *Hölderlin. Gedenkschriften zu seinem 100. Todestag* (1943) Tübingen: J.B.C. Mohr, pp. 267-324. *GA* 4 (1981), pp. 79-151.

        [D]   *Elucidations of Hölderlin's Poetry* (2000) Amherst: Humanity Books, pp. 101-173. {R4}

171.   [A]   (A)   "Remembrance of the Poet" (1949) [Douglas Scott].

                (B)   "Homecoming / To Kindred Ones" (2000) [Keith Hoeller].

        [B]   "Heimkunft / An die Verwandten": Lecture given at the University of Freiburg on June 6, 1943, on the 100th anniversary of the death of Friedrich Hölderlin.

        [C]   *Erläuterungen zu Hölderlins Dichtung* (1944): *GA* 4 (1981), pp. 9-31.

[D]   (A)   *Existence and Being* (1949) Washington: Regnery Gateway, 1988, pp. 232-269.

       (B)   *Elucidations of Hölderlin's Poetry* (2000) Amherst: Humanity Books, pp. 23-49. {R5}

172. [A]   (A)   "Review of Ernst Cassirer's *Mythical Thought*" (1976) [James G. Hart and John C. Maraldo].

       (B)   "Ernst Cassirer: Philosophy of Symbolic Forms. Part Two: Mythical Thought. Berlin, 1925" (1997) [Peter Warnek].

  [B]   "Besprechung: Ernst Cassirers *Philosophie der symbolischen Formen. 2. Teil: Das mythische Denken* [1925]": Book review published in 1928.

  [C]   *Deutsche Literaturzeitung* (Berlin) 21, 1928, pp. 1000-1012. Reprinted in *Kant und das Problem der Metaphysik* (4th ed., 1973). *GA* 3 (1991), pp. 255-270.

  [D]   (A)   *The Piety of Thinking* (1976) Bloomington: Indiana University Press, pp. 32-45.

       (B)   *Kant and the Problem of Metaphysics* (1997) Bloomington: Indiana University Press, pp. 180-190 (based on the 5th expanded edition of Heidegger's text). {R6}

173. [A]   *Schelling's Treatise on the Essence of Human Freedom* (1985) [Joan Stambaugh].

  [B]   "Schellings Abhandlung über das Wesen der menschlichen Freiheit": Lecture course given during the Summer Semester 1936, University of Freiburg, with excerpts from the manuscripts of an advanced seminar on Schelling (Summer Semester 1941) (pp. 165-189) and selected seminar notes on Schelling from the years 1941 to 1943 (pp. 189-194).

  [C]   *Schellings Abhandlung über das Wesen der menschlichen Freiheit* (1971) Tübingen: Niemeyer. *GA* 42 (1988). The seminar material has been published in *GA* 49 (1991).

  [D]   *Schelling's Treatise on the Essence of Human Freedom* (1985) Athens: Ohio University Press. {S1}

174. [A]   "Science and Reflection" (1977) [William Lovitt].

[B]   "Wissenschaft und Besinnung": Lecture first given May 15,
       1953, at a conference held by the Arbeitsgemeinschaft
       Wissenschaftlicher near Freiburg. Revised for presentation on
       August 4, 1953, to a small group.

[C]   *Börsenblatt für den Deutschen Buchhandel* (Frankfurt) 10
       (29), 1954, pp. 321-330 (original version). Reprinted in
       Vorträge und Aufsätze I (1954) Pfullingen: Neske, 1978, pp.
       37-62 (revised version). *GA* 7 (2000), pp. 37-65.

[D]   *The Question Concerning Technology and Other Essays*
       (1977) New York: Harper and Row, 1982, pp. 155-182. {S2}

175.   [A]   "Sketches for a History of Being as Metaphysics" (1973)
              [Joan Stambaugh].

       [B]   "Entwürfe zur Geschichte des Seins als Metaphysik": Notes
              on Nietzsche written in 1941.

       [C]   *Nietzsche* II (1961) Pfullingen: Neske, pp. 458-480 [Part IX].
              GA 6.2 (1997), pp. 417-438.

       [D]   *The End of Philosophy* (1973) New York: Harper and Row,
              pp. 55-74. {S3}

176.   [A]   *Sojourns. The Journey to Greece* (2005) [John Panteleimon
              Manoussakis].

       [B]   Text written in Greece, 1962.

       [C]   *Aufenthalte* (1989) Frankfurt: Klostermann.

       [D]   *Sojourns. The Journey to Greece* (2005) Albany: SUNY
              Press. {S4}

177.   [A]   "Summary of a Seminar on the Lecture 'Time and Being'"
              (1972) [Joan Stambaugh].

       [B]   "Seminar Protokoll zu Heideggers Vorlesung 'Zeit und Sein'":
              Transcript of a six-session seminar given September 11-13,
              1962, in Todtnauberg, on the lecture "On Time and Being"
              (see (T5)), written by Alfredo Guzzoni and edited by
              Heidegger.

       [C]   *Zur Sache des Denkens* (1969) Tübingen: Niemeyer, pp. 27-
              58. *GA* 14 (2007) 31-64.

       [D]   *On Time and Being* (1972) New York: Harper and Row, 1978,
              pp. 25-54. {S5}

178. [A] "The Teacher Meets the Tower Warden at the Door to the
           Tower Stairway" (2010) [Bret W. Davis].
      [B] "Die Lehrer trifft den Türmer an der Tür zum Turmaufgang":
           Dialogue written in 1944-45.
      [C] *GA* 77 (1995), pp. 161-202.
      [D] *Country Path Conversations* (2010) Bloomington: Indiana
           University Press, pp. 105-131. {T8}

179. [A] (A) ^"The Thing" (1971) [Albert Hofstadter].
           (B) "Bremen Lectures. *Insight into That Which Is*: "The
                Indication" and "The Thing" (2009) [Jerome Veith].
           (C) "The Thing" (2012) [Andrew J. Mitchell].
      [B] "Das Ding": First of four lectures in the series "Einblick in das
           was ist," originally given December 1, 1949, Bremen Club.
           The first seven seven paragraphs of the lecture were given a
           separate heading in the 1950 manuscript version as "Der
           Hinweis" (published in (B) as "The Indication" and in (C) as
           "The Point of Reference").
      [C] *Gestalt und Gedanke* (Munich) 1, 1951, pp. 128-148.
           Reprinted with an epilogue written June 18, 1950, "A Letter to
           a Young Student [Hartmut Buchner]," in *Vorträge und
           Aufsätze* II (1954) Pfullingen: Neske, 1978, pp. 37-59. *GA* 7
           (2000), pp. 165-187. The lecture, an "Anhang," and a
           "Nachtrag" appear in *GA* 79 (1994), pp. 5-23. The letter is
           omitted (see *GA* 7 [2000], pp. 184-187).
      [D] (A) *Poetry, Language, Thought* (1971) New York:
                Harper and Row, 1975, pp. 165-186. Includes the
                letter. A CD version (2005) for the blind is available.
           (B) Günther Figal (ed.), *The Heidegger Reader* (2009)
                New Haven: Yale University Press, pp. 253-267.
                Omits the letter, marginalia, "Anhang" and
                "Nachtrag."
           (C) *Bremen and Freiburg Lectures* (2012) Bloomington:
                Indiana University Press, pp. 3-20. Omits the letter
                but contains marginalia, Heidegger's "Anhang" (pp.
                21-22), and "Nachtrag" (p. 10, n. 1). {T1}

180. [A] ^"The Thinker as Poet" (1971) [Albert Hofstadter].

[B]   "Aus der Erfahrung des Denkens": Text written during 1947.

[C]   Privately printed on the occasion of the 25th anniversary of
        the construction of the Todtnauberg retreat, the text was
        published as *Aus der Erfahrung des Denkens* (1954)
        Pfullingen: Neske. *GA* 13 (1983), pp. 75-86.

[D]   *Poetry, Language, Thought* (1971) New York: Harper and
        Row, 1975, pp. 1-14. Reprinted in Manfred Stassen (ed.),
        Martin Heidegger. Philosophical and Political Essays (2003)
        New York: Continuum, pp. 19-23. A CD version (2005) for
        the blind is available. {T2}

181.   [A]   "Thoughts" (1976) [Keith Hoeller].

        [B]   "Gedachtes. Für René Char in freundschaftlichen Gedenken ":
                Five poems written in 1970: "Zeit," "Wege," "Winke,"
                "Ortschaft," "Cézanne," "Vorspiel," "Dank".

        [C]   Dominique Fourcade (ed.), *Hommage à René Char* (1971)
                Paris: Edition de L'Herne, pp. 169-187. Reprinted in *GA* 13
                (1983), pp. 221-224, and in *GA* 81 (2007), pp. 325-328. (See
                {C12} for the last of several version of the poem.)

        [D]   * *Philosophy Today* (Celina) 20 (4), 1976, pp. 286-290. {T3}

182.   [A]   "Time and Being" (1972) [Joan Stambaugh].

        [B]   ^"Zeit und Sein": Lecture given January 31, 1962, at the
                University of Freiburg.

        [C]   *L'Endurance de la Pensée. Festschrift für Jean Beaufret*
                (1968) Paris: Plon, pp. 12-71. Reprinted in *Zur Sache des
                Denkens* (1969) Tübingen: Niemeyer, pp. 1-25. *GA* 14 (2007),
                pp. 3-30. Available on CD: *Von der Sache des Denkens.
                Vorträge, Reden und Gespräche* (Munich: Der Hörverlag,
                2000).

        [D]   *On Time and Being* (1972) New York: Harper and Row, 1978,
                pp. 1-24. {T5}

183.   [A]   "Traditional Language and Technological Language" (1998)
                [Wanda Torres Gregory].

        [B]   "Überlieferte Sprache und Technische Sprache": Lecture
                given July 18, 1962, Comburg (Schwäbische Hall).

[C]   *Überlieferte Sprache und Technische Sprache* (1989) St. Gallen: Erker Verlag.

[D]   "Traditional Language and Technological Language," in *Journal of Philosophical Research* (Notre Dame) 23, 1998, pp. 129-145. {T6}

184. [A]   (A)   "The Turning" (1971) [Kenneth R. Maly].
            (B)   "The Turning" (1977) [William Lovitt].
            (C)   "The Turn" (2012) [Andrew W. Mitchell].

      [B]   "Die Kehre": The last of four lectures in the series "Einblick in das was ist," originally given December 1, 1949, at the Bremen Club.

      [C]   *Die Technik und die Kehre* (1962) Pfullingen: Neske, pp. 37-47. *GA* 79 (1994), pp. 68-77.

      [D]   (A)   *Research in Phenomenology* (Pittsburgh) 1, 1971, pp. 3-16.

            (B)   *The Question Concerning Technology and Other Essays* (1977) New York: Harper and Row, 1982, pp. 36-49.

            (C)   *Bremen and Freiburg Lectures* (2012) Bloomington: IndianaUniversity Press, pp. 44-63. Contains marginalia from *GA* 79 (1994). {T7}

185. [A]   "The Understanding of Time in Phenomenology and in the Thinking of the Being-Question" (1979) [Thomas Sheehan and Frederick Elliston].

      [B]   "Über das Zeitverständnis in der Phänomenologie und im Denken der Seinsfrage": Essay written in 1968 in commemoration of the 30th anniversary of the death of Edmund Husserl.

      [C]   Helmut Gehrig (ed.), *Phänomenologie — lebendig oder tot?* (1969) Karlsruhe: Badenia, p. 47. *GA* 14 (2007), pp. 145-149.

      [D]   *The Southwestern Journal of Philosophy* (Norman) 10 (2), 1979, pp. 199-201. {U1}

186. [A]   "Vita, with Accompanying Letter to Georg Misch" (2007) [Theodore Kisiel].

      [B]   Handwritten text, dated June 30, 1922.

[C]   Vita only in *GA* 16 (2000), pp. 41-45
[D]   Theodore Kisiel and Thomas Sheehan (eds.), *Becoming Heidegger. On the Trail of His Early Occasional Writings, 1910-1927* (2007) Evanston: Northwestern University Press, pp. 104-109 (letter, pp. 104-106; vita: pp. 106-109). {V1}

187.   [A]   "The Want of Holy Names" (1985) [Bernhard Radloff].
       [B]   "Der Fehl heiliger Namen": Essay written in 1974, dedicated to Hugo Friedrich.
       [C]   *Contre Toute Attente* (St. Julien du Sault) 2/3, 1981, pp. 40-55 (with a French translation by Roger Munier and Philippe Lacoue-Labarthe). *GA* 13 (1983), pp. 231-235.
       [D]   *Man and World* (Dordrecht) 18, 1985, pp. 261-267. {W1}

188.   [A]   "The War-Triduum in Messkirch" (2007) [Theodore Kisiel]
       [B]   "Das Kriegstriduum in Meßkirch": Newspaper article.
       [C]   *Heuberger Volksblatt* (Meßkirch) 17, January 13, 1915.
       [D]   Theodore Kisiel and Thomas Sheehan (eds.), *Becoming Heidegger. On the Trail of His Early Occasional Writings, 1910-1927* (2007) Evanston: Northwestern University Press, pp. 47-50. {W16}

189.   [A]   (A)   "The Way Back into the Ground of Metaphysics": Introduction [1949] to "What Is Metaphysics?" (1956) [Walter Kaufmann].
              (B)   "Introduction to 'What Is Metaphysics?'" (1998) [William McNeill].
       [B]   "Einleitung zu `Was ist Metaphysik?'. Der Rückgang in den Grund der Metaphysik": Introductory essay for the inaugural lecture (1929), written for the 5th edition (1949) of the lecture (see {W6}).
       [C]   *Was ist Metaphysik?* (1929) Frankfurt: Klostermann, pp. 7-23. Reprinted in *Wegmarken* (1967): *GA* 9 (1976), pp. 365-383.
       [D]   (A)   Walter Kaufmann (ed.), *Existentialism from Dostoevsky to Sartre* (1956; rev. ed., 1975) New York: New American Library, 1984, pp. 265-279 (beginning with the revised edition). Reprinted in William Barrett and Henry D. Aiken (eds.),

Philosophy in the Twentieth Century. An Anthology (1962) New York: Random House, 1982, Vol. 3, pp. 206-218. Excerpt of Kaufman edition (pp. 211-212), reprinted in Richard Ellmann and Charles Feidelson (eds.), *The Modern Tradition. Backgrounds of Modern Literature* (New York: Oxford University Press, 1965), pp. 879-880.

(B)   *Pathmarks* (1998) Cambridge: Cambridge University Press, pp. 277-290. {W2}

190.   [A]   (A)   "The Way to Language" (1971) [Peter D. Hertz].
              (B)   "The Way to Language" (1993) [David Farrell Krell].
       [B]   "Der Weg zur Sprache": Essay based on a lecture first given on January 23, 1959. Original title "Die Sprache."
       [C]   *Gestalt und Gedanke* (Munich) 4, 1959, pp. 137-170. Reprinted with a few changes in *Unterwegs zur Sprache* (1959): *GA* 12 (1985), pp. 227-257.
       [D]   (A)   *On the Way to Language* (1971) New York: Harper and Row, 1982, pp. 111-136.
              (B)   *Basic Writings* (1977; rev. ed., 1993) San Francisco: HarperSanFrancisco, pp. 397-426 (rev. ed.). {W3}

191.   [A]   (A)   ^"What Are Poets For?" (1971) [Albert Hofstadter].
              (B)   "Why Poets?" (2002) [Kenneth Haynes].
       [B]   "Wozu Dichter?": Lecture given December 29, 1946, in remembrance of the 20th anniversary of the death of Rainer Maria Rilke
       [C]   *Holzwege* (1950): *GA* 5 (1977), pp. 269-320
       [D]   (A)   Poetry, Language, Thought (1971) New York: Harper and Row, 1975, pp. 91-142. A CD verison (2005) for the blind is available.
              (B)   Off the Beaten Track (2002) Cambridge: Cambridge University Press, pp. 200-241. {W4}

192.   [A]   *What Is Called Thinking?* (1968) [Fred D. Wieck and J. Glenn Gray].

[B] ^"Was heißt Denken?": Lecture course given during the Winter Semester 1951-52 and Summer Semester 1952, University of Freiburg.

[C] *Was heißt Denken?* (1954) Tübingen: Niemeyer. *GA* 8 (2002). In May 1952, Bavarian Radio broadcast Heidegger's reading of an address entitled "Was heißt Denken?" which contained material that had served as the basis of the opening lectures of the course and some that was not presented (see *GA* 8 [2002], pp. 5-23 and 253 ff.). The address appeared in *Merkur* (Berlin) 6, 1952, pp. 601-611. *GA* 7 (2000), pp. 127-143. Available on CD: *Von der Sache des Denkens. Vorträge, Reden und Gespräche* (Munich: Der Hörverlag, 2000), 1(2).

[D] *What Is Called Thinking?* (1968) New York: Harper and Row, 1976. Excerpts reprinted in Richard Zaner and Don Ihde (eds.), *Phenomenology and Existentialism* (1977) New York: G.P. Putnam, pp. 326-332 [Part II, Lecture V] and *Basic Writings* (1977; rev. ed., 1993) San Francisco: HarperSanFrancisco, pp. 369-391(rev. ed.) [Part I, Lecture I; Part II, Lecture II, excluding the "Summary and Transition," under the title "What Calls for Thinking?"]. Part II, Summary and Transition of Lectures I, III, and IX and excerpt from Lecture XI (pp. 122-25, 143-47, 214-15, 244) reprinted in Manfred Stassen (ed.), *Martin Heidegger. Philosophical and Political Essays* (2003) New York: Continuum, pp. 80-86. {W5}

193. [A] (A) "What Is Metaphysics?" (1949) [R.F.C. Hull and Alan Crick].

    (B) "What Is Metaphysics?" (1977) [David Farrell Krell].

    (C) "What Is Metaphysics?" (1998) [William McNeill and David Farrell Krell].

    (D) "Martin Heidegger's Inaugural Lecture at Freiburg University. A Reading of Heidegger's 'What Is Metaphysics?'" (2001) [Thomas Sheehan].

  [B] ^"Was ist Metaphysik?": Heidegger's inaugural lecture to the faculties of the University of Freiburg, given on July 24, 1929. The text was expanded for the Fourth Edition (1943) of the work with the addition of a "Nachwort" (see {P13}). The

"Nachwort" was revised and an introduction, "Einleitung. Der Rückgang in der Grund der Metaphysik," was added for the Fifth Edition (1949) (see. See {W2}).

[C]   *Was ist Metaphysik?* (1929) Frankfurt: Klostermann. Reprinted in *Wegmarken* (1967): *GA* 9 (1976), pp. 103-122. A sound book (Klostermann, 1981) is available.

[D]   (A)   *Existence and Being* (1949) Washington: Regnery Gateway, 1988, pp. 325-349. Reprinted in James L. Jarrett and Sterling M. McMurrin (eds), *Contemporary Philosophy* (1954) New York: Holt, Rinehart and Winston, pp. 448-458. Reprinted in Walter Kaufmann (ed.), *Existentialism from Dostoevsky to Sartre* (1956; rev. ed., 1975) New York: New American Library, 1984, pp. 242-264 (beginning with the revised edition). Reprinted in *Twentieth Century Philosophy and Religion* [Great Books of the Western World, Vol. 55, ed. Mortimer Adler] (2nd ed., 1990) Chicago: Encyclopedia Britannica, Inc., pp. 296-310. Reprinted with "footnotes deleted and postscript omitted" in Diane Barsoum Raymond (ed.), *Existentialism and the Philosophical Tradition* (1991) Englewood Cliffs: Prentice-Hall, pp. 251-264.

        (B)   *Basic Writings* (1977; rev. ed., 1993) San Francisco: HarperSanFrancisco, pp. 93-110 (rev. ed.).

        (C)   *Pathmarks* (1998) Cambridge: Cambridge University Press, pp. 82-96.

        (D)   *The New Yearbook for Phenomenology and Phenomenological Research* (Seattle) 1, 2001, pp. 181-201. A translation of the first edition (1929) text, with textual differences compared to (C) and Heidegger's marginal notes to the several editions of the work. {W6}

194.   [A]   (A)   *What Is Philosophy?* (1958) [William Kluback and Jean T. Wilde].

        (B)   "Philosophy--What Is It?" (1962) [Jean T. Wilde and William Kimmel].

(C)   *What Is That--Philosophy?* (1991) [Eva T.H. Brann].

[B]   "Was ist das -- die Philosophie?": Lecture given in Cérisy-la-Salle in August 1955.

[C]   *Was ist das -- die Philosophie?* (1956) Pfullingen: Neske. *GA* 11 (2006), pp. 3-26

[D]   (A)   * *What Is Philosophy?* (1958) New York: Twayne, 1989.

(B)   Jean T. Wilde and William Kimmel (eds.), *The Search for Being* (1962) New York: Twayne, pp. 493-507 (revised excerpt [pp. 41-97] of (A)).

(C)   *What Is That--Philosophy?* (1991) Annapolis: St. John's College. {W7}

195.   [A]   *What Is a Thing?* (1967) [W.B. Barton, Jr. and Vera Deutsch].

[B]   "Grundfragen der Metaphysik": Lecture course given during the Winter Semester 1935-36, University of Freiburg.

[C]   *Die Frage nach dem Ding. Zu Kants Lehre von der transzendentalen Grundsätzen* (1962) Tübingen: Niemeyer. *GA* 41 (1984).

[D]   *What Is a Thing?* (1967) Washington: Regnery Gateway, 1985. A slightly modified translation of Section B 5 (a-f$_3$) (pp. 66-108), "The Characteristics of Modern Science in Contrast to Ancient and Medieval Science," is reprinted in *Basic Writings* (1977; rev. ed., 1993) San Francisco: HarperSanFrancisco, pp. 271-305 (rev. ed.), under the title "Modern Science, Metaphysics, and Mathematics."{W8}

196.   [A]   (A)   "Who Is Nietzsche's Zarathustra?" (1967) [Bernd Magnus].

(B)   "Who Is Nietzsche's Zarathustra?" (1984) [David Farrell Krell].

[B]   "Wer ist Nietzsches Zarathustra?": Lecture given May 8, 1953, at the Bremen Club.

[C]   *Vorträge und Aufsätze* I (1954) Pfullingen: Neske, 1978, pp. 93-118. *GA* 7 (2000), pp. 99-124.

[D]   (A)   *The Review of Metaphysics* (Washington) 20, 1967, pp. 411-431. Reprinted in David B. Allison (ed.), *The New Nietzsche: Contemporary Styles of*

Interpretation (1977) New York: Dell Publishing Company, 1985, pp. 64-79.

(B) *Nietzsche*, Volume II: *The Eternal Recurrence of the Same* (1984) New York: Harper and Row, pp. 211-233 [Part Two]. The HarperCollins paperback reprint (1991) of all four volumes of *Nietzsche* combines Volumes I and II. An audio (CD) version of all volumes of *Nietzsche* in this translation series is available. {W9}

197. [A] (A) "Why Do I Stay in the Provinces?" (1977) [Thomas Sheehan].

(B) "Creative Lanscape: Why Do We Stay in the Provinces? (1994) [Thomas Sheehan].

[B] "Schöpferische Landschaft: Warum bleiben wir in der Provinz?": Essay written in the fall of 1933.

[C] *Der Alemanne* (Freiburg), March 7, 1934, p. 1. *GA* 13 (1983), pp. 9-13.

[D] (A) *Listening* (Dubuque) 12 (3), 1977, pp. 122-124. Reprinted in Thomas Sheehan (ed.), *Heidegger. The Man and the Thinker* (1981) Chicago: Precedent Publishing Company, pp. 27-30, and in Manfred Stassen (ed.), *Martin Heidegger. Philosophical and Political Essays* (2003) New York: Continuum, pp. 16-18.

(B) *Vice Versa* (Montreal) 43 (1993), pp. 35-36, as "Why Do I Remain in the Provinces?" Reprinted in Anton Kaes, Martin Jay and Edward Dimendberg (eds.), *The Weimar Republic Sourcebook* (1994) Berkeley: University of California Press, pp. 426-428. {W10}

198. [A] (A) "Wilhelm Dilthey's Research and the Struggle for a Historical Worldview"(2002) [Charles Bambach].

(B) "Wilhelm Dilthey's Research and the Current Struggle for a Historical Worldview" (2007) [Theodore Kisiel].

[B]   "Wilhelm Diltheys Forschungsarbeit und der Kampf um eine
         historische Weltanschauung": Walter Bröcker's transcript of a
         lecture series given April 16-21, 1925, in Kassel.

[C]   Frithjof Rodi, "Wilhelm Diltheys Forschungsarbeit und der
         Kampf um eine historische Weltanschauung," in *Dilthey-
         Jahrbuch* 8, 1992-93, pp. 123-30, 143-180. (Cf. *GA* 16 [2000],
         pp. 49-51.)

[D]   (A)   *Supplements. From the Earliest Essays to* Being and
                 Time *and Beyond* (2002) Albany: SUNY Press, pp.
                 147-176.

         (B)   Theodore Kisiel and Thomas Sheehan (eds.),
                 *Becoming Heidegger. On the Trail of His Early
                 Occasional Writings, 1910-1927* (2007) Evanston:
                 Northwestern University Press, pp. 241-274 (excerpt,
                 translating [C] pp. 143-180). {W11}

199.   [A]   (A)   "The Will to Power as Art. First Section: 'Nietzsche
                        as Metaphysical Thinker'" (1973) [Joan Stambaugh].

                (B)   "The Will to Power as Art" (1979) [David Farrell
                        Krell].

       [B]   "Nietzsche: Der Wille zur Macht als Kunst": Heidegger's first
                lecture course on Nietzsche, given during the Winter Semester
                1936-37, University of Freiburg. First Section: "Nietzsche als
                metaphysicher Denker."

       [C]   *Nietzsche* I (1961) Pfullingen: Neske, pp. 11-254 [Part I], First
                Section, pp. 11-15. A substantially revised version of the text
                has been published in *GA* 43 (1985), pp. 3-7. *Nietzsche* I and
                II (1961) reprinted as *GA* 6.1 (1996) and *GA* 6.2 (1997).

       [D]   (A)   Robert C. Solomon (ed.), *Nietzsche. A Collection of
                        Critical Essays* (1973) New York: Doubleday, pp.
                        105-108.

                (B)   *Nietzsche*, Volume I: *The Will to Power as Art*
                        (1979) New York: Harper and Row. The
                        HarperCollins paperback reprint (1991) of all four
                        volumes of *Nietzsche* combines Volumes I and II.
                        Section 15, "Kant's Doctrine of the Beautiful: Its
                        Misinterpretation by Schopenhauer and Nietzsche"
                        (*GA* 6.1 [1997], pp. 106-114), was reprinted in Peter

Sedgwick (ed.), *Nietzsche. A Critical Reader* (1995) Oxford: Blackwell, pp. 104-110. An audio (CD) version of all volumes of *Nietzsche* in this translation series is available. {W12}

200.   [A]   "The Will to Power as Knowledge" (1987) [Joan Stambaugh].
        [B]   "Nietzsches Lehre vom Willen zur Macht als Erkenntnis": Heidegger's third lecture course on Nietzsche, given during the Summer Semester 1939 at the University of Freiburg.
        [C]   *Nietzsche* I (1961) Pfullingen: Neske, pp. 473-658 [Part III]. A substantially revised version of the text has been published as *Nietzsches Lehre vom Willen zur Macht als Erkenntnis*: *GA* 47 (1989). *Nietzsche* I and II (1961) reprinted as *GA* 6.1 (1996) and *GA* 6.2 (1997).
        [D]   *Nietzsche*, Volume III: *The Will to Power as Knowledge and as Metaphysics* (1987) New York: Harper and Row, pp. 1-158 [Part One]. The translation was somewhat modified by David Farrell Krell, the editor of *Nietzsche* (p. viii). The first section of this text, "Nietzsche als Denker der Vollendung der Metaphysik" (*Nietzsche* I [1961], pp. 473-481), was published in a translation by Joan Stambaugh, in 1973, under the title "Nietzsche as Metaphysician," in Robert C. Solomon (ed.), *Nietzsche* (1973) New York: Doubleday, pp. 108-113. The HarperCollins paperback reprint (1991) of all four volumes of *Nietzsche* combines Volumes III and IV. An audio (CD) version of all volumes of *Nietzsche* in this translation series is available. {W13}

201.   [A]   (A)   "The Word of Nietzsche: 'God Is Dead'" (1977) [William Lovitt].
               (B)   "Nietzsche's Word: 'God Is Dead'" (2002) [KennethHaynes].
        [B]   "Nietzsches Wort 'Gott ist tot'": Lecture written in 1943, based on the Nietzsche courses (1936-40) at the University of Freiburg.
        [C]   *Holzwege* (1950): *GA* 5 (1977), pp. 209-267.

[D]   (A)   *The Question Concerning Technology and Other Essays* (1977) New York: Harper and Row, 1982, pp. 53-112.

        (B)   *Off the Beaten Track* (2002) Cambridge: Cambridge University Press, pp. 157-199. {W14}

202.   [A]   "Words" (1971) [Peter D. Hertz].

        [B]   "Dichten und Denken. Zu Stefan Georges Gedicht `Das Wort'' ": Lecture given May 11, 1958 in Vienna. Revised title: "Das Wort."

        [C]   *Unterwegs zur Sprache* (1959): *GA* 12 (1985), pp. 205-225.

        [D]   *On the Way to Language* (1971) New York: Harper and Row, 1982, pp. 139-156. {W15}

203.   [A]   (A)   *Zollikon Seminars. Protocols – Seminars - Letters* (2001) [Franz Mayr and Richard Askay].

                (B)   "Martin Heidegger's Zollikon Seminars" (1978-79) [Brian Kenny].

                (C)   "On Adequate Understanding of Daseinsanalysis" and "Marginalia an Phenomenology, Transcendence and Care" (1988) [Michael Eldred].

        [B]   (A)   *Zollikoner Seminare. Protokolle - Zwiegespräche - Briefe*: Texts from 1947-1971 (edited by Medard Boss), includes records of seminars for medical students and residents in psychiatry from the University of Zurich Psychiatric Clinic, and conversations with and letters from Heidegger.

                (B)   Excerpts from the protocol of Heidegger's seminar on January 26, 1961. Includes Heidegger's marginalia toBoss's *Grundriß der Medizin: Ansätze zu einer phänomenologischen Physiologie, Psychologie, Therapie und zu phänomenologischen Physiologie, Psychologie, Therapie und zu einer daseinsgemäßen Präventiv-Medizin in der modernen Industriegesellschaft*, by Medard Boss (1971) Bern: Huber, and translated as *Existential Foundations of Medicine and Psychology* (1979) New York: Jason Aronson.

(C)   "Protokollen - Gespräche": Excerpts from seminars
           of March 8, 1965; November 23, 1965; November
           28-30, 1965; July 14, 1969.

[C]   (A)   *Zollikoner Seminare. Protokolle—Gespräche—Briefe*
              (1987) Frankfurt: Klostermann, 1994.

       (B)   The quoted protocol is summarized in [C](A),
              pp. 8-9.

       (C)   [C] (A): pp. 150-152, 157, 236-238, 238-242, 253,
              254-256, 259, 286-287.

[D]   (A)   *Zollikon Seminars. Protocols, Seminars, Letters*
              (2001) Evanston: Northwestern University Press,
              2001.

       (B)   *Review of Existential Psychology and Psychiatry*
              (Pittsburgh) 16 (1-3), 1978-79, pp. 7-20. Reprinted in
              Keith Hoeller (ed.), *Heidegger and Psychology*
              (1988) Seattle: Review of Existential Psychology and
              Psychiatry, pp. 7-20.

       (C)   *The Humanistic Psychologist* (Carrollton) 16(1),
              1988, pp. 75-98 and 218-223. The excerpts
              correspond to pp. 115-116, 120-121, 188-191, 203,
              204-205, 205-206, 207, 227-228 and 191-194 of the
              complete work. {Z1}

C. SUPPLEMENTAL BIBLIOGRAPHY: HEIDEGGER AND POLITICS

204. [A]   (A)   "Documents from the Denazification Proceedings
                    Concerning Martin Heidegger" (1991) [Jason M.
                    Wirth].
              (B)   "Letter to the Rector of Freiburg University,
                    November 4, 1945" (1991) [Richard Wolin].
       [B]   Letters, written November 4, 1945, and December 15, 1945,
              following Heidegger's appearance before the denazification
              committee.
       [C]   Letter of November 4, 1945: Karl Augustus Moehling, *Martin
              Heidegger and the Nazi Party: An Examination* (Ph.D.
              dissertation, Northern Illinois University, 1972), Appendix B,
              pp. 264-268; letter of December 15, 1945: *Archiv für
              Christlich-Demokratische Politik* (St. Augustin). Reprinted in
              GA 16 (2000), pp. 397-404 and 409-415 (as "Antrag auf die
              Wiederstellung in die Lehrtätigkeit (Reintegrierung)" and
              "Erläuterungen und Grundsätzliches").
       [D]   (A)   * *Graduate Faculty Philosophy Journal* (New York)
                    14 (2)-15 (1), 1991, pp. 535-556. (Contains letters of
                    November 4, 1945, and December 15, 1945.)
              (B)   Richard Wolin (ed.), *The Heidegger Controversy*
                    (1991) Cambridge: MIT Press, 1993, pp. 61-66.
                    (Contains only letter of November 4, 1945.) {S-D1}

205. [A]   "The Jewish Contamination of German Spiritual Life–Letter
              to Victor Schwoerer" (2003) [Manfred Stassen].
       [B]   "Brief an Victor Schwoerer vom 02.10.1929": Letter to deputy
              secretary general of the *Notgemeinshcaft der deutschen
              Wissenschaft,* Victor Schwoerer.
       [C]   Ulrich Sieg, "Die Verjudung des deutschen Geistes," in *Die
              Zeit,* #52, December 22, 1989, p. 50.
       [D]   Manfred Stassen (ed.), *Martin Heidegger. Philosophical and
              Political Essays* (2003) New York: Continuum, p. 1. {S-J1}

206. [A]   Letter to Carl Schmitt (1987) [NN].
       [B]   Letter, dated August 22, 1933, Freiburg im Bresigau.

[C]   "Heidegger and Schmitt: The Bottom Line," in *Telos* , #72, Summer 1987, p. 132 (n. **). *GA* 16 (2000), p. 156 (as "Hier ist es lleider sehr trostlos (22. August 1933)").

[D]   * [C] p. 132. {S-L1}

207.   [A]   *Nature, History, State 1933-1934* (2013) [Gregory Fried and Richard Polt].

[B]   "Über Wesen und Begriff von Natur, Geschichte und Staat": Übung aus dem Wintersemester 1933/34": Selections from students' notes, seminar series, November 3, 1933 - February 23, 1934, University of Freiburg (reviewd by Heidegger).

[C]   Alfred Denker and Holgar Zaborowski (eds.), *Heidegger-Jahrbuch: Heidegger und der Nationalsozialismus I, Dokmente* 4 (Freiburg im Breisgau: Alber, 2009), 53-88.

[D]   *Nature, History, State 1933-1934* (London: Bloomsbury, 2013), 13-64 {S-N1}

208.   [A]   *On Hegel's Philosophy of Right* (2014) [Andrew J. Mitchell]

[B]   "Hegel 'Rechtsphilosophie' WS 1934/35": Seminar notes.

[C]   *GA* 86 (2011), pp. 55-184.

[D]   *On Hegel's Philosophy of Right* (2014) New York: Bloomsburg Academic,101-195. {S-O2}

209.   [A]   "On My Relation to National Socialism" (1982) [Frank Meklenberg].

[B]   "Brief an *Münchner Süddeutschen Zeitung*: Letter of June 24, 1950, in response to a newspaper article "Hanfstaengel contra Heidegger" published June 14, 1950.

[C]   *Münchner Süddeutschen Zeitung* (Munich), June 24, 1950. *GA* 16 (2000), pp. 452-53 (as "Betr. die Notiz 'Hanfstaengl contra Heidegger' in der Müncher Süddeutschen Zeitung vom Mittwoch, den 14. Juni 1950").

[D]   *Semiotext(e)* (New York) 4 (2), 1982, pp. 253-54. {S-O1}

210.   [A]   (A)   "The Rectorate 1933/34: Facts and Thoughts" (1985) [Karsten Harries].

        (B)   "The Rectorate 1933/34: Facts and Thoughts" (1990) [Lisa Harries].

[B]   "Das Rektorat 1933/34. Tatsachen und Gedanken (1945)":
         Essay written in 1945.

[C]   Hermann Heidegger (ed.), *Die Selbstbehauptung der*
         deutschen Universität / Das Rektorat 1933/34. Tatsachen und
         Gedanken (1983) Frankfurt: Klostermann, pp. 21-43. *GA* 16
         (2000), pp. 372-394.

[D]   (A)   *The Review of Metaphysics* (Washington) 38, 1985,
                  pp. 481-502.

         (B)   Günther Neske and Emil Kettering (eds.), *Martin*
                  Heidegger and National Socialism (1990) New York:
                  Paragon House, pp. 15-32. {S-R1}

211.   [A]   (A)   "The Self-Assertion of the German University:
                          Address, Delivered on the Solemn Assumption of the
                          Rectorate of the University [of] Freiburg" (1985)
                          [Karsten Harries].

                 (B)   "The Self-Assertion of the German University"
                          (1990) [Lisa Harries].

                 (C)   "The Self-Assertion of the German University"
                          (1991) [William S. Lewis].

                 (D)   "Rectorship Address. *The Self-Assertion of the*
                          German University" (2009) [Jerome Veith].

       [B]   "Die Selbstbehauptung der deutschen Universität":
                Heidegger's rectorial address, given May 27, 1933.

       [C]   *Die Selbstbehauptung der deutschen Universität. Rede,*
                gehalten bei der feierlichen Übernahme des Rektorats der
                Universität Freiburg i. Br. am 27.5.1933 (1933) Breslau:
                Korn. Reprinted in Hermann Heidegger (ed.), *Die*
                Selbstbehauptung der deutschen Universität / Das Rektorat
                1933/34. Tatsachen und Gedanken (1983) Frankfurt:
                Klostermann, pp. 9-19. *GA* 16 (2000), pp. 107-117.

       [D]   (A)   *The Review of Metaphysics* (Washington) 38, 1985,
                          pp. 470-480. Reprinted in Manfred Stassen (ed.),
                          Martin Heidegger. Philosophical and Political
                          Essays (2003) New York: Continuum, pp. 2-11.

                 (B)   Günther Neske and Emil Kettering (eds.), *Martin*
                          Heidegger and National Socialism (1990) New York:
                          Paragon House, pp. 5-13.

(C)   Richard Wolin (ed.), *The Heidegger Controversy. A Critical Reader* (1991) Cambridge: MIT Press, 1993, pp. 29-39. A newspaper article (*Freiburger Zeitung* (Freiburg), May 29, 1933, p. 1) reporting on the address was translated in Dagobert Runes (ed.), *German Existentialism* (1965) New York: Philosophical Library, pp. 148-50 (translation by the editor). See {S-S2}.

(D)   Günther Figal (ed.), *The Heidegger Reader* (2009) New Haven: Yale University Press, pp. 108-116. {S-S1}

212.   [A/B]   Speeches and newspaper articles from the period May 27, 1933 to February 1, 1934.

(A)   Dagobert Runes (1965).

(B)   William S. Lewis (1988).

[C]   (1) "Schlageterfeier der Freiburger Universität [University of Freiburg's Schlageter Celebration]," speech [May 26, 1933], in *Der Alemanne* (Freiburg), May 27, 1933, p. 6; (2) "Arbeitsdienst und Universität [Labor Service and the University]," newspaper article, *Freiburger Studentenzeitung*, June 20, 1933, p. 1; (3) "Die Universität im Neuen Reich [The University in the New State]," speech [June 30, 1933], in the *Heidelberger Neueste Nachrichten*, July 1, 1933, p. 4; (4) "Deutschen Studenten [German Students]," newspaper article, *Freiburger Studentenzeitung*, November 3, 1933, p. 1; (5) "Deutsche Männer und Frauen! [German Men and Women!]," newspaper article, *Freiburger Studentenzeitung*, November 10, 1933, p. 1; (6) "Ansprache am 11. November 1933 in Leipzig," speech [November 11, 1933], published in *Bekenntnis der Professoren an den deutschen Universitäten und Hochschulen zu Adolf Hitler und dem nationalsozialistischen Staat. Überreicht vom Nationalsozialistischen Lehrerbund [Pledge of German University Professors and High School Teachers to Adolf Hitler and the National Socialist State. Given by the National Socialist Teachers' Association]* (Dresden), November 11, 1933, pp. 13-14; (7) "Das Geleitwort der Universität

[Prefatory Word from the University]," newspaper article, published in *150 Jahre Freiburger Zeitung* (Freiburg), January 6, 1934, p. 10; (8) "Der Ruf zum Arbeitsdienst [Call to Labor Service]," newspaper article, *Freiburger Studentenzeitung*, January 23, 1934, p. 1; and (9) "Nationalsozialistische Wissensschulung [National Socialist Education]," speech [January 22, 1934], published in *Der Alemanne* (Freiburg), February 1, 1934, p. 9. All reprinted in Guido Schneeberger (ed.), *Nachlese zu Heidegger. Dokumente zu seinem Leben und Denken, mit zwei Bildtafeln* (1962) Bern: Suhr, (1) pp. 47-49, (2) pp. 63-64, (3) pp. 73-75, (4) pp. 135-36, (5) pp. 144-46, (6) pp. 148-50, (7) p. 171, (8) pp. 180-181, and (9) pp. 198-202. *GA* 16 (2000) reprints (1) [pp. 759-760, as "Gedenkworte zu Schlageter (26. Mai 1933 vor der Universität"], (2) [pp. 125-126, as "Arbeitsdienst und Universität"], (3) [pp. 761-762, as "Die Universität im neuen Reich (30. Juni 1933)"], (4) [pp. 184-185, as "Zum Semestergeinn vgl. Universitätsführer Wintersemestere 1933/34"], (5) [pp. 188-189, as "Aufruf zur Wahl (10. November 1933"], (6) [pp. 190-193, as "Ansprache am 11. November 1933 in Leipzig"], (7) [p. 227, as "Das Geleitwort der Universität [150 Jahre "Freiburger Zeitung"]], (8) [pp. 238-239, as "Der Ruf zum Arbeitsdienst"], and (9) [pp. 232-237, as "Zur Eröffnung der Schullungkurse für die Notstandsarbeiter der Stadt an der Universität (22. Januar 1934)"]. {W10}.

[D] (A) *German Existentialism* (1965) New York: Philosophical Library, pp. 21-42. Includes excerpts of six of the texts in [C]: (2)-(4), (6), and (8)-(9); and extracts from twelve newspaper articles reporting on Heidegger. Item (9) reprinted in Manfred Stassen (ed.), *Martin Heidegger. Philosophical and Political Essays* (2003) New York: Continuum, pp. 12-15.

   (B) *New German Critique* (Ithaca) 45, Fall 1988, pp. 96-114. Reprinted in Richard Wolin (ed.), *The Heidegger Controversy. A Critical Reader* (1991) Cambridge: MIT Press, 1993, pp. 40-60. {S-S2}

D. LETTERS

Included here are, first, volumes of collected correspondence followed by entries containing a series of letters to an individual and, finally, single letters to individuals, each set arranged alphabetically by the addresse's name. A number of unpublished letters appear in Heinrich Wiegand Petzet, *Encounters and Dialogues with Martin Heidegger, 1929-1976* (Chicago: University of Chicago Press, 1993), translated by Parvis Emad and Kenneth Maly, and Hugo Ott, *Heidegger. A Political Life* (London: Basic Books, 1993)[1], translated by Allan Blunden. Excerpts from other previously unpublished letters and archival material have been published in the papers of Theodore Kisiel and in his fundamental source for Heidegger scholarship, *The Genesis of Heidegger's Being and Time* (Berkeley: University of California Press, 1993); Thomas Sheehan's paper, "Heidegger's *Lehrjahre*," in John Sallis, G. Moneta and Jacques Taminiaux (eds.), *The Collegium Phaenomenologicum. The First Ten Years* (Dordrecht: Kluwer, 1988), pp. 77-137;[2] Thomas Sheehan and Richard E. Palmer (eds.), *Psychological and Transcendental Phenomenology and the Confrontation with Heidegger (1927-1931)* (Dordrecht: Kluwer, 1997);[3] and Theodore Kisiel and Thomas Sheehan (eds.), *Becoming Heidegger. On the Trail of His Early Occasional Wrirings, 1910-1927* (Evanston: Northwestern University Press, 2007).[4] A number of letters to Medard Boss are published in {Z1}, pp. 235-291.

a. Collections

213.   [A]   *Letters 1925-1975. Hannah Arendt and Martin Heidegger* (2004) [Andrew Shields].

---

[1] Letters to Matthäus Lang, May 30, 1928 (p. 52); Karl Jaspers, July 14, 1923 (p. 183), July 1, 1935 (p. 37), May 16, 1936 (p. 267), April 8, 1950 (p. 24), and February 19, 1953 (p. 36) (all in {H6} (A)); Viktor Schwoerer, October 2, 1929 (p. 378) (see {S-J1}); and Josef Sauer, March 17, 1912 (pp. 70-71). See also pp. 29-30, 77, 95, 157, 195, 214-15, 238, 239, 249 and 333.

[2] See {L12} [D](A).

[3] Includes fragments from letters to Karl Löwith, Karl Jaspers, Georg Misch and Elisabeth Blochmann (pp. 17, 25, 140-142).

[4] See {H6} [D](B), {L12} [D](C), {L18} [D](C), {L20} [D](C)-(D), {L29}.

        [B]   Correspondence between Heidegger and Arendt from
February 10, 1925 to July 30, 1975.
        [C]   Ursula Ludz (ed.), *Hannah Arendt / Martin Heidegger. Briefe
1925 bis 1975* (1998) Frankfurt: Klostermann.
        [D]   *Letters 1925-1975. Hannah Arendt and Martin Heidegger*
(2004) New York: Harcourt. {L23}

214.   [A]   *Letters to His Wife 1915-1970* (2008) [R.D.V. Glasgow].
        [B]   Letters to Elfriede Petri Heidegger.
        [C]   *"Mein liebes Seelchen!" Briefe Martin Heideggers an seine
Frau Elfriede 1915-1970* (2005) München: Deutsche Verlags-
Anstalt.
        [D]   *Letters to His Wife 1915-1970*(2008) Cambridge: Polity Press.
{L28}

215.   [A]   (A)   *The Heidegger-Jaspers Correspondence (1929-1963)*
(2003) [Gary F. Aylesworth].
                    (B)   Letters to Karl Jaspers (2007) [Theodore Kisiel and
Thomas Sheehan].
        [B]   Correspondence between Heidegger and Karl Jaspers.
        [C]   Walter Biemel and Hans Saner (eds.), *Martin Heidegger/Karl
Jaspers Briefwechsel 1920-1963* (1990) Frankfurt:
Klostermann.
        [D]   (A)   *The Heidegger-Jaspers Correspondence (1920-1963)*
(2003) Amherst: Humanity Books.
                    (B)   Theodore Kisiel and Thomas Sheehan (eds.),
*Becoming Heidegger. On the Trail of His Early
Occasional Writings, 1910-1927* (2007) Evanston:
Northwestern University Press, pp. 373 and 378
(letters of July 14, 1923 and May 4, 1926). {H6}

b. Selections

216.   [A]   (A)   "Letters to Elisabeth Blochmann" (1991) [Frank
W.H. Edler].
                    (B)   Excerpt of letters September 12, 1929 and Januaray
19, 1933 (1993) [Allan Blunden].

(C)   May 1, 1919: Martin Heidegger to Elisabeth
         Blochmann (2007) [Theodore Kisiel].

[B]   Letters from the Heidegger-Blochmann
         correspondence, 1919-1933.

[C]   Joachim Storck (ed.), *Martin Heidegger—Elisabeth
         Blochmann. Briefwechsel 1918-1969* (1989) Marbach:
         Deutsche Schillergesellschaft, pp. 31-33 (letter #22), pp. 36-
         39 (letter #25), pp. 45-46 (letter #32), pp. 49-50 (letter #35),
         pp. 52-53 (letter #37), pp. 55-58 (letters #40 and #42), pp. 60-
         63 (letters #46 and #47), pp. 69-70 (letter #57), pp. 73-74
         (letter #61), pp. 76-77 (letter #64).

[D]   (A)   *Graduate Faculty Philosophy Journal* (New York)
                 14 (2) - 15 (1), 1991, pp. 563-577. Excerpts from
                 letters in [C]: #25 (September 20, 1930, Freiburg),
                 #32 (December 20, 1931, Freiburg), #35 (May 25,
                 1932, Freiburg), #37 (June 22, 1932, Freiburg), #40
                 (December 19, 1932, Freiburg), #42 (January 19,
                 1933, Freiburg), #46 (March 30, 1933, Freiburg), #47
                 (April 12, 1933, Freiburg), #57 (August 30, 1933,
                 Todtnauberg retreat), #61 (September 19, 1933,
                 Meßkirch), and #64 (October 16, 1933, Freiburg).

         (B)   Hugo Ott, *Martin Heidegger. A Political Life* (1993)
                 London: Basic Books, pp. 377-78. Letters of
                 September 12, 1929 and January 19, 1933 (letters
                 #22 and #42 in [C]).

         (C)   Theodore Kisiel and Thomas Sheehan (eds.),
                 *Becoming Heidegger. On the Trail of His Early
                 Occasional Writings, 1910-1927* (2007) Evanston:
                 Northwestern University Press, p. 366 (excerpt of
                 letter of May 1, 1919, [C], p. 16). {L18}

217. [A]   Letters to Karl Löwith.
         (A)   (1970) [R. Philip O'Hara].
         (B)   (a)   (1988) [Richard Wolin and Melissa J. Fox].
                 (b)   (1994) [Elizabeth King].
         (C)   (1995) [Gary Steiner].
         (D)   (2007) [Theodore Kisiel].

[B] (A)   "Auszüge aus Briefen Heideggers an Karl Löwith
           1921-29": Letters dated August 19, 1921; March 26,
           1924; August 21, 1924; June 30, 1925; August 20,
           1927; February 3, 1929; September 3, 1929.
     (B)   Five brief excerpts from (A).
     (C)   Letter of August 19, 1921.
     (D)   Letters dated October 20, 1920; August 19, 1921;
           February 20, 1923; May 8, 1923; August 20, 1927.
[C] (A)   Hans-Georg Gadamer (ed.), *Die Frage Martin
           Heideggers* (1969) Heidelberg: Winter, pp. 36-39.
           Reprinted in Karl Löwith, *Aufsätze und Vorträge
           1930-1970* (1971) Stuttgart: W. Kohlhammer, pp.
           189-203.
     (B)   Karl Löwith, "Les Implications Politiques de la
           Philosophie de l'Existence chez Heidegger," in *Les
           Temps Modernes* (Paris) 14, 1946, pp. 343-360. This
           is a French translation by Joseph Rovan of an edited
           version of Löwith's essay, which was written in1939
           and first published in German in *Heidegger--Denker
           in dürftiger Zeit: Zur Stellung der Philosophie im 20.
           Jahrhundert* (1984) Stuttgart: J.B. Metzler, pp. 61-
           68. The complete text of the essay appeared as
           "Martin Heideggers Philosophie der Zeit (1919-
           1936)," in Löwith's *Mein Leben in Deutschland vor
           und nach 1933: Ein Bericht* (1986) Stuttgart: J.B.
           Metzler, pp. 27-42.
     (C)   Dietrich Papenfuss and Otto Pöggeler (eds.), *Zur
           philosophischen Aktualität Heideggers*, Vol. 2: *Im
           Gespräch der Zeit* (1990) Frankfurt: Klostermann,
           pp. 235-239. Letter of August 19, 1921, reprinted
           (edited by Theodore Kisiel) in Theodore Kisiel and
           Thomas Sheehan (eds.), *Becoming Heidegger. On the
           Trail of His Early Occasional Writings, 1910-1927*
           (2007) Evanston: Northwestern University Press, pp.
           299-303.
     (D)   Unpublished transcript of the letter (October 20,
           1920, edited by Klaus Stichweh); see (C) (August 19,
           1921); unpublished transcript of the letter (February

20, 1923, edited by Klaus Stichweh); unpublished transcript of the letter (May 8 1923, edited by Klaus Stichweh); see (C) (August 20, 1927).

[D]   (A)   Karl Löwith, "The Nature of Man and the World of Nature. For Heidegger's 80th Birthday," *The Southern Journal of Philosophy* (Memphis) 8 (4), 1970, pp. 309-318. Reprinted in Edward G. Ballard and Charles Scott (eds.), *Martin Heidegger: In Europe and America* (1973) The Hague: Martinus Nijhoff, pp. 37-46 (excerpts).

      (B)   (a)   Karl Löwith, "The Political Implications of Heidegger's Philosophy," in *New German Critique* (Ithaca) 45, Fall 1988, pp. 117-134. Reprinted in Richard Wolin (ed.), *The Heidegger Controversy. A Critical Reader* (1991) New York: Columbia University Press, pp. 167-185.

             (b)   Karl Löwith, "Martin Heidegger's Philosophy of Time (1919-1936)," in *My Life in Germany Before and After 1933: A Report* (1992) Urbana: University of Illinois Press, pp. 27-33.

      (C)   Gary Steiner and Richard Wolin (eds.), *Martin Heidegger and European Nihilism* (1995) New York: Columbia University Press, pp. 235-239. Reprinted (edited by Theodore Kisiel) in Theodore Kisiel and Thomas Sheehan (eds.), *Becoming Heidegger. On the Trail of His Early Occasional Writings, 1910-1927* (2007) Evanston: Northwestern University Press, pp. 99-102.

      (D)   Theodore Kisiel and Thomas Sheehan (eds.), *Becoming Heidegger. On the Trail of His Early Occasional Writings, 1910-1927* (2007) Evanston: Northwestern University Press, pp. 368, 99-102, 368 (excerpt), 372 (excerpts), 299-303. {L20}

218.   [A]   (A)   Letters to Emil Staiger (1981) [Arthur A. Grugan].

(B)   "An Exchange of Letters between Emil Staiger and
         Martin Heidegger" (1990) [Berel Lang and Christine
         Ebel].

[B]   "Briefe an Emil Staiger": Letters written in the autumn of
         1950 and December 28, 1950, to Emil Staiger about a poem
         by Eduard Mörike, "Auf eine Lampe."

[C]   Emil Staiger, "Zu einem Vers von Mörike. Ein Briefwechsel
         mit Heidegger," *Trivium* (Zürich) 9 (1), 1951, pp. 1-16.
         Reprinted in Emil Staiger, *Die Kunst der Interpretation*
         (1963) Zürich: Atlantis Verlag, pp. 34-49. *GA* 13 (1983), pp.
         93-109.

[D]   (A)   Emil Staiger, "The Staiger-Heidegger
                  Correspondence," *Man and World* (Dordrecht) 14,
                  1981, pp. 291-307.
         (B)   "A 1951 Dialogue on Interpretation: Emil Staiger,
                  Martin Heidegger, Leo Spitzer," in *Publications of
                  the Modern Language Association* 105 (3), 1990, pp.
                  420-427. {L19}

c. Single Letters

219. [A]   "Letter to Jean Beaufret" (1988) [Steven Davis].
      [B]   "Brief an Jean Beaufret:" Letter written February 22, 1975,
               Freiburg. A French translation by Jean Beaufret, "La Question
               Portant Fondamentalment sur l'Être-même," follows the letter.
      [C]   *Heidegger Studies* (Berlin) 3/4, 1987-88, pp. 3-4.
      [D]   * [C] pp. 5-6. {L15}

220. [A]   Letter from Martin Heidegger [to Albert Borgmann] (1970)
               [Albert Borgmann].
      [B]   "Gruß und Dank an die Teilnehmer der Heidegger-Konferenz
               in Honolulu auf Hawai [sic] 17.-21. November 1969 (Brief an
               Albert Borgmann)": Letter written July 4, 1969, to participants
               at a conference on "Heidegger and Eastern Thought,"
               University of Honolulu, Hawaii, November 17-21, 1969. All
               but the concluding paragraph of the German text was read.
      [C]   *GA* 16 (2000), pp. 721-722.

[D]   Winfield E. Nagley, "Introduction to the Symposium and Reading of a Letter from Martin Heidegger," *Philosophy East and West* (Honolulu) 20, 1970, p. 221. {L7}

221.   [A]   Letter to Medard Boss [excerpt] (1963) [Ludwig B. Lefebre].
       [B]   Excerpt from a letter, no date. The passage does not appear among the letters included in {Z1}. It is likely from a letter written earlier than 1957.
       [C]   Medard Boss, *Psychoanalyse und Daseinsanalytik* (1957) Bern: Huber.
       [D]   Medard Boss, *Psychoanalysis and Daseinsanalysis* (1963) New York: Basic Books, p. 36, n. 4. {L21}

222.   [A]   "Letter to Alcopley [Alfred L. Copley]" (1963) [William Barrett].
       [B]   "Brief an Alcopley": Letter written in 1959.
       [C]   Alfred L. Copley, *Heidegger und Hisamatsu und ein Zuhörende* (1963) Kyoto: Bokubi Verlag, pp. 34-35, 84. Also contains the transcript of a dialogue between Heidegger and Hisamatsu Hoseki by Copley. Reprinted in *GA* 16 (2000), p. 562 as "Aus einmen Brief Heideggers an L. Alcopley [sic]" (see {A8}).
       [D]   * [C] p. 37. {L8}

223.   [A]   Letter to David L. Edwards (1965) [John Macquarrie].
       [B]   "Brief an David L. Edwards": Letter written January 28, 1965, to the director of the SCM [Student Christian Movement] Press, London, the first publisher of *Being and Time*.
       [C]   John Macquarrie, *Heidegger and Christianity* (1994) London: Continuum, pp. 111-112.
       [D]   * [C] p. 111. {L17}

224.   [A]   Letter to Manfred [S.] Frings (1964) [Thomas Sheehan].
       [B]   "Brief an Manfred [S.] Frings": Letter written August 6, 1964.
       [C]   German text unpublished.
       [D]   Translator's introductory note to Max Scheler, "Reality and Resistance: On *Being and Time*, Section 43," in *Listening* (Dubuque) 12 (3), 1977, p. 61. Reprinted in Thomas Sheehan

(ed.), *Heidegger. The Man and the Thinker* (1981) Chicago: Precedent Publishing, p. 133. {L11}

225. [A]   "A Letter from Heidegger [to Manfred S. Frings]" (1968) [William J. Richardson].
      [B]   "Grußwort an das Heidegger-Symposion Chicago 11./12. Nov. 1966": Letter written October 20, 1966.
      [C]   Manfred S. Frings (ed.), *Heidegger and the Quest for Truth* (1968) Chicago: Quadrangle Books, pp. 19-21. Reprinted in *GA* 16 (2000), pp. 684-686.
      [D]   * [C] pp. 17-19. {L5}

226. [A]   Letter to J. Glenn Gray and Joan Stambaugh [excerpts] (1973) [Joan Stambaugh].
      [B]   "Brief an J. Glenn Gray and Joan Stambaugh": Responses written in the summer of 1970 to questions posed by the co-editors of the projected English *Works* of Martin Heidegger.
      [C]   German text unpublished.
      [D]   *The End of Philosophy* (1973) New York: Harper and Row, pp. xi-xiv. {L10}

227. [A]   "Heidegger's Letter to the Boss's Daughter [Elisabeth Husserl]" (1988) [Russell A. Berman and Paul Piccone].
      [B]   "Brief Martin Heideggers an Elisabeth Husserl": Letter of April 24, 1919, to Elli Husserl.
      [C]   "Brief Martin Heideggers an Elisabeth Husserl," in *Aut Aut* (Scandicci) 223-24, January-April, 1988, pp. 6-11. Includes an Italian translation by Renato Cristin.
      [D]   *Telos* (New York) #77, Fall 1988, pp. 125-127. {H8}

228. [A]   Letter to Edmund Husserl (2007) [Theodore Kisiel and Thomas Sheehan].
      [B]   Excerpt of letter of April 14, 1922.
      [C]   Karl Schuhmann (ed.), *Husserliana. Briefwechsel* [Part 3] (1994) Dordrecht: Kluwer, Vol. 4, pp. 136-137.
      [D]   Theodore Kisiel and Thomas Sheehan (eds.), *Becoming Heidegger. On the Trail of His Early Occasional Writings,*

1910-1927(2007) Evanston: Northwestern University Press, pp. 369-370. {L29}

229.   [A]   (A)   "Letter to Edmund Husserl" (1977) [Thomas Sheehan].

               (B)   "Heidegger's Letter and Appendices [to Draft B of the *Encyclopaedia Britannica* article `Phenomenology']" (1997) [Thomas Sheehan].

        [B]   "Brief an Edmund Husserl vom 22. Oktober 1927": Letter written October 22, 1927, to accompany "The Idea of Phenomenology" (see {I1}).

        [C]   Edmund Husserl, *Phänomenologische Psychologie* [Husserliana 9] (1962) The Hague: Martinus Nijhoff, 1968, pp. 600-601. *GA* 14 (2007), pp. 129-130.

        [D]   (A)   *Listening* (Dubuque) 12 (3), 1977, pp. 118-119.

               (B)   Thomas Sheehan and Richard E. Palmer (eds.), *Psychological and Transcendental Phenomenology and the Confrontation with Heidegger (1927-1931)* Dordrecht: Kluwer, 1997, pp. 136-137. {L9}

230.   [A]   (A)   Letter to Father Engelbert Krebs (1998) [Thomas Sheehan].

               (B)   Letter to Father Engelbert Krebs (1988) [Allan Blunden].

               (C)   July 14, 1914: Martin Heidegger to Engelbert Krebs (2007) [Thomas Sheehan].

        [B]   Letter of July 14, 1914. Ott gives the date of the letter as July 19, 1914.

        [C]   Hugo Ott, *Martin Heidegger. Unterwegs zur seiner Biographie* (1988) Frankfurt: Campus, p. 83.

        [D]   (A)   Thomas Sheehan, "Heidegger's *Lehrjahre*," in John Sallis, G. Moneta and Jacques Taminiaux (eds.) *The Collegium Phaenomenologicum: The FirstTen Years* [*Phaenomenologica* 105] (1988) Dordrecht: Kluwer, p. 113.

               (B)   Hugo Ott, *Martin Heidegger. A Political Life* (1993) New York: Basic Books, p. 81.

(C)   Theodore Kisiel and Thomas Sheehan (eds.),
           Becoming Heidegger. On the Trail of His Early
           Occasional Writings, 1910-1927 (2007) Evanston:
           Northwestern University Press, pp. 351-352. {L12}

231. [A]   (A)   Letter to Father Engelbert Krebs (1988) [John van
                    Buren].
             (B)   Letter to Englebert Krebs (1993) [Thomas Sheehan].
             (C)   Letter to Engelbert Krebs (1993) [Allan Blunden].
      [B]   "Brief an Engelbert Krebs": Letter written January 9, 1919.
      [C]   Bernhard Casper, "Martin Heidegger und die Theologische
             Fakultät Freiburg 1909-1923," *Freiburger Diözesan-Archiv*
             (Freiburg) 100, 1980, pp. 534-541. Reprinted in Hugo Ott,
             Martin Heidegger. Unterwegs zu seiner Biographie (1988)
             Frankfurt: Campus, pp. 106-107.
      [D]   (A)   John van Buren, "The Young Heidegger," McMaster
                    University, 1989, pp. 573-574. This is the author's
                    doctoral dissertation.
             (B)   Charles Guignon (ed.), *Cambridge Companion to*
                    Heidegger(1993) Cambridge: Cambridge University
                    Press, p. 70.
             (C)   Hugo Ott, *Martin Heidegger. A Political Life* (1993)
                    New York: Basic Books, p.
                    81-83. {L13}

232. [A]   Letter to Herbert Marcuse (1991) [Richard Wolin].
      [B]   "Brief an Herbert Marcuse": Letter written January 20, 1948.
      [C]   *GA* 16 (2000), p. 430-431.
      [D]   "Herbert Marcuse and Martin Heidegger. An Exchange of
             Letters," *New German Critique* (Ithaca) 53, 1991, pp. 30-31.
             Reprinted in Richard Wolin (ed.), *The Heidegger*
             Controversy. A Critical Reader (1991) Cambridge: MIT
             Press, 1993, pp. 163-64. {L14}

233. [A]   "A Letter from Martin Heidegger [to Arthur H.
             Schrynemakers" (1970) [Arthur H. Schrynemakers].
      [B]   "Grußwort an das Symposion über Heideggers Philosophie an
             der Duquesne-Universität in Pittsburgh (15.-16. Oktober

1966)": Letter written September 20, 1966, for the American
Heidegger Conference, Duquesne University, Pittsburgh.

[C]   John Sallis (ed.), *Heidegger and the Path of Thinking* (1970)
Pittsburgh: Duquesne University Press, pp. 9-10. *GA* 16
(2000), pp. 650-651.

[D]   * [C] pp. 10-11. {L6}

E. UNPUBLISHED TRANSLATIONS

234.   [A]   "Heidegger's Last Seminar" (1995) [Iain Thompson].
       [B]   "Nachtrag" to "Die Herkunft des Denkens": Postscript to
             Heidegger's 1973 seminar in Zähringen including a reflection
             on Parmenides' Fragment 1. Those in attendance, whose notes
             were the basis for the published texts of the seminars, were
             Jean Beaufret, François Fédier, François Vezin, Henri-Xavier
             Mongis and Jacques Taminiaux. The notes were in French and
             the seminar was first published in French in 1976. The
             German text, which is the basis of the translation, is by Curt
             Ochwadt.
       [C]   *GA* 15 (1986), pp. 401-407.
       [D]   http://wagner.edu/psychology/files/2013/01/Heidegger-Letter-
             On-Humanism-Translation-GROTH.pdf U-H1}

235.   [A]   "Letter on 'Humanism'" (1995) [Miles Groth].
       [B]   "Brief über den 'Humanismus'": Text based on a letter to Jean
             Beaufret written in 1946.
       [C]   *Wegmarken* (1967): *GA* 9 (1976), pp. 313-364. See {L4} for
             details on the text.
       [D]   http://www.wagner.edu/dept/psychology/grothfiles/pubs.htm
             {U-L1}

236.   [A]   "What Is Metaphysics" (1995) [Miles Groth].
       [B]   Texts of Heidegger's Freiburg inaugural lecture, "Was ist
             Metaphysik?" (1929), the 1943 "Nachwort" (revised, 1949),
             and "Einleitung: Der Rückgang in den Grund der Metaphysik"
             (1949) as Heidegger published them beginning in 1955 as a
             booklet (7th edition). The parts are presented in the order in
             which intended them to be read (introduction, lecture,
             postscript). See the entries above corresponding to the three
             elements of the booklet. See {W2}, {W6} and {P13}.
       [C]   Was ist Metaphysik? (1955) Frankfurt: Klostermann [7th
             edition]. Wegmarken (1967): *GA* 9 (1976), pp. 365-383, 103-
             122 and 303-312. The translator worked from the 11th edition
             (1975).

[D]   https://wagner.edu/psychology/files/2013/01/Heidegger-
        What-Is-Metaphysics-Translation-GROTH.pdf {U-W1}

F. TRANSLATORS BY ALPHANUMERIC CODE OF ITEM (1949-2015)

The translators are keyed to entries identified by a alphanumeric code found at the end of each entry {} in the bibliography.

Adamczewski, Zygmunt	O9
Alexander, Edwin Michael	Q3
Alter, Maria P.	O10
Anderson, John M.	C8, M3
Arel, Joseph	H15
Arendt, Hannah	A8
Askay, Richard	P15, Z1
Aylesworth, Gary E.	B1, H6
Bambach, Charles	W11
Barlow, John	P9
Barrett, William	L8
Barton, Jr., W.B.	W8
Baur, Michael	P6
Berman, Russell A.	H8
Blunden, Allan	C5, C11, G1, J3, L12, L13, L18, O3
Borgmann, Albert	L7
Bossert, Phillip J.	P24
Bowles, Brian Hansford	B6, P25
Brann, Eva	W7
Brogan, Walter	A6
Braunstein, Phillip Jacques	A12, I6
Bunch, Aaron	A10, D2, P24
Campbell, Scott M.	B8
Capobianco, Richard	O19
Caputo, John D.	O10
Capuzzi, Frank	A4, E6, L4, L25, M9, N2, N3, N4
Churchill, James S.	E9, K1
Colony, Tracy	P7
Crick, Alan	O7, P13, W6
Dahlstrom, Daniel	I4
Davis, Bret W.	A11, E8, T8
Davis, Julia	H12

Metcalf, Robert D.	B10
NN	L4, P2, S-L1
Murthy, B. Srinirasa	M1
Novak, Joseph A	I1
O'Hara, R. Philip	L20
O'Meara, Thomas F.	H14, P2
Osers, Ewald	E7, G1
Pambrun, Robert	M1
Peck, John	E7
Piccone, Paul	H8
Pohl, William	K3
Polt, Richard	F6, I3, O20, S-N1
Powell, Jeffrey	H16
Protevi, John	C9, F1, G3, J2, L24, O2, P3, P26
Radloff, Bernhard	W1
Raffoul, Francois	F3
Richardson, William J.	E7, L5, L16, O10
Robbins, Harold J.	D2
Robinson, Edward	B5
Rojcewicz, Richard	B2, B9, B12, C6, E10, P1, P5, P10
Runes, Dagobert	S-S2
Sadler, Ted	E2, E3, I7, O1, P28
Sallis, John	H2, M8, O7
Schendler, David	O10
Schrynemakers, Arthur H.	L6
Schrynemakers, Therese	C10
Schuwer, André	B2, P1, P10
Scott, Douglas	H11, P17, R5
Seibert, Charles	A7, H9
Seigfried, Hans	R2
Sheehan, Thomas	C10, C11, F2, H6, H14, I1, I2, L2, L9, L11, L12, L13, L29, L30, O4, P2, P9, U1, W6, W10
Shields, Andrew	L23
Skinner, Alex	C13
Slade, Francis	C1

G. TRANSLATORS BY TITLE OF WORK (1949-2015)

Adamczewski, Zygmunt
"On the Way to Being. Reflecting on Conversations with Martin
Heidegger" (1970)
Alexander, Edwin Michael
"Martin Heidegger's *The Question about Technic*. A Translation and
Commentary" (1973)
Alter, Maria P.
"Only a God Can Save Us: *Der Spiegel's* Interview with Martin Heidegger
on September 23, 1966" (1976)
Anderson, John M.
"Conversation on a Country Path about Thinking" (1966)
"Memorial Address" (1966)
Arel, Joseph
Hegel (2015)
Arendt, Hannah
"Art and Thinking" (1963)
Askay, Richard
Zollikon Seminars. Protocols, Seminars, Letters (2001)
"A Word on Hölderlin's Poetry" (2001)
Aylesworth, Gary
Basic Concepts (1993)
Bambach, Charles
"Wilhelm Dilthey's Research and the Struggle for a Historical Worldview"
(2002)
Barlow, John
"Plato's Doctrine of Truth" (1962)
Barrett, William
"Letter to Alcopley" (1963)
Barton, Jr., W.B.
What Is a Thing? (1967)
Baur, Michael
"Phenomenological Interpretations with Respect to Aristotle: Indication of
the Hermeneutical Situation" (1992)
Berman, Russell A.
"Heidegger's Letter to the Boss's Daughter" (1988)

Blunden, Allan
  Letter to Father Englesbert Krebs (1988)
  "Consolation" (1993)
  "Résumé" (1993)
  "Gethsemane Hours" (1993)
  "July Night" (1993)
  Letter to Engelbert Krebs (1993)
  Excerpt of a letter written September 12, 1929 (1993)
  "On Still Paths" (1993)
Borgmann, Albert
  Letter from Martin Heidegger (1970)
Bossert, Phillip J.
  "The Problem of Reality in Modern Philosophy" (1973)
Bowles, Brian Hansford
  "Being-There and Being True According to Aristotle" (2007)
  "The Problem of Sin in Luther" (2007)
Brann, Eva
  What Is That--Philosophy? (1991)
Brogan, Walter
  Aristotle's Metaphysics Θ *1-3. On the Essence and
    Actuality of Force* (1995)
Braunstein, Phillip Jacques
  "Appendix to *Nietzsche's Metaphysics*" (2011)
  Introduction to Philosophy—Thinking and Poetizing (2011)
Bunch, Aaron
  "Author's Notice" (2007)
  "Supplements to *The Doctrine of Categories and Meaning in Duns Scotus*
    ["Author's Notice" and "Conclusion: The Problem of
    Categories"] (2007)
  "The Problem of Reality in Modern Philosophy" (2007)
Campbell, Scott M.
  Basic Problems of Phenomenology (1919/1920)
Capobianco, Richard
  "On the Question Concerning the Determination of the Matter for
    Thinking" (2010).
John Caputo
  "Only a God Can Save Us: *Der Spiegel's* Interview with Martin
    Heidegger" (1976)

Capuzzi, Frank

"Aletheia (Heraclitus, Fragment B 16)" (1975)

"Logos (Heraclitus, Fragment B 50" (1975)

"Moira (Parmenides VIII, 34-41)" (1975)

"Letter on Humanism" (1977)

Nietzsche (1979-1987)

"Nihilism as Determined by the History of Being" (1982)

"European Nihilism" (1982)

"Nietzsche's Metaphysics" (1987)

Churchill, James S.

Kant and the Problem of Metaphysics (1962)

"Editor's Foreword" to Edmund Husserl, *The Phenomenology of Inner Time Consciousness [1905]*" (1964)

Colony, Tracy

Phenomenology of Intuition and Expression (2010)

Crick, Alan

"On the Essence of Truth" (1949)

"Postscript" to "What Is Metaphysics?" (1949)

"What Is Metaphysics?" (1949)

Dahlstrom, Daniel

Introduction to Phenomenological Research (2005)

Davis, Bret W.

"Ἀγχιβασιν: A Triadic Conversation on a Country Path between a Scientist, a Scholar and a Guide" (2010)

"Evening Conversation: In a Prisoner of War Camp in Russia, between a Younger and Older Man" (2010)

"The Teacher Meets the Tower Warden at the Door to the Tower Stairway" (2010)

Davis, Julia

Hölderlin's Hymn "The Ister" (1996)

Davis, Steven

"Letter to Jean Beaufret" (1988)

de Deugd, Cornelis

[*Being and Time*]. Sein und Zeit. *An Informal Paraphrase of Sections 1-53, with Certain Omissions as Noted* (1955)

de Man, Paul

"Hölderlin and the Essence of Poetry" (1959)

Deely, John N.
  "The Idea of Phenomenology" (1970)
Deutsch, Vera
  What Is a Thing? (1967)
Dreyfus, Hubert
  [*Being and Time*]. Sein und Zeit. *An Informal Paraphrase of Sections 1-53,
    with Certain Omissions as Noted* (1955)
Ebel, Christine
  "An Exchange of Letters between Emil Staiger and Martin
    Heidegger" (1990)
Edler, Frank
  "Letters to Elisabeth Blochmann" (1991)
Eldred, Michael
  "On Adequate Understanding of Daseinsanalysis" and "Marginalia on
    Phenomenology, Transcendence and Care" (1988)
Elliston, Frederick
  "The Understanding of Time in Phenomenology and in the Thinking of the
    Being-Question" (1979)
Emad, Parvis
  "The Basic Question of Being as Such" (1986)
  Hegel's Phenomenology of Spirit (1988)
  Phenomenological Interpretation of Kant's Critique of Pure Reason (1997)
  Contributions to Philosophy: From Enowning (1999)
  Mindfulness (2006)
Farin, Ingo
  The Concept of Time [The First Draft of Being and Time] (2011)
Feuerhahn, Niels
  Hegel (2015)
Foltz, Bruce V.
  "Hebel—Friend of the House" (1983)
Fox, Melissa J.
  Letters to Karl Löwith (1988)
Freund, E. Hans
  "Memorial Address" (1966)
  "Conversation on a Country Path about Thinking" (1966)
Fried, Gregory
  Introduction to Metaphysics (2000)
  "The Fundamental Question of Philosophy" (2010)

"On the Essence of Truth" (2010)
Nature, History, State 1933/1934 (2013)
Fritsch, Matthias
  "Augustine and Neo-Platonism" (2004)
  "Introduction to the Phenomenology of Religious Life (2004)
  "The Philosophical Foundations of of Medieval Mysticism" (2004)
Gill, Gerry
  "The Problem of a Non-objectifying Thinking and Speaking in
    Contemporary Theology" (1968)
Glasgow, R.D.V.
  Letters to His Wife 1915-1970 (2008)
Göbel, Marie
  "On the Question Concerning the Determination of the Matter for
    Thinking" (2010).
Gosetti-Ferencei, Jennifer Anna
  "Augustine and Neo-Platonism" (2004)
  "Introduction to the Phenomenology of Religious Life (2004)
  "The Philosophical Foundations of Medieval Mysticism" (2004)
Gray, J. Glenn
  What Is Called Thinking? (1968)
  Hegel's Concept of Experience (1970)
  "Being and Time: Introduction" (1977)
  "Letter on Humanism" (1977)
  "More founding than poetry . . ." (1977)
Gregory, Wanda Torres
  "Traditional Language and Technological Language" (1998)
  *On the Essence of Language The Metaphysics of Language and the
    Essencing of the Word. Concerning Herder's Treatise* On the Origin of
    Language (2004)
  Logic as the Question Concerning the Essence of Language (2009)
Grene, Marjorie
  "The Age of the World View" (1951)
Groth, Miles
  "Adalbert Stifter's `Ice Tale'" (1993)
  "Letter on 'Humanism'" (1995)
  "What Is Metaphysics" (1995)
  "Acknowledgment on the Conferment of the National Hebel
    Memorial Prize" (1997)

Grugan, Arthur A.
    Letters to Emil Staiger (1981)
Gualiardo, Vincent
    "Martin Heidegger: An Interview" (1971)
Hamburg, Carl H.
    "A Cassirer-Heidegger Seminar" (1964)
Harries, Karsten
    "The Rectorate 1933/34: Facts and Thoughts" (1985)
    "The Self-Assertion of the German University: Address, Delivered on the
        Solemn Assumption of the Rectorate of the University [of]
        Freiburg" (1985)
Harries, Lisa
    "A Greeting to the Symposium in Beirut in November 1974" (1990)
    "Martin Heidegger in Conversation with Richard Wisser" (1990)
    "*Der Spiegel* Interview with Martin Heidegger" (1990)
    "The Rectorate 1933/34: Facts and Thoughts" (1990)
    "The Self-Assertion of the German University" (1990)
Hart, James G.
    "Conversation with Martin Heidegger" (1976)
    "Phenomenology and Theology" (1976)
    "Principles of Thinking" (1976)
    "Review of Ernst Cassirer's *Mythical Thought*" (1976)
Haynes, Kenneth
    "Why Poets?" (2002)
Heim, Michael
    "Hebel—Friend of the House" (1983)
    "Max Scheler: In Memoriam" (1984)
    The Metaphysical Foundations of Logic (1984)
    "From the Last Marburg Lecture Course" (1998)
Hertz, Peter D.
    "A Dialogue on Language" (1971)
    "Language in the Poem. A Discussion on Georg Trakl's Poetic Work"
        (1971)
    "The Nature of Language" (1971)
    "The Way to Language" (1971)
    "Words" (1971)
Hoeller, Keith
    "The Principle of Ground" (1974)

"Thoughts" (1976)
"As When on a Holiday . . ." (2000)
"A Glimpse into Heidegger's Study" (2000)
"Hölderlin and the Essence of Poetry" (2000)
"Hölderlin's Heaven and Earth" (2000)
"The Poem" (2000)
"Preface to a Reading of Hölderlin's Poems" (2000)
"Prefaces to *Elucidations of Hölderlin's Poetry* (2000)
"Preface to a Repetition of the Address 'Homecoming'" (2000)
"Remembrance" (2000)
"Homecoming / To Kindred Ones" (2000)
Hofstadter, Albert
"The Origin of the Work of Art" (1965)
"Building Dwelling Thinking" (1971)
"Language" (1971)
" . . . Poetically Man Dwells . . ." (1971)
"The Thing" (1971)
"The Thinker as Poet" (1971)
"What Are Poets For?" (1971)
The Basic Problems of Phenomenology (1982)
Hull, R.F.C.
"On the Essence of Truth" (1949)
"Postscript" to "What Is Metaphysics?" (1949)
"What Is Metaphysics?" (1949)
Ireland, Julia
*Hölderlins Hymnen "Germanien" und "Der Rhein"*I (2014)
Kalary, Thomas
Mindfulness (2006)
"Poverty" (2011)
Kaufmann, Walter
"What Is Metaphysics?" (1956)
Kenny, Brian
"Martin Heidegger's Zollikon Seminars" (1978)
Kimmel, William
"On the Essence of the Ground" (1962)
"Philosophy -- What Is It?" (1962)
King, Elizabeth
[Heidegger/Löwith Correspondence] Letters to Karl Löwith (1994)

Kisiel, Theodore
   History of the Concept of Time (1985)
   [Heidegger/Jaspers Correspondence] Letter of May 4, 1926 (2007)
   "Critical Comments on Karl Jaspers's *Psychology of Worldviews* (2007)
   "The Concept of Time" (2007)
   "The Concept of Time in the Science of History" (2007)
   "'Heidegger, Martin': Lexicon Article Attributed to Rudolf
       Bultmann" (2007)
   [Heidegger/Blochmann Correspondence] May 1, 1919: Martin Heidegger to
       Elisabeth Blochmann (2007)
   [Heidegger/Löwith Correspondence] Letters of October 20, 1920, February
       20, 1923, and May 8, 1923 (2007)
   Letter to Edmund Husserl (2007)
   "The War-Triduum in Messkirch" (2007)
   "On the Essence of Truth [Pentecost Monday, 1926]" (2007)
   "Phenomenological Interpretations with Respect to Aristotle: Indication of
       the Hermeneutical Situation" (2007)
   "On Schleiermacher's Second Speech, 'On the Essence of
       Religion' " (2007)
   "Question and Judgment" (2007)
   "Recent Research in Logic" (2007)
   "Vita, with Accompanying Letter to Georg Misch" (2007)
   "Wilhelm Dilthey's Research and the Current Struggle for a Historical
       Worldview" (2007)
   "On a Philosophical Orientation for Academics" (2007)
   "The Problem of Sin in Luther" (2007)
Klein, Jr., Ted E.
   "Kant's Thesis about Being" (1973)
Kluback, William
   The Question of Being (1958)
   What Is Philosophy? (1958)
Krell, David Farrell
   "The Anaximander Fragment" (1975)
   "Logos (Heraclitus, Fragment B 50" (1975)
   "What Is Metaphysics?" (1977)
   "Being and Time: Introduction" (1977)
   "The End of Philosophy and the Task of Thinking" (1977)
   "The Will to Power as Art" (1979)

Nietzsche (1979-1987)

"The Eternal Recurrence of the Same" (1984)

"Who Is Nietzsche's Zarathustra?" (1984)

"The Eternal Recurrence of the Same and the Will to Power" (1987)

"The Way to Language" (1993)

"Letter on `Humanism'" (1998)

Lang, Berel

"An Exchange of Letters between Emil Staiger and Martin
   Heidegger" (1990)

Lefebre, Ludwig B.

Letter to Medard Boss [excerpt] (1963)

Leidecker, Kurt F.

"The Onto-theo-logical Nature of Metaphysics" (1960)

"The Principle of Identity" (1960)

Lewis, William S.

Speeches and newspaper articles from the period May 27, 1933 and
   February 1, 1934 (1988)

"The Self-Assertion of the German University" (1991)

Lilly, Reginald

"The Principle of Reason" (1991)

The Principle of Reason (1991)

Lohner, Edgar

"Letter on Humanism" (1962)

Lovitt, William

"The Age of the World Picture" (1977)

"The Question Concerning Technology" (1977)

"Science and Reflection" (1977)

"The Turning" (1977)

"The Word of Nietzsche: `God Is Dead'" (1977)

"A Heidegger Seminar on Hegel's *Differenzschrift*" (1980)

Macquarrie, John

Being and Time (1962)

Letter to David L. Edwards (1965)

"From the Last Marburg Lecture Course" (1971)

Magnus, Bernd

"Who Is Nietzsche's Zarathustra?" (1967)

Malick, Terrence

The Essence of Reasons (1969)

Maly, Kenneth
    "The Turning" (1971)
    "The Basic Question of Being as Such" (1986)
    Hegel's Phenomenology of Spirit (1988)
    Phenomenological Interpretation of Kant's Critique of Pure Reason (1997)
    Contributions to Philosophy: From Enowning (1999)
Manheim, Ralph
    An Introduction to Metaphysics (1959)
Manoussakis, John Panteleinon
    Sojourns. The Journey to Greece (2005)
Maraldo, John C.
    "Conversation with Martin Heidegger" (1976)
    "Phenomenology and Theology" (1976)
    "Principles of Thinking" (1976)
    "The Theological Discussion of `The Problem of a Non-objectifying
        Thinking and Speaking in Contemporary Theology'--Some Pointers to
        Its Major Aspects" (1976)
    "Review of Ernst Cassirer's *Mythical Thought*" (1976)
Mayr, Franz
    Zollikon Seminars. Protocols, Seminars, Letters (2001)
    "A Word on Hölderlin's Poetry" (2001)
McNeill, William
    "The Concept of Time" (1992)
    *The Fundamental Concepts of Metaphysics. World, Finitude,
        Solitude* (1995)
    Hölderlin's Hymn "The Ister" (1996)
    Hölderlins Hymnen "Germanien" und "Der Rhein" (2014)
    "From the Last Marburg Lecture Course" (1998)
    "Hegel and the Greeks" (1998)
    The History of Beyng (2015)
    "Kant's Thesis about Being" (1998)
    "Letter on `Humanism'" (1998)
    "On the Essence and Concept of *phusis* in Aristotle's *Physics* B, 1" (1998)
    "On the Essence of Ground" (1998)
    "On the Essence of Truth" (1998)
    "Phenomenology and Theology" (1998)
    "Plato's Doctrine of Truth" (1998)
    "Postscript" to "What Is Metaphysics?" (1998)

"Preface" to *Pathmarks* (1998)
"The Theological Discussion of `The Problem of a Non-objectifying
    Thinking and Speaking in Contemporary Theology'--Some Pointers to
    Its Major Aspects" (1998)
"On the Question of Being" (1998)
"Introduction to `What Is Metaphysics?'" (1998)
"What Is Metaphysics?" (1998)
Meklenberg, Frank
    "On My Relation to National Socialism" (1982)
Metcalf, Robert
    "Hegel and the Greeks" (1998)
    Basic Concepts of Aristotelian Philosophy (2009)
Mexia, Berit
    "The Fieldpath" (1986)
Mitchell, Andrew
    Four Seminars (2003)
    Bremen and Freiburg Lectures. Insight Into That Which Is and *Basic
    Principles of Thinking* (2012)
    On Hegel's Philosophy of Right (2014)
NN
    ["Letter on Humanism":] "The Meaning of `Humanism'" (1949)
    ["The Pathway":] "The Field Path. A Meditation" (1950)
    Letter to Carl Schmitt (1987)
Murthy, B. Srinirasa
    "Martin Heidegger in Conversation" (1977)
Novak, Joseph A
    "The Idea of Phenomenology" (1970)
O'Hara, R. Philip
    Letters to Karl Löwith (1970)
O'Meara, Thomas F.
    "The Pathway" (1967)
    "Homeland. Festival Address at a Centennial Celebration" (1971)
Osers, Ewald
    "Evening Walk on Reichenau" (1998)
    "Gethsemane Hours" (1998)
Pambrun, Robert
    "Martin Heidegger: An Interview" (1971)

Peck, John
    "Evening on the Reichenau" (1970)
Piccone, Paul
    "Heidegger's Letter to the Boss's Daughter" (1988)
Pohl, William
    "Kant's Thesis about Being" (1973)
Polt, Richard
    Introduction to Metaphysics (2000)
    "The Fundamental Question of Philosophy" (2010)
    "On the Essence of Truth" (2010)
    Nature, History, State 1933-1934 (2013)
Powell, Richard
    The History of Beyng (2015)
Protevi, John
    "Cüppers, Ad. Jos. *Sealed Lips: The Story of the Irish Folk Life in the
        19ᵗʰ Century*" (1991)
    "Förster, Fr. W. *Authority and Freedom: Observations on the Cultural
        Problem of the Church*" (1991)
    "Gredt, Jos. O.S.B. *Elements of Aristotelian-Thomistic Philosophy*, vol. 1:
        Logic, Philos. Nat. Edit. II (1991)
    "Jörgensen, Joh. *Travelogue: Light and Dark Nature and Spirit*" (1991)
    "*Library of Valuable Novellas and Stories,* vol. 9, O. Hellinghaus,
        ed." (1991)
    "On a Philosophical Orientation for Academics" (1991, 2007)
    "*Per mortem ad vitam* (Thoughts on Johannes Jörgensen's *Lies of Life and
        Truth of Life*" (1991)
    "Psychology of Religion and the Subconscious" (1991)
Radloff, Bernhard
    "The Want of Holy Names" (1985)
Raffoul, Francois
    Four Seminars (2003)
Richardson, William J.
    "Eventide on Reichenau" (1963)
    Letter to William J. Richardson (1963)
    "A Letter from Heidegger" (1968)
    "'Only a God Can Save Us': The *Spiegel* Interview with Martin
        Heidegger" (1981)

Robbins, Harold J.
  Duns Scotus' Theory of the Categories and of Meaning (1978)
Robinson, Edward
  Being and Time (1962)
Rojcewicz, Richard
  Parmenides (1992)
  Basic Questions of Philosophy (1994)
  Plato's Sophist (1997)
  *Phenomenological Interpretations of Aristotle: Initiation into
      Phenomenological Research* (2001)
  Basic Concepts of Ancient Philosophy (2008)
  Contributions to Philosophy (Of the Event) (2012)
  The Event (2013)
  *The Beginning of Western Philosophy. Interpretation of Anaximander
      and Parmenides* (2015)
Runes, Dagobert
  Speeches and newspaper articles from the period May 27, 1933 and
      February 1, 1934 (1965)
Sadler, Ted
  "On the Nature of the University and Academic Study" (2000)
  "The Idea of Philosophy and the Problem of Worldview" (2000)
  "Phenomenology and Transcendental Philosophy of Value" (2000)
  The Essence of Human Freedom. An Introduction to Philosophy (2002)
  The Essence of Truth. On Plato's Cave Allegory and Theaetetus (2002)
Sallis, John
  "Modern Natural Science and Technology" (1977)
  "On the Essence of Truth" (1977)
  "Hegel and the Greeks" (1998)
Schalow, Frank
  "Poverty"
Schendler, David
  "Only a God Can Save Us Now" (1977)
Schrynemakers, Arthur H.
  "A Letter from Martin Heidegger" (1970)
Schrynemakers, Therese
  "*Curriculum vitae*" (1965)
Schuwer, André
  Parmenides (1992)

Basic Questions of Philosophy (1994)
Plato's Sophist (1997)
Scott, Douglas
 "Hölderlin and the Essence of Poetry" (1949)
 "Prefatory Remark to a Repetition of the Address" (1949)
 "Remembrance of the Poet" (1949)
Seibert, Charles
 "Art and Space" (1973)
 Heraclitus Seminar 1966/67 (1979)
Seigfried, Hans
 "A Recollection" (1970)
Sheehan, Thomas
 Letter to Manfred Frings (1964)
 "Messkirch's Seventh Centennial" (1973)
 "The Pathway" (1973)
 "Language" (1976)
 "On the Being and Concept of *phusis* in Aristotle's *Physics* B, 1" (1976)
 "The Idea of Phenomenology" (1977)
 " . . . a Letter to Edmund Husserl" (1977)
 "Why Do I Stay in the Provinces?" (1977)
 "The Understanding of Time in Phenomenology and in the Thinking of the
  Being-Question" (1979)
 "In Memory of Max Scheler" (1981)
 Letter to Father Engelbert Krebs (1988)
 "Plato's Doctrine of Truth" (1998)
 "Martin Heidegger's Inaugural Lecture at Freiburg University. A Reading
  of Heidegger's 'What Is Metaphysics?'" (2001)
 "For Edmund Husserl on His Seventieth Birthday" (1997, 2007)
 "Curriculum vitae 1913" (1988, 2007)
 "Curriculum vitae 1915" (1988, 2007)
 [Heidegger/Jaspers Correspondence] Letter of July 14, 1923 (2007)
 Letter to Edmund Husserl (2007)
 Logic. The Question of Truth (2010)
Shields, Andrew
 Letters 1925-1975 [Hannah Arendt and Martin Heidegger] (2004)
Skinner, Alex
 The Concept of Time [The First Draft of Being and Time] (2011)

Slade, Francis
"A Discussion Between Ernst Cassirer and Martin Heidegger" (1971)
Stambaugh, Joan
   Letter to Manfred Frings (1964)
   "The Onto-theo-logical Constitution of Metaphysics" (1969)
   "The Principle of Identity" (1969)
   "The End of Philosophy and the Task of Thinking" (1972)
   "My Way to Phenomenology" (1972)
   "Summary of a Seminar on the Lecture `Time and Being'" (1972)
   "Time and Being" (1972)
   Letter to J. Glenn Gray and Joan Stambaugh [excerpts] (1973)
   "The Will to Power as Art": First Section: "Nietzsche as
        Metaphysical Thinker" (1973)
   "Overcoming Metaphysics" (1973)
   "Recollection in Metaphysics" (1973)
   "Metaphysics as History of Being" (1973)
   "Sketches for a History of Being as Metaphysics" (1973)
   "Being and Time: Introduction" (1977)
   Nietzsche (1979-1987)
   Schelling's Treatise on the Essence of Human Freedom (1985)
   "The Will to Power as Knowledge" (1987)
   Being and Time (1996)
Stassen, Manfred
   "The Jewish Contamination of German Spiritual Life–Letter to Victor
        Schwoerer" (2003)
Steiner, Gary
   Letters to Karl Löwith (1995)
Stewart, Roderick
   "Signification and Radical Subjectivity in Heidegger's
        Habilitationsschrift" (1979)
   "The Problem of the Categories" (1979)
Taft, Richard
   "Davos Disputation Between Ernst Cassirer and Martin Heidegger" (1990)
   Kant and the Problem of Metaphysics (1990, 1997)
   "Kant's *Critique of Pure Reason* and the Task of a Laying of the Ground of
        Metaphysics" (1990)
   "Notes on the Kantbook" (1997)
   "On Debrecht's and Cassirer's Critiques of the Kantbook (1997)

"On the History of the Philosophical Chair Since 1866 (1977)
Tanzer, Mark B.
  Basic Concepts of Aristotelian Philosophy (2009)
Taylor, Harry S.
  "The Concept of Time in the Science of History" (1978)
Thompson, Iain
  "Heidegger's Last Seminar" (1995)
Trahern, Robert J.
  [*Being and Time*]. Sein und Zeit. *An Informal Paraphrase of Sections 1-53,
    with Certain Omissions as Noted* (1955)
Uffelmann, Hans W.
  "The Concept of Time in the Science of History" (1978)
Unna, Yvonne
  *On the Essence of Language The Metaphysics of Language and the
    Essencing of the Word. Concerning Herder's Treatise* On the Origin of
    Language (2004)
  Logic as the Question Concerning the Essence of Language (2009)
Vallega-Neu, Daniel
  Contributions to Philosophy (Of the Event) (2012)
van Buren, John
  Letter to Father Engelbert Krebs (1988)
  "*Per mortem ad vitam* (Thoughts on Johannes Jörgensen's *Lies of Life and
    Truth of Life*" (1991)
  "Comments on Karl Jaspers's *Psychology of Worldviews*" (1998)
  Ontology--The Hermeneutics of Facticity (1999)
  "Author's Book Notice" (2002)
  "The Concept of Time in the Science of History" (2002)
  "Phenomenological Interpretations in Connection with Aristotle: An
    Indication of the Hermeneutical Situation" (2002)
  "Conclusion: The Problem of Categories" (2002)
  "The Problem of Reality in Modern Philosophy" (2002)
  "The Problem of Sin in Luther" (2002)
Veith, Jerome
  "The Age of the World Picture" (2009)
  "Art and Space" (2009)
  "As When on a Holiday . . ." (2009)
  "Cézanne [from the series *Gdachtes* for René Char. L'Herne 1971. *Last
    Version 1974*)" (2009)

"*Ereignis*" (2009)

"The Projection of Being in Science and Art" (2009)

"Description of the Situation. *Fundemental Attunement*" (2009)

"The *Ge-Stell*" (2009)

"Hölderlin and the Essence of Poetry" (2009)

"The Language of Johann Peter Hebel" (2009)

Letter to Father William J. Richardson (2009)

"*Logos* and Langauge" (2009)

"The Problem of *Being and Time*" and "Transcendence" (2009)

"On Nietzsche" (2009)

"On the Origin of the Work of Art. *First Version*" (2009)

"On Ernst Jünger [(1) and (2)]" (2009)

"*Der Spiegel* Interview with Martin Heidegger" (2009)

"Indication of the Hermeneutical Situation" (2009)

"The Principle of Identity" (2009)

"Bremen Lectures. *Insight into That Which Is*: "The Indication" and "The Thing" (2009)

"The Environmental Experience" (2009)

"Rectorship Address. *The Self-Assertion of the German University*" (2009)

Walker, Nicholas

    The Fundamental Concepts of Metaphysics. World, Finitude, Solitude (1995)

Warnek, Peter

    Aristotle's Metaphysics Θ *1-3. On the Essence and Actuality of Force* (1995)

    "Ernst Cassirer: Philosophy of Symbolic Forms. Part Two: Mythical Thought. Berlin, 1925" (1997)

    Kant and the Problem of Metaphysics [5th edition text, Appendix II] (1997)

Wieck, Fred D.

    What Is Called Thinking? (1968)

    Hegel's Concept of Experience (1970)

Wild, John

    [*Being and Time*]. Sein und Zeit. *An Informal Paraphrase of Sections 1-53, with Certain Omissions as Noted* (1955)

Wilde, Jean T.

    The Question of Being (1958)

    What Is Philosophy? (1958)

    "On the Essence of the Ground" (1962)

Wirth, Jason M.
"Documents from the Denazification Proceedings Concerning Martin
	Heidegger" (1991)
Wolin, Richard
Letters to Karl Löwith (1988)
Letter to Herbert Marcuse (1991)
"Letter to the Rector of Freiburg University, November 4, 1945" (1991)
Young, Julian
"The Age of the World Picture" (2002)
"Anaximander's Saying" (2002)
"The Origin of the Work of Art" (2002)
Zisselsberger, Markus
"Of the Origin of the Work of Art (first elaboration)" (2008)

II. GERMAN TEXTS TRANSLATED INTO ENGLISH (1949-2015): ALPHABETICAL

"Abendgang auf der Reichenau": Poem written in 1916.

"Abendgespräch in einem Kriegsgefangenenlager in Rußland zwischen einem Jüngeren und einem Älteren": Dialogue dated May 8, 1945.

"Adalbert Stifters `Eisgeschichte'": Lecture broadcast on Radio Zürich, January 26, 1964.

"Αγχιβασιν. Ein Gespräch selbstdritt auf einem Feldweg zwischen einem Forscher, einem Gelehrten und einem Weisen": Dialogue dated April 7, 1945.

"Andenken": Essay contributed to Paul Luckholm (ed.), *Hölderlin. Gedenkschrfiten zu seinem 100. Todestag*, 1942.

"Der Anfang der abendländischen Philosophie, Auslegung des Anaximander und Parmenides": Lecture course given during the Summer Semester 1932, University of Freiburg.

"Anmerkungen zu Karl Jaspers *Psychologie der Weltanschauungen*": Review article, 1919-21.

"Ansprache zum Heimatabend": Speech given in Meßkirch. July 22, 1961.

"Antrittsrede": Address at the Heidelberg Academy of Sciences, Fall 1957, on being admitted to the Academy.

"Die Armut": Address given June 27, 1945, Hausen.

"Auf stillen Pfaden": Poem written in early 1911.

Aufenthalte: Text written in Greece, 1962.

"Aufzeichnungen zum Kantbuch": Notes form 1929 on, found in Heidegger's copy of the first edition of *Kant und das Problem der Metaphysik*"Aufzeichnungen zu *Nietzsches Metaphysik*": Notes for the essay "Nietzsches Metaphysik,"1940.

"Augustinus under der Neoplatonismus": Lecture course given during Summer Semester, 1921, University of Freiburg.

"Aus der Erfahrung des Denkens": Text written during 1947.

"Aus der letzten Marburger Vorlesung": Text based on §5 of the lecture course "Logik," given during the Summer Semester 1928, University of Marburg.

"Aus einem Gespräch von der Sprache. Zwischen einem Japaner und einem Fragenden [From a Conversation on Language. Between a Japanese and a Questioner]": Dialogue from the years 1953-54.

"Auszüge aus Briefen Heideggers an Karl Löwith 1921-29": Excerpts of letters
    to Karl Löwith, dated August 19, 1921; March 26, 1924; August 21, 1924;
    June 30, 1925; August 20, 1927; February 3, 1929; September 3, 1929.
"The Basic Question of Being as Such": Text dictated to Jean Beaufret in
    September 1946 (no German text given).
"Bauen Wohnen Denken": Lecture given August 5, 1951, Darmstadt.
"Der Begriff der Zeit": Lecture delivered to the Marburg Theological Society on
    July 25, 1924.
"Der Begriff der Zeit": Text of unpublished review article for the *Deutsche
    Vierteljahrsheft für Literaturwissenschaft und Geistesgeschichte*, 1924.
"Die Begründung des neuzeitlichen Weltbildes durch die Metaphysik": Lecture
    given June 9, 1938, Freiburg. Revised title: "Die Zeit des Weltbildes"
    (1950)
"Beiträge zur Philosophie (Vom Ereignis)": Ruminations from 1936-38.
Besinnung: Text from 1938-39.
"Besprechung: Ernst Cassirers *Philosophie der symbolischen Formen*. 2. Teil:
    Das mythische Denken [1925]": Book review, 1928.
"Bibliotehek wertvoller Novellen und Erzählungen. Herausgegeben von Prof.
    Dr. O. Hellinghaus": Book review, January 1913.
"Ein Blick in die Werkstatt": Marginal notes to the texts of the second and third
    versions of Hölderlin's "Griechenland" in the *Grosse Stuttgarter Ausgabe*
    of Hölderlin's works, edited by Friedrich Beissner, 1959.
"Brief über den Humanismus": Text based on a letter to Jean Beaufret written in
    1946.
"Brief an Jean Beaufret": Letter dated February 22, 1975, Freiburg. A French
    translation by Jean Beaufret, "La Question Portant Fondamentalment sur
    l'Être-même," follows the letter.
"Briefe an Elisabeth Blochmann": Letters 1929-1933, from the Heidegger-
    Blochmann correspondence.
"Brief an Albert Borgmann": Letter dated July 4, 1969, to participants in the
    conference on "Heidegger and Eastern Thought," University of Honolulu,
    Hawaii, held November 17-21, 1969.
"Brief an Rudolf Bultmann": Letter to Rudolf Bultmann, December 31, 1927.
"Brief an Alfred L. Copley": Letter, 1959.
"Brief an David L. Edwards": Letter dated January 28, 1965, to the director of
    the SCM (Student Christian Movement) Press, London.
"Brief an Manfred Frings": Letter dated August 6, 1964.
"Brief an Manfred S. Frings": Letter dated October 20, 1966.

"Brief an Edmund Husserl": Letter dated October 22, 1927, to accompany "The
    Idea of Phenomenology."

"Brief Martin Heideggers an Elisabeth Husserl": Letter of April 24, 1919, to Elli
    Husserl.

"Brief an Engelbert Krebs": Letter dated January 9, 1919.

"Brief an Englebert Krebs": Letter dated July 14, 1919.

"Brief an Herbert Marcuse": Letter dated January 20, 1948.

"Brief an William J. Richardson": Letter dated early April, 1962, Freiburg.

"Brief an Carl Schmitt": Letter dated August 22, 1933.

"Brief an Arthur H. Schrynemakers": Letter dated September 20, 1966, for the
    Heidegger Circle conference, Duquesne University, Pittsburgh.

"Brief an Victor Schwoerer vom 02.10.1929": Letter to Deputy Secretary
    General of the Notgemeinschaft detuschen Gesellschaft, 1929.

"Brief an Joan Stambaugh and J. Glenn Gray": Excerpts from a letter in
    response to questions posed by the co-editors of the projected English
    Works of Martin Heidegger, Summer 1970.

"Brief an *Münchner Süddeutschen Zeitung*": Letter dated June 14, 1950, in
    response to "Hanfstaengel contra Heidegger," printed in the *Münchner
    Süddeutschen Zeitung* (Munich).

"Briefe an Emil Staiger": Letters from autumn of 1950 and December 28, 1950
    to Emil Staiger on a poem by Eduard Mörike, "Auf eine Lampe."

"Briefe": Letters to the Denazification Committee: November 4, 1945, and
    December 15, 1945, following Heidegger's appearance before the
    committee.

"Cézanne (spätere Fassung)": Last version of "Cézanne" (1974). Original
    version published in "Gedachtes. Für René Char in freundschaftlichen
    Gedenken" (see below).

"Cüppers, Ad. Jos. *Versiegelte Lippen*. Erzählungen aus dem irischen
    Volksleben des 19. Jahrhunderts": Book review, December 1910.

Curriculum vitae: Document written to accompany his *Habilitationsschrift, Die
    Kategorien- und Bedeutungslehre des Duns Scotus*, 1915.

"Dank bei der Verleihung des staatlichen Hebelgedenkenpreises": Address
    given May 10, 1960, acknowledging the Hebel National Memorial Prize on
    the occasion of the 200th anniversary of the birth of Johann Peter Hebel.

"Dasein und Wahrsein nach Aristoteles (Interpretation von Buch VI [der]
    Nikomachischen Ethik): Transcript of a lecture given in December 1924.

"Davoser Disputation zwischen Ernst Cassirer und Martin Heidegger [Protokoll
    der `Arbeitsgemeinschaft Cassirer-Heidegger']": Summary of seminar

discussions held March 17-April 4, 1929, Davos Academy, prepared by Otto Bollnow and Joachim Ritter.

"Davoser Vorträge: Kants *Kritik der reinen Vernunft* und die Aufgabe einer Grundlegung der Metaphysik": Heidegger's summary of three lectures given in March 1929, at the Davos Academy.

"Dichten und Denken. Zu Stefan Georges Gedicht `Das Wort'": Lecture given May 11, 1958, in Vienna. Revised title: "Das Wort" (1959)

" . . . dichterisch wohnet der Mensch . . .": Lecture given on October 6, 1951, Bühlerhöhe.

"Das Ding": First of four lectures in the series "Einblick in das was ist," originally given December 1, 1949, at the Bremen Club.

"Edmund Husserl zum 70. Geburtstag": Address given on April 8, 1929, on the occasion of the presentation to Husserl of a *Festschrift* in his honor.

"Einführung in die Metaphysik": Lecture course given during the Summer Semester 1935, University of Freiburg.

"Einführung in die phänomenologische Forschung": Lecture course given during the Winter Semester 1923-24, University of Marburg.

"Einige Hinweise auf Hauptgeschichtspunkte für das theologische Gespräch über `Das Problem eines nichtobjectivierenden Denkens und Sprechens in der heutigen Theologie'": Letter written March 11, 1964, to participants at a conference held April 9-11, 1964, Drew University.

"Einleitung in die Philosophie. Denken und Dichten": Lecture course "Nietzsches Metaphysik" begun during the Winter Semester 1944, University of Freiburg, but discontinued in November after the second session.

"Einleitung in die Phänomenologie der Religion": Lecture course given during the Winter Semester 1920-21, University of Freiburg.

"Einleitung zu `Was ist Metaphysik?'. Der Rückgang in den Grund der Metaphysik": Introduction to the inaugural lecture, written for the 5th edition (1949).

"Das Ende der Philosophie und die Aufgabe des Denkens": Lecture given during a colloquium on Kierkegaard in Paris, April 21-23, 1964.

"Entwürfe zur Geschichte des Seins als Metaphysik": Notes on Nietzsche written in 1941.

"Das Ereignis": Text from 1941-42.

"Die Erinnerung in die Metaphysik": Essay written in 1941.

"Eräuterung der 'Einleitung' zu Hegels 'Phänomenologie des Geistes (1942)'": Treatises prepared for presentation to a small group of scholars.

"Die ewige Wiederkehr des Gleichen und der Wille zur Macht": A two-lecture conclusion to the first three courses on Nietzsche given at the University of Freiburg. These lectures were never presented.

"Der Fehl heiliger Namen": A text written in 1974, dedicated to Hugo Friedrich.

"Förster, Fr. W. *Autorität und Freiheit. Betrachtungen zum Kulturproblem der Kirche*": Book review from May 1910.

"Frage und Urteil": Lecture, July 10, 1915.

"Gedachtes. Für René Char in freundschaftlichen Gedenken": Seven short poems written in 1970: "Zeit," "Wege," "Winke," "Ortschaft," "Cézanne," "Vorspiel," "Dank".

"Die Gefahr": Third lecture in the series "Einblick in das was Ist," given December 1, 1949, at the Bremen Club.

"Gelassenheit. Bodenständigkeit im Atomzeitalter": Address given October 30, 1955, on the 175th anniversary of the birth of the composer Conradin Kreuzer, Meßkirch.

"Georg Trakl. Eine Erörterung seines Gedichtes": Essay written in 1953. Revised title: "Die Sprache im Gedicht. Eine Erörterung von Georg Trakls Gedicht" (1959).

"Die Geschichte des Seyns (1938/40)": Text from 1938-40.

"Geschichte des Zeitbegriffs. Prolegomena zur Geschichte des Zeitbegriffs": Lecture course given during the Summer Semester 1925, University of Marburg.

"Gespräch mit Martin Heidegger": Protocol of informal discussions at the Protestant Academy of Hofgeismar, held in early December, 1953, recorded by Hermann Noack, corrected and completed by Heidegger in 1973.

"Gespräch mit Zygmunt Adamcsewski": Record of Heidegger 's conversations with Zygmunt Adamczewski in Freiburg and Todtnauberg, October 1968.

"Das Ge-Stell": The second of four lectures first presented in the series "Einblick in das was ist," given December 1, 1949, at the Bremen Club. A revised and expanded version with the title "Die Frage nach der Technik" was given on November 18, 1953 at the Bavarian Academy of Fine Arts, Munich.

"Das Gedicht": Lecture given August 25, 1968, in honor of Friedrich Ernst Jünger's birthday.

"Gredt, Jos., O.S.B. *Elementa Aristotelico-Thomisticae.* Vol. I. Logica, Philos.at. Edit II": Book review, March 1912.

"Grundbegriffe": Lecture course given during the Winter Semester 1941, University of Freiburg.

"Grundbegriffe der antiken Philosophie": Lecture course given during the Summer Semester 1926, University of Marburg.

"Grundbegriffe der aristotelischen Philosophie": Lecture course given during the Summer Semester 1924, University of Marburg.

"Die Grundbegriffe der Metaphysik. Welt, Endlichkiet, Vereinzelung": Lecture course given during the Winter Semester 1929-30, University of Freiburg.

"Die Grundfrage der Philosphie": Lecture course given Summer Semester 1933 at the University of Freiburg.

"Grundfragen der Metaphysik": Lecture course given during the Winter Semester 1935-36 at the University of Freiburg.

"Grundfragen der Philosophie: Vom Wesen der Wahrheit (*aletheia* und *poiesis*": Lecture course given during the Winter Semester 1937-38, University of Freiburg.

"Die Grundprobleme der Phänomenologie": Lecture course given during the Summer Semester 1927, University of Marburg.

"Grundprobleme der Phänomenologie": Lecture course given during the Winter Semester 1919-20, University of Freiburg.

Grundsätze des Denkens: Series of five lectures given at the University of Freiburg, 1957.

"Grundsätze des Denkens": First in the series of lectures *Grundsätze des Denken* given in 1957 at the University of Freiburg. Revised in 1958 as a contribution in honor of the 75th birthday of Viktor Emil von Gebsattel.

"Ein Grußwort für das Symposion in Beirut November 1974": Letter written in 1974 for participants in a conference at the Goethe Institute in Beirut, Lebanon.

Hannah Arendt / Martin Heidegger. Briefe 1925 bis 1975: Correspondence, 1925-1975, with Hannah Arendt.

Hebel—der Hausfreund: Expanded version of an address "Gespräch mit Hebel beim `Schatz-kästlein' zum Hebeltag 1956."

"Hegel. 'Rechtsphilosophie' WS 1934/35: Seminar, Winter Semester, 1934-35, University of Freiburg.

"Hegel und die Griechen": Lecture given at the Heidelberg Academy of Sciences, July 26, 1958. An earlier version (Aix-en-Provence, March 20, 1958) was published in a French translation, by Jean Beaufret and Pierre-Paul Sagave, in *Cahiers du Sud* (Paris) 47 (No. 349), January 1959, 355-368.

"Hegels Phänomenologie des Geistes": Lecture course given during the Winter Semester 1930-31, University of Freiburg.

"Hegels Begriff der Erfahrung": Text written in 1942-43, based on a series of seminars devoted to Hegel's *Phänomenologie des Geistes* given at the University of Freiburg.

"Heimkunft / An die Verwandten": Lecture given at the University of Freiburg on June 6, 1943, on the 100th anniversary of the death of Friedrich Hölderlin.

Heraklit. Martin Heidegger-Eugen Fink. Seminar 1966/67: Seminar on Heraclitus, with Eugen Fink, given during the Winter Semester 1966-67, University of Freiburg.

"Heraklit": Text written in 1954 for a *Festschrift* based on material from the lecture course "Der Anfang des abendländischen Denkens," prepared for the Summer Semester 1943, University of Freiburg. Revised title: "Aletheia (Heraklit, Fragment 16)" (1954).

Heraklit. Der Anfang des abendländischen Denkens. Logik. Heraklits Lehre vom Logos: Lecture course given Summer Semester 1944.

"Die Herkunft des Denkens": Preface (973) to a text on Parmenides Fragment 1, line 29 (*aletheies eukyleos atremos etor*) from the seminar in Zähringen.

"Hölderlin und das Wesen der Dichtung": Lecture given April 2, 1936, Rome.

"Hölderlins Himmel und Erde": Lecture given June 6, 1959, for the Munich Hölderlin Society.

"Hölderlins Hymnen: 'Der Ister'": Lecture course given during the Summer Semester 1942, University of Freiburg.

Hölderlins Hymnen "Germanien" und "Der Rhein": Lecture course given during the Winter Semester 1934-35, University of Freiburg.

"Die Idee der Philosophie und das Weltanschauungsproblem": Lecture course given during the Wartime Semester 1919, University of Freiburg.

"In memoriam Max Scheler": Eulogy on the death of Max Scheler, given on May 21, during the Summer Semester 1928, University of Marburg.

"Interpretation Platonishcer Dialoge ("*Sophistes, Philebus*)": Lecture course given during the Winter Semester 1924-25, University of Marburg.

"Interpretationen aus der antiken Philosophie: Aristoteles, *Metaphysik*, IX (*dynamis-energeia*)": Lecture course given during the Summer Semester 1931, University of Freiburg.

"Jörgensen, Joh. *Das Reisebuch*. Licht und dunkle Natur und Geist": Book review, January 1911.

"Julinacht": Poem, Summer of 1911.

"Kant und das Problem der Metaphysik": Lecture course given during the Winter Semester 1925-26, University of Marburg.

"Kants These über das Sein": Lecture given May 17, 1961, Kiel.

Die Kategorien- und Bedeutungslehre des Duns Scotus: *Habilitationsschrift*, University of Freiburg, 1915.

"Die Kehre": The last of four lectures in the series "Einblick in das was ist," originally given December 1, 1949, at the Bremen Club.

"Κοινόν. Aus der Geschichte des Seyns (1939/40)": Text from 1939-40.

"Das Kriegstriduum in Messkirch": Newspaper article, January 13, 1915.

"Die Kunst und das Denken": Colloquy with Hoseki Shin'ichi Hisamatsu on May 18, 1958, University of Freiburg, transcribed by Alfredo Guzzoni.

"Lebenslauf": *Curriculum vitae* (1913) appended to Heidegger's doctoral dissertation (1914), University of Freiburg.

"Die Lehrer trifft den Türmer an der Tür zum Turmaufgang": Dialogue written in 1944-45.

"Logik: Die Frage nach der Wahrheit": Lecture course given during the Winter Semester, 1925-26, University of Marburg.

"Logik": Lecture course given during the Summer Semester 1928, University of Marburg.

"Logik als die Frage nach dem Wesen der Sprache": Lecture course given Summer Semester 1934, University of Freiburg.

"Logos (Heraklit, Fragment 50)": Essay written in 1944, based on the lecture course "Logik. Heraklits Lehre vom Logos" given during the Summer Semester 1944, University of Freiburg.

Martin Heidegger/Karl Jaspers Briefwechsel: 1920-1963: Correspondence, 1920-1963, with Karl Jaspers.

"Martin Heidegger im Gespräch:" Transcript of a conversation between Martin Heidegger and Richard Wisser, filmed on September 17, 1969, for broadcast on television [ZDF].

"Mein Weg in die Phänomenologie": Essay written in 1963 in honor of the publisher Hermann Niemeyer. Supplement added in 1969.

"Die Metaphysik als Geschichte des Seins": Essay written in 1941, Freiburg.

"Moira (Parmenides VIII, 34-41)": Undelivered portion of the lecture course "Was heißt Denken?," given during Winter Semester 1951-52 and Summer Semester 1952, University of Freiburg. It is a supplement to Part II, Lecture XI.

"Nachwort [1943] zu `Was ist Metaphysik?'": Postscript to the inaugural address, added in 1943 for the 4th edition of the lecture. Revised in 1949 for the 5th edition.

"Die Negativität. Eine Auseinandersetzung mit Hegel aus dem Ansatz in der Negativität (1938/39, 1941)." Treatise prepared for presentation to a small group of scholars.

"Neuere Forschungen über Logik": Review essay, 1912.

"Neuzeitliche Naturwissenschaft und moderne Technik": Letter written April 11, 1976, to the participants of 10th Heidegger Circle conference, held May 14-16, 1976, DePaul University, Chicago, Illinois.

"Nietzsche: Der europäische Nihilismus": Heidegger's fourth and last course on Nietzsche, given during the second trimester of 1940, University of Freiburg.

"Nietzsche: *Der Wille zur Macht* als Kunst": Heidegger's first lecture course on Nietzsche, given during the Winter Semester 1936-37, University of Freiburg.

"Nietzsches Metaphysik": Essay from 1940, once thought to be material for a lecture course prepared in 1940 for the Winter Semester of 1941-42, University of Freiburg, but not given.

"Nietzsches metaphysische Grundstellung im abendländischen Denken. Die ewige Wiederkehr des Gleichen": Heidegger's second lecture course on Nietzsche, given during the Summer Semester 1937, University of Freiburg.

"Nietzsches Wort `Gott ist tot'": Lecture written in 1943, based on the Nietzsche courses (1936-40) given at the University of Freiburg.

"Nietzsches Lehre vom Willen zur Macht als Erkenntnis": Heidegger's third lecture course on Nietzsche, given during the Summer Semester 1939, University of Freiburg.

"Nur noch ein Gott kann uns retten": Transcript of an interview with Heidegger on September 23, 1966. Published in 1976 in *Der Spiegel*.

"Oelbergstunden": Poem written in early 1911.

"Ontologie (Hermeneutik der Faktizität)": Lecture course given during the Summer Semester 1923, University of Freiburg.

"Die onto-theo-logische Verfassung der Metaphysik": The concluding lecture for a seminar during the winter semester 1956-57 on Hegel's *Science of Logic*, given on February 24, 1957 in Todtnauberg.

"Parmenides": Lecture course given during the Winter Semester 1942-43, University of Freiburg.

"Parmenides: *aletheies eukyleos atremos etor* ": Text of essay from the seminar in Zähringen, 1973.

"Per mortem ad vitam (Gedanken über Jörgensens *Lebenslüge und Lebenswahrheit*": Book review essay written in March 1910.

"Phänomenologie der Anschauung und des Ausdrucks": Lecture course given during the Summer Semester 1920, University of Freiburg.

"Phänomenologie und Theologie": Lecture given March 9, 1927 in Tübingen. A preface was added, in 1970, for the first German publication of the lecture.

"Phänomenologie und tranzendentale Wertphilosophie: Lecture course given during the Summer Semester 1919, University of Freiburg.

"Phänomenologische Interpretation von Kants *Kritik der reinen Vernunft*": Lecture course given during the Winter Semester 1927-28, Marburg University.

"Phänomenologische Interpretationen zu Aristoteles (Anzeige der hermeneutischen Situation)": Manuscript, written in the fall of 1922, outlining current and future research, submitted as part Heidegger's application for a full-time teaching position.

"Die Philosophien Grundlagen der mittelalterischen Mystik": Course scheduled for Winter Semester, 1918-19, University of Freiburg, but not given.

"Platons Lehre von der Wahrheit": Text written in 1940 for a private lecture, related to the lecture course "Vom Wesen der Wahrheit" given during the Winter Semester 1930-31, University of Freiburg.

"Das Problem der Sünde bei Luther": Student transcript of a two-part talk given in Rudolf Bultmann's seminar on "The Ethics of St. Paul" on February 14 and 21, 1924.

"Protokol": Excerpts from the protocol of Heidegger's seminar on January 26, 1961, for medical students and psychiatric residents from the Zurich Psychiatric University Clinic, given with Medard Boss in Zollikon (Zürich), Switzerland. Includes marginalia to the manuscript for *Grundriß der Medizin: Ansätze zu einer phänomenologischen Physiologie, Psychologie, Therapie und zu einer daseinsgemäßen Präventiv-Medizin in der modernen Industriegesellschaft*, by Medard Boss.

"Protokollen - Gespräche": Excerpts from protocols of conversations with Medard Boss, seminar transcripts and ancillary texts prepared for meetings with Boss and his students in Zollikon (Zürich) on the meaning of Heidegger's work for psychiatry and psychotherapy: March 8, 1965; November 23, 1965; November 28-30, 1965; July 14, 1969.

"Raum, Mensch und Sprache": Revised version of a lecture given October 3, 1964, at the Galerie im Erker, St. Gallen, Switzerland.

"Das Realitätsproblem in der modernen Philosophie": Heidegger's first published paper, 1912.

"Das Rektorat 1933/34: Tatsachen und Gedanken": Essay written in 1945.

"Religionspsychologie und Unterbewußtsein": Essay from March 1912.

"Der Satz vom Grund": Lecture course given during the Winter Semester 1955-56, University of Freiburg.

"Der Satz vom Grund": Lecture given May 25, 1956, at the Bremen Club and October 24, 1956, at the University of Vienna.

"Der Satz der Identität": Lecture given June 27, 1957, at the University of Freiburg, on the occasion of the 500th anniversary of the founding of the university. Third in the lecture series *Grundsätze des Denkens*.

"Schelling, *Über das Wesen der menschlichen Freiheit*": Lecture course given during the Summer Semester 1936, University of Freiburg, with excerpts from the manuscripts of an advanced seminar on Schelling (Summer Semester 1941) and selected seminar notes on Schelling from the years 1941 to 1943.

"Schöpferische Landschaft: Warum bleiben wir in der Provinz?": Text written in the Autumn, 1933.

Sein und Zeit: Dedicated April 8, 1926, Todtnauberg.

"Die seinsgeschichtliche Bestimmung des Nihilismus": Essay written during the years 1944-46.

"Seinsverlassenheit und Irrnis": Notes on Nietzsche from the years 1936-46.

"Selbstanzeige. *Die Kategorien- und Bedeutungslehre des Duns Scotus*: Journal book notice of Heidegger's *Habilitationsschrift*, 1917.

"Die Selbstbehauptung der deutschen Universität": Heidegger's rectorial address, given May 27, 1933.

"Seminar in Le Thor 1966": Protocol of the first seminar held in Provence.

"Seminar in Le Thor": Protocol of the eight sessions of the second seminar held August 30-September 8, 1968, Provence. A French translation appeared in 1976.

"Seminar in Le Thor 1969": Final seminar held in Provence.

"Seminar in Zähringen 1973": Seminar held at Heidegger's home in Freiburg.

"Seminar Protokoll zu Heideggers Vorlesung `Zeit und Sein'": Transcript of a six-session seminar given September 11-13, 1962, in Todtnauberg, prepared by Alfredo Guzzoni and edited by Heidegger.

"Sprache": Verse written in 1972 sent to Raymond Panikkar, University of California, Santa Barbara, in March 1976.

"Die Sprache": Lecture given October 7, 1950, Bühlerhöhe.

"Die Sprache Johann Peter Hebels": Essay from 1955.

"Der Spruch des Anaximander": Essay written in 1946, Todtnauberg.

"Stiftender als Dichgten . . .": Poem written in Fall,1974.

"Trost": Poem written in early 1915.

"Über das Wesen der Universität und das akademischen Studiums": Lecture course given during the Summer Semester 1919, University of Freiburg.

"Über das Zeitverständnis in der Phänomenologie und im Denken der Seinsfrage": Essay written in 1969 in commemoration of the 30th anniversary of the death of Edmund Husserl.

"Überlieferte Sprache und Technische Sprache": Lecture given July 18, 1962, Comburg (Schwäbische Hall).

"Der Ursprung des Kunstwerkes": Lecture given November 13, 1935 in Freiburg. Expanded to a series of three lectures given November 17 and 24, 1936, and December 1, 1936, in Frankfurt. A "Zusatz" was added in 1956. An earlier version, "Vom Ursprung des Kunstwerkes: Erste Ausarbeitung," has been published and translated.

"Vom Ursprung des Kunstwerkes: Erste Ausarbeitung": First version of "Der Ursprung des Kunstwerkes."

"Versuch einer zweiten Bearbeitung. Einleitung. Die Idee der Phänomenologie und der Rückgang auf das Bewusstsein": Article written in 1927 for the Fourteenth Edition of the *Encyclopaedia Britannica*.

"V*ita*" [with Accompanying Letter to Georg Misch]: June 30, 1922.

"Vom Wesen und Begriff der *phusis*. Aristoteles *Physik* B,1": Text written in 1939 for a seminar entitled "Über die *phusis* bei Aristoteles," given the First Trimester 1940, University of Freiburg.

"Vom Wesen der menschlichen Freiheit: Einleitung in die Philosophie": Lecture course given during the Summer Semester of 1930, University of Freiburg.

"Vom Wesen der Sprache. Die Metaphysik der Sprache und die Wesung des Wortes. Zu herders Abhandlung "'Über den Ursprung der Sprache'": Notes for a graduate seminar given during Summer Semester 1939, University of Freiburg.

"Vom Wesen der Wahrheit": Lecture written in 1930.

"Vom Wesen der Wahrheit ("Höhlengleichnis" und *Theätet*, über *pseudos*)": Lecture course given during the Winter Semester of 1930-31, University of Freiburg.

"Vom Wesen der Wahrheit": Lecture course given Winter Semester 1933-34, University of Freiburg.

"Vom Wesen des Grundes": Essay written in 1929 for a *Festschrift* celebrating the 70th birthday of Edmund Husserl. The third edition (1949) of the book was supplemented with a "Vorwort."

"Vorbemerkung": Prefatory note to the first edition of *Wegmarken*, Freiburg im Breisgau, early Summer 1967.

"Vorbemerkung zur Wiederholung der Rede": Introductory remarks to the lecture ""Heimkunft / An die Verwandten," given on June 21, 1943, University of Freiburg.

"Vorbemerkungen des Herausgebers ("Einleitung")": Introduction to Heidegger's edition of Husserl's lectures on the inner consciousness of time, written in 1928.

"Vortrag gehalten con Prof. Martin Heidegger am Pfingstmontag 1926 in Marburg vor der Akademischen Vereinigung": Lecture, 1926.

"Vorwort": Preface to the 2nd Edition (1951) of *Erläuterungen zu Hölderlins Dichtung*.

"Vorwort zur Lesung von Hölderlins Gedichten": Introductory remarks for the recording *Heidegger ließt Hölderlin*, 1963.

"Was heißt Denken?": Lecture course given during the Winter Semester 1951-52 and Summer Semester 1952, University of Freiburg.

"Was ist Metaphysik?" (1998[15]): Heidegger's inaugural lecture to the faculties of the University of Freiburg, given on July 24, 1929. The text was expanded for the Fourth Edition (1943) of the work with the addition of a "Nachwort." The "Nachwort" was revised and an introduction, "Einleitung. Der Rückgang in der Grund der Metaphysik," was added for the Fifth Edition (1949).

"Was ist das -- die Philosophie?": Lecture given in Cérisy-la-Salle in August 1955.

"Der Weg zur Sprache": Revised title of "Die Sprache," a lecture first given in January 1959.

"Wer ist Nietzsches Zarathustra?": Lecture given May 8, 1953, at the Bremen Club.

"Das Wesen der Sprache": Text of a lecture series given December 4 and 18, 1957, and February 5, 1958, at the University of Freiburg.

"Wie wenn am Feiertage . . .": Lecture on Hölderlin, 1939.

"Wilhelm Diltheys Forschungsarbeit und der Kampf um eine historische Weltanschauung": Walter Bröcker's transcript of a lecture series given April 16-21, 1925, in Kassel.

"Wissenschaft und Besinnung": Lecture first given May 15, 1953, at a conference held by the Arbeitsgemeinschaft wissenschaftlicher Sortimenter near Freiburg. Revised for a presentation on August 4, 1953.

"Wozu Dichter?": Private lecture given December 29, 1946, in remembrance of the 20th anniversary of the death of Rainer Maria Rilke.

"Zeit und Sein": Lecture given January 31, 1962, at the University of Freiburg.

"Der Zeitbegriff in der Geschichtswissenschaft": Trial lecture for the *venia legendi* at the University of Freiburg, presented to the philosophy faculty on July 27, 1915.

"Zu Ernst Jünger": Two texts on Ernst Jünger from 1939-40.

"Zur Erörterung der Gelassenheit. Aus einem Feldweggespräch über das Denken": Part of a long discussion from the years 1944-45.

"Zur Frage nach der Bestimmung der Sache des Denkens": Text based on an address given October 230, 1965, in Amriswil, in honor of Ludwig Binswanger as "Das Ende des Denkens in der Gestalt der Philosophie."

"Zur Geschichte des philosophischen Lehrstules seit 1866": An account of the development of the Marburg School of Kant studies.

"Zu Odebrechts und Cassirers Kritik des Kantbuches": Notes found in Heidegger's copy of the first edition of *Kant und das Problem der Meatphysik* on reviews of the book published by Ernst Cassirer (in *Kantstudien* (Berlin) 1-2, 1931, pp. 1-26) and Rudolf Odebrecht (in *Blätter für deutsche Philosophie* (Heidelberg) 6(1), 1931-32, pp. 132-135).

"Zur philosophischen Orientierung für Akademiker": Review article, March 1911.

Zur Seinsfrage: Contribution written in 1955 for a volume dedicated to Ernst Jünger. Original title "Über `die Linie'."

"Zur Zuspruch des Feldweges": Essay written in 1949. Revised title: "Der Feldweg" (1950).

III. GERMAN TEXTS TRANSLATED (1949-2015):
DATE OF COMPOSITION (1910-1976)

1910

"*Per mortem ad vitam*. (Gedanken über Jörgensens 'Lebenslüge und Lebenswahrheit')": Review article, March 1910.

"Förster, Fr. W. *Autoritäy und Freiheit*": Review article, May 1910.

"Cüppers, Ad. Jos. *Versiegelte Lippen*. Erzählungen aus dem irischen Volksleben des 19. Jahrhunderts": Review article, (December 1910).

1911

"Jörgensen, Joh. *Das Reisebuch*. Licht und dunkle Natur und Geist": Review article, January 1911.

"Zur philosophischen Orientierung für Akademiker": Review article, March 1911.

"Auf stillen Pfaden": Poem, early 1911.

"Oelbergstunden": Poem, early 1911.

"Julinacht": Poem, early 1911.

1912

"Religionspsychologie und Unterbebusstsein": Article, March 1912.

"Gredt, Jos., O.S.B. *Elementa Aristotelico-Thomisticae*. Vol. I. Logica, Philos.at. Edit II": Book review, March 1912.

"Das Realitätsproblem in der modernen Philosophie": Heidegger's first published paper (1912).

"Neuere Forschungen über Logik": Review essay, 1912.

1913

"*Bibliotehek wertvoller Novellen und Erzählungen*. Herausgegeben von Prof. Dr. O. Hellinghaus": Book review, January 1913.

1914

"Lebenslauf": *Curriculum vitae* (1913) appended to Heidegger's doctoral dissertation (1914), University of Freiburg.

1915

"Das Kriegstriduum in Messkirch": Newspaper article, January 13, 1915.

Die Kategorien- und Bedeutungslehre des Duns Scotus: *Habilitationsschrift*
[Faculty Thesis], University of Freiburg (1915).

Curriculum vitae: Written to accompany *Die Kategorien- und Bedeutungslehre des Duns Scotus* (1915).

"Trost": Poem, early 1915.

"Frage und Urteil": Lecture, July 10, 1915.

"Der Zeitbegriff in der Geschichtswissenschaft": *Probevorlesung* [trial lecture] for the *venia legendi* [right to lecture] at the University of Freiburg, presented to the philosophy faculty on July 27, 1915.

1916

"Abendgang auf der Reichenau": Poem written in 1916.

1917

"Selbstanzeige. *Die Kategorien- und Bedeutungslehre des Duns Scotus*": Journal book notice of the author's *Habilitationsschrift*.

1918

"Die Philosophien Grundlagen der mittelalterischen Mystik": Course scheduled for Winter Semester, University of Freiburg, but not given.

1919

Brief an Engelbert Krebs: Letter, January 9, 1919.

"Brief Martin Heideggers an Elisabeth Husserl": Letter, April 24, 1919.

Brief an Englebert Krebs: Letter, July 14, 1919.

"Die Idee der Philosophie und das Weltanschauungsproblem": Lecture course given during the Kriegnotssemester [wartime semester] 1919, University of Freiburg.

"Phänomenologie und tranzendentale Wertphilosophie": Lecture course given during the Summer Semester 1919, University of Freiburg.

"Über das Wesen der Universität und das akademischen Studiums": Lecture course given during the Summer Semester 1919, University of Freiburg.

1919-20

"Grundprobleme der Phänomenologie" Lecture course given during the Winter Semester 1919-21, University of Freiburg.

1919-21

"Anmerkungen zu Karl Jaspers *Psychologie der Weltanschauungen*": Review article, 1919-21.

1920

Martin Heidegger/Karl Jaspers Briefwechsel: 1920-1963: Correspondence with Karl Jaspers.

"Phänomenologie der Anschauung und des Ausdrucks": Lecture notes for a course given during the Summer Semester 1920, University of Freiburg.

"Einleitung in die Phänomenologie der Religion": Lecture course given during the Winter Semester 1920-21, University of Freiburg.

"Augustinus under der Neoplatonismus": Lecture course given during Winter Semester, University of Freiburg.

1921-29

"Auszüge [7] aus Briefen Heideggers an Karl Löwith": Letters (excerpts) dated August 19, 1921; March 26, 1924; August 21, 1924; June 30, 1925; August 20, 1927; February 3, 1929; September 3, 1929.

1922

"V*ita*, with Accompanying Letter to Georg Misch": June 30, 1922.

"Phänomenologische Interpretationen zu Aristoteles (Anzeige der hermeneutischen Situation)": Manuscript, written in the fall of 1922, outlining current and future research and submitted as part Heidegger's application for a full-time teaching position.

1923

"Ontologie (Hermeneutik der Faktizität)": Lecture course given during the Summer Semester of 1923, University of Freiburg.

"Einführung in die phänomenologische Forschung": Lecture course given during the Winter Semester 1923-24, University of Marburg.

1924

"Das Problem der Sünde bei Luther": Student transcript of a two-part talk given in Rudolf Bultmann's seminar on "The Ethics of St. Paul" on February 14 and 21, 1924.

"Der Begriff der Zeit": Lecture given at the Marburg Theological Society on
   July 25, 1924.
"Interpretation Platonishcer Dialoge ("*Sophistes, Philebus*)": Lecture course
   given during the Winter Semester 1924-25, University of Marburg.
"Grundbegriffe der aristotelischen Philosophie": Lecture course given during
   the Summer Semester 1924, University of Marburg.
"Der Begriff der Zeit": Text of unpublished review article written in 1924 for
   the *Deutsche Vierteljahrsheft für Literaturwissenschaft und
   Geistesgeschichte*.
"Dasein und Wahrsein nach Aristoteles (Interpretation von Buch VI [der]
   Nikomachischen Ethik)": Transcript of a lecture given in December 1924.

1925

"Wilhelm Diltheys Forschungsarbeit und der Kampf um eine historische
   Weltanschauung": Walter Bröcker's transcript of a lecture series given
   April 16-21, 1925, in Kassel.
"Geschichte des Zeitbegriffs. Prolegomena zur Geschichte des Zeitbegriffs":
   Lecture course given during the Summer Semester 1925, University of
   Marburg.
Hannah Arendt / Martin Heidegger. Briefe 1925 bis 1975: Correspondence with
   Hannah Arendt.

1925-26

"Kant und das Problem der Metaphysik": Lecture course given during the
   Winter Semester 1925-26, University of Marburg.
"Logik: Die Frage nach der Wahrheit": Lecture course given during the Winter
   Semester 1925-26, University of Marburg.

1926

"Grundbegriffe der antiken Philosophie": Lecture course given during the
   Summer Semester 1926, University of Marburg.
"Vortrag gehalten con Prof. Martin Heidegger am Pfingstmontag 1926 in
   Marburg vor der Akademischen Vereinigung": Lecture for Penetost
   Monday, 1926, at the Marburg Academic Association.
Sein und Zeit: Dedicated April 18, 1926, Todnauberg.

1927

"Phänomenologie und Theologie": Lecture given March 9, 1927, in Tübingen. A preface ["Vorwort"] was added, in 1970, for the first German publication of the lecture.

"Versuch einer zweiten Bearbeitung. Einleitung. Die Idee der Phänomenologie und der Rückgang auf das Bewusstsein": Article written in 1927 for the Fourteenth Edition of the *EncyclopÆdia Britannica*.

"Die Grundprobleme der Phänomenologie": Lecture course given during the Summer Semester 1927, University of Marburg.

"Phänomenologische Interpretation von Kants *Kritik der reinen Vernunft*": Lecture course given during the Winter Semester 1927-28, University of Marburg.

"Zur Geschichte des philosophischen Lehrstules seit 1866": An account of the development of the Marburg School of Kant studies.

Brief an Edmund Husserl: Letter to Edmund Husserl dated October 22, 1927, to accompany the text of "The Idea of Phenomenology."

"Brief an Rudolf Bultmann": Letter to Rudolf Bultmann, December 31, 1927.

1928

"Besprechung: Ernst Cassirers *Philosophie der symbolischen Formen*. 2. Teil: *Das mythische Denken* [1925]": Book review, 1928.

"Logik": Lecture course given during the Summer Semester 1928, University of Marburg.

"In memoriam Max Scheler": Eulogy on the death of Max Scheler, given on May 21, 1928, during the Summer Semester, University of Marburg.

"Aus der letzten Marburger Vorlesung": Text based on §5 of the lecture course "Logik," given during the Summer Semester 1928, University of Marburg.

"Vorbemerkungen des Herausgebers ("Einleitung")": Introduction to Heidegger's edition of Husserl's lecture on inner consciousness of time.

1929

"Davoser Disputation zwischen Ernst Cassirer und Martin Heidegger": Summary of seminar discussions held March 17-April 4, 1929, Davos Academy, prepared by Otto Bollnow and Joachim Ritter.

"Davoser Vorträge: Kants *Kritik der reinen Vernunft* und die Aufgabe einer Grundlegung der Metaphysik": Heidegger's summary of three lectures given in March 1929, at the Davos Academy.

"Edmund Husserl zum 70. Geburtstag": Address given on April 8, 1929, on the
occasion of the presentation to Husserl of a *Festschrift* in his honor.

"Was ist Metaphysik?": Inaugural lecture to the faculties of the University of
Freiburg, given on July 24, 1929. The text was expanded for the Fourth
Edition (1943) of the work with the addition of a "Nachwort." The
"Nachwort" was revised and "Einleitung. Der Rückgang in der Grund der
Metaphysik" was added for the Fifth Edition (1949).

"Vom Wesen des Grundes": Essay written in 1929 for a Festschrift celebrating
the 70th birthday of Edmund Husserl. The third edition (1949) of the book
was supplemented with a "Vorwort."

"Brief an Victor Schwoerer vom 02.10.1929": Letter to Deputy Secretary
General of the Notgemeinschaft deutschen Gesellschaft.

"Die Grundbegriffe der Metaphysik. Welt – Endlichkiet - Vereinzelung":
Lecture course given during the Winter Semester 1929-30, University of
Freiburg.

"Aufzeichnungen zum Kantbuch": Notes form 1929 on, found in Heidegger's
copy of the first edition of *Kant und das Problem der Metaphysik*.

1929-33

Briefe an Elisabeth Blochmann: Correspondence (1929-1933) with Elisabeth
Blochmann.

1930

"Vom Wesen der Wahrheit": Lecture written in 1930.

"Vom Wesen der menschilichen Freiheit. Einleitung in die Philosophie":
Lecture course given during the Summer Semester 1930, University of
Freiburg.

"Hegels Phänomenologie des Geistes": Lecture course given during the Winter
Semester 1930-31, University of Freiburg.

1931

"Interpretationen aus der antiken Philosophie: Aristoteles, *Metaphysik*, IX
(*dynamis-energeia*)": Lecture course given during the Summer Semester
1931, University of Freiburg.

"Vom Wesen der Wahrheit ("Höhlengleichnis" und *Theätet*, über *pseudos*)":
Lecture course given during the Winter Semester 1930-31, University of
Freiburg.

"Zu Odebrechts und Cassirers Kritik des Kantbuches": Notes found in
Heidegger's copy of the first edition of *Kant und das Problem der
Meatphysik* on reviews of the book published by Ernst Cassirer (in
Kantstudien (Berlin) 1-2, 1931, pp. 1-26) and Rudolf Odebrecht (in *Blätter
für deutsche Philosophie* (Heidelberg) 6(1), 1931-32, pp. 132-135).

1932
"Der Anfang der abendländischen Philosophie, Auslegung des Anaximander
und Parmenides": Lecture course given during the Summer Semester 1932,
University of Freiburg.

1933
"Die Selbstbehauptung der deutschen Universität": Rectorial address, given
May 27, 1933.
"Brief an Carl Schmitt": Letter to Carl Schmitt, August 22, 1933.
"Schöpferische Landschaft: Warum bleiben wir in der Provinz?": Text written in
the Fall of 1933.
"Die Grundfrage der Philosophie": Lecture courses given Summer Semester
1933, University of Freiburg.

1933-34
"Vom Wesen der Wahrheit": Lecture course given Winter Semester 1933-34,
University of Freiburg.

1934
"Logik als die Frage nach dem Wesen der Sprache": Lecture course given
Summer Semester 1934, University of Freiburg.

1934-35
Hölderlins Hymnen "Germanien" und "Der Rhein": Lecture course given
during the Winter Semester 1934-35, University of Freiburg.
"Hegel. 'Rechtsphilosophie' WS 1934/35: Seminar given Winter Semester
1934/35, University of Freiburg.w

1935
"Einführung in die Metaphysik": Lecture course given during the Summer
Semester 1935, University of Freiburg.

"Der Ursprung des Kunstwerkes": Lecture given November 13, 1935 in
    Freiburg. Expanded to a series of three lectures given November 17 and 24,
    1936, and December 1, 1936, in Frankfurt. A "Zusatz" was added in 1956.
    An earlier version "Of the Origin of the Work of Art (first elaboration)"
    was published (see below).
"Grundfragen der Metaphysik": Lecture course given during the Winter
    Semester 1935-36, University of Freiburg.

1936

"Hölderlin und das Wesen der Dichtung": Lecture given April 2, 1936, Rome.
"Schelling, *Über das Wesen der menschlichen Freiheit*": Lecture course given
    during the Summer Semester 1936, University of Freiburg, with excerpts
    from the manuscripts of an advanced seminar on Schelling (Summer
    Semester 1941) and selected seminar notes on Schelling from the years
    1941 to 1943.
"Nietzsche: *Der Wille zur Macht* (als Kunst)": Heidegger's first lecture course
    on Nietzsche, given during the Winter Semester 1936-37, University of
    Freiburg. First Section: "Nietzsche als metaphysicher Denker."

1936-38

"Beiträge zur Philosophie (Vom Ereignis)": Ruminations from 1936-38.

1936-46

"Seinsverlassenheit und Irrnis": Notes on Nietzsche from the years 1936-46.

1937

"Nietzsches metaphysische Grundstellung im abendländischen Denken. Die
    Lehre vom ewige Wiederkehr des Gleichen": Heidegger's second lecture
    course on Nietzsche, given during the Summer Semester 1937, University
    of Freiburg.

1937-38

"Grundfragen der Philosophie: Vom Wesen der Wahrheit (*aletheia* und *poiesis*":
    Lecture course given during the Winter Semester 1937-38, University of
    Freiburg.

1938

"Die Begründung des neuzeitlichen Weltbildes durch die Metaphysik": Lecture given June 9, 1938, Freiburg. Revised title (1950): "Die Zeit des Weltbildes."

1938-39

Besinnung: Text from 1938-39.

"Die Negativität. Eine Auseinandersetzung mit Hegel aus dem Ansatz in der Negativität": Treatise prepared for presentation to a small group of scholars. Includes a text from 1941. Published with "Erläuterung der 'Einleitung' zu Hegels 'Phänomenologie des Geistes'."

1938-40

"Die Geschichte des Seyns (1938/40)": Text from 1938-40.

1939

"Nietzsches Lehre vom Willen zur Macht als Erkenntnis": Third lecture course on Nietzsche, given during the Summer Semester 1939, University of Freiburg.

"Vom Wesen der Sprache. Die Metaphysik der Sprache und die Wesung des Wortes. Zu herders Abhandlung "'Über den Ursprung der Sprache'": Notes for a graduate seminar given during Summer Semester 1939, University of Freiburg.

"Vom Wesen und Begriff der *phusis* Aristoteles *Physik* B,1": Text written for a seminar entitled "Über die *phusis* bei Aristoteles," given the First Trimester 1940, University of Freiburg.

"Die ewige Wiederkehr des Gleichen und der Wille zur Macht": A two-lecture conclusion to the first three courses on Nietzsche given at the University of Freiburg. These lectures were never presented.

"Wie wenn am Feiertage . . .": Lecture on Hölderlin.

1939-40

"Κοινόν. Aus der Geschichte des Seyns (1939/40)": Text from 1939-40.

1940

"Nietzsche: Der europäische Nihilismus": Heidegger's fourthand last course on
Nietzsche, given during the SecondTrimester of 1940, University of
Freiburg.

"Nietzsches Metaphysik": Essay from 1940, thought to be a lecture course for
the Winter Semester of 1941-42, University of Freiburg, but not given.

"Platons Lehre von der Wahrheit": Text written in 1940 for a private lecture,
related to the lecture course "Vom Wesen der Wahrheit" given during the
Winter Semester 1930-31, University of Freiburg.

1941

"Grundbegriffe": Lecture course given during the Winter Semester 1941,
University of Freiburg.

"Entwürfe zur Geschichte des Seins als Metaphysik": Notes on Nietzsche
written in 1941.

"Die Erinnerung in die Metaphysik": Essay written in 1941.

"Die Metaphysik als Geschichte des Seins": Essay written in 1941, Freiburg.

"Die Negativität. Eine Auseinandersetzung mit Hegel aus dem Ansatz in der
Negativität": Treatise prepared for presentation to a small group of scholars.
Includes a text prepared in 1938/39. Published with "Erläuterung der
'Einleitung' zu Hegels 'Phänomenologie des Geistes'."

1941-42

"Das Ereignis: Text from 1941-42.

1942

"Hölderlins Hymnen 'Der Ister'": Lecture course given during the Summer
Semester 1942, University of Freiburg.

"Andenken": Essay on Hölderlin.

"Parmenides": Lecture course given during the Winter Semester 1942-43,
University of Freiburg.

"Erläuterung der 'Einleitung' zu Hegels 'Phänomenologie des Geistes'":
Treatise prepared for presentation to a small group of scholars. Published
with "Die Negativität. Eine Auseinandersetzung mit Hegel aus dem Ansatz
in der Negativität (1938/39, 1941).

1942-43

"Hegels Begriff der Erfahrung": Text written in 1942-43, based on a series of seminars devoted to Hegel's *Phänomenologie des Geistes* given at the University of Freiburg.

1943

"Heimkunft / An die Verwandten": Address given at the University of Freiburg on June 6, 1943 on the 100th anniversary of the death of Friedrich Hölderlin.

"Nietzsches Wort `Gott ist tot'": Lecture written in 1943, based on the Nietzsche courses (1936-40) at the University of Freiburg.

"Nachwort [1943] zu `Was ist Metaphysik?'": Postscript to the inaugural address, added in 1943 for the 4th edition of the lecture. Revised in 1949 for the 5th edition.

"Vorbemerkung zur Wiederholung der Rede": Introductory remarks to the lecture "Heimkunft / An die Verwandten," given on June 21, 1943, University of Freiburg im Bresigau.

1944

"Logos (Heraklit, Fragment 50)": Essay written in 1944, based on the lecture course "Logik. Heraklits Lehre vom Logos," given during the Summer Semester 1944, University of Freiburg.

"Einleitung in die Philosophie. Denken und Dichten": Lecture course "Nietzsches Metaphysik," begun for the Winter Semester 1944, University of Freiburg, but discontinued in November after the second session.

1944-45

"Zur Erörterung der Gelassenheit. Aus einem Feldweggespräch über das Denken": Part of a long discussion from the years 1944-45. Published in its complete form as "Αγχιβασιν. Ein Gespräch selbstdritt auf einem Feldweg zwischen einem Forscher, einem Gelehrten und einem Weisen."

"Die Lehrer trifft den Türmer an der Tür zum Turmaufgang": Dialogue written in 1944-45.

1944-46

"Die seinsgeschichtliche Bestimmung des Nihilismus": Essay written during 1944-46.

1945

"Das Rektorat 1933/34: Tatsachen und Gedanken": Essay, 1945."Ἀγχιβασιν.
    Ein Gespräch selbstdritt auf einem Feldweg zwischen einem Forscher,
    einem Gelehrten und einem Weisen": Dialogue dated April 7, 1945.
"Abendgespräch in einem Kriegsgefangenenlager in Rußland zwischen einem
    Jüngeren und einem Älteren": Dialogue, May 8, 1945.
"Die Armut": Address given June 27, 1945, Hausen (near
    Beuron Archabbey)
Briefe: Letters to the Denazification Committee, November 4, 1945, and
    December 15, 1945, following Heidegger's appearance before the
    committee.

1946

"Der Spruch des Anaximander": Essay, 1946, Todtnauberg.
"Brief über den Humanismus": Text based on a letter to Jean Beaufret, 1946.
"Wozu Dichter?": Lecture given December 29, 1946, in remembrance of the
    20th anniversary of the death of Rainer Maria Rilke.

1947

"Aus der Erfahrung des Denkens": Text written during 1947.

1948

Brief an Herbert Marcuse: Letter dated January 20, 1948.

1949

"Einleitung zu `Was ist Metaphysik?'. Der Rückgang in den Grund der
    Metaphysik": Introduction essay to the inaugural address, written for the
    5th edition (1949).
"Zur Zuspruch des Feldweges": Essay written in 1949. Revised title: "Der
    Feldweg" (1950).
"Das Ding": First of four lectures in the series "Einblick in das was ist,"
    originally given December 1, 1949, Bremen Club.
"Das Ge-Stell": Second of four lectures first presented in the series "Einblick in
    das was ist," originally given December 1, 1949 at the Bremen Club. A
    revised and expanded version with the title "Die Frage nach der Technik"
    was given on November 18, 1953 at the Bavarian Academy of Fine Arts,
    Munich.

"Die Gefahr": Third of four lectures in the series "Einblick in das was ist," originally given December 1, 1949, Bremen Club.

"Die Kehre": Last of four lectures in the series "Einblick in das was ist," originally given December 1, 1949 at the Bremen Club.

1950

Brief an *Münchner Süddeutschen Zeitung*: Letter, June 14, 1950, in response to "Hanfstaengel contra Heidegger," printed in the *Münchner Süddeutschen Zeitung* (Munich).

Briefe an Emil Staiger: Letters dated Autumn 1950 and December 28, 1950, to Emil Staiger on a poem by Eduard Mörike, "Auf eine Lampe."

"Die Sprache": Lecture given October 7, 1950, Bühlerhöhe.

1951

"Bauen Wohnen Denken": Lecture given August 5, 1951, Darmstadt.

" . . . dichterisch wohnet der Mensch . . .": Lecture given October 6, 1951, Bühlerhöhe.

"Vorwort": Preface to 2nd Edition of *Erläuterungen zu Hölderlins Dichtung*.

1951-52

"Was heißt Denken?": Lecture course given during the Winter Semester 1951-52 and Summer Semester 1952, University of Freiburg.

"Moira (Parmenides VIII, 34-41)": Undelivered portion (supplement to Part II, Lecture XI)of the lecture course "Was heißt Denken?," given during Winter Semester 1951-52 and Summer Semester 1952, University of Freiburg.

1953

"Wer ist Nietzsches Zarathustra?": Lecture given May 8, 1953, at the Bremen Club.

"Wissenschaft und Besinnung": Lecture first given May 15, 1953, at a conference held by the Arbeitsgemeinschaft wissenschaftlicher Sortimenter, Freiburg. Revised for presentation on August 4, 1953.

"Georg Trakl. Eine Erörterung seines Gedichtes": Essay written in 1953. Revised title, "Die Sprache im Gedicht. Eine Erörterung von Georg Trakls Gedicht" (1959).

"Gespräch mit Martin Heidegger": Protocol of informal discussions at the
    Protestant Academy of Hofgeismar, held in early December, 1953, recorded
    by Hermann Noack, corrected and completed by Heidegger in 1973.

1953-54

"Aus einem Gespräch von der Sprache. Zwischen einem Japaner und einem
    Fragenden": Dialogue from the years 1953-54.

1954

"Heraklit": Text written in 1954 for a *Festschrift* based on material from the
    lecture course "Der Anfang des abendländischen Denkens," prepared for the
    Summer Semester 1943, University of Freiburg. Revised title: "Aletheia
    (Heraklit, Fragment 16)" (1954).

1955

"Was ist das -- die Philosophie?": Lecture given in Cérisy-la-Salle, August
    1955.
"Gelassenheit. Bodenständigkeit im Atomzeitalter": Address given October 30,
    1955, on the 175th anniversary of the birth of the composer Conradin
    Kreuzer, Meßkirch.
Zur Seinsfrage (original title "Über `die Linie')": Contribution written to a
    volume dedicated to Ernst Jünger.

1955-56

"Der Satz vom Grund": Lecture course given during the Winter Semester 1955-
    56, University of Freiburg.

1956

Hebel—der Hausfreund: Expanded version of "Gespräch mit Hebel beim
    `Schatz-kästlein' zum Hebeltag 1956."
"Der Satz vom Grund": Lecture given May 25, 1956, at the Bremen Club and
    October 24, 1956, at the University of Vienna. Included with the
    publication of Heidegger's course of the same name given during the
    Winter Semester 1955-56, University of Freiburg.

1957

"Die onto-theo-logische Verfassung der Metaphysik": Concluding lecture for a seminar during the winter semester 1956-57 on Hegel's *Science of Logic*, given on February 24, 1957, in Todtnauberg.

Grundsatze des Denkens: Five lectures, University of Freiburg.

"Grundsätze des Denkens": First lecture in the series *Grundsätze des Denkens*, revised in 1958 as a contribution in honor of the 75th birthday of Viktor Emil von Gebsattel.

"Der Satz der Identität": Third lecture in the series *Grundsätze des* Denkens, given June 27, 1957, University of Freiburg, on the occasion of the 500th anniversary of the founding of the university.

"Antrittsrede": Address at the Heidelberg Academy of Sciences, Fall 1957, on being admitted to the Academy.

1957-58

"Das Wesen der Sprache": Texts from a series of lectures given December 4 and 18, 1957 and February 5, 1958, University of Freiburg.

1958

"Dichten und Denken. Zu Stefan Georges Gedicht 'Das Wort'": Lecture given May 11, 1958, in Vienna. Revised title: "Das Wort" (1959).

"Die Kunst und das Denken": Colloquy with Hoseki Shin'ichi Hisamatsu held on May 18, 1958, University of Freiburg, transcribed by Alfredo Guzzoni.

Brief an Alfred L. Copley: Letter, 1959.

"Hegel und die Griechen": Lecture given at the Heidelberg Academy of Sciences, July 26, 1958. An earlier version (Aix-en-Provence, March 20, 1958) was published in a French translation, by Jean Beaufret and Pierre-Paul Sagave, in *Cahiers du Sud* (Paris) 47 (No. 349), January 1959, 355-368.

1959

"Der Weg zur Sprache": Revised version of "Die Sprache," a lecture first given in January 1959.

"Hölderlins Himmel und Erde": Lecture given June 6, 1959, for the Munich Hölderlin Society.

"Ein Blick in die Werkstatt": Marginal notes to the texts of the second and third versions of Hölderlin's "Griechenland" in the *Grosse Stuttgarter Ausgabe* of Hölderlin's works, edited by Friedrich Beissner.

1960

"Dank bei der Verleihung des staatlichen Hebelgedenkenpreises": Lecture given in acknowledgement of receiving the Hebel National Memorial Prize, May 10, 1960, the 200th anniversary of the birth of Johann Peter Hebel.

1961

"Protokol": Excerpts of the protocol of Heidegger's seminar on January 26, 1961, for medical students and psychiatric residents from the Zurich Psychiatric University Clinic, given with Medard Boss in Zollikon (Zürich), Switzerland. Includes marginalia to the manuscript for *Grundriß der Medizin: Ansätze zu einer phänomenologischen Physiologie, Psychologie, Therapie und zu einer daseinsgemäßen Präventiv-Medizin in der modernen Industriegesellschaft*, by Medard Boss.
"Kants These über das Sein": Lecture given May 17, 1961, Kiel.
"Ansprache zum Heimatabend": Address given July 22, 1961, Meßkirch.

1962

"Zeit und Sein": Lecture given January 31, 1962, University of Freiburg.
Brief an William J. Richardson: Letter written in early April, 1962, Freiburg.
"Überlieferte Sprache und Technische Sprache": Lecture given July 18, 1962, Comburg (Schwäbische Hall).
"Seminar Protokoll zu Heideggers Vorlesung `Zeit und Sein'": Transcript of a six-session seminar given September 11-13, 1962, Todtnauberg, prepared by Alfredo Guzzoni and edited by Heidegger.
Aufenthalte: Text written during a visit to Greece.

1963

"Mein Weg in die Phänomenologie": Essay in honor of the publisher Hermann Niemeyer. Supplement added in 1969.
"Vorwort zur Lesung von Hölderlins Gedichten": Introductory remarks for the recording *Heidegger ließt Hölderlin*.

1964

"Adalbert Stifters `Eisgeschichte'": Text of broadcast lecture on Radio Zürich, January 26, 1964.

"Einige Hinweise auf Hauptgeschichtspunkte für das theologische Gespräch über `Das Problem eines nichtobjectivierenden Denkens und Sprechens in der heutigen Theologie'": Letter, March 11, 1964, to participants of a conference held April 9-11, 1964, Drew University.

"Das Ende der Philosophie und die Aufgabe des Denkens": Lecture given during a colloquium on Kierkegaard in Paris, April 21-23, 1964.

Brief an Manfred Frings: Letter, August 6, 1964.

"Raum, Mensch und Sprache": Lecture given October 3, 1964, at the Galerie im Erker, St. Gallen, Switzerland.

1965

Brief an David L. Edwards: Letter to the director of SCM [Student Christian Movement] Press, London, January 28, 1965.

1965-69

"Protokollen - Gespräche": Excerpts from protocols of conversations with Medard Boss, seminar transcripts and ancillary texts prepared for meetings with Boss and his students in Zollikon (Zürich) on the meaning of Heidegger's work for psychiatry and psychotherapy: March 8, 1965; November 23, 1965; November 28-30, 1965; July 14, 1969.

1966

"Seminar in Le Thor 1966": Seminar held in Provence.

Brief an Arthur H. Schrynemakers: Letter, September 20, 1966, for the American Heidegger Conference, Duquesne University, Pittsburgh.

"Nur noch ein Gott kann uns retten": Transcript of an interview with Heidegger audio-taped on September 23, 1966.

Brief an Manfred S. Frings: Letter, October 20, 1966.

1966-67

Heraklit. Martin Heidegger-Eugen Fink. Seminar 1966/67: Seminar on Heraclitus, with Eugen Fink, given during the Winter Semester 1966-67, University of Freiburg.

1967

"Vorbemerkung": Prefatory note to the first edition of *Wegmarken*, Freiburg, early Summer 1967.

1968

"Seminar in Le Thor": Protocol of the eight sessions of the second seminar held August 30 - September 8, 1968, in Provence.

"Gespräch mit Zygmunt Adamcsewski": Transcript of Heidegger 's conversations with Zygmunt Adamczewski in Freiburg and Todtnauberg, October 1968.

"Das Gedicht": Lecture given August 25, 1968, in honor of Friedrich Ernst Jünger's birthday.

"Zur Frage nach der Bestimmung der Sache des Denkens": Text based on an address given October 23, 1965, in Amriswil, in honor of Ludwig Binswanger as "Das Ende des Denkens in der Gestalt der Philosophie."

1969

"Seminar in Le Thor 1969": Protocol of the third seminar held in Provence.

Brief an Albert Borgmann: Letter dated July 4, 1969, for participants in the conference on "Heidegger and Eastern Thought," University of Honolulu, Hawaii, November 17-21, 1969.

"Martin Heidegger im Gespräch:" Transcript of a conversation on September 17, 1969, between Martin Heidegger and Richard Wisser, filmed for broadcast on television [ZDF].

"Über das Zeitverständnis in der Phänomenologie und im Denken der Seinsfrage": Essay written in 1969 in commemoration of the 30th anniversary of the death of Edmund Husserl.

1970

Brief an Joan Stambaugh and J. Glenn Gray: Excerpts from a letter written in Summer 1970, in response to questions posed by the co-editors of the projected English *Works* of Martin Heidegger.

"Gedachtes. Für René Char in freundschaftlichen Gedenken" ("Zeit," "Wege," "Winke," "Ortschaft," "Cézanne," "Vorspiel," "Dank"): Seven short poems written in 1970.

1972

"Sprache": Verse written in 1972, sent to Raymond Panikkar, University of California, Santa Barbara, in March 1976.

1973

Seminar in Zähringen: Seminar at Heidegger's home.

"Die Herkunft des Denkens": Preface to a text on Parmenides' Fragment 1 (line 29: *aletheies eukyleos atremos etor*) from the seminar in Zähringen.

"Parmenides: *aletheies eukyleos atremos etor* ": Text from the seminar in Zähringen.

1974

"Der Fehl heiliger Namen": Text written in 1974, dedicated to Hugo Friedrich.

"Ein Grußwort für das Symposion in Beirut November 1974": Letter to participants in a conference at the Goethe Institute in Beirut, Lebanon.

"Stiftender als Dichten . . .": Poem.

1975

"Brief an Jean Beaufret": Letter dated February 22, 1975, Freiburg. A French translation by Jean Beaufret, "La Question Portant Fondamentalment sur l'Être-même," follows the letter.

1976

"Neuzeitliche Naturwissenschaft und moderne Technik": Letter written April 11, 1976, sent to the participants of the 10th Heidegger Circle conference, held May 14-16, 1976, DePaul University, Chicago, Illinois.

IV. CONTENTS OF THE HEIDEGGER *GESAMTAUSGABE* (1975-2015) BY VOLUME NUMBER

Titles that have been fully * or partially (*) translated are marked and appear in the Primary Bibliography. Some volumes are in two parts (6.1, 6.2; 73.1, 73.2; 84.1, 84.2) and some bear combined volumes numbering (29/30, 36/37, 56/57). In all 102 volumes have been announced. Only 13 volumes remain unpublished: 72, 80, 82, 84.2, 89, 91, 92, 93, 98, 99, 100, 101 and 102 as of April 1, 2016.

Volumes published: 89
Volumes remaining: 13.

I. PUBLISHED WRITINGS (1910-1976)

1   Frühe Schriften (*)

Das Realitätsproblem in der modernen Philosophie (1912)*
Neuere Forschungen über Logik (1912) *
Besprechungen (1913/14)
Die Lehre vom Urteil im Psychologismus (1913)
Die Kategorien- und Bedeutungslehre des Duns Scotus (1915)*
Selbstanzeige (1917)*
Der Zeitbegriff in der Geschichtswissenschaft (1916)*

2   Sein und Zeit *

Einleitung

Erster Teil
Die Interpretation des Daseins auf die Zeitlichkeit und die Explikation der Zeit als des transzendentalen Horizontes der frage nach dem Sein

Erster Abschnitt
Die vorbereitende Fundamentalanalyse des Daseins

Zweiter Abschnitt
Dasein und Zeitlichkeit

3   Kant und das Problem der Metaphysik *

Einleitung
Erster Abschnitt
    Die Grundlegung der Metaphysik im Ansatz
Zweiter Abschnitt
    Die Grundlegung der Metaphysik in der Durchfüllung
Dritter Abschnitt
    Die Grundlegung der Metaphysik in ihrer Ursprünglichkeit
Vierter Abschnitt
    Die Grundlegung der Metaphysik in einer Wiederholung
Anhang
    I. Aufzeichnungen zum Kantbuch
    II. Ernst Cassirer, Philosophie der symbolischen Formen. 2 Teil: Das
    mythische Denken
    III. Davoser Vorträge
    IV. Davoser Disputation zwischen Ernst Cassirer und Martin
Heidegger
    V. Odebrechts und Cassirers Kritik des Kantbuches
    VI. Geschichte des philosophischen Lehrstules seit 1866

4   Erläuterungen zu Hölderlins Dichtung *

"Heimkunft / An die Verwandten"
Hölderlin und das Wesen der Dichtung
"Wie wenn am Feiertage . . ."
"Andenken"
Hölderlins Erde und Himmel
Das Gedicht
Anhang
    Vorbemerkung zur Wiederholung des Rede
    Vorwort zur Lesung von Hölderlins Gedichten
    Ein Blick in die Werkstatt

5   Holzwege *

Der Ursprung des Kunstwerkes (1935/36)

Die Zeit des Weltbildes (1938)
Hegels Begriff der Erfahrung (1942/43)
Nietzsches Wort "Gott ist tot" (1943)
Wozu Dichter? (1946)
Der Spruch des Anaximander (1946)

6.1   Nietzsche I *

I.   Der Wille zur macht als Kunst
II.   Der ewige Widerkehr des Gleichen
III.   Der Wille zur macht als Erkenntnis

6.2   Nietzsche II *

IV.   Die ewige Wiederkehr des Gleichen und der Wille zur Macht
V.   Der europäische Nihilismus
VI.   Nietzsches Metaphysik
VII.   Die seinsgeschichtliches bestimmung des Nihilismus
VIII.   Die Metaphysik als Geschichte des Seins
IX.   Entwürfe zur Geschichte des Seins als Metaphysik
X.   Die Erinnerung in die Metaphysik

7   Vorträge und Aufsätze *

I   Die Frage nach der Technik (1953)
        Wissenschaft und Besinnung (1953)
        Überwindung der Metaphysik (1936-46)
        Wer ist Nietzsches Zarathustra? (1953)
II   Was heißt Denken? (1952)
        Bauen Wohnen Denken (1951)
        Das Ding (1950)
        "...dichterisch wohnet der Mensch . .." (1951)
III   Logos (Heraklit, Fragment 50) (1951)
        Moira (Parmenides, Fragment VIII, 34-41) (1952)
        Aletheia (Heraklit, Fragment 16) (1954)

8   Was heißt Denken? *

Die Vorlesung im Wintersemester 1951/52 mit Stundenübergängen
Die Vorlesung im Sommersemester 1952 mit Stundenübergängen
Anhang
  Bisher unveröffentlicher Textabschnitt as der IX. Vorlesungsstunde in
Wintersemester 1951/52
  Letzte, nicht Vorgetragende Vorlesung (Zwölfte Stunde) aus dem
Sommersemester 1952

9   Wegmarken *

Anmerkungen zu Karl Jaspers "Psychologie der Weltanschauungen" (1919/21)
Phänomenologie und Theologie (1927)
Aus der letzten Marburger Vorlesung (1928)
Was ist Metaphysik? (1929)
Vom Wesen des Grundes (1929)
Vom Wesen der Wahrheit (1930)
Platons Lehre von der Wahrheit (1931/32, 1940)
Vom Wesen und Begriff der physis. Aristoteles, Physik B,1 (1939)
Nachwort zu "Was ist Metaphysik?" (1943, 1949)
Brief über den Humanismus (1946)
Einleitung zu "Was ist Metaphysik?" (1949)
Zur Seinsfrage (1955)
Hegel und die Griechen (1958)
Kants These über das Sein (1961)

10   Der Satz vom Grund *

Vorlesung
Vortrag

11   Identität und Diffrenz (*)

Was ist das – die Philosophie? (1955)*
Identität und Differenz (1957)*
  Der Satz der Identität (1957)*
  Die onto-theo-logische Verfassung der Metaphysik (1956-57)*
Die Kehre (1949)*
Grundsätze des Denkens (1957)*

Ein Vorwort. Brief an Pater William J. Richardson (1962)*
Brief an Takehiko Kojima (1963)

12   Unterwegs zur Sprache *

Die Sprache (1950)
Die Sprache im Gedicht (1952)
Aus einem Gespräch von der Sprache (1953/54)
Das Wesen der Sprache (1957/58)
Das Wort (1958)
Der Weg zur Sprache (1959)

13   Aus der Erfahrung des Denkens. 1910-1976 (*)

Abraham a Sankta Clara (1910)
Frühe Gedichte (1910-1916) *
Schöpferische Landschaft: Warum bleiben wir in der Provinz? (1933)*
Wege zur Aussprache (1937)
Winke (1941)*
Chorlied aus der Antigone des Sophokles (1943)
Zur Erörterung der Gelassenheit. Aus einem Feldweggespräch über das Denken
(1944/45)*
Aus der Erfahrung des Denkens (1947)*
Der Feldweg (1949)*
Holzwege ("Dem künftigen Menschen . . .") (1949)
Zu einem Vers von Mörike. Ein Briefwechsel mit Martin Heidegger von Emil
Staiger (1951)*
Was heißt Lesen? (1954)
Vom Geheimnis des Glockenturms (1954)
Für das Langenharder Hebelbuch (1954)
Über die Sixtina (1955)
Die Sprache Johann Peter Hebels (1955)*
Begegnungen mit Ortega y Gasset (1955)
Was ist die Zeit? (1956)
Hebel - der Hausfreund (1957)*
Aufzeichnungen aus der Werkstatt (1959)
Sprache und Heimat (1960)
Über Igor Strawinsky (1962)

Für René Char (1963)
Adalbert Stifters "Eisgeschichte" (1964)*
Wink in das Gewesen (1966)
Die Kunst und der Raum (1969)*
Zeichen (1969)
Das Wohnen des Menschen (1970)
Gedachtes (1970)*
Rimbaud vivant (1972)
Sprache (1972)*
Der Fehl heiliger Namen (1974)*
Fridolin Wiplingers letzter Besuch (1974)
Erhardt Kästner zum Gedächtnis (1975)
Grußwort von Martin Heidegger (1976)

14   Zur Sache des Denkens (2007) (*)

Zeit und Sein*
Protokoll zu einmen Seminar über den Vortrag "Zeit und Sein"*
Das Ende der Philosophie und die Aufgabe des Denkens*
Mein Weg in die Phänomenologie*
  Hinweise
  Beilagen
Selbstanzeige: Martin Heidegger, Sein und Zeit I. Hälfte (1927)*
Brief an Edmund Husserl vom 22. Oktober 1927*
Vorbemerkung des Herausgebers von Edmund Husserls Vorlesung zur
Phänomenologie des inneren Zeitbebusstseins*
Ankündigung und zwei Vorworte zur Freiburger Antrittsvorlesng "Was ist
Metaphysik?"
Über das Zeitverständnis in der Phänomenologie und im Denken der
Seinsfrage*

15   *Seminare* (1986) (*)

Martin Heidegger - Eugen Fink: Heraklit*
Vier Seminare
        Le Thor 1966*
        Le Thor 1968*
        Le Thor 1969*

     Zähringen 1973*
Nachtrag*
Anhang
Zürcher Seminar (1951)

16   Reden und andere Zeugnisse eines Lebensweges [2000] (*)

Per mortem ad vitam (Gedanken über ˆJörgensensˆ˝ Lebenslüge und Lebenswahrheit")*
Förster, Fr. W. *Autorität und Freiheit* (Brtrachtungen zum Kulturproblem der Kirche)*
Cüppers, Ad. Jos. *Versiegelte Lippen*. Erzählung aus dem irischen Volksleben des 19. Jahrhunderts*
Jörgensen, Joh. *Das Reisebuch*. Licht und Dunkel in Natur und Geist*
Zur philosophischen Orientierung für Akademiker (März 1911)*
Auf stillen Pfaden*
Julinacht*
Religionspsychologie und Unterbewußtsein*
Gredt, Jos., O.S.B. Elementa Philosophiae Aristotelico-Thomistiscae*
Bibliothek wertvoller Novellen und Erzählungen (Januar 1913)*
Lebenslauf*
Trost*
Lebenslauf (Zur Habilitation)*
Vita*
Wilhelm Diltheys Forschungsarbeit und der Kampf um eine historische Weltanschauung*
Edmund Husserl zum 70. Geburtstag*
Die Selbstbehauptung der deutschen Universität*
Arbeitsdienst und Universität*
Hier ist es leider sehr trosdtlos (22. August 1933) [to Carl Schmitt]*
Zum Semestergeinn vgl. Universitätsführer Wintersemestere 1933/34*
Aufruf zur Wahl (10. November 1933)*
Ansprache am 11. November 1933 in Leipzig*
Das Geleitwort der Universität [150 Jahre "Freiburger Zeitung"]*
Der Ruf zum Arbeitsdienst*
Zur Eröffnung der Schullungkurse für die Notstandsarbeiter der Stadt an der Universität (22. Januar 1934)*
Das Rektorat 1933/34: Tatsachen und Gedanken*

Antrag auf die Wiedereinstellung in die Lehrtätigkeit (Reintegrierung)*
Erläuterungen und Grundsätzliches*
Zu 1933-1945 (Brief an Marcuse, 20. Januar 1948*
Betr. die Notiz 'Hanfstaengl contra Heidegger' in der Müncher Süddeutschen
Zeitung vom Mittwoch, den 14. Juni 1950
Gelassenheit*
Die Kunst und das Denken*
Aus einem Brief Heideggers an L. Alcopley [sic]*
Dank bei der Verleihung des staatlichen Hebelgedenkenpreises*
700 Jahre Meßkirch (Ansprache zum Heimatabend am 22. Juli 1961))*
Spiegel-Gespräch mit Martin Heidegger (23. September 1966)*
Grußwort an das Symposium über Heideggers Philosophie an der Duquesne-
Universität in Pittsburgh 15.-16. Oktober 1966 [to Arthur H. Schrynemakers] *
Spiegel-Gespräch mit Martin Heidegger*
Grußwort an das Heidegger-Symposium Chicago 11./12. November 1966 [to
Manfred S. Frings]*
Martin Heidegger im Gespräch [to Manfred S. Frings]*
Gruß und Dank an die Teilnehmer der Heidegger-Konferenz in Honolulu auf
Hawai [sic] [to Albert Borgmann]*
Ein Grußwort für das Symposium in Beirut November 1974*
Grußwort an die Teilnehmer des zehnten Colloquiums vom 14.-16. Mai 1976 in
Chicago*
Worte Hölderlins
Gedenkwort zu Schlageter (26. Mai 1933 vor der Universität)*
Die Universität im neuen Reich (30. Juni 1933)*

II. LECTURE COURSES (1919-1944)

MARBURG LECTURE COURSES (1923-1928)

17 Einführung in die phänomenologische Forschung *

Vorbemerkung
Erster Teil
PHAINOMENON und LOGOS bei Aristoteles und Husserls Selbstauslegung
der Phänomenologie
Zweiter Teil
Rückgang zu Descartes und der ihn bestimmenden scholastischen Ontologie

Dritter Teil
Nachweis der versäumnisses der Seinsfrage als Aufweis des Daseins
Anhang

18   Grundbegriffe der aristotelischen Philosophie *

I. Der Vorlesungstext auf der Grundlage der studentischen Nachschriften
Einleitung - Der philologische Absicht der Vorlesung und deren
Voraussetzungen
          Erster Teil - Dasein als In-der-Welt-sein
Erstes Kapitel - Definition
Zweites Kapitel - Die aristotelische Bestimmung des Daseins des Menschens als
zoon praktike im Sinne einer psyches energeia
Drittes Kapitel - Grundmöglichkeit des Miteinandersprechens am Leitfaden der
Rhetorik
          Zweiter Teil - Begrifflichkeit
Erstes Kapitel - Das Daseins des Menschens als die Bodenständigkeit der
Begrifflichkeit
Zweites Kapitel - kinesis als eines radikalen Ergreifens der Ausgelegtheit des
Daseins

II. Der Vorlesungstex auf der Grundlage der Erhaltenen Teile der Handschrift
[1-9, 24-28]
Anhang - Beilage 1-8

19   Platon: Sophistes *

Nachruf auf Paul Natorp
Vorbetrachtung
Einleitender Teil
Die Gewinnung der *aletheia* als des Bodens der platonishcen Seinsforschung
          Überleitung
          Die Fixierung des thematischen Feldes im Ausgang vom *aletheia*

Hauptteil
Die platonische Seinsforschung
          Erster Abschnitt

Die Suche nach dem *logos* der faktischen Existenz des Sophisten ("Sophistes" 219a-237b)
> Zweiter Abschnitt

Ontologishe Erörterung. Das Sein des Nicht-Seienden (236e-264b)
Anhang

20   Prolegomena zur Geschichte des Zeitbegriffs *

Einleitung
Vorbereitender Teil
Sein und Aufgabe der phänomenologischen Forschung
Hauptteil
Analyse des Zeitphänomens und Gewinnung des Zeitbegriffs
> Erster Abschnitt
> Die vorbereitende Deskription des Feldes, in dem das Phänomen der Zeit sichtbar wird
> Zweiter Abschnitt
> Die Freilegung der Zeit selbst

21   Logik. Die Frage nach der Wahrheit *

Einleitung
Vorbetrachtung
Die gegenwärtige Lage der philosophischen Logik. Psychologismus und Wahrheitsfrage
> Erstes Hauptstück

Das Wahrheitsproblem im entscheidenden Anfang der philosophierenden Logik und die Wurzeln der traditionellen Logik
> Zweites Hauptstück

Die radikalisierte Frage: Was ist Wahrheit? Wiederholung der Analyse der Falschheit auf ihre Temporalität

22   Die Grundbegriffe der antiken Philosophie *

Vorbemerkungen
Erster Teil
Allgemeine Einführung in die antike Philosophie
Zweiter Teil

Zweiter Teil
Die Analytik der Begriffe in der transzendentalen Logik

26 Metaphysische Anfangsgründe der Logik im Ausgang von Leibniz *
Einleitung
Erstes Hauptstück
Destruktion der Leibnizschen Urteilslehre auf die metaphysischen
Grundprobleme
Zweites Hauptstück
Die Metaphysik des Satzes vom Grunde als des Grundproblems der Logik

FREIBURG LECTURE COURSES (1928-1944)

27 Einleitung in die Philosophie

Einführung
Erster Abschnitt
Philosophie und Wissenschaft
Zweiter Abschnitt
Philosophie und Weltanschauung

28 Der deutsche Idealismus (Fichte, Schelling, Hegel) und die
philosophische Problemlage der Gegenwart

Einleitung
Erster Teil
Die Enthüllung der philosophischen Grundtendentzen der gegenwart
Zweiter Teil
Die Auseinandersetzung mit dem deutschen Idealismus
    Erster Abschnitt
    Fichte
    Zweiter Abschnitt
    Zwischenbetrachtung über den frühen Schelling
    Dritter Abschnitt
    Hegel
Beilagen
Ergänzungen (aus einer Nachschrift)

Anhang
Einführung in das akademische Studium [1929]

29/30   Die Grundbegriffe der Metaphysik. Welt - Endlichkeit -Einsamkeit *

Vorbetrachtung
Erster Teil
Die Weckung einer Grundstimmung unseres Philosophierens
Zweiter Teil
Das wirkliche Fragen der aus der Grundstimmung der tiefen Langeweile zu
entwickelnden metaphysischen Frage. Die Frage: Was ist Welt?
Für Eugen Fink zum sechzigsten Geburtstag

31   Vom Wesen der menschlichen Freiheit. Einleitung in die Philosophie *

Vorbetrachtung
Erster Teil
Positive Bestimmung der Philosophie aus dem Gehalt der Freiheitsfrage. Das
Problem der menschlichen Freiheit und die Grundfrage der Philosophie
Zweiter Teil
Kausalität und Freiheit. Transzendentale und praktische Freiheit bei Kant
Schluß
Die eigentliche ontologische Dimension der Freiheit. Die Verwurzelung der
Seinsfrage in der Frage nach dem Wesen der menschlichen Freiheit. Freiheit als
Grund der Kausalität

32   Hegels Phänomenologie des Geistes *

Einleitung
Erster Teil
Bewußtsein
Zweiter Teil
Selbstbewußtsein

33   Aristoteles, Metaphysik Θ 1-3. Von Wesen und Wirklichkeit der Kraft *

Einleitender Teil

Das Aristotelische Fragen nach der Vielfalt und Einheit des Seins
Hauptteil
Erster Abschnitt
  Metaphysik Θ 1. Die Einheit des Wesen der *dynamis kata kinesis* der auf
Bewegung hin verstandenen Kraft
Zweiter Abschnitt
  Metaphysik Θ 2. Die Einteilung der *dynamis kata kinesis* zwecks Aufhellung
ihres Wesens
Dritter Abschnitt
  Metaphysik Θ 3. Die Wirklichkeit der *dynamis kata kinesis* oder der
Vermögens

34   Vom Wesen der Wahrheit. Zu Platons Höhlengleichnis und Theätet *

Einleitende Betrachtungen
Erster Teil
  Der Wink in das "Wesen" der ALETHEIA. Eine Auslegung des
Höhlengleichnisses in Platons Politeia
Zweiter Teil
  Eine Auslegung von Platons "Theätet" in Absicht auf die Frage nach dem
Wesen der Unwahrheit
Anhang
Zusätze aus Heideggers Entwürfen

35   Der Anfang der abendländischen Philosophie. Auslegung des

Anaximander und Parmenides
Erster Teil
  Der Spruch des Anaximander von Milet. 6./5/ Jahrhundert
Zweiter Teil
  Zwischenbetrachtung
Dritter Teil
  Das "Lehrgedicht" des Parmenides aus Elea 6./5. Jahrhundert
Schluss
Anhang

36/37   Sein und Wahrheit *

Die Grundfrage der Philosophie (Sommersemester 1933) [Hegel]
Vom Wesen der Wahrheit (Wintersemester 1933/34) [Plato]
Anhang I (Aufzeichnungen und Entwürfe zur Vorlesung, Sommersemester 1933)
Anhang II (Aufzeichnungen und Entwürfe zur Vorlesung, Wintersemester 1933/34)

38   Logik als die Frage nach dem Wesen der Sprache *

Einleitung
Erster Teil
  Die Frage nach dem Wesen der Sprache als Grund- und Leitfrage aller Logik
Zweiter Teil
  Die Ursprüngliche Zeit als der Boden aller bisherigen Fragen und die Wiederaufnahme der Fragereihe und umgekehrter Richtung

39   Hölderlins Hymnen "Germanien" und "Der Rhein"

Vorbemerkung
Einleitung
Erster Teil
  "Germanien"
Zweiter Teil
  "Der Rhein"

40   Einführung in die Metaphysik *

Erstes Kapitel
  Die Grundfrage der Metaphysik
Zweites Kapitel
  Zur Grammatik und Etymologie des Wortes "Sein"
          A. Die Grammatik des Wortes "Sein"
          B. Die Etymologie des Wortes "Sein"
Drittes Kapitel
  Die Frage nach dem Wesen des Seins
Viertes Kapitel
  Die Beschränkung des Seins
          A. Sein und Werden

B. Sein und Schein
C. Sein und Denken
D. Sein und Sollen
Anhang
Zur Kritik der Vorlesung
Erste Fassung der Handschriftseiten 31-36

41 Die Frage nach dem Ding. Zu Kants Lehre von der transzendentalen Grundsätzen *

Vorbereitender Teil
Verschiedene Weisen, nach dem Ding zu fragen
Hauptteil
Kants Weise, nach dem Ding zu fragen
Erstes Kapitel
 Der geschichtliche Boden, auf dem Kants "Kritik der reinen Vernunft" ruht
Zweites Kapitel
 Die Dingfrage in Kants Hauptwerk
Schluß
Anhang

42 Schelling: Vom Wesen der menschlichen Freiheit (1809) *

Vorbetrachtung
Erster Teil
 Zur Möglichkeit eines Systems der Freiheit. Die Einleitung von Schellings
Abhandlung
Zweiter Teil
 Metaphysik des Bösen als Grundlegung eines System der Freiheit. Die
Hauptuntersuchung der Freiheitsabhandlung
Schlußbemerkungen

43 Nietzsche: Der Wille zur Macht als Kunst *

Vorbetrachtung
Erster Teil
 Wille zur Macht. Die Gestalt von Nietzsches denkerischer Grundstellung und
ihre Herkunft aus der Überlieferten Metaphysik

Zweiter Teil
Kunst und Wahrheit. Nietzsches Ästhetik und die Tradition des Platonismus
Anhang
A. Zur Vorlesung und Nietzsche im Ganzen
B. Zu den beiden Vorlesungen über Nietzsche Wintersemester 1936/37 und Sommersemester 1937 im Ganzen
C. Der Zusammenhang der Vorlesungen aus dem Wintersemester 1936/37 und den Sommersemester 1937
D. Anmerkung zu den Nietzsche-Vorlesungen
"Nietzsches Werke" (Großoktavausgabe) aus Martin Heideggers Besitz

44   Nietzsches metaphysische Grundstellung im abendländischen Denken. Die ewige Wiederkehr des Gleichen *

Einleitung
Erster Teil
   Vorläufige Darstellung der Lehre von der ewigen Wiederkunft des Gleichen nach ihrer Entstehung, ihrer Gestalt und ihrem Bereich
Zweiter Teil
   Das Wesen einer metaphysischen Grundstellung und ihre bisherige Möglichkeit in der Geschichte der abendländischen Philosophie
Anhang

45   Grundfragen der Philosophie. Ausgewählte "Probleme" der "Logik" *

Vorbereitender Teil
Das Wesen der Philosophie und die Frage nach der Wahrheit
Hauptteil
Grundsätzliches über die Wahrheitsfrage
Anhang
Die Wahrheitsfrage
Aus dem ersten Entwurf
      I. Grundsätzliches über die Wahrheitsfrage
      II. Der Vorsprung in die Wesung der Wahrheit
      III. Die Erinnerung an den ersten Aufschein des Wesens der Wahrheit
      als *aletheia* (Unverborgenheit)
Beilage

[46]   Zur Auslegung von Nietzsches II. Unzeitgemäßer Betrachtung "Vom Nutzen und Nachteil der Historie für das Leben"

47   Nietzsches Lehre vom Willen zur Macht als Erkenntnis *

Einleitung
Der Denker und sein "Hauptwerk"
Erster Teil
  Erster Durchblick durch Nietzsches Wahrheitsbestimmung. Vordeutung auf den metaphysischen Umkreis des Willens zur Macht
Zweiter Teil
  Von Nietzsches Wahrheitsbegriff zum Wesen des Willens zur Macht. Die Wahrheit als eine notwendige Bedingung für das Leben
Dritter Teil
  Die ewige Wiederkehr des Gleichen und der Wille zur Macht
Anhang
Überarbeitete Fassung der letzten Vorlesungsstunde im Sommersemester 1939 über "Nietzsches Lehre vom Willen zur Macht als Erkenntnis"
Nietzsches Lehre vom Willen zur Macht. Gang
Nietzsches Biologismus
Der Gedanke des Wertes

48   Nietzsche: Der europäische Nihilismus *

Einleitung
Erster Teil
  Der Wertgedanke in der Metaphysik des Willens zur macht und das verborgene Wesen des Nihilismus als das Grundgeschehen der abendländischen Geschichte
Zweiter Teil
  Die Frage nach dem Ursprung des Wertgedankens aus einem ursprünglicheren Verstehender Metaphysik im Ausblick auf das Verhältnis des Menschen zum Seienden
Dritter Teil
  Der Wesenswandel der Wahrheit und des Seins als der verborgene Grund des Vorrangs der Subjektivität und ihrer Entfaltung. Nietzsches aus dem wertgedanken gedachte Metaphysik der Subjektivität des Willens zur Macht als Vollendung der abendländischen Metaphysik

Schluß
Der vergessene Unterschied des Seins und des Seienden und das Ende der
abendländischen Philosophie als Metaphysik
Anhang

49   Die Metaphysik des deutschen Idealismus (Schelling). Zur erneuten
            Auslegung con Schelling: Philosophische Untersuchungen über das
            Wesen der menschlichen Freiheit und die damit zusammenhängenden
            Gegenstände (1809)

Einleitung
Die Notwendigkeit eines geschichtlichen Denkens
Erster Teil
  Vorbetrachtung über die Unterscheidung von Grund und Existenz
Zweiter Teil
  Zur Auslegung des Kernstückes, "Der Erläuterung der Unterscheidung" von
Grund und Existenz
Abschluß
Durchblick
Wiederholungen und Gang der Auslegung
Anhang
  Vorblicke und Richtlinien
  Zwischenbetrachtung über Hegel
  Zur Auseinandersetzung mit der Metaphysik des deutschen Idealismus
und der Metaphysik überhaupt
  Durchblick durch den Wandel des Seins als "Wirklichkeit"
Beilage (Leibniz)

50   1. Nietzsches Metaphysik 2. Einleitung in die Philosophie. Denken
            und Dichten *

1. Nietzsches Metaphysik *
Einleitung
Hauptteil
Die fünf Grundworte der Metaphysik Nietzsches
Anhang
Aufzeichnungen zu Nietzsches Metaphysik *

2. Einleitung in die Philosophie. Denken und Dichten *
Einleitung
Einleitung in die Philosophie als Anleitung zum eigentliche Denken durch den
Denker. Nietzsche und den Dichter Hölderlin
Denken und Dichten. Überlegungen zur Vorlesung
Anhang
  Zweite Fassung der Wiederholung zu: Einleitung in die Philosophie. Denken
und Dichten
  Wiederholung zu Seite 105f. [Nietzsche. Zum Verhältnis von Denken und
Dichten]
  Zweite Fassung der Manuskriptseiten 4 und 5 zu: *Denken und Dichten.
Überlegungen zur Vorlesung* [Vorfragen zur Besinnung auf Denken und
Dichten]
  Zwei fragmentarische Fassungen der Manuskriptseite 12
  Notizen zur Vorlesung: Einleitung in die Philosophie. Denken und Dichten

51 Grundbegriffe *

Einleitung
Erster Teil
Das Bedenken des Spruches. Der Unterschied zwischen Seiendem und Sein
  Erster Abschnitt
    Die Erörterung des "ist", des Seienden im Ganzen
  Zweiter Abschnitt
    Leitworte für die Besinnung auf das Sein
  Dritter Abschnitt
    Sein und Mensch
Zweiter Teil
Das anfängliche Sagen des Seins im Spruch des Anaximander

52 Hölderlins Hymne "Andenken"

Vorbetrachtungen
Hauptteil
"Andenken"
Anhang
Aufbau der Auslegung der genannten Dichtungen

53   Hölderlins Hymne "Der Ister" *

Erster Teil
   Das Dichten des Wesens der Ströme--die Ister-Hymne
Zweiter Teil
   Die griechische Deutung des menschen in Sophokles' Antigone
Dritter Teil
   Hölderlins Dichten des Wesens des Dichters als Halbgott
Schlußbemerkung
   "Giebt es auf Erden ein Maas?"

54   Parmenides *

Einleitung
Erster Teil
   Die dritte Weisung des übersetzende Wortes *aletheia*: Der seinsgeschichtliche
Bereich der Gegensätzlichkeit von *aletheia* und *lethe*
Zweiter Teil
   Die vierte Weisung des übersetzenden Wortes *aletheia*. Das Offene und das
Freie der Lichtung des Seins. Die Göttin "Wahrheit"
Zusatz

55   Heraklit. 1. Der Anfang des abendländischen Denkens. 2. Logik.
                Heraklits Lehre vom Logos (*)

1. Der Anfang des abendländischen Denkens
Vorbetrachtung
Einleitung
Hauptteil
Die Wahrheit des Seins

2. Logik. Heraklits Lehre vom Logos
Vorbemerkung
Erster Abschnitt
Logik: Ihr Name und ihre Sache
Zweiter Abschnitt (*)
Das Wegbleiben des ursprünglichen *logos* und die Wege des Zugangs
Dritter Abschnitt

Rückgang in die ursprüngliche Gegend der Logik

EARLY FREIBURG LECTURE COURSES (1919-1923)

56/57   Zur Bestimmung der Philosophie *

1. Die Idee der Philosophie und das Weltanschauungsproblem
Vorbetrachtung
Wissenschaft und Universitätsreform
Einleitung
Erster Teil
  Die Idee der Philosophie als Wissenschaft
Zweiter Teil
  Phänomenologie als vortheoretische Urwissenschaft

2. Phänomenologie und transzendentale Wertphilosophie
Einleitung
Erster Teil
  Problemgeschichtliche Darlegungen
Zweiter Teil
  Kritische Betrachtungen
Anhang
Über das Wesen der Universität und des akademischen Studiums
Nachschrift von Oskar Becker

58   Grundprobleme der Phänomenologie (1919/20)

Vorbetrachtung
Erster Abschnitt
  Das Leben als Ursprungsgebiet der Phänomenologie
Zweiter Abschnitt
  Phänomenologie a;s Ursprungswissenschaft des faktischen Lebens an sich
Anhang A
I. Rekonstruktion des Schlußteiles der Vorlesung aus Heideggers eigenen
Aufzeichnungen
II. Beilagen
Anhang B

I. Ergänzungen zu ausgearbeiten Vorlesung aus der Nachschrift von Oskar Becker

II. Der Schlußteil der Vorlesung in der Nachschrift von Oskar Becker

59   Phänomenologie der Anschauung und des Ausdrucks. Theorie der philosophischen Begriffsbildung *

Einleitung
Erster Teil
  Zur Destruktion des Aprioriproblems
Zweiter Teil
  Zur Destruktion des Erlebnisproblems
Beilagen

60   Phänomenologie des religiosen Lebens *

1. Einleitung in die Phänomenologie der Religion (1920/21)
Erster Teil
  Methodische Einleitung. Philosophie, Faktische Lebenserfahrung and Religionsphänomenologie
Zweiter Teil
  Phänomenologische Explikation konkreter religiöser Phänomene im Anschluß an Paulinische Briefe
Anhang

2. Augustinus und der Neuplatonismus (1921)
Einleitender Teil
Augustinus-Anfassungen
Hauptteil
Phänomenologische Interpretation von Confessiones Liber X
Anhang I
Anhang II

3. Die philosophischen Grundlagen der mittelalterischen Mystik (1918/1919)

61   Phänomenologische Interpretationen zu Aristoteles. Einführung in die phänomenologische Forschung *

Einleitung
I. Teil
Aristoteles und Aristoteles-Rezeption
II. Teil
Was ist Philosophie?
1. Kapitel
Die Definitionsaufgabe
2. Kapitel
Die Aneignung der Verstehenssituation
III. Teil
Das faktische Leben
1. Kapitel
Grundkategorien des lebens
2. Kapitel
Die Ruinanz
Anhang I
Voraussetzung
Anhang II
Lose Blätter

62   Phänomenologische Interpretationen ausgewählte Abhandlungen des
        Aristoteles zur Ontologie und Logik (*)

Vorbemerkung zu den Aristotelesinterpretationen
Erstes Kapitel
Zweites Kapitel
Drittes Kapitel
Anhang I
Anhang II
Anhang III – Phänomenologische Interpretatonen zu Aristoteles (Anzeige
        der hermeneutischen Situation). Ausarbeitung für die Marburger und
        die Göttinger Philosophische Fakultät (Herbst 1922) *

63   Ontologie (Hermeneutik der Faktizität) *

Einleitung
Hermeneutik der Faktizität
Vorwort

I. Teil
Wege der Auslegung des Daseins in seiner Jeweiligkeit
II. Teil
Der phänomenologische Weg der Hermeneutik der Faktizität
Anhang

III. UNPUBLISHED TREATISES, ADDRESSES, THOUGHTS

64   Der Begriff der Zeit (2004) *

Der Begriff der Zeit
I. Die Fragestellung Diltheys und Torcks Grundtendenz
II. Die ursprünglichen Seinscharakterr des Daseins
III. Dasein und Zeitlichketi
IV. Zeitlichkeit und Geschichtlichkeit
Der Begriff der Zeit (Vortrag)

65   Beiträge der Philosophie (Vom Ereignis) *

I.   Vorblick
II.   Der Anklang
III.   Das Zuspiel
IV.   Der Sprung
V.   Die Gründung
 a. Da-sein und Seinsentwurf
 b. Das Da-sein
 c. Das Wesen der Wahrheit
 d. Der Zeit-Raum als der Ab-grund
 e. Die Wesung der Wahrheit als Bergung
VI.   Die Zu-künftigen
VII.   Der letzte Gott
VIII.   Das Seyn

66   Besinnung *

I. Einleitung
II. Der Vorsprung in die Einzigkeit des Seyns
III. Die Philosophie

BIBLIOGRAPHY: ENGLISH TRANSLATIONS OF HEIDEGGER

IV. Zum Entwurf des Seyns
V. Wahrheit und Wissen
VI. Das Seyn
VII. Das Seyn und der Mensch
VIII. Das Seyn und der Mensch
IX. Der Anthropomorphismus
X. Geschichte
XI. Die Technik
XII. Historie und Technik
XIII. Seyn und Macht
XIV. Das Seyn und das Sein
XV. Das Denken des Seyns
XVI. Die Seynsvergessenheit
XVII. Die Seynsgeschichte
XVIII. Götter
XIX. Die Irre
XX. Zur Geschichte der Metaphysik
XXI. Die metaphysische Warumfrage
XXII. Seyn und "Werden"
XXIII. Das Sein als Wirklichkeit
XXIV. Das Seyn und die "Negativität"
XXV. Sein und Denken. Sein und Zeit
XXVI. Eine Sammlung des Besinnens
XXVII. Das Seynsgeschichtliche Denken und die Seinsfrage
XXVIII. Der Seynsgeschichtliche Begriff der Metaphysik
Anhang

67   Metaphysik und Nihilismus

1. Die Überwindung der Metaphysik (1938-39)
Die Überwindung der Metaphysik
Die Überwindung Metaphysik. I. Fortsetzung
  I. Die Unterscheidung
  II. Zum Begriff der Metaphysik
  III. Kunst und Metaphysik
  IV. Metaphysik und "Weltanschauung"
  V. "Sein und Zeit". In der Geschichte des Seyns, sofern sie als
Überwindung der Metaphysik erfahren wird

Die Überwindung der Metaphysik. II. Fortsetzung
  I. Die Vollendung der Metaphysik. Seinsverlassenheit und Verwüstung
  II. Der seynsgeschichtliche Ursprung der Metaphysik. Der Ursprung der
Metaphysik und das erstanfängliche Wesen der Wahrheit
  III. Die Metaphysik. Die einzelnen Grundstellungen der Metaphysik

2. Das Wesen der Nihilismus (1946-48)

Anhang
Beilagen zu: Das Wesen der Nihilismus

68   Hegel

1. Die Negativität. Eine Auseinandersetzung mit Hegel aus dem Ansatz in
der Negativität
Anhang

2. Erläuterung der "Einleitung" zu Hegels "Phänomenologie des Geistes"
Anhang

69   Die Geschichte des Seyns

1. Die Geschichte des Seyns (1938/40)
Teil I.
  I. Die Geschichte des Seyns
  II. Wider-Spruch dun Wiederlegung
  III. Gang. Die Geschichte des Seyns
  IV. Die Vollendung der Metaphysik. Die Seinsverlassenheit
  V. TO KOINON
  VI. Der Austrag. Das Wesen der Macht. Das Notwendige
  VII. Das Wesen der Geschichte. "Anfang". "Seyn"
  VIII. Das Seyn und der letzte Gott
  IX. Wesen der Geschichte
  X. Das Eigentum
Teil II.
  XI. Das Gefüge des Sagens
  XII. Die Geschichte des Seyns (Da-sein)
  XIII. Das Seynsgeschichtliche Denken

2. KOINON. Aus der Geschichte des Seyns (1939/40)
koinon. Aus der Geschichte des Seyns
Entwurf zu koinon. Zur Geschichte des Seyns
Anhang
Beilagen zu: Die geschichte des Seyns (1938/40)
Beilagen zu: Koinon. Aus der Geschichte des Seyns (1939/40)

70   Über den Anfang

Das Vorwort
I. Die Anfängnis des Anfangs
II. Der Anfang und das Anfängliche Denken. Das Erdenken des Anfangs
III. Ereignis und Da-sein
IV. Die Auslegung und der Dichter
V. Die Seynsgeschichte
VI. Sein und Zeit and das anfängliche Denken als Geschichte des Seyns

71   Das Ereignis

Vorworte
I. Der errste Anfang
  A. Der erste Anfang. Aletheia
  B. doxa
  C. Anaximander
  D. Das abendländischee Denken. Die Reflexion. Das Da-seyn
  E. Unterwegs zum ersten Anfang. Die vorbereitung des seynsgeschichtlichen
Denkens. Auf der Brücke zum Bleiben
  F. Der erste Anfang
  G. Der erste Anfang
  E. Der Fortgang des ersten Anfangs in den Beginn der Metaphysik
II. Der Anklang
  A. Der Anklang. Durckblick
  B. Die Zeichen des Übergangs. Die Vorbeigang. Das
Inzwischen der Seynsgeschichte
  C. Die Neuzeit und und das Abendland
  D. Die Metaphysik. Der Zwischenfall zwischen dem ersten und dem anderen
Anfang. Der Übergang (seine Zeichen)

E. Der Wille zum Willen

III. Der Unterscheid

IV. Die Verwindung

V. Das Ereignis. Der Wortschatz seines Wesens

VI. Das Ereignis

VII. Das Ereignis und das Menschenwesen

VIII. Das Da-seyn

   A. Der seynsgeschichtliche Mensch und das Da-seyn (die Instaändigkeit)

   B. Das Da-seyn. Der Zeit-Raum. Da-sein und "Reflexion" Inständigkeit und die Stimmung

   C. Stimmung und Da-sein. Der Schmeriz der Fragwürdigkeit des Seyns

IX. Der andere Anfang

X. Weisungen in das Ereignis

   A. Der Austrag des Unterschieds (der Unterscheidung). Die Erfahrung als der Schmerz "des" Abschieds

   B. Das seynsgeschichtlichte Denken. Der Austrag der Unterschieds (der Unterschediung). Die Sorge des Ab-grundes. Der Holzweg. Das Denken und das Wort

   C. Zur ersten Erläuterung der Grundworte. Die "Wahr-heit" (zu: Sage des ersten Anfangs). Das "Wesen" und die "Wesung". Die Geschichte und das Geschicht.

XI. Dase seynsgeschichtliche Denken (Denken und DIchten)

   A. Die Erfahrung des Fragwürdigen. Der Sprung. Die Auseinandersetzung. Die Klärung des Tuns. Das Wissen des Denkens.

   B. Der Anfang und die Aufmerksamkeit

   C. Die Sage des Anfangs

   D. Denken und Erkennen. Denken und Dichten.

   E. Dichten und Denken

   F. Der Dichter und der Denker

   G. "Anmerkungen" und "Auslegung"

      a. Das Denke zu Hölderlin "Auslegung"

      b. "Anmerkungen" und "Auslegung"

[72]   Die Stege des Anfangs (1944)

73.1   Zum Ereignis-Denken (1932-1976)

I   Zerklüftung und Aletheia

II Die Seinsfrage und das Ereignis
III Das Da-sein
IV Wesen des Entwurfs – Vorgehen
V Abschied. Eine Reihe von Manuskripte zum Ereignis (1943-1945)

73.2   Zum Ereignis-Denken (1932-1976)

Zu Ereignis VI. Ontologische Differenz und Unterschied

74   Zum Wesen der Sprache und Zur Frage nach der Kunst [2010[1]]

Erster Teil: Zum Wesen der Sprache
  Die Sage
  Das Wort. Vom Wesen der Sprache
  Das Wort – Das Zeichen – Das Gespräch – Die Sprache
Zweiter Teil: Zur Frage nach der Kunst
  Zur Frage nach der Kunst
  Kunst und Raum
  Das Kunstwerk und die "Kunstgeschichte"
  Besinnung auf Wesen und Haltung der kunstgeschichtlichen "Wissenschaft"

75   Zu Hölderlin. Griechenlandreisen

Aufsätzse und Dialog
Griechenlandreisen
Aufzeichnungen und Entwürfe
Anhang

76   Leitgedanken zur Entstehung der Metaphysik, der neuzeitlichen
          Wissenschaft under modernen Technik

I. Teil: Abhandlungen und Entwürfe zur Entstehung der Metaphysik
II. Teil: Abhandlungen und Entwürfe zur Entstehung der neuzeitlichen
Wissenschaft
III. Teil: Abhandlungen un Entwürfe zur Entstehung der modernen Technik
Anhang

77   Feldweg-Gespräche *

Αγχιβασιν. Ein Gespräch selbstdritt auf einem Feldweg zwischen einem
Forscher, einem Gelehrten und einem Weisen
Der Lehrer trifft den Türmer an der Tür zum Turmaufgang
Abendgespräch in einem Kriegsgefangenenlager in Rußland zwischen einem
Jüngeren und einem Älteren

78   Der Spruch des Anaximander

Einleitung
Vorbereitende Einführung in das zu Denkende
Erstes Kapitel
  Der erste Teil des Spruches
Zweites Kapitel
  Der zweite Teil des Spruches
Drittes Kapital
  Das Verhältnis der beiden Teile des Spruches. Das Rätselwort *gar*
Anhang I
Anhang II

79   Bremer und Freiburger Vorträge. 1. Einblick in das was ist. 2.
           Grundsätze des Denkens *

Einblick in das was ist
  Das Ding*
  Das Ge-Stell*
  Die Gefahr*
  Die Kehre*
Grundsätze des Denkens*

[80]   Vorträge

81   Gedachtes (*)

Frühe Gedichte – Briefe – Gedachtes (1910-1975)
Aus der Erfahrung des Denkens*
Gedachtes für das Vermächtnis eines Denkens
Vereinzeltes

IV. HINTS AND NOTES

[82]   Zu eigenen Veröffentlichungen

83   Seminare: Platon – Aristoteles - Augustinus

I Aristoteles, Physik L 1-3 [SS 1928]
II Platon, Parmenides [WS 1930/31]
III Augustinus, Conessiones XI (de tempore) [WS 1930/31]
IV Platons Phaidros [SS 1932]
V Aristoteles, Physik L und Z [SS 1944]
VI Übungen im Lesen: Über die Kausalität
    Übungen im Lesen: Aristoteles, Physik B1, L 1-3 [SS 1951]
Anhang I Protokolle zu "Aristotlees, Physik L 1-3 [SS 1928]
  Toni Rübesamen
  Simon Moser
  Paul Jakoby
  Lisolette Richter
  Ernst Fuchs
  Richard Haug
  Wilhelm Weischedel
  Hans Reiner
Anhang II Protokolle zu "Augustinus, Confessiones XI {de tempore)"
  Ulrich von Loessel
  Heinz Lehmann
  Otti Cordier
  Robert Oertel
  Albert Leyendecker
  Eberhard Hasper
  Gertrud Philipson
  Gerhard Stallman
  Balduin Noll
  Erich Hassinger
  Werner Heidinger
  Rita Scmitz
  Heinz L. Matzat
Anhang III Protokolle zu "Platons Phaidros"
  Badiun Noll

Heinz L. Matzat
Franz Anton Doll
Ulrich Steffen
Hilde Matt
Ulrich von Loessel
Alfred Schmitz
Anhang IV Protokolle zu "Aristoteles, Metaphysik L und Z"
  Walter Biemel
  A. Guggenberger
Anhang V Protokolle zu "Übungen im Lesen: Über die Kausalität"
  Ernst Tugendhat
Anhang VI Protokolle zu "Übungen im Lesen: Aristoteles, Physik B1, L 1-3"
  Ernst Tugendhat
Anhang VII Protokolle zu "Übungen im Lesen: Aristoteles, Physik L und
Metaphysik Theta 10" von vershiedenen Studenten"
Anhang VIII Ptotkolle zu "Übungen im Lesen: Übungen im Lesen: Aristoteles,
Physik L und Metaphysik Theta 10" Ernst Tugendhat

84.1   Seminare: Leibniz – Kant – Schiller
         [Teil 1: Sommersemester 1931 bis Wintersemester 1935/36]

Kant. Uber die Fortschritte der Metaphysik [Sommersemester 1931]
Kants tranzendentale Dialektik und die praktische Philosophie [Wintersemester
1931/32]
Hauptstücke aus Kants Kritik der reieen Vernunft [Sommersemester 1934]
Leibnizens Weltbegriff und der deutsche Idealismus (Monadologie)
[Wintersemester 1935/36]
Anhang

85   Vom Wesen der Sprache. Die Metaphysik der Sprache und die Weisung
        des Wortes zu Herders Abhandlung "Über den Ursprung der Sprache" *

I. Zur Auslegung von Herder, über den Ursprung der Sprache
II. Konstruktion des Ursprungs der Sprache in der Weise des Gebrauchs der
freiwerkenden Besinnung
III. Zur Auseinandersetzung mit Herder
IV. Vom Wesen der Sprache
V. Zu Herder, über den Ursprung der Sprache

VI. Philosophie der Sprache
VII. Übergang
VIII. Metaphysik der Sprache und der Übergang
IX. Stefan George
X. Sprache - Freiheit - Wort
XI. Über die Ursprungsfrage und die Herdersche Upsprungsbetrachtung als metaphysische
XII. Disposition
XIII. Ursprungsfrage
XIV. Von Herder zu Grimm (Metaphysik und Sprachwissenschaft)
XV. Sagen und Hören - Laut und Stille
XVI. Horchen als Mitte des Sensorium Commune
XVII. "Gefühl" und "Gehör" bei Herder. Tönen und Lauten
XVIII. "Das Schaf Blökt"
XIX. Sprache und Vernunft
Anhang
Seminarprotokolle

86   Seminare. Hegel – Schelling

Aristoteles-Hegel-Seminar SS 1927

Schelling. Über das Wesen der menschlichen Freiheit WS 1927/28

Hegel. "Rechtsphilosophie" WS 1934/35
   I. Hegel – Staat
   [II. Gewaltenteilung und Verfassung. Verfassung des nationalsozialistischen Staats
   III. Bürgerliche Gesellschaft und Staat]
   IV. Abstraktes Recht und Moralität
   [V. Hegels Systematik. Staat – Geist –Volk]
   VI. Übungen über Hegel – Staat
   VII. Freiheit und Wille im Allgemeinen
   VIII. Recht und Staat
   [IX. Hegels Rechtsphilosophie]
   X. Grundsätzliches zur Staatslehre
      A. Sorge – Staat – Seyn
      B. Autorität – Herrschaft – Macht – Gewalten. Ihre

Metaphysik und Wahrheit
   C. Das Politische. Gesinnung – Verfassung – (Staat)

Schelling und der Deutsche Idealismus 1941-1943
   I. "Die Metaphysik des Deutschen Idealiismus"
   II. Zu Schellings "Freiheitsabhandlung"

Zu Hegel. Phänomenologie des Geistes SS 1942
   [I. Einleitung in das tranzendentale Wesen der absoluten Metaphysik]
   II. Die Vorrede zur Phänomenologie des Geistes
   III. Die Negativität. Die Unterscheidung. Die Un-Endlichkeit. Das Ein-Fache
   IV. Das Selbstbewusstsein. Die Subjectität
   V. Zu Hegel. Die Phänomenologie des Geistes (Text Ed. Hoffmeister) (Das Wesen der "Metaphysik")
   VI. Die Einleitung. Zur Phänomenologie des Geistes
   VII. Mitgehende Auslegung des Beginns. "Die sinnliches Gewissheit". Die sinnliche Gewissheit. Durchblicke
   VIII. Hegel über die Sprache
   IX. Die Wahrnehmung
   X. Der Entwurf der "Unkehrung" des "Bewusstseins". Die tranzendentale Konstruktion. Vgl. Über das "Bewusstsein"
   XI. Hegel – Geist. Bewusstsein. Begriff. Wiklichkeit. Kopernikanische Wendung
   XII. Hegels Begriff der "Erfahrung abgehoben gegen die empeiria des Aristoteles und gegn den Begriff der "Erfahrung" bei Kant

Zu Hegel. Logik des Wissens WS 1955/56
   I. Hegel – Der Satz vom Grund. Logik des Wesens.
   II. Die Reflexionsbestimmungen
   III. Zu Hegel
   IV. Wahrheit des Seins

Gespräch von der Sache des Denkens mit Hegel WS 1956/57

Anhang I [Hegel]
Anhang II Protokolle und Mitschiften
Anhang III Vorlesungen und Seminarübungen

87   Nietszche. Seminare 1937 und 1944

1. Nietzsches metaphysiche Grundstellung (Sein und Schein)
2. Skizzen zu "Grundbegriffe des Denkens"
Anhang I
Anhang II

88   Seminare (Übungen) 1937/38 und 1941/42 *
    1. Die metaphysischen Grundstellungden des abendländischen
    Denkens
    2. Einübung in das philosophische Denken
    Die metaphysischen Grundstellungden des abendländischen Denkens
    (Metaphysik)

1. Die metaphysischen Grundstellungen abendländischen Denkens (Metaphysik)
        Übungen im Wintersemester 1937/38)

I. Die metaphysischen Grundstellungden des abendländischen Denkens (Die
Entfaltung der Leitfrage)
II. Die Leitfrage der abendländischen Metaphysik und der Rückgand in die
Grundfrage
III. Die Besinnung auf die Leitfrage und ihre Überwindung
IV. Zu Plaons metaphysischer Grundstellung
V. Der Übergang von der griechischen Metaphysik zur Neuzeitlichen: Das
Christentum
VI. Descartes' metaphysische Grundstellung
VII. Leibnizens metaphysiche Grundstellung
VIII. Kants metaphysiche Grundstellung
IX. Der deutsche Idealismus und die Leitfragenbehandlung
X. Schelling: Die negative und positive Philosophie

2. Einübung in das philosophische Denken (Übungen im Wintersemester
1941/42)

I. Einübung in das philosophische Denken
II. Heraklit, Frg. 7 – Nietzsche, der Wille zur Macht, N. 493
III. Richtigkeit – Gewissheit (Vergegenständlichung und Quantenmechanik)
IV. Die Selbigkti (Identität) – (Das Eine) – *hen*

V. "Das Wachsbeispiel" aus Descartes' *Meditationen*

Anhang
I. Ergänzungen
II. Seminaprotokolle

[89]   Zollikoner Seminare (*)

90   Zu Ernst Jünger (*)

I. Aufzeichnungen zu Ernst Jünger
  I. "Der Arbeiter"
  II. "Marmorklippen"
  III. Ernst Jüngers Blendung und wesentliche Grenze zufolge der metaphysischen Grundstellung Nietzsches
  IV. Der Wider-spruch zur metaphysik
  V. Wesen und Begriff der Arbeit (Technik und Arbeit)
  VI. Bürger und Arbeiter
  VII. Das Elementare
  VIII. "Gestalt" und Sein. Die Gestalt des Arbeiters
  IX. Das Wesen der Freiheit. Die neuzeitliche Freiheit – als Freiheitsanspruch
  X. Macht als Repräsentation des Arbeietrs
  XI. Die Arbeit als Prinzip des Wirkens des menschentuns (Der Meisterung der Welt = Materie). Die Zeichnung des Arbeiters
  XII. Der Typus als die Höchste Form der Subjektivität. Die Typik und die Technik
  XIII. Die organische Konstruktion
  XIV. Die Kunst

II. Zaussprache über Ernst Jünger
  I. Ernst Jünger, Der Arbeiter. 1932. Zur Einführung 1939/40
  II. Zu Ernst Jünger 1939/40
  III. Von Ernst Jünger 1939/40 *
  IV. Zu Ernst Jünger 1939/40 *
  V. Ernst Jünger

Anhang
Ein brief an einzelne Krieger

"Gestalt" 1954
    I. "Herrschaft"
    II. Arbeit
    III. Gestalt
    IV. Ernst Jünger
    V. Die Freyheit und das Böse
Randbemerkungen in Schriften Ernst Jüngers

[91]   Ergämzungen und Denksplitter

[92]   Ausgewählte Briefe I

[93]   Ausgewählte Briefe II

94   Überlegungen II-VI (Schwarze Hefte 1931-1938)

Winke X Überlegungen (II) und Anweisungen
Überlegungen und Winke III
Überlegungen IV
Überlegungen V
Überlegungen VI

95   Überlegungen VII-XI (Schwarze Hefte 1938/39)

Überlegungen VII
Überlegungen VIII
Überlegungen IX
Überlegungen X
Überlegungen XI

96   Überlegungen XII-XV (Schwarze Hefte 1939-1941)

Überlegungen XII
Überlegungen XIII
Überlegungen XIV
Überlegungen XV

97   Anmerkungen I-V (Schwarze Hefte 1942-1948)

V. LECTURE COURSES (1915-1955) AND SEMINARS (1927-1957): DATE OF COMPOSITION

Number and title in parentheses refer to the volume in the *Gesamtausgabe* (1975-2014).

[1915-1930 follows Kisiel and Sheehan (2007)⁵]

1915	Die Grundlinien der antiken und scholastischen Philosophie. WS
1916	Der deutsche Idealismus. SS
	Grundfragen der Logik. WS
1918	Die philosophischen Grundlagen der mittelalterischen Mystik. WS (60: Phänomenologie des religiösen Lebens)⁶
1919	Die Idee der Philosophie und das Weltanschauungsproblem. Kriegsnotsemester (56/57: Zur Bestimmung der Philosophie)
	Phänomenologie und transzendentale Wertphilosophie. SS (56/57: *Zur Bestimmung der Philosophie*)
	Über das Wesen der Universität und des akademischen Studiums. SS (56/57: Zur Bestimmung der Philosophie)
	Grundprobleme der Phänomenologie. WS (58: *Grundprobleme der Phänomenologie*)
1920	Phänomenologie der Anschauung und des Ausdrucks. Theorie der philosophischen Begriffsbildung. SS (59: *Phänomenologie der Anschauung und des Ausdrucks. Theorie der philosophischen Begriffsbildung*)
	Einleitung in die Phänomenologie des religiösen Lebens. WS (60: Phänomenologie des religiösen Lebens)
1921	Augustinus und der Neuplatonismus. SS (60: Phänomenologie des religiösen Lebens)
	Phänomenologische Interpretationen zu Aristoteles. Einführung im Anschluss an Aristotles, *de* anmia, WS (61:

---

⁵ Theodore Kisiel and Thomas Sheehan (eds.), *Becoming Heidegger. On the Trail of His Early Occasional Wrirings, 1910-1927* (Evanston: Northwestern University Press, 2007).

⁶ This course was not given.

	Phänomenologische Interpretationen zu Aristoteles. Einführung in die phänomenologische Forschung)
1922	Phänomenologische Interpretationen ausgewählter Abhandlungen des Aristoteles zur Ontologie und Logik. SS (62: *Phänomenologische Interpretationen ausgewählte Abhandlungen des Aristoteles zur Ontologie und Logik)* Ausarbeitung für die Marburger und die Göttinger Philosophische Fakultät (Autumn 1922) (62: Phänomenologische Interpretationen ausgewählte Abhandlungen des Aristoteles zur Ontologie und Logik)
1923	Ontologie. Hermeneutik der Faktizität. SS (63: *Ontologie (Hermeneutik der Faktizität)*) Einführung in die phänomenologische Forschung. Der Beginn der neuzeitlichen Philosophie. WS (17: Einführung in die phänomenologische Forschung)
1924	Grundbegriffe der aristotelischen Philosophie. SS (18: *Grundbegriffe der aristotelischen Philosophie)* Interpretation Platonischer Dialoge (*Sophistes, Philebus*). WS (19: *Platon: Sophistes)*
1925	Geschichte des Zeitbegriffs. Prolegomena zur Phänomenologie von Geschichte und Natur. SS (20: Prolegomena zur Geschichte des Zeitbegriffs) Logik: Die Frage nach der Wahrheit. WS (21: *Logik. Die Frage nach der Wahrheit)*.
1926	Die Grundbegriffe der antiken Philosophie. SS (22: *Die Grundbegriffe der antiken Philosophie)* Geschichte der Philosophie von Thomas v. Aquin bis Kant. WS (23: *Geschichte der Philosophie von Thomas von Aquin bis Kant)*
1927	Die Grundprobleme der Phänomenologie. SS (24: *Die Grundprobleme der Phänomenologie)* Phänomenologische Interpretation von Kants *Kritik der reinen Vernunft*. WS (25: *Phänomenologische Interpretation von Kants Kritik der reinen Vernunft)*
1928	Logik. SS (26: *Metaphysische Anfangsgründe der Logik im Ausgang der Leibniz)* Einleitung in die Philosophie. WS (27: *Einleitung in die Philosophie)*

1929	Einführung in die akademische Studium. SS (28: *Der deutsche Idealismus (Fichte, Schelling, Hegel)* und die philosophische Problemlage der Gegenwart ("Einführung in das akademische Studium"))
	Die Grundbegriffe der Metaphysik. Welt – Endlichkeit – Vereinzelung. WS (GA 29/30: *Die Grundbegriffe der Metaphysik. Welt-Endlichkeit*)
1930	Vom Wesen der menschlichen Freiheit. Einleitung in die Philosophie SS (31: *Vom Wesen der menschlichen Freiheit. Einleitung in die Philosophie*)
	Hegels Phänomenologie des Geistes. WS (32: *Hegels Phänomenologie des Geistes* [1980¹,1988²])

[1931-1955 follows Richardson (2003 [1963][7]) with annotations by Heidegger, adjusted to GA volumes' publication titles]

1931	Interpretationen aus der antiken Philosophie: Aristoteles, *Metaphysik*, IX (*dynamis-energeia*). SS (33: *Aristoteles, Metaphysik Θ 1-3. Von Wesen und Wirklichkeit der Kraft*)
	Kant. Uber die Fortschritte der Metaphysik [Sommersemester 1931
1931/32	Vom Wesen der Wahrheit ("Höhlengleichnis" und *Theätet*, über *pseudos*). WS (34: *Vom Wesen der Wahrheit. Zu Platons Höhlengleichnis und Theätet*)
	Kants tranzendentale Dialektik und die praktische Philosophie 1 [Wintersemester 1931/32]
1932	Der Anfang der abendländischen Philosophie: Anaximander und Parmenides. SS (35: *Der Anfang der abendländischen Philosophie. Auslegung des Anaximander und Parmenides*)
1933	Die Grundfrage der Philosophie. SS 1933 (36/37: *Sein und Wahrheit*)
1933/34	Vom Wesen der Wahrheit. WS 1933/34 (36/37: *Sein und Wahrheit*)

---

[7] William J. Richardson, *Heidegger. Through Phenomenology to Thought*, 4th ed., New York: Fordham University Press, 2003 (1963).

	[Über Wesen und Begriff von Natur, Geschichte und Staat: Übung aus dem Wintersemester 1933/34. WS 1933/34 (*Heidegger-Jahrbuch* 4 (2009), 53-88.]
1934	Über Logik als Frage nach der Sprache. SS (38: *Logik als die Frage nach dem Wesen der Sprache*)
	Hölderlins Hymnen ("Der Rhein" und "Germanien"). WS (39: *Hölderlins Hymnen "Germanien" und "Der Rhein"*)
	Hauptstücke aus Kants Kritik der reieen Vernunft [Sommersemester 1934]
1934/35	*Hölderlins Hymnen "Germanien" und "Der Rhein"* WS (39: *Hölderlins Hymnen "Germanien" und "Der Rhein"*)
1935	Einführung in die Metaphysik. SS (40: *Einführung in die Metaphysik*)
	Grundfrage der Metaphysik. WS (41: *Die Frage nach dem Ding. Zu Kants Lehre von den transzendentalen Grundsätzen*)
1935/36	Leibnizens Weltbegriff und der deutsche Idealismus (Monadologie) [Wintersemester 1935/36]
1936	Schelling, Über das Wesen der menschlichen Freiheit. SS (42: *Schelling: Vom Wesen der menschlichen Freiheit (1809))*
	Nietzsche, *Der Wille zur Macht* (als Kunst). WS (43: *Nietzsche: Der Wilfle zur Macht als Kunst*)
1937	Nietzsches metaphysische Grundstellung im abendländischen Denken: Die Lehre von der ewige Wiederkehr des Gleichen. SS (44: *Nietzsches metaphysische Grundstellung im abendländischen Denken: Die ewige Wiederkehr des Gleichen*)
	Grundfragen der Philosophie: Vom Wesen der Wahrheit (*aletheia* und *poiesis*). WS (45: *Grundfragen der Philosophie. Ausgewählte "Probleme" der "Logik"*)
	Seminare (Übungen): Die metaphysischen Grundstellungden des abendländischen Denkens (1937/38). WS (88: *Seminare (Übungen) 1937/38 und 1941/42 1. Die metaphysischen Grundstellungden des abendländischen Denkens 2. Einübung in das philosophische Denken*)
1938	Einleitung in die Philosophie. WS (46: *Zur Auslegung von Nietzsches II. Unzeitgemäßer Betrachtung "Vom Nutzen und Nachteil der Historie für das Leben"*)

1939	Nietzsches Lehre vom Willen zur Macht als Erkenntnis. SS (47: *Nietzsches Lehre vom Willen zur Macht als Erkenntnis*) [Kunst und Technik. WS]
1940	Nietzsche: Der europäische Nihilismus. Second Trimester (48: *Nietzsche: Der europäische Nihilismus*) [Grundfragen der Philosophie. WS]
1941	Die Metaphysik als Deutschen Idealismus: *Philosophische Untersuchungen über das Wesen der menschlichen Freiheit).* First Trimester (49: *Die Metaphysik des deutschen Idealismus (Schelling)*) Grundbegriffe. SS (51: *Grundbegriffe*) Nietzsches Metaphysik. WS (50: *1. Nietzsches Metaphysik. 2. Einleitung in die Philosophie. Denken und Dichten*)[8] Hölderlins "Andenken". WS (52: *Hölderlins Hymne "Andenken"*)
1941/42	Einübung in das philosophische Denken WS (88: *Seminare (Übungen)1937/38 und 1941/42 1. Die metaphysischen Grundstellungden des abendländischen Denkens 2. Einübung in das philosophische Denken*)
1942	Hölderlins Hymne "Der Ister". SS (53: *Hölderlins Hymne "Der Ister"*) Parmenides. WS (54: *Parmenides*)
1943	Heraklit. Der Anfang des abendlaänischen Denkens (55: *Herakit. Der Anfang des abendländischen Denkens. 2. Logik. Heraklits Lehre zum Logos*)
1944	Logik (Heraklits Lehre vom *logos*). SS (55: *Herakit. Der Anfang des abendländischen Denkens. 2. Logik. Heraklits Lehre zum Logos*) Einleitung in die Philosophie. Denken und Dichten. (Nach der 3. Stunde am achten November abgebrochen, weil durch die Parteileitung zum Volkssturm eingezogen). WS (50: *1. Nietzsches Metaphysik. 2. Einleitung in die Philosophie. Denken und Dichten*)[9]

---

[8] An essay from 1940.

[9] Only the first two sessions were given before Heidegger was dismissed as a

1951	Was heißt Denken?. WS (8: *Was heißt Denken?*)
1952	Was heißt Denken?. SS (8: *Was heißt Denken?*)
1955	Der Satz vom Grund. WS (10: *Der Satz vom Grund*)

SEMINARS

1927 Aristoteles-Hegel-Seminar SS (86: *Seminare. Hegel – Schelling*)

1927-28 Schelling. Über das Wesen der menschlichen Freiheit WS (86: *Seminare. Hegel – Schelling*)

1928 Aristoteles, Physik L 1-3 (83: *Seminare. Platon – Aristoteles – Augustinus*)

1930-31 Platon, Parmenides (83: *Seminare. Platon – Aristoteles – Augustinus*)
Augustinus, Confessiones XI (de tempore) (83: *Seminare. Platon – Aristoteles – Augustinus*)

1932 Platons Phaidros (83: *Seminare. Platon – Aristoteles – Augustinus*)

1934-35 Hegel. "Rechtsphilosophie" WS (86: *Seminare. Hegel – Schelling*)

1937 Nietsches metaphysische Grundstellung (Sein und Schein) (87: *Nietzsche Seminare 1937 und 1944*)

1937-38 Die metaphysichen Grundstellungen des abendländischen Denkens (Metaphysik) WS (88: *Seminare (Übungen)1937/38 und 1941/42*
1. Die metaphysischen Grundstellungden des abendländischen Denkens
2. Einübung in das philosophische Denken)

1939 Vom Wesen der Sprache. Die Metaphysik der Sprache und die Ursprung der Sprache"

1940 "Über die Φύσις bei Aristoteles" (9: *Wegmarken*)

1941-42 Einübung in das philosophische Denken WS (88: *Seminare (Übungen)1937/38 und 1941/42*
1. Die metaphysischen Grundstellungden des abendländischen Denkens

professor and his status as tenured professor was at an end.

	2. Einübung in das philosophische Denken)
1941-1943	Schelling under der deutsche Idealismus (86: *Seminare. Hegel – Schelling)* Die Metaphysik des deutschen Idealismus Zu Schellings "Freiheitsabhandlung"
1942	Zu Hegel. Phänomenologie des Geistes SS (86: *Seminare. Hegel – Schelling)*
1944	Skizzen zu "Grundbegriffe des Denkens": (87: *Nietzsche. Seminare 1937 und 1944)* Aristoteles, Metaphysik L und Z (83: *Seminare. Platon – Aristoteles – Augustinus)*
1950-51	Übungen im Lesen: Über die Kausalität (83: *Seminare. Platon – Aristoteles – Augustinus)*
1951	Übungen im Lesen: Aristoteles, Physik B 1, L 1-3 (83: *Seminare. Platon – Aristoteles – Augustinus)*
1951-52	Zürich (15: *Seminare)* Protokolle zu "Übungen im Lesen: Aristoteles, Physik L und Metaphysik Theta 10 (83: *Seminare. Platon – Aristoteles – Augustinus)*
1955-56	Zu Hegel. Logik des Wissens WS (86: *Seminare. Hegel – Schelling)*
1956-57	Gespräch von der Sache des Denkens mit Hegel WS (86: *Seminare. Hegel – Schelling)*
1966	Le Thor (I) (15: *Seminare)*
1966-67	Heraklit (with Eugen Fink) WS (15: *Seminare)*
1968	Le Thor (II) (15: *Seminare)*
1969	Le Thor (III) (15: *Seminare)*
1973	Zähringen (15: *Seminare)*

VI. LECTURE COURSES (1919-1955) AND SEMINARS (1927-1973): DATE OF FIRST PUBLICATION IN GERMAN (1953-2014)

LECTURE COURSES

1953
GA 40 Einführung in die Metaphysik
SS 1935, University of Freiburg
(Petra Jaeger)

1961
GA 43 Nietzsche: Der Wille zur Macht als Kunst [1961, earlier version]
WS 1936/37, University of Freiburg
(Bernd Heimbüchel)

GA 44 Nietzsches metaphysische Grundstellung im abendländischen
Denken: Die ewige Wiederkehr des Gleichen [1961, earlier version]
SS 1937, University of Freiburg
(Marion Heinz)

GA 47 Nietzsches Lehre vom Willen zur Macht als Erkenntnis [1961, earlier
version]
SS 1939, University of Freiburg
(Eberhard Hanser)

GA 48 Nietzsche: Der europäische Nihilismus [1961, earlier version]
Second Trimester 1940, University of Freiburg
(Petra Jaeger)

1962
GA 41 Grundfrage der Metaphysik (published Die Frage nach dem Ding.
Zu Kants Lehre von den transzenentalen Grundsätzaen)
WS 1935/36, University of Freiburg
(Petra Jaeger)

1971

GA 42 Schelling: Vom Wesen der menschlichen Freiheit (1809)
SS 1936, University of Freiburg
(Ingrid Schüßler)

1975

GA 24 Die Grundprobleme der Phänomenologie
SS 1927, University of Marburg
(Friedrich-Wilhelm von Herrmann)

1976

GA 21 Logik. Die Frage nach der Wahrheit
WS 1925/26, University of Marburg
(Walter Biemel)

1977

GA 25 Phänomenologische Interpretation von Kants Kritik der reinen Vernunft
WS 1927/28, University of Freiburg
(Ingtraud Görland)

1978

GA 26 Logik (published as Metaphysische Anfangsgründe der Logik im
Ausgang der Leibniz)
SS 1928, Marburg University
(Klaus Held)

1979

GA 39 Hölderlins Hymnen "Germanien" und "Der Rhein"
WS 1934/35, University of Freiburg
(Susanne Ziegler)

GA 55 Heraklit. 1. Der Anfang des abendländischen Denkens. 2. Logik.
Heraklits Lehre zum Logos
1. SS 1943, University of Freiburg. 2. SS 1944, University of Freiburg
(Manfred S. Frings)

1980

GA 32 Hegels Phänomenologie des Geistes
WS 1930/31, University of Freiburg
(Ingtraud Görland)

1981

GA 51 Grundbegriffe
SS 1941, University of Freiburg
(Petra Jaeger)

GA 33 Interpretationen aus der antiken Philosophie: Aristoteles, Metaphysik,
IX (dynamis-energeia) (published as Aristoteles, Metaphysik _ 1-3. Von Wesen
und Wirklichkeit der Kraft
WS 1931, University of Freiburg
(Heinrich Hüni)

1982

GA 31 Vom Wesen der menschlichen Freiheit. Einleitung in die Philosophie
SS 1930, University of Freiburg
(Hartmut Tietjen)

GA 52 Hölderlins Hymne "Andenken"
WS 1941/42, University of Freiburg
(Curd Ochwadt)

GA 54 Parmenides
WS 1942/43, University of Freiburg
(Manfred S. Frings)

1983

GA 29/30 Die Grundbegriffe der Metaphysik..Welt—Endlichkeit—Einsamkeit
WS 1929/30, University of Freiburg
(Friedrich-Wilhelm von Herrmann)

1984

GA 45 Grundfragen der Philosophie. Ausgewählte "Probleme" der "Logik"
WS 1937/38, University of Freiburg
(Friedrich-Wilhelm von Herrmann)

GA 53 Hölderlins Hymne "Der Ister"
SS 1942, University of Freiburg
(Walter Biemel)

1985
GA 61 Phänomenologische Interpretationenen zu Aristoteles. Einführung in die phänomenologische Forschung
WS 1921/22, University of Freiburg
(Walter Bröcker and Käte Bröcker-Oltmanns)

1987
GA 56/57 Zur Bestimmung der Philosophie.
1. Die Idee derPhilosophie und das Weltanschauungsproblem.
2. Phänomenologie und transzendentale Wertphilosophie [mit einer Nachschrift der Vorlesung "Über das Wesen der Universität und des akademischen Studiums"]
"Kriegsnotsemester [War Emergency Semester]" 1919 and SS 1919, University of Freiburg
(Bernd Heimbüchel)

1988
GA 63 Ontologie (Hermeneutik der Faktizität) [1988]
SS 1923, University of Freiburg
(Käte Bröcker-Oltmanns)

GA 20 Prolegomena zur Geschichte des Zeitbegriffs [1979; 2nd ed., 1988]
SS 1925, Freiburg University
(Petra Jaeger)

GA 34 Vom Wesen der Wahrheit. Zu Platons Höhlengleichnis und Theätet
WS 1931/32, University of Freiburg
(Hermann Mörchen)

1990
GA 50 1. Nietzsches Metaphysik. 2. Einleitung in die Philosophie. Denken und Dichten
WS 1941/42 [not given] and WS 1944/45, University of Freiburg

(Petra Jaeger)
[The first text was determined to be an essay and not lecture course material. The second is a fragment of two sessions worth of material. Heidegger was dismissed as a professor in November 1944.]

1991

GA 49 Die Metaphysik des deutschen Idealismus (Schelling)
First Trimester 1941 and Seminar SS 1941, University of Freiburg
(Günther Seibold)

1992

GA 19 Interpretation Platonischer Dialoge (Sophistes, Philebus).(published as Platon: Sophistes
WS 1924/25, University of Marburg
(Ingeborg Schüßler)

1993

GA 59 Phänomenologie der Anschauung und des Ausdrucks. Theorie der philosophischen Begriffsbildung
SS 1920, University of Freiburg
(Claudius Strube)

GA 58 Grundprobleme der Phänomenologie (1919/20)
WS 1919/20, University of Freiburg
(Hans-Helmuth Gander)

GA 22 Die Grundbegriffe der antiken Philosophie
SS 1926, University of Marburg
(Franz-Karl Blust)

1994

GA 17 Einführung in die phänomenologische Forschung
WS 1923/24, University of Marburg
(Friedrich-Wilhelm von Herrmann)

1995

GA 60 Phänomenologie des religiösen Lebens
1. Einleitung in die Phänomenologie der Religion (1920/21)

2. Augustinus und der Neuplatonismus (1921)
3. Die philosophischen Grundlagen der mittelalterischen Mystik (1918/1919)
(1. Matthias Jung and Thomas Reghely
2. Claudius Strube
3. Claudius Strube)

1996

GA 27 Einleitung in die Philosophie
WS 1928/29, University of Freiburg
(Otto Saame and Ina Saame-Speidel)

1997

GA 28 Der deutsche Idealismus (Fichte, Schelling, Hegel) und die
philosophische Problemlage der Gegenwart ("Einführung in das akademische
Studium")
SS 1929, University of Freiburg
(Claudius Strube)

GA 10 Der Satz vom Grund
Volesung. Der Satz vom Grund
Vortrag. Der Satz vom Grund
WS 1955/56, University of Freiburg
(Petra Jaeger)

1998

GA 38 Logik als die Frage nach dem Wesen der Sprache
SS 1934, University of Freiburg
(Günther Seubold)

2001

GA 36/3 Sein und Wahrheit
1. Die Grundfrage der Philosophie.
2. Vom Wesen der Wahrheit
SS 1933, University of Freiburg
WS 1933/34, University of Freiburg
(Hartmut Tietjen)

2002

GA 8 Was heisst Denken? [2002]
WS 1951/52, SS 1952, University of Freiburg
(Paola-Ludovika Coriando)

GA 18 Grundbegriffe der aristotelischen Philosophie [2002]
SS 1924, University of Marburg
(Mark Michalski)

2003
GA 46 Einleitung in die Philosophie (published as Zur Auslegung von
Nietzsches II. Unzeitgemäßer Betrachtung "Vom Nutzen und Nachteil der
Historie für das Leben"
WS 1938/39, University of Freiburg
(Hans-Joachim Friedrich)

2004
GA 87 Nietzsche. Seminare 1937 und 1944.
SS 1937, University of Freiburg
SS1944, University of Freiburg
(Peter von Ruckjteschell)

2005
GA 62 Phänomenologische Interpretationen ausgewählte Abhandlungen des
Aristoteles zur Ontologie und Logik
[Phänomenologische Interpretationen zu Aristoteles (Anzeige der
hermeneutischen Situation) Ausarbeitung für die Marburger und die Göttinger
Philosophische Fakultät Autumn 1922]
SS 1922, University of Freiburg
(Günther Neumann)

2006
GA 23 Geschichte der Philosophie von Thomas von Aquin bis Kant
WS 1926/27, Marburg University
(Helmuth Vetter)

2008
GA 88 Seminare (Übungen) 1937/38 und 1941/42
1. Die metaphysischen Grundstellungden des abendländischen Denkens

2. Einübung in das philosophische Denken
WS 1937/38, Freiburg University
WS 1941/42, Freiburg University
(Alfred Denker)

2011
GA 86 Seminare. Hegel – Schelling [1927-1957]
(Peter Trawny)
2012

GA 35 Der Anfang der abendländischen Philosophie Auslegung des
Anaximander und Parmenides
SS 1932, Freiburg University
(Peter Trawny)

SEMINARS

1976
GA 9 Über die Φύσις bei Aristoteles

1986
GA 15
Zürich (1951-52)
Heraklit (with Eugen Fink)
WS 1966-67
Le Thor (I) (1966)
Le Thor (II) (1968)
Le Thor (III) (1969)
Zähringen (1973)
(Curd Ochwadt)

2004
GA 85 Vom Wesen der Sprache. Die Metaphysik der Sprache und die Wesung
des Wortes. Zu Herders Abhandlung "Über den Ursprung der Sprache"

2011
GA 86 Seminare. Hegel – Schelling

Aristoteles-Hegel-Seminar
SS 1927, University of Freiburg

Schelling. Über das Wesen der menschlichen Freiheit
WS 1927-28, University of Freiburg

Hegel. "Rechtsphilosophie"
WS 1934-35, University of Freiburg

Schelling under der deutsche Idealismus
"Die Metaphysik des deutschen Idealismus"
Zu Schellings "Freiheitsabhandlung"
1941-43, University of Freiburg

Zu Hegel. Phänomenologie des Geistes
SS 1942, University of Freiburg

Zu Hegel. Logik des Wissens
WS 1955-56, University of Freiburg

Gespräch von der Sache des Denkens mit Hegel
WS 1956-57, University of Freiburg
(Peter Trawny)

2012
GA 83 Seminare: Platon – Aristoteles - Augustinus

Aristoteles, Physik L 1-3
SS 1928, University of Marburg

Platon, Parmenides
WS 1930/31, University of Freiburg

Augustinus, Conessiones XI (de tempore)
WS 1930/31, University of Freiburg

Platons Phaidros
SS 1932, University of Freiburg

Der Anfang der abendländischen Philosophie, Auslegung des Anaximander und Parmenides
SS 1932, University of Freiburg.

Aristoteles, Physik L und Z
SS 1944, University of Freiburg

Übungen im Lesen: Über die Kausalität
Übungen im Lesen: Aristoteles, Physik B1, L 1-3
SS 1951, University of Freiburg

2013
GA 84.1
Kant. Uber die Fortschritte der Metaphysik [Sommersemester 1931]
Kants tranzendentale Dialektik und die praktische Philosophie [Wintersemester 1931/32]
Hauptstücke aus Kants Kritik der reieen Vernunft [Sommersemester 1934]
Leibnizens Weltbegriff und der deutsche Idealismus (Monadologie) [Wintersemester 1935/36]

2014
GA 39
Hölderlins Hymnen "Germanien" und "Der Rhein"
WS 1934/35, University of Freiburg

GA 86
Seminar. Hegel. "Rechrsphilosophie" WS 1934/35
WS 1934/35, University of Freiburg

VI. LECTURE COURSES (1919-1955) AND SEMINARS (1927-1973): DATE OF FIRST PUBLICATION IN GERMAN (1953-2014)
LECTURE COURSES

1953
GA 40 Einführung in die Metaphysik
SS 1935, University of Freiburg
(Petra Jaeger)

1961
GA 43 Nietzsche: Der Wille zur Macht als Kunst [1961, earlier version]
WS 1936/37, University of Freiburg
(Bernd Heimbüchel)

GA 44 Nietzsches metaphysische Grundstellung im abendländischen
Denken: Die ewige Wiederkehr des Gleichen [1961, earlier version]
SS 1937, University of Freiburg
(Marion Heinz)

GA 47 Nietzsches Lehre vom Willen zur Macht als Erkenntnis [1961, earlier
version]
SS 1939, University of Freiburg
(Eberhard Hanser)

Second Trimester 1940, University of Freiburg
(Petra Jaeger)

1962
GA 41 Grundfrage der Metaphysik (published Die Frage nach dem Ding.
Zu Kants Lehre von den transzenentalen Grundsätzaen)
WS 1935/36, University of Freiburg
(Petra Jaeger)

1971
GA 42 Schelling: Vom Wesen der menschlichen Freiheit (1809)
SS 1936, University of Freiburg
(Ingrid Schüßler)

1975

GA 24 Die Grundprobleme der Phänomenologie
SS 1927, University of Marburg
(Friedrich-Wilhelm von Herrmann)

1976

GA 21 Logik. Die Frage nach der Wahrheit
WS 1925/26, University of Marburg
(Walter Biemel)

1977

GA 25 Phänomenologische Interpretation von Kants Kritik der reinen Vernunft
WS 1927/28, University of Freiburg
(Ingtraud Görland)

1978

GA 26 Logik (published as Metaphysische Anfangsgründe der Logik im
Ausgang der Leibniz)
SS 1928, Marburg University
(Klaus Held)

1979

GA 39 Hölderlins Hymnen "Germanien" und "Der Rhein"
WS 1934/35, University of Freiburg
(Susanne Ziegler)

GA 55 Heraklit. 1. Der Anfang des abendländischen Denkens. 2. Logik.
Heraklits Lehre zum Logos
1. SS 1943, University of Freiburg. 2. SS 1944, University of Freiburg
(Manfred S. Frings)

1980

GA 32 Hegels Phänomenologie des Geistes
WS 1930/31, University of Freiburg
(Ingtraud Görland)

1981
GA 51 Grundbegriffe
SS 1941, University of Freiburg
(Petra Jaeger)

GA 33 Interpretationen aus der antiken Philosophie: Aristoteles, Metaphysik,
IX (dynamis-energeia) (published as Aristoteles, Metaphysik _ 1-3. Von Wesen
und Wirklichkeit der Kraft
WS 1931, University of Freiburg
(Heinrich Hüni)

1982
GA 31 Vom Wesen der menschlichen Freiheit. Einleitung in die Philosophie
SS 1930, University of Freiburg
(Hartmut Tietjen)

GA 52 Hölderlins Hymne "Andenken"
WS 1941/42, University of Freiburg
(Curd Ochwadt)

GA 54 Parmenides
WS 1942/43, University of Freiburg
(Manfred S. Frings)

1983
GA 29/30 Die Grundbegriffe der Metaphysik..Welt—Endlichkeit—Einsamkeit
WS 1929/30, University of Freiburg
(Friedrich-Wilhelm von Herrmann)

1984
GA 45 Grundfragen der Philosophie. Ausgewählte "Probleme" der "Logik"
WS 1937/38, University of Freiburg
(Friedrich-Wilhelm von Herrmann)

GA 53 Hölderlins Hymne "Der Ister"
SS 1942, University of Freiburg
(Walter Biemel)

1985

GA 61 Phänomenologische Interpretationenen zu Aristoteles. Einführung in die phänomenologische Forschung
WS 1921/22, University of Freiburg
(Walter Bröcker and Käte Bröcker-Oltmanns)

1987

GA 56/57 Zur Bestimmung der Philosophie.
1. Die Idee derPhilosophie und das Weltanschauungsproblem.
2. Phänomenologie und transzendentale Wertphilosophie [mit einer Nachschrift der Vorlesung "Über das Wesen der Universität und des akademischen Studiums"]
"Kriegsnotsemester [War Emergency Semester]" 1919 and SS 1919, University of Freiburg
(Bernd Heimbüchel)

1988

GA 63 Ontologie (Hermeneutik der Faktizität)
SS 1923, University of Freiburg
(Käte Bröcker-Oltmanns)

GA 20 Prolegomena zur Geschichte des Zeitbegriffs
SS 1925, Freiburg University
(Petra Jaeger)

GA 34 Vom Wesen der Wahrheit. Zu Platons Höhlengleichnis und Theätet
WS 1931/32, University of Freiburg
(Hermann Mörchen)

1990

GA 50 1. Nietzsches Metaphysik. 2. Einleitung in die Philosophie. Denken und Dichten
WS 1941/42 [not given] and WS 1944/45, University of Freiburg
(Petra Jaeger)
[The first text was determined to be an essay and not lecture course material. The second is a fragment of two sessions worth of material. Heidegger was dismissed as a professor in November 1944.]

1991

GA 49 Die Metaphysik des deutschen Idealismus (Schelling)
First Trimester 1941 and Seminar SS 1941, University of Freiburg
(Günther Seibold)

1992

GA 19 Interpretation Platonischer Dialoge (*Sophistes, Philebus*).(published as
Platon: Sophistes
WS 1924/25, University of Marburg
(Ingeborg Schüßler)

1993

GA 59 Phänomenologie der Anschauung und des Ausdrucks. Theorie der
philosophischen Begriffsbildung
SS 1920, University of Freiburg
(Claudius Strube)

GA 58 Grundprobleme der Phänomenologie (1919/20)
WS 1919/20, University of Freiburg
(Hans-Helmuth Gander)

GA 22 Die Grundbegriffe der antiken Philosophie
SS 1926, University of Marburg
(Franz-Karl Blust)

1994

GA 17 Einführung in die phänomenologische Forschung
WS 1923/24, University of Marburg
(Friedrich-Wilhelm von Herrmann)

1995

GA 60 Phänomenologie des religiösen Lebens
1. Einleitung in die Phänomenologie der Religion (1920/21)
2. Augustinus und der Neuplatonismus (1921)
3. Die philosophischen Grundlagen der mittelalterischen Mystik (1918/1919)
(1. Matthias Jung and Thomas Reghely
2. Claudius Strube
3. Claudius Strube)

1996
GA 27 Einletung in die Philosophie
WS 1928/29, University of Freiburg
(Otto Saame and Ina Saame-Speidel)

1997
GA 28 Der deutsche Idealismus (Fichte, Schelling, Hegel) und die
philosophische Problemlage der Gegenwart ("Einführung in das akademische
Studium")
SS 1929, University of Freiburg
(Claudius Strube)

GA 10 Der Satz vom Grund
Volesung. Der Satz vom Grund
Vortrag. Der Satz vom Grund
WS 1955/56, University of Freiburg
(Petra Jaeger)

1998
GA 38 Logik als die Frage nach dem Wesen der Sprache
SS 1934, University of Freiburg
(Günther Seubold)

2001
GA 36/3 Sein und Wahrheit
1. Die Grundfrage der Philosophie.
2. Vom Wesen der Wahrheit
SS 1933, University of Freiburg
WS 1933/34, University of Freiburg
(Hartmut Tietjen)

2002
GA 8 Was heisst Denken?
WS 1951/52, SS 1952, University of Freiburg
(Paola-Ludovika Coriando)

GA 18 Grundbegriffe der aristotelischen Philosophie [2002]
SS 1924, University of Marburg
(Mark Michalski)

2003
GA 46 Einleitung in die Philosophie (published as Zur Auslegung von
Nietzsches II. Unzeitgemäßer Betrachtung "Vom Nutzen und Nachteil der
Historie für das Leben"
WS 1938/39, University of Freiburg
(Hans-Joachim Friedrich)

2004
GA 87 Nietzsche. Seminare 1937 und 1944.
SS 1937, University of Freiburg
SS1944, University of Freiburg
(Peter von Ruckjteschell)

2005
GA 62 Phänomenologische Interpretationen ausgewählte Abhandlungen des
Aristoteles zur Ontologie und Logik
[Phänomenologische Interpretationen zu Aristoteles (Anzeige der
hermeneutischen Situation) Ausarbeitung für die Marburger und die Göttinger
Philosophische Fakultät Autumn 1922]
SS 1922, University of Freiburg
(Günther Neumann)

2006
GA 23 Geschichte der Philosophie von Thomas von Aquin bis Kant
WS 1926/27, Marburg University
(Helmuth Vetter)

2008
GA 88 Seminare (Übungen) 1937/38 und 1941/42
1. Die metaphysischen Grundstellungden des abendländischen Denkens
2. Einübung in das philosophische Denken
WS 1937/38, Freiburg University
WS 1941/42, Freiburg University
(Alfred Denker)

2011
GA 86 Seminare. Hegel – Schelling [1927-1957]
(Peter Trawny)

2012
GA 35 Der Anfang der abendländischen Philosophie Auslegung des
Anaximander und Parmenides
SS 1932, Freiburg University
(Peter Trawny)

SEMINARS

1976
GA 9 Über die Φύσις bei Aristoteles

1986
GA 15
Zürich (1951-52)
Heraklit (with Eugen Fink)
WS 1966-67
Le Thor (I) (1966)
Le Thor (II) (1968)
Le Thor (III) (1969)
Zähringen (1973)
(Curd Ochwadt)

2004
GA 85 Vom Wesen der Sprache. Die Metaphysik der Sprache und die Wesung
des Wortes. Zu Herders Abhandlung "Über den Ursprung der Sprache"

2011
GA 86
Seminare. Hegel – Schelling

Aristoteles-Hegel-Seminar
SS 1927, University of Freiburg
Schelling. Über das Wesen der menschlichen Freiheit
WS 1927-28, University of Freiburg

Hegel. "Rechtsphilosophie"
WS 1934-35, University of Freiburg
Schelling under der deutsche Idealismus
"Die Metaphysik des deutschen Idealismus"
Zu Schellings "Freiheitsabhandlung"
1941-43, University of Freiburg
Zu Hegel. Phänomenologie des Geistes
SS 1942, University of Freiburg
Zu Hegel. Logik des Wissens
WS 1955-56, University of Freiburg
Gespräch von der Sache des Denkens mit Hegel
WS 1956-57, University of Freiburg
(Peter Trawny)

2012

GA 83 Seminare: Platon – Aristoteles – Augustinus

Aristoteles, Physik L 1-3
SS 1928, University of Marburg
Platon, Parmenides
WS 1930/31, University of Freiburg
Augustinus, Conessiones XI (de tempore)
WS 1930/31, University of Freiburg
Platons Phaidros
SS 1932, University of Freiburg
Der Anfang der abendländischen Philosophie, Auslegung des Anaximander und
Parmenides
SS 1932, University of Freiburg.
Aristoteles, Physik L und Z
SS 1944, University of Freiburg
Übungen im Lesen: Über die Kausalität
Übungen im Lesen: Aristoteles, Physik B1, L 1-3
SS 1951, University of Freiburg

2013

GA 84.1 Seminare. Kant – Leibniz – Schiller

Kant. Uber die Fortschritte der Metaphysik [Sommersemester 1931]Kants tranzendentale Dialektik und die praktische Philosophie [Wintersemester 1931/32]
Hauptstücke aus Kants Kritik der reieen Vernunft [Sommersemester 1934]
Leibnizens Weltbegriff und der deutsche Idealismus (Monadologie) [Wintersemester 1935/36]

2014

GA 39
Hölderlins Hymnen "Germanien" und "Der Rhein"
WS 1934/35, University of Freiburg

GA 86
Seminar. Hegel. "Rechrsphilosophie" WS 1934/35
WS 1934/35, University of Freiburg

VII. VIDEO AND AUDIO RECORDINGS (1955-2009)

(1) VIDEO

1.   *Martin Heidegger im Denken Unterwegs* (Baden-Baden: Südwestfunk
        VHS 1975; DVD 2004)

(2) AUDIO

A. Heidegger Reading

I.   "Der Satz der Identität": Heidegger reads the lecture recorded live on
        June 27, 1957 at the University of Freiburg on a recording (1957)
        Pfullingen: Neske. Available as the CD *Martin Heidegger. Der Satz
        der Identität* (Stuttgardt: Klett-Cotta, 1997) and in the CD set *Von der
        Sache des Denkens. Vorträge, Reden und Gespräche* (Munich: Der
        Hörverlag, 2000; 2009), 3(5). See {P20}.

II.   "Hölderlins Erde und Himmel": Heidegger reads the lecture recorded
        live on January 18, 1960 at the University of Heidelberg on a recording
        (1960) Pfullingen: Neske. Available as the CD *Hölderlins Himmel und
        Erde* (Stuttgardt: Klett-Cotta, 1997; 2002, 2007). See {H13}.

III   *Martin Heidegger* ließt *Hölderlin* : Studio recording of Heidegger
        reading "Ermunterung," "Die Wanderung," "Heimkunft."
        "Friedensfeier," " Der Ister." "Was ist Gott?," "Was ist der Menschen
        Leben?," "Aber in Hütten wohnet," "Wie Meeresküsten," and
        "Heimath." A preliminary "Anmerkung" is provided, published first in
        the fifth edition of the book and GA 4 (1981) as "Vorwort zur Lesung
        von Hölderins Gedichten," pp.195-197. The LP *Heidegger ließt
        Hölderlin* appeared in 1963 (Pfullingen: Neske). A CD followed in
        1997 (Stuttgart: Klett-Cotta). See {P15}.

IV   "Gelassenheit. Bodenständigkeit im Atomzeitalter": Recorded October
        30, 1955. Released as an LP in 1955 by Telefunken and in 1959 by
        Teldec as *Zum Atomzeitalter. Gedenkrede anläßlich einer Konradin-
        Kreutzer-Feier gehalten am 30.10.55 in Meßkirch.*Now available in the
        CD set *Von der Sache des Denkens. Vorträge, Reden und Gespräche*
        (Munich: Der Hörverlag, 2000; 2009), 5(7). See (M3}.

V   "Martin Heidegger im Gespräch mit Richard Wisser": Audio of a
         conversation between Heidegger and Richard Wisser filmed on
         September 17, 1969, for broadcast on television [ZDF] available in the
         CD set *Von der Sache des Denkens. Vorträge, Reden und Gespräche*
         (Munich: Der Hörverlag, 2000; 2009), 1(1). See {M1}.

VI   "Was heißt Denken?": Address given in May 1952 on Bavarian Radio
         and served as the basis of the opening lectures of the course "Was heißt
         Denken," a lecture course given during the Winter Semester 1951-52
         and Summer Semester 1952 at the University of Freiburg. Available as
         the CD *Was* heißt Denken? (Auditorium Netzwerk, 2009) and in the
         CD set *Von der Sache des Denkens. Vorträge, Reden und Gespräche*
         (Munich: Der Hörverlag, 2000; 2009), 1(2). See {W5}.

VII   "Zeit und Sein": Lecture given January 31, 1962 at the University of
         Freiburg. Available in the CD set, *Von der Sache des Denkens.
         Vorträge, Reden und Gespräche* (Munich: Der Hörverlag, 2000; 2009),
         2(3). See {T5}.

VIII   +"Dankrede anläßlich der Verleihung der Ehrenbürgerschaft der Stadt
         Meßkirch": Address given on September 27, 1959. Test printed in
         GA16 (2000), pp. 558-561. Available in the CD set *Von der Sache des
         Denkens. Vorträge, Reden und Gespräche* (Munich: Der Hörverlag,
         2000; 2009), 3(4).

IX   "Die Sprache": Lecture given on January 23, 1959. Availabe in the CD
         set *Von der Sache des Denkens. Vorträge, Reden und Gespräche*
         (Munich: Der Hörverlag, 2000; 2009), 4(6). See {W3}.

X   "Der Feldweg": Lecture written in 1949, revised in 1950. Recorded
         December 12, 1952. Available in the CD set *Von der Sache des
         Denkens. Vorträge, Reden und Gespräche* (Munich: Der Hörverlag,
         2000; 2009), 1(1). See {P2}.

XI   "Bauen Wohnen Denken": Lecture broadcast in 1951 on
         Westduetschen Rundfunks Köln, A CD is included with Eduard Führ
         (ed.), *Bauen und Wohnen : Martin Heideggers Grundlegung einer
         Phänomenologie der Architektur* (Munich: Waxmann Verlag, 2000).
         See {B7}.

XII   "Hebel—der Hausfreund": Expanded version of "Gespräch mit Hebel
         beim `Schatz-kästlein' zum Hebeltag 1956," an address given May 9,
         1956, in Lörrach. See "Rede auf Hebel" in GA 13, pp. 434-545. See
         {H1}.

XIII   "Die Kunst und der Raum": Revised version of a lecture "Raum,
         Mensch und Sprache" given October 3, 1964, at the Galerie im Erker,
         St. Gallen, Switzerland. Available as an LP (St. Gallen: Erker 1969,
         1978). See {A7}.

B. Sound Books

(i) German

XIV   "Der Ursprung des Kunstwerkes": Lecture given November 13, 1935,
         in Freiburg, expanded to a series of three lectures given November 17
         and 24, 1936, and December 1, 1936, in Frankfurt. Reclam (1977). See
         {O13}.
XV   "Was ist Metaphysik?": Heidegger's inaugural lecture to the faculties
         of the University of Freiburg, given on July 24, 1929. Klostermann
         (1981). See {W6}.

(ii) English

XVI   *Introduction to Metaphysics:* Fried/Polt translation (2000). CD
         (Princeton: Recording for the Blind and Dyslexic, 2005). See {I3}.
XVII   *Poetry, Language, Thought:* Hofstadter translation (1971). CD
         (Princeton: Recording for the Blind and Dyslexic, 2005). See {T2,
         O132, W4, B7, T1, L1, P12}.
XVIII   *The Metaphysical Foundations of Logic.* CD (Princeton: Recording for
         the Blind and Dyslexic, 2008). See {M5}.
XIX   *History of the Concept of Time* (CD) (Princeton: Recording for the
         Blind and Dyslexic, 2008). See {H10}.
XX   *The Basic Problems of Phenomenology* (CD) (Princeton: Recording for
         the Blind and Dyslexic, 2008). See {B3}.
XXI   *Nietzsche.* Volumes 1. *The Will to Power as Art* (CD) (Princeton:
         Recording for the Blind and Dyslexic, 2008). See {N2}.
XXII   *Nietzsche.* Volume 2. *The Eternal Recurrence of the Same* (CD)
         (Princeton: Recording for the Blind and Dyslexic, 2008). See {N2}.
XXIII   *Nietzsche.* Volumes 3. *The Will to Power as Knowledge and as
         Metaphysics* (CD) (Princeton: Recording for the Blind and Dyslexic,
         2008). See {N2}.

XXIV   *Nietzsche.* Volumes 4. *Nihilism* (CD) (Princeton: Recording for the Blind and Dyslexic, 2008). See {N2}

XXV   *Existence and Being* (CD) (Princeton: Recording for the Blind and Dyslexic, 2008). See {H11, O17, P7, P 13, R5, W6}.

Printed in Great Britain
by Amazon